Praise for the first edition of thi

"Stienstra is bluntly honest in his assessments. He does not make the jobs glamorous when they are not...,Those who are looking for a career change would do well to obtain a copy for an honest and detailed account of what 50 outdoor jobs are all about."—Gary Moore, Journal-Opinion, *Bradford, VT*

"...a really unique book...just the ticket for anyone looking for an occupational change of pace...It's also a great source book...whether you're looking for a part-time venture or a full-time career."—Ron Kolodziej, The Recorder, *Amsterdam, NY*

"Stienstra pulls no punches, describing the joys as well as the downsides of outdoor careers and soliciting the comments of various people deeply involved in the careers he writes about."— Bob Gooch, Virginian Review, *Covington, VA*

"...easy reading, often witty, with some delightful anecdotes...recommended reading for people who love the outdoors."—Camping & RV

"Every career counselor in the U.S. should have a copy of this book."—Columbia Basin Herald, *Moses Lake, WA*

"...filled with useful background on outdoors positions...Sick of the rat race? Stienstra's book can help you make wise choices."—The Times Leader, *Wilkes-Barre, PA*

"...a marvelously helpful resource guide...in an interesting and effective format."—West Hawaii Today

"...Stienstra has chosen wisely when it comes to interviewing sterling representatives of the careers he covers...a most useful and interesting book."—The Herald, *Rock Hill, SC*

"This is a straightforward, informative book filled with factual career tips and pitfalls...Stienstra's entertaining, casual style helps make this more than a 'how to get the job you want' book."—Commercial Appeal, *Memphis, TN*

There's a place for everybody.
There's always one more way
to do things, and that's your way.
You have a right to try that.

—Waylon Jennings

CREDITS

Research Editor: Janet Connaughton
Editorial: The New Careers Center, Inc.
Cover Design: Shannon Bodie, Lightbourne Images

SUNSHINE JOBS
Career Opportunities
Working Outdoors

by Tom Stienstra
and Robyn Schlueter

Live Oak Publications
Boulder, CO
(303) 447-1087

Live Oak Publications
PO Box 2193
Boulder, CO 80306
(303) 447-1087

Distributed by Publishers Group West

Library of Congress Cataloging-in-Publication Data

Stienstra, Tom.
   Sunshine jobs: career opportunities working outdoors/ by Tom
Stienstra and Robyn Schlueter. --Careers in the outdoors.
      p. cm.
Originally published: Careers in the outdoors. San Francisco, CA
Foghorn Press, c 1992.
   Includes bibliographical references.
ISBN 0-911781-15-3 (trade paper)
1. Outdoor life--Vocational guidance--United States--Handbooks,
   manuals, etc.-- 2. Occupations--United States--Handbooks,
   manuals, etc.   I. Schlueter, Robyn. II. Title.
   HF5382.5.U5S69   1997
   331.7'02--dc21   96-51898
                                            CIP

Disclaimer

Table of Contents

Introduction

People who have careers in the outdoors have their lives filled with adventure, and are not only happy in their work, but are paid well for it. Sound good? It is.

It turns out that there are many paths to the same truth. In researching this book, my assistant Robyn Schlueter and I found 50 outdoor careers from a diverse spectrum of interests, requirements, financial risks and rewards. The jobs span from photographer to park ranger, from surfing instructor to hydrologist, from tackle shop owner to radio show host. Take a good look and see what attracts you. It turns out there are many options, whether you are planning a career start, a career change, or want a seasonal job, retirement income, or some bonus cash on weekends. Always remember: You decide.

To provide an inside look at what is possible, we interviewed more than 100 outdoor career professionals across North America. In their own words, they tell you each job's requirements, prospects, benefits, pay, negatives, and future. Also included is an overview of each job and a capsule summary, as well as where to write for more information or networking.

Remember that you have two ears and one mouth because it is twice as hard to listen as it is to talk. So listen closely to what these professionals have to say because they will tell you what you need to know. As you shop through the book for possibilities, you may see how people can make a pro-active choice as to how they wish to spend their lives. Because of that, the individual who takes the initiative to learn a craft, then moves forward with resolve and enthusiasm, will soar off to success.

The opposite of that, you may otherwise discover, is to start every day as a prisoner of hope. When I quit my job as a sportswriter in the 1970s, I floundered about for nearly a year trying to become an outdoors writer because I had no idea of how to go about my new mission or where to turn for help. Many can empathize, regardless of the field. This book will solve similar dilemmas for newcomers to an outdoor field. So do your homework and plan your strategy from start to finish, and then make the commitment to take your trail as far as it will go.

The outdoors is good for the soul. An outdoor-related job can be rewarding on all levels—physically, mentally, spiritually and financially. Along with spiritual strength, physical health and love, having a fulfilling career is one of the best ways there is to improve your life.

Onward with your quest!

—*Tom Stienstra*

Bicycle Tour Leader

Dreams—It's got to be a dream to get paid to go bicycling in the country's most idyllic settings, but there you are, surrounded by happy, vacationing admirers, pedaling away every day, with your lodging paid for at country inns. How cushy can it get?

Nightmares—It rains, your knee hurts, everybody keeps getting flat tires, and not only that, nobody appreciates your stamina, or jokes either. Finally, you knew the money would be bad, but not this bad. Hey, you've been shooting a day's pay in one night, easy.

Realities—Great adventures, beautiful country, and new friends are the rewards if you can get along well with strangers, and not be too pushy. Good physical conditioning is a given, so is handiness with bikes, which have a way of breaking. The money? Well, you can't win 'em all. While becoming a bicycle tour leader won't lead you to riches and a pension, it provides a unique opportunity for students on summer break or a stopover for others in career transition. It's much easier for a female than a male to get hired. Rarely you will even find a wealthy eccentric (who is also a biking nut) taking a stab at it.

What it's all about—Bicycle tours are designed so participants see the most beautiful parts of America while pedaling down back roads by day, then staying at comfortable country inns by night. Some people say there is no better way to see Vermont in the fall, upstate New York in the spring or Tahoe in summer.

That is why people who sign up to take part in these tours arrive in such good spirits, making the job of tour leader quite easy, at least for the first few days of each week-long stint. All you need is to be able to fix bicycles, be in good physical condition, and be able to get along with all kinds of people. It also helps if you don't need to make much money, because bicycle tour leaders typically make peanuts, like $50 a day, sometimes even less, and only in rare cases $100 per day. A bonus is that your lodging and meals are paid for, which helps financial overhead. Just make sure your expenses don't surpass income, and if they don't, then you might want to check this job out. Money is rarely the measure of any experience, and being a bicycle tour leader is a good example of that.

A basic truth about the outdoors is that the slower you go, the more you will enjoy it. The slowness order goes like this: jet, airplane, car, motorcycle, bicycle, horseback, feet. Bicycle is situated just about perfectly, not so fast (and engine powered) so as to force you to miss details, but not so slow as to reduce the amount of country you can see. Bike tours commonly cover 40 or 50 miles a day, and you get the chance to get in touch with your surroundings on an intimate basis.

After awhile, you will be in such good condition that it will become routine to pedal up a five-mile hill, to turn in a 75-mile day, or to laugh and talk while pushing out the last miles of the day into a headwind. A key to remember is that as a bike tour leader, you are not allowed to expect the same stamina from your group, or worst of all, to show off or to tell them how wonderful you are.

Right there is the key. Participants in these tours say the number one thing they hate is being pressured by a tour leader to cover a certain amount of distance in an unreasonable, specified amount of time. It gets worse if a member of the group is tired, becomes disenchanted with an upcoming hill, and then is told by the tour leader, "OK, time to grunt it out; let's get those pedals moving and wheels rotating. This hill isn't for wimps!"

You'd be better off saying, "Maybe we should take a break and get prepared for this next hill. How do you feel about it?"

That might sound simple enough, but this business of seeing it through another's eyes can be difficult, especially for college-age males who take their athletic vigor for granted. That is one reason why females have the edge in securing a tour leader position; according to the owners of tour companies, females are more considerate of the guests than their male counterparts. "I wish my entire crew of tour leaders were young women," said one. "They tend to get along better with the groups. But they're hard to find."

Openings for this summer job are not difficult come by, providing you get your name, abilities and resume to the owners of bike tour companies by mid-March or April, when most tour leaders are selected. If you are making contact by mail, it is a good idea to include a photograph of yourself. Even though doing good beats looking good, appearance counts for plenty any time you're dealing with the public.

Bicycle tours may be an offshoot of the fitness trend, and in the long run, that bodes well for the industry. Another plus is that every year, more and more people who live in cities realize the wonders available in the great outdoors, and ponder over what they are missing. A bicycle tour can hold particular fascination for them. The same is true for the person who might consider a job as a tour leader. If the yearning is there, take a summer or two and try it on for size. After all, it beats working.

Career Case Study

Claudette Bourque, Massachusetts
Claudette Bourque, a grandmother of three, guides bicycle tours for Bike Vermont in the summer months and works as a swimming instructor for the YMCA in the winter. She also guides year-round for Outdoor Vacations for Women Over 40, leading bicycling, hiking, cross-country skiing, snowshoeing and canoeing trips. Claudette worked for 15 years as a bookkeeper before deciding to move on to the field of outdoor adventure. She now resides in Gardner, Massachusetts.

Requirements—You need to be a bicyclist yourself, first of all. It helps to have experienced some trips yourself, so you know what a tour is like. You also have to have some knowledge of bike repair. You should be a very enthusiastic person with some knowledge about group dynamics. People skills are very important, because you're with groups of people for days at a time. It's important to be in fairly good physical condition, because you're biking between 20 and 50 miles per day, up and down hills, for four or five days a week.

Prospects—Guide jobs are fairly easy to find because the rate of turnover is so high. Many bike tour guides are people who are in transition in their lives, and most don't stay for more than a couple of seasons. There are some, like myself, who return every season, but that is the exception rather than the rule.

Benefits—Probably the number one benefit for me is working with people on vacation. I don't run into many difficult people; for the most part, they're looking to relax and have fun, and you can have fun along with them. You can create new friends. Through them you can also learn a lot about the country, because people come from every state, as well as Canada. Another great benefit is just being outdoors, bicycling and exercising at the same time that I'm working.

Pay—A beginning guide's salary is not very high, but remember that all expenses are paid; room and board is always provided at the inns. The actual daily wage is probably between $40 and $50. For returning guides, that usually goes up in $5 (per day) increments per year. We also receive a yearly bonus based on the number of days we've worked.

Negatives—I don't find many negatives in the job, even when it rains. Sometimes you have to be responsible for getting people into a positive mood when there's bad weather, though. That's where experience comes in handy.
You don't always get as much private time as you might like when you're touring. Sometimes I just want to get a bowl of popcorn and go for a walk rather than sit at a big dinner table at the inn and socialize.

The future—I feel the prospects are very good, because people are becoming more concerned about health and fitness, as well as the environment. Bicycling is becoming a popular alternative to driving in order to avoid pollution.

Career Case Study

Jill Johnson, California

Jill Johnson is a bicycle tour leader with Backroads Bicycle Touring, which is based in Berkeley, California. They specialize in week-long tours.

Requirements—I think the most important requirement is to be a people-oriented person, because you're constantly dealing with so many different kinds of personalities. You're also serving as a liaison between your guests and the staffs of the hotels and restaurants that you deal with on the road. There's a lot of interaction with the general public as well, because we're very visible on the road.

You have to be very well organized. A tour leader has so many details to be responsible for. It's up to the leaders to make sure the guests have an enjoyable experience. There are other areas of knowledge that are learned mostly while on the job, but it would be beneficial to have some previous background in them. One of those is bike mechanics, because you will always need to be repairing and maintaining equipment. Another is food preparation. The leaders are the ones who prepare picnics for the guests, and on the camping trips we cook all three meals. You also need a special driver's license to drive the passenger van.

Prospects—It depends on where you are and which company you want to work for. There are a number of companies throughout the U.S., Europe and Canada. Some are small, mom-and-pop-type businesses, and some are quite large. I would think that the smaller ones have a lower rate of turnover simply because they are often very tightly knit, family-run groups. Backroads, the firm that I work for, has a large number of employees and a very thorough hiring and training program. I know that the number of people who applied this year was higher than it ever has been. It's a really unique sort of job, and I think that there are a lot of people out there who want to be involved in this type of activity and be paid for it.

Benefits—The two main bonuses are the travel experience and the people you deal with. When I say people, I also mean the other leaders who you work with. They are just as interesting and exciting as the people you lead. It's very rewarding. Like any job, you follow certain guidelines, but with each trip you're creating something really special for the people you're with. Each leader leaves their mark, and each one is different.

Pay—The pay is not why you'd seek this job out. For the first year, a beginning guide can expect to earn about $40 to $50 per day, depending on what type of trip it is. There's a pretty significant jump from the first to the second year. That's sort of an incentive to come back. After the second year, the increments of increase get smaller. You might go from getting an extra $15 a day one year to only $5 more per day the next year. There are other things that come into play; when you start gaining other responsibilities such as paperwork and training, you have the opportunity to earn extra money.

Comparatively, the pay isn't great, but it is very possible to save while you're on the road. Your expenses are minimal and can be nonexistent if you want them to be. All of your lodging and meals are covered by the business, and unless you want to buy a glass of wine or something that's not covered, you don't have to spend any of your own money. On most trips there's no time to think about shopping or spending money anyway.

Negatives—Being on the road all the time is sometimes really hard. For some that's a positive thing, but as time goes by, it can become a bigger and bigger burden. Many leaders are on the road so much that they don't bother keeping an apartment, so when they come back, they're jumping from couch to couch and living out of a duffel bag. They may not have any sort of home base, and that can be unsettling.

The future—During the years I've been with Backroads, I've seen the business grow. I think that the outdoor field as a whole is growing, and I don't think there's an end in sight. People are looking for more active vacation opportunities, things that they can participate in rather than sedentary activities like beach-sitting. And I believe that as long as there are people interested in the outdoors, there will be a need for people to guide them.

References

Bike Centennial, 150 East Pine Street, Missoula, MT 59802; (406) 721-1776.

The League of American Bicyclists, 190 West Ostend, Ste 120, Baltimore, MD 21230; (410) 539-3399 or (800) 288-BIKE.

Backroads, 801 Cedar Street, Berkeley, CA 94710; (510)527-1889, extension 117 or (800) 462-2848.

Vermont Bike Touring, Box 711, Bristol, VT 05443; (802) 453-4811 or (800) 245-3868.

Bush Pilot

Dreams—Bush pilots fly in awesome wild country to the best fishing and hunting spots in the world, have a great adventure every day of the summer, get to catch huge fish any time they want, are paid very well, and command instant respect.

Nightmares—What if the weather socks in and your clients demand a refund worth thousands? Or an engine part breaks and you can't fly? Or the kid in back throws up on you? You can't get any customers and no lodge wants you, and not only that, the mosquitoes eat you alive. And when will you ever get out of the back country?

Realities—It's expensive to get a commercial pilot's license, $15,000 to $20,000, and you need a lot of flying time to be qualified to work for a lodge. That done, the pay is good, overhead can be nil, and you get a bald eagle's view of the wildest country in North America.

What it's all about—My dad told me that the second-best feeling in the world is flying. The first-best, he explained, is. . . landing. Heh, heh, heh. Flying a bush plane, a plane with floats instead of wheels, is more than simply using a transport vehicle to get you and your customers to the best places to fish and hunt in North America. It's the process itself that is exciting, rewarding and just plain fun. The pay is good, the adventures are unmatched, and it's an excellent outlet for people who need a challenge that requires both intellect and physical ability.

As a bush pilot, you pick up wide-eyed vacationers at a dock, then fly them off into wild country, make your landing on a lake or river, let them out for their fishing or hunting vacation, and off you go again. Whether you say "Be back tonight" or "Be back in a week," you are up, up and away, having the time of your life. Maybe you'll even land on a secret lake of yours and catch a few giant fish before heading off again.

Most bush pilots say things like, "I've got the best job in the world," and they mean it. It is an ideal occupation for all ages, whether you're a young person looking for full-time summer work, a middle-aged professional looking for a career change, or someone near retirement who wants adventure, and to be paid well for it in the bargain. The prerequisites, however, are many.

You must pass a series of tests, checkrides and flying hours in order to qualify to carry passengers for hire under the laws of the Federal Aviation Administration. In addition, many lodge owners in Alaska have more stringent requirements for their pilots. In any case, the more flying experience, the better. One of the drawbacks is coming up with the dough to pay for the flying experience.

For starters, you will need a pilot's license. If you have the aptitude for flying and do your ground work, you can get a pilot's license in about six months, going through about $5,000 for plane rental and tutoring instruction. After a year of logging hours, most pilots will obtain an instrument rating, which costs another $5,000. Then you will need a seaplane rating ($1,500). Some pilots get a twin engine rating ($5,000), a commercial rating ($1,000), and since they have gone that far, spend another $1,500 and become a Certified Flight Instructor. The more experience and levels of certification you have, the easier it is to get hired. You always get paid back.

Of course, each of these flying levels requires a lot of home-work. But if you know you are going to take it all the way, your best bet is to arrange a package deal from a flight-based operator at a general aviation airport. With a package that includes plane rental, tutoring and tests, you can become a professional pilot for $15,000 to $20,000. Pilots already working for the airlines or the military have it easier. They can get their seaplane rating, then head north to Alaska or Canada.

As a certified pilot with commercial and seaplane ratings, you have three basic options: 1) You can work for a lodge, which provides everything you need and pays you about $1,000 per week. 2) You can work as an independent with your own plane, flying vacationers to their destinations, which pays about $400 to $600 per flight, sometimes more. 3) You can work as a semi-outfitter, setting up a number of outposts with boats and tents, then flying customers and dropping them off for three days to a week.

Each has it benefits, but working for a lodge is probably the best deal. You get a lot of flying in, the lodge provides the plane, makes all repairs, pays you well, and often will include food and lodging for the season. Your overhead is almost nil. The bad part is living the camp life all summer. After a while, if you survive the mosquitoes, it starts to grind on you.

The opposite end of the spectrum is working for yourself. That means owning your own bush plane in quality condition, such as a Cessna 206, 185 or a Beaver (figure $100,000 to $200,000), paying for all the maintenance work (about $5,000 per season), insurance ($5,000), and gas and oil ($2.50 per gallon). You can make $500 per flight, which a group of four vacationers split up and think is a deal. There can be a steady stream of clients, too, thanks to the remote Forest Service cabins in Tongas National Forest in Alaska that rent out for $20 a night and have become so popular. This is no mystery, however, and other pilots with the same idea will compete for those jobs.

The other option is becoming a quasi-outfitter, where you set up outposts with boats, motors, tents, cooking gear and food, then fly in guests for short stays. Because of government regulation, this is more successful in Canada than in the U.S. You can clear $1,000 per week per guest, but the headaches are many, especially if a grizzly decides to destroy the outpost, or worse, take a bite out of somebody.

Of course, the key is to get yourself in a position where you will be flying a lot. You will get to know the country, find the lakes with the best fishing, and you'll be doing it in Alaska or Canada, where the word "frontier" still has meaning. The view from the pilot's seat of the expanses of the northern wildlands is a reminder of the greatness possible on earth.

A lot of people complain a lot about this planet, but at last look, it's still the best one around. Bush pilots are reminded of that every time they reach cruising altitude, take a moment, and gaze down at it all.

Career Case Study

Arnie Johnson, Alaska
Arnie Johnson has owned and operated Mountain
Aviation in Sitka, Alaska since 1983. He has worked as
a bush pilot in Alaska and Montana since 1977, and has
had the opportunity to explore some of the country's

most beautiful territory. He lives in Sitka with his wife and four children.

Requirements—The first thing you've got to have is a commercial license. To break in, you start with 200 hours of flight time, then you submit your application to an aviation company and hopefully find someone to train you. Here at Mountain Aviation, we spend a week just on ground training: learning about the operations manual, transporting hazardous material, how the airplane works, and dealing with people. The airtime required depends on the individual.

You have to really get to know the area you're working in, and that can take a lot of time. But the number one consideration is attitude. I'd say 90 percent of the job is being willing to work and get out there and do it. You've got to like the country, like to fly, and have a good sense of responsibility and basic common sense. If you have a bad attitude, it's just not going to work out.

Having a good rapport with the customers is important, too. You deal with so many types of people, from loggers and miners to senators and congressmen. If you're able to get along with customers and make them feel comfortable, they'll keep coming back. You have to talk to them, tell them what's going on. I find that it really helps to be talkative, especially if the passenger is a little uneasy. If a customer is nervous about flying, it makes it even worse to sit there with a totally silent pilot.

Prospects—It depends on where you are. The smaller companies like mine tend to have a very low rate of turnover because we have the same guys working here year after year. But the larger businesses, which have many employees, have a much higher turnover rate, and there are more opportunities. It depends on location too; for instance, in the Ketchikan area, the competition is fierce because there are more people and the demand is higher.

Benefits—You're getting paid for something you love to do. I couldn't buy the experience of flying around here. In terms of scenery, we get to go on million-dollar flights all the time. To me it's more pleasure than work. I've always said that if it ever becomes a job, I'll go out and get a real job. But it hasn't yet.

Pay—A trainee with some flight time but no experience in the area will start out at about $825 a week, based on a five-day week. Once established, an experienced pilot will make about $1000 per week.

Negatives—You have to work long hours. We try to fly from 7 a.m. to 7 p.m., and we generally work really hard. The FAA only allows us to fly so many hours in a day, but some days you're working harder at it because of weather conditions and such. The summer season is when we do the bulk of our flying, so we have to work really hard to carry over through the winter months.

It can be hard on families, especially if you're a helicopter pilot. If you're flying a plane, you can finish your flight and go home, but helicopter pilots tend to want to keep their craft with them, and that requires staying overnight. I'm gone for weeks and sometimes months at a time. That can be kind of hard on the kids. Other negatives are bad weather and grumpy passengers, but those you can usually deal with pretty easily.

The future—I think there are a lot of people out there who are interested in flying; it sounds like such an exciting job. And there are a lot of experienced pilots working for airlines who want to try something different. The interest is there, and there always will be a need for bush pilots in Alaska. In the interior, there are no roads; the only way to get around is by plane or helicopter.

Career Case Study

Niall McGraph, British Columbia
Niall McGraph, 22, has worked as a bush pilot in Canada since 1989. He enjoys traveling the "beautiful and untouched" western coast of Canada, and is an avid skier and runner during the off-season. Niall lives in Belaculah, British Columbia.

Requirements—Basically you need a commercial pilot's license and a float endorsement, which allows you to fly sea planes. When you go to work for a company, that's usually what you'll be flying. By the time you get both your licenses, you'll have a total of about 250 hours of flight time.

You have to be confident. Most people who hop into the airplane for the first time are a little nervous, and you have to show them that you know what you're doing.

Prospects—The market is very competitive. The company I work for employs about seven pilots, and right now we're receiving ten resumes per day. There's a low rate of turnover. The career is getting more professional, which is good. It takes away from the public's view that bush pilots are these crazy guys.

Benefits—I love getting up to go to work every day. I don't know a lot of people who can say that. I get to go out and get paid to do my favorite hobby. And the pay's not too bad.

Pay—It all depends on the amount of experience you have, but that's kind of a Catch-22. You need experience to get a job, but you need a job to get experience. I know a lot of guys who fly for free, in exchange for room and board, just so they can get experience. When you start flying, you can make about $1000 a month. As you gain experience, you can make upwards of $40,000 a year. If you go into the airlines, the pay fluctuates even more, but it goes pretty high.

Negatives—It's only seasonal, and the days are long. You usually work seven days a week during the season, at least ten hours a day. A lot of bush pilots work for fishing camps or lodges, and they're always flying. It can be pretty stressful.

The future—I don't think it'll be expanding very much; I don't see a great increase in job openings, but it'll be a long time before areas like Alaska and the western coast of Canada will be accessible by any other form of travel.

I do think the industry in general is becoming more professional. Pilots are starting to make this a career rather than a stepping stone to working for a major airline.

References

Alaska Air Carriers Association, 4040 B Street, Anchorage, AK 99503; (907) 277-0071.

Canadian Aircraft Owners and Pilots Association (COPA), 75 Albert Street, Ste 1001, Ottawa, Canada K1P5E7; (613) 236-4901.

Aircraft Owners and Pilots Association (AOPA), 421 Aviation Way, Frederick, MD 21701; (800) 659-2170.

For a list of certificated pilot schools write: Supt. of Documents, US Government Printing Office, Washington, DC 20402.

Canoe Rental Service

Dreams—You "work" six months a year, then have a six month vacation, and pull down about $40,000. You canoe when you want and where you want. Maybe you guide now and then and become known as the Legendary Paddler of The North Woods. The big question: "What exotic vacation should we take this year, dear?"

Nightmares—When business is bad, it seems like there isn't a humanoid on the planet who is going to walk through the door. Then when business is good, you have no time to go canoeing yourself. You're working every day, with too many loose ends, too many whiners, too many questions. Are we having fun yet?

Realities—You must have a good location, either near a world-class water or a decent river near a city, to pull in customers. That done, figure on spending $50,000 to get started, then earning $20,000 to $40,000 per year. You have to be detail- oriented in the short run (how does that shuttle work?) and astute in the long run (how much does that canoe sell for?). Do it right and you won't have regrets.

What it's all about—On a lake, canoe paddling is so quiet. On a windless day, all you hear is the sound of paddles dipping in the water, with silent little whirlpools left behind with each stroke. Even deer sipping at the lake's edge don't know you're there.

On a river, canoeing requires a distinct lack of effort. It is the current that sends you downstream, and you and your partner spend your efforts guiding the boat through riffles, around sweepers and eddies, keeping a lookout for submerged boulders. All the way, there is a sensation of freedom as the river sails you along.

That is ironic, because running a canoe rental service is nothing like that. It isn't quiet, and it takes a lot of effort. And if you don't watch it, you won't get to canoe at all yourself because you will be working seven days a week trying to keep your customers happy. You actually don't have a choice with the latter; they won't stop asking questions until you have virtually planned their entire trip for them.

But the rewards make the business satisfying for the people who can pull it off. You only have to work five or six months a year, during which you make $20,000 to $40,000. That leaves a long off-season to earn more with another job, or just play. It also means that when summer arrives, you have to score big, or the winter will feel colder than Bismarck, North Dakota.

The three keys with this business are quite simple: location, location and location. That is why some people go bankrupt and others, using the same business techniques, get rich. If your rental service is not based within close proximity to a world-class canoeing destination—or a decent river near a metropolitan area—it can be tough to get enough customers to pay the freight.

Examples of premium locations include the Bowron Lakes Circuit in British Columbia, or the Boundary Waters and Quetico in northern Minnesota and southern Ontario. There are many others, of course. Examples of decent canoeing rivers near a metropolitan area include the Russian River north of the San Francisco Bay Area, or the Moose River in New York. Get the picture? The biggest mistake well-intentioned people make when starting a business like this is failing to project customer traffic accurately. If you can't get a handle on it, you are better off buying an existing successful business, although it may cost you a hundred thousand, maybe more.

The do-it-yourself method is a lot cheaper, of course, but more risky. Figure about $50,000 to get started with a building lease, canoes and associated equipment, insurance, and employees. Then plan on plenty of public relations work to get the word out to the public. If you are the type who would prefer to live in a cave and never answer to anybody, forget it.

Sure, you are certainly your own boss. But as others who run small businesses realize, you also become a prisoner of your customers. If you set up near an area loaded with quality lakes, this means helping people plan canoe camping trips, showing each one how to secure the canoe to the top of their car, and then explaining in detail the best areas to visit. If you set up near a river, it means arranging shuttles, lessons and helping to match the ability of paddlers to appropriate sections of river.

The logistics can be an ordeal for anybody but clear thinkers who enjoy both the process and the people. If you have that kind of mind, then you will also be able to schedule in plenty of canoeing time yourself, perhaps occasionally guiding tours (a way to make some extra bucks).

If you develop skills as a photographer, writer, seminar leader or speaker, you can make bonus money at your leisure in the off-season by communicating the canoeing experience. Another way to add to your income is to sell canoes and canoeing equipment. Many people take their first canoe trip with a distinct degree of curiosity and awe. When they discover how enjoyable it is, they not only come back for more, but are often ready to buy. If you step in and sell them a canoe and the accessories (paddles, lifejackets, lead rope), you can make an extra $250 to $400 a pop.

Success has a way of overshadowing all the little griefs, the weather, the inevitable whiners, the lost paddle, and the periods where you work every day for weeks. Of course, every career has its nits, and you learn to ride them out. The smiling faces of happy customers returning to say "thanks" is another bonus. No matter how tired you get, that has a way of inspiring you onward to another day.

Career Case Study

Beth Tickner, New York

Beth and her husband Dan have owned Tickner's Moose River Canoe Outfitters since 1989. Her past experience includes working for Vail Associates in Colorado and for a real estate development company. She enjoys traveling, canoeing, rowing and tennis, and has a great love for animals. The Tickners have one young son, and live in Old Forge, New York, in the Adirondack Mountains.

Requirements—Educationally, someone who's interested in getting into the field might concentrate on a background in business or marketing. A working knowledge of accounting would be helpful as well. But the most important requisite is experience; you have to have actual experience in canoeing and camping and a strong general sense of the outdoors. You must be very knowledge-able about the area you're working in. People are renting canoes and camping gear from you, and they need your help on trip planning and itineraries.

I think it helps to be a real people person. Most people who come to you are on vacation. They may want everything planned out in detail for them, so you have to have numerous conversations with them. Or sometimes because they are on vacation they have a lot of time to shoot the breeze. Either way, patience is a virtue. Because we live next door to our business, we often find people knocking at the door at any time of the day.

You have to be flexible and able to deal with things as they come. If you stick to set rules, you could lose a lot of business, and in the canoe business you take everything you can get.

Prospects—I would say that the market is really good right now, especially with the current awareness of the environment. The most important consideration for a new business is location. Ideally, it should be situated on or close to the water, in an area with heavy tourism. The problem is that those factors make land and taxes very expensive, and the profit margin can be minimal until you have built up your name, clientele and business.

Benefits—I enjoy being my own boss and the sense of achievement after all the hours of sweat. Because we are located in a climate where winter limits our business to being open only seven months of the year, I enjoy spending the winter months at home with my son, working on the upcoming season. Also, my husband and I are able to raise our son together and work at the same time in a beautiful environment.

And of course, we have quite a selection of boats to go out and experience all the places we tell our customers about.

Pay—When you first start out, you're not going to make any profit, because you've got to pay for your equipment and worry about all your start-up fees such as insurance, licensing, things like that. The amount of capital you need to get established depends on whether you're going to buy or lease a place, and whether you're going to be a retail business or deal only with rentals. If you're going to lease and strictly rent, I'd say you'd need at least $50,000 to get set up. If you decide to include retail sales, that figure would be significantly higher to cover inventory costs.

Your income is what you decide your salary is going to be.

Most owners make it fairly low to avoid other costs that are involved in payroll expense. After that, it's all in how much business you pull in and how you handle your cash flow. Once you get established, you could probably expect to start at $20,000 a season, depending on how long your season is. In this particular area, we have a five-month season, and we only do strong business in July and August, so we really have to hustle in the summer to cover the off-season.

Negatives—You never know if you're going to make it, because you're so weather-dependent. The season is so short that rainy weekends cannot be made up financially. Running a small business can be very expensive because of the cost of operation. You try to do as much as you can by yourself to keep the bills down, so that can be very time-consuming.

You can end up being really burned out by the end of the season. You work and work and work intensely for five or six months, and then you're sick of dealing with people and you don't even want to look at another canoe. Then you have a long winter and you can't wait to get back.

The future—People will always want to canoe. What's hard to foresee are the political and financial considerations: how much land is going to be available, whether potential areas will be accessible or not, what the cost of liability insurance will be, what the weather in future seasons will be. Uncontrollable circumstances may make it difficult.

Career Case Study

Don Waterberry, California
Don Waterberry is general manager of Trowbridge Recreation, a canoe rental company, and has been with the business off and on since 1968. He enjoys fishing, motorcycling, bicycling and walking. He and his wife and two sons live in Healdsburg, California.

Requirements—I don't think you need an extensive education. I went straight from high school into the business. The two most important qualities you can have are experience and determination. It takes a special person to be in a managerial position. Some people can be around the business for years and years and never have what it takes to be a manager.

You can't be too high strung; if you let the little things get to you, you'll never make it. You have to be able to organize well. There are so many things to deal with—canoes strung out on miles of river, vehicles shuttling people back and forth, reservations, people asking questions. You also need to know the value of having good people working for you. You can't do it by yourself, and quality employees can really improve your business.

You have to be able to relate to everybody. We get all kinds of people in here: rich, poor, non-English-speaking. If you have the ability to get along with everybody, no matter who they are, you will be much more successful. It's important to remember that you'll be dealing with thousands of people, all with different levels of knowledge. Some people will come in and know exactly what to do; others are like children—you have to lead them through every step. You can't get testy with beginners.

Prospects—You have to know your local market. I know that in this area, there's one other rental business besides us, and a new guy trying to break in would have a mighty tough time. Cost is very prohibitive. There are so many start-up expenses: You have to buy your fleet, and canoes are not cheap; you have to pay for insurance, hire employees, get permits to launch and pull in canoes. The costs would be unbelievable. And it takes a long time before you can begin to make much money.

A more practical business, I would think, would be not just renting boats, but also doing retail sales. But that would take even more money to get started.

Benefits—I love working outdoors and being my own boss. I couldn't see myself sitting in an office all the time. I'm sure many people would be envious of the schedule I have: I work for six months, then basically do what I want for six months. I enjoy working with a lot of people. You meet so many different, interesting types. The variety keeps you from ever getting bored. Every day brings new experiences and different things to do.

Pay—Many people start out as clerks, making around $5 an hour. It doesn't go up much until you reach management level; high pay, even for a foreman who's been around for years, is about $7.50 an hour. I make about $35,000 a year right now, but included in that is my house and a company car. It's not a high-paying job; you do it for the personal satisfaction, not the paycheck.

Negatives—The hours during the season are very long. I work 12 hours a day, seven days a week from April to October. You really have to concentrate and make your income for the whole year in a short period of time.

Occasionally people move in and want to stop the canoes running on the river, much like the people who move next door to an airport and want the planes to stop flying. That can be a hassle, but it's fairly rare and not too hard to deal with.

The future—For a while in the '80s, business seemed to be slowing, but recently we've begun to grow fairly rapidly. People today want to do outdoor things, and canoeing is a relatively inexpensive family vacation. We charge $32, and you can't even take a family to the movies for that price. The rivers seem to be more enjoyable for recreation these days. The water is cleaner, there is more wildlife around, and as people gain ecological awareness, fewer people are using the rivers in negative ways.

References

North American Paddle Sports Association (NAPSA), 12455 North Wauwatosa Road, Mequon, WI 53097; (800) 755-5228.

Professional Paddle Sports Association, PO Box 248, Butler, KY 41006; (606) 472-2205.

Canoe & Kayak Magazine, PO Box 3146, Kirkland, WA 98083; (206) 827-6363.

Paddler Magazine, PO Box 1341, Eagle, ID 83616; (208) 939-4500.

Coast Guard

Dreams—Other people have blood in their veins; you have sea water. You love your job, are paid well for it, and have a great variety of tasks awaiting, such as rescuing people, piloting ships or stopping a drug shipment. All the while, you and the sea are one. It's a tight outfit, and you like the fit, maybe for a lifetime.

Nightmares—The budget is short again. That means you're stuck on land and can't even do your job. When you complain, you almost get thrown in the brig. At sea, when boaters see "Coast Guard," they're almost never happy to see you, figuring you're going to bust them for something. They're right. Heaven forbid if you get seasick when writing a ticket.

Realities—It's a good solid outfit, a little heavy in officious attitude, with openings available to quality individuals. Once in, don't blow the deal with your big mouth. Satisfaction rates high for those who get enough time on the water. It's another story if you get assigned a job you don't like, or the budget is tight. The key to satisfaction: If you love the open sea, always try to remember that every time you look at it.

What it's all about—Some people are just naturally attuned to water, big water, be it the Atlantic Ocean, Pacific Ocean, Gulf of Mexico or Great Lakes. These people feel a special aura from the vast expanse of the sea, and it has a dramatic soothing effect on their temperament. Once it gets in your blood, you've got to have it. Ah, the feeling of a good ship cutting a path through the wide-open spaces of the sea . . . it has a way of casting all of life's troubles aside, like a deckhand tossing off the mooring rope.

That is how it is for many who work for the U.S. Coast Guard, regardless of their assigned duties. All differences are transcended by their bonded passion for the sea. If you have ever felt it, you know exactly what this career is about.

There are so many choices. One of the real attractions with the Coast Guard is the ability to match your talent with the job. Within the Coast Guard are hundreds of positions: radar specialist, radio work, pilotage, search and rescue, inspections, surveillance, drug interdiction, patrol, safety, accident investigation... the list goes on. It's a take-your-pick deal. Well, almost. Sometimes you get your pick until an admiral decides to pick for you.

They want the best you can offer. To get a job here requires intellect as well as aptitude, labor as well as infatuation, inner drive as well as passion. You also have to be a team player, because there is no bureaucracy like government bureaucracy, especially in a tight outfit that prides itself on officious behavior like the Coast Guard. Of course, another must is that you have to be able to keep from donating your dinner to Davy Jones' Locker on a regular basis, heh, heh, heh.

Newcomers must complete the Coast Guard's formal training program. To be considered for that, you have to demonstrate that you have potential as a good prospect. Good grades in school can help. So can your depth of knowledge of the specific job you desire. Personality counts big, and so does appearance. The Coast Guard avoids prospects with a history of rocking the boat, and any whiners need not apply.

But what they are looking for most of all is a general commitment to excellence. The best rewards come for those who master a specialty, and then as an authority on it, become indispensable to the operation. So the best suggestion is to do exactly that: Select a specific interest, then do everything possible to master it. Your superiors will notice. That's how positions get filled and promotions awarded.

A career in the Coast Guard is rewarding on many levels, including the personal satisfaction of being on the water, the good feeling that comes with rescue work or keeping people safe, and also the pay that comes with the job. Cadets usually start out in the $25,000 range (typical start-up pay for government work), then top out at $50,000. The pay can go higher, if you gain a captainship or are appointed to a policy-making position.

While many rewarding careers in the Coast Guard are available that have nothing to do with running boats, it is the idea of captaining a large craft that often provides the most compelling attraction for newcomers. If this is your calling, become proficient in all areas of navigation, but become the best at a particular pursuit, such as pilotage. You will eventually have a chance to demonstrate that mastery, particularly if you are posted at a busy harbor that gets fog and wind, where boats have many hazards to navigate—like San Francisco or New York.

When you develop a reputation as one who just plain knows their stuff, you will be in demand and put on the promotion track. The Coast Guard is not without major problems, unfortunately. The biggest is intermittent funding, with outlays varying from year to year depending on the latest groping on the federal budget by Congress and the White House. There have been cases where a Coast Guard boat has gone down for repair and the harbor was left for weeks on end without a single patrol or rescue boat because of insufficient funds.

As a rescue specialist stuck on land, what could be more frustrating than being unable to answer a radio call for help? Nothing. Well, maybe nothing. What might be more frustrating is trying to discuss and solve the problem with the top Coast Guard dogs. Some of these fellows are remarkable, clear-thinking individuals, rising to the top from years of extraordinary work. But many seem like nothing more than regressive appointees, bureaucrats buried in paper, muddling about like lost rowboats in a thick fog. Remember, this is not only government, but also technically the military. If you are progressive, smart and have ideas to improve operations, these guys can drive you nuts and jeopardize your career.

Oh yeah? How? Well, remember this: The nail that stands up gets hammered down. So you learn. Learn where your boundary of authority is, then don't step beyond it, an essential with the Coast Guard. Instead, do your job, and do it well. Become a master at a specialty. The pay is decent, but more importantly, you will be in touch with the wide-open sea. Always remember that it is your love of big water that attracted you to the Coast Guard. Through good and bad, that love is something that lasts.

Career Case Study

Peggy Thurber, California
Lieutenant Commander Peggy Thurber has been with

the U.S. Coast Guard since 1980. She worked previously
as an elementary school teacher in New York. Peggy is
married, has two children, and lives in Walnut Creek,
California, where she enjoys music and gardening.

Requirements—There are several ways to get into the Coast Guard. I was an elementary school teacher before I came in. I already had a bachelor's degree, and I went through Officer Candidates School (OCS). But some people go through the academy and get their degree there, and some get enlisted. Some people come in with a direct commission without going through all the channels. It really depends on what you want to do.

To start out, officers in the Coast Guard are not really specialists. There is a point where you become specialized to some degree, but we are basically interchangeable as far as capability is concerned.

Prospects—Competition is very intense, especially in the officer corps. It's also pretty competitive for enlisted people, but they can generally stay where they are as long as they're performing well. In the officer corps, you only get a certain number of chances to get promoted when an opening comes up, and if you don't, you're basically out.

I know that the Coast Guard Academy is the only academy that accepts people by merit based on aptitude and high school grades rather than appointments. But they have more applicants than they need, so they can afford to be pretty picky. As far as job security goes, I feel a little more safe in my job than I might out in the civilian sector. There's a certain stability that's lacking in the private sector, especially when the economy is down.

Benefits—It's never boring. I feel like I get a chance to do a lot of things that most people don't even think about doing. For example, I was down in the middle of an oil pollution spill recently; I flew down in a Coast Guard helicopter, was right out there in the middle of things working, and then I flew back in a private aircraft. I've crawled around big tank ships and ran around on Coast Guard boats. Every day is different.

Working with people in the maritime industry is generally very enjoyable. The people that I work for and those who work for me are really high caliber people, very professional.

Of all the armed services, the Coast Guard seems to be way ahead. It's an ideal position for a woman; I'd recommend the Coast Guard to any woman who was interested in joining the armed services. Every other branch has restrictions for women's jobs, but the Coast Guard has no such limitations.

Pay—The pay really varies depending on what kind of position you hold. The pay scale is the same as all the other branches of the armed services. It depends on if you're enlisted or commissioned, and from there you move up. You get 30 days a year of vacation and unlimited sick leave, which are both great benefits, if you get a chance to take them. They offer good medical and retirement benefits as well.

Negatives—Long hours are to be expected. You're on duty seven days a week, 24 hours a day. I find that I'm away from home more than I'd like, and that's even more true for someone who's working on a boat. An integral part of the Coast Guard is transferring, which gives you a chance to see new places, but it can be a real pain in the neck. If you don't like moving around, you won't like the Coast Guard. You're going to have to relocate about every three to four years, sometimes more often depending on the job.

The future—As far as marine safety is concerned, we're being driven a lot by the Valdez oil spill. The whole area of pollution response and prevention is really on the cutting edge, and we've seen new jobs and funding open up because of it. The Coast Guard has improved greatly since I first started. I hope it will continue to improve and expand in its efforts.

Career Case Study

Donald Bunn, New York
Donald Bunn has been affiliated with the Coast Guard since 1969 and is now a Lieutenant Commander. Between periods of active duty, he worked for the Washington Metropolitan Area Transit Authority as an auditor and budget analyst. He lives with his wife on Governors Island, New York.

Requirements—You must have a high school education; in some situations they'll accept a GED with 15 college credits. You have to be at least 17 years of age, with your parent's permission. You have to be in good health. This is a military operation, so you're subject to many requirements.

The normal avenue is to go through basic training for eight weeks, where you're taught the history of the Coast Guard, the basics of seamanship, firefighting skills, nautical terminology, and basic survival skills for a military environment, such as how to make your bed, how to march, how to address your superior officers. You're also put through a rigorous physical conditioning program.

After you complete basic training, you either go to school or get assigned to the field, depending on what you want to get into. There aren't as many schools in the Coast Guard as in other branches of the military. We don't have as many divisions of specialized tasking as, say, the Navy, because we're operating on a much smaller scale. The Coast Guard operates under the Department of Transportation rather than the Department of Defense, so many things are a bit different.

Different positions require different qualifications. For example, the person responsible for a search and rescue vessel is accountable for the 41-foot boat and the crew. He has to know all about the duties of his crewmen, be familiar with search and rescue, know the navigational Rules of The Road, have firefighting skills, and know how to work all the various electronic equipment on board. The necessary skills are going to be quite a bit different, of course, for someone who works in our public affairs department.

Prospects—There are many different jobs available within the Coast Guard. There are people who drive boats, people who fly planes, damage controlmen, radiomen, health service specialists, cooks, and electronics technicians. There are people who fix the boats and people who run the boats.

Advancement depends on the field you're going into. Some ratings advance more quickly than others. We don't have many positions for public affairs specialists, for example, so those who come in and like the position stay there, which means that vacancies are not created very often. But often someone will go through the ranks and become an electronics technician, realize they can make more money out in the civilian world, and leave, opening a job for someone new.

We are the only branch of the military that doesn't put restrictions on the assignment of females. The Coast Guard has a peacetime mission, but we also have a wartime mission, and an integral part of any member's duty is possibly being assigned to a unit that could be involved in combat.

Benefits—There are advantages to being a small branch of the military. The smaller service gives a greater sense of family.

I like the variety. I've had the opportunity to travel all over the world; I've worked in Honolulu, the Philippines, Vietnam, California, Maryland, Ohio, Washington D.C. and New York City. The multi-mission concept is really good. We have a definite peacetime and definite wartime mission. We're ready for both at all times. It's a "renaissance man" kind of concept—we have to know a little about everything.

I like the fact that as an enlisted member, I was awarded jobs that had a high level of responsibility. That's still true today. On the human side, it's rewarding to know that we're serving the public. We're rendering first aid, fighting fires and saving lives.

Pay—The pay scale and the benefits are identical to the other branches of armed services. It's based on grade level and longevity. When you come out of boot camp, you're making $880.50 a month, plus a subsistence pay of $210 a month. If you're married and live off the base, you receive an additional $302 month for what is called BAQ pay. Subsistence and BAQ pay are not currently taxed, which is very nice.

As an officer, you can make around $1,500 a month, topping out at about $2,000 after a few years. It goes up proportionately from there. I am a Lieutenant Commander with over 20 years in, and I make $3,739 a month, plus BAQ.

Compensation in dollars and cents is below what a civilian would make in a comparable job, but you have to look at the benefits. Everyone, regardless of rank, gets 30 vacation days per year. I have to admit that I've seen some erosion of benefits over the years, but they're still not bad. Retirement benefits are not what they used to be, unfortunately. VA education benefits are pretty nice. You have to look at the overall compensation packet.

Negatives—It seems like the Coast Guard is always fighting to improve its annual budget. It's tough, because we're only paid once for all the hats we wear. When the budget is cut, the same tasking remains and sometimes it even increases. There's no cushion. The infrastructure starts to suffer. There's little budget to offer incentives or special training. There are fewer family housing options.

It's frustrating to me that we're not always recognized as a military organization. A large part of the public doesn't know what we do. Many don't know we're a branch of the military and that we have law enforcement authority. The multi-mission approach is great, but we need to be recognized. We are involved in law enforcement, fisheries and military missions.

The future—The bright spot in the Coast Guard is the marine field. That's actually been born out of disaster, since the Exxon Valdez spill and other major pollution catastrophes. More regulations have been put into effect, and the Coast Guard has been authorized to increase its manpower. With more concern over regulations to contain and prevent the pollution of our natural resources, I think the expansion potential is very good.

Reference

Coast Guard Information Center, 14180 Dallas Parkway, Dallas, TX 75240-9795; (800) 424-8883, extension 5003.

US Coast Guard Academy, Director of Admissions, 15 Mohegan Avenue, New London, CT 06320-9807; (203) 444-8505.

For the address of the nearest Coast Guard recruiting office, phone (800)438-8724.

Commercial
Fisherman

Dreams—Being a commercial fisherman is exciting and unpredictable, with the reward as clear as the big fish on your hook. Ah, you are literally the captain of your ship, deciding everything—where to venture next, what to fish for, when to anchor for the night. You are an example for all, independent and rugged, seeing the world on your own terms.

Nightmares—If the fish don't bite, you're in a hell of a mess. It gets a lot worse if you try to make up for some bad days by fishing in storms. After all, there are no return trips from Davy Jones' Locker. Boats are real money sponges, keeping overhead high. But the worst are the weeks of isolation at sea, and the personal difficulties that isolation creates with your boatmates.

Realities—With training as a deckhand, you will know what you're getting into: long hours at sea, hard work, wildly oscillating paychecks, and a dangerous risk with marginal weather. Mastering seamanship skills comes with the territory. The future will demand the flexibility to leave cold markets behind, and always the ability to enjoy the wind in your face and the magic of a sunrise at sea.

What it's all about—There is no greater prisoner of hope than a commercial fisherman. On the briny blue, everything is in a state of flux, and it gives rise to continual prayer over the winds, seas and swells; over the fish, birds and bait; and over abundance, market and price. When you get done praying about those, you will start hoping about problems back on the mainland: the condition and care of spawning habitat, the political chicanery that affects fish populations, and inevitably, the mirage-like vision of a romantic companion who is supposed to be waiting for you back at the port. That romantic companion is usually a female, because this job is nearly 100 percent male.

You don't become a commercial fisherman part way. You are in or you are out. This has nothing to do with how much time you spend at it—many do quite well on a part-time basis—but rather your state of mind. Every successful commercial fisherman feels that this job is something he just "has to do." If you don't feel that way, too, then you will feel like a square peg in a round hole if you make a run at it.

So a key from the start is to ask, "Why do I want to do this?" If the answer is because you heard that you could work a summer on a commercial fishing boat in Alaska and make a quick $75,000, well, that's the wrong reason (and we'll explain why shortly). If the reason is because you love the sea and its rhythms, and every dawn's light on the brine inspires the hopes of nature's greatest promises, then this is the job for you.

That's because when all is done—from a 10-mile run uphill against a norther, to fouled lines, to the smell of fish guts, to the fish won't bite, to the lonely nights—you will still love your job. Because after all, you love the sea.

The notion of a quick summer hit off Alaska's Kenai is a pipe-dream that should be quashed, and quick. While it is true that some young people do make the trip north, get hired on, and then clear maybe $100,000 in a summer, the fact is that you may have almost as good a chance of dying at sea. According to the U.S. Department of Commerce, the most dangerous job in America is that of a commercial fisherman in Alaska. Boats go out and don't come back. Happens all the time.

It is also very difficult to get such a lucrative job anyway (if it were easy, everybody would do it, right?). Unless you have an insider's connection to a long-established captain who knows about Alaska's fickle weather, you are better off with your feet firmly planted on land. The best way to get started is as a hand at a fair-weather port on either coast, making $15,000 to $20,000 in the process. See the life as it is, live it, and if you still like it, then maybe it is time to invest in a boat, berth, insurance and licenses. You can get in as cheap as $25,000 to $30,000, but figuring $40,000 to $50,000 is more appropriate, and if you want to roll the dice for the big time off Alaska, it can cost a quarter million bucks just to get a fishing permit.

Obviously, the price to get in varies according to locale and target species. Like any career, you must know your trade. When it comes to commercial fishing, there is a lot to know. In fact, you will never stop learning, because Neptune is always coming up with new lessons. A full comprehension of weather, navigation skills and government regulations is absolutely required. Then to make any money, you have to know how to catch fish, keep them fresh, and just as importantly, sell them at a fair price. Starting out green is a mistake; always learn as a deckhand.

There are two additional factors that cannot be minimized. One is the danger; the other is the isolation. The danger is real, particularly in northern harbors. In Crescent City, California, for instance, nearly every winter a crab fisherman is lost at sea while trying to fish an extra day in rough seas. There are many such harbors on both coasts where this occurs.

Then there is the isolation. Some people just can't handle it. Six weeks on a boat can turn some guys into candidates for a sanitarium; it can be worse than jail, with absolutely no female contact. Then there is the bizarre dynamic for commercial fisher-men with families. They return from the sea and discover the homefront runs just fine without them, except for the inevitable: "How much money did you make?"

What is an absolute key for the future of this job is for commercial fishermen to have the flexibility to fish different species in different areas, and the astuteness to recognize when a fishery is going flat and then switch over to something prosperous before getting burned. This is a business with tremendous peaks and valleys. You can be standing on top of Mt. Whitney one year, then be banished by Neptune to the Death Valley of fishing the next. Most commercial fishermen are always worrying about this. But there is always one saving grace. You see, they always have next year to hope for.

Career Case Study

Jake Dykstra, Rhode Island
Jake Dykstra worked as a commercial fisherman for six
years, then retired and sailed the Caribbean for three.
He has been active with the Point Judith Fisherman's

Co-Op in Rhode Island for 40 years, and remains active representing fisheries. He lives in Kingston, Rhode Island.

Requirements—Some say you've got to have a strong back and a weak mind. It is primarily a physical job. You have to be very physically fit. Some people say that the best skippers think like a fish, and I would agree that that's an asset. If you know where the fish are and how they operate, you're going to have one up on the other guys. That skill doesn't put you as far ahead these days, though, because the new electronic equipment does a lot of thinking for you.

A fisherman is essentially a small businessman and he has to run his business accordingly, so business skills are necessary. I've seen skippers who outfished and made more money than anyone else around but still went broke because they spent unwisely. Bills tend to catch up with you much more quickly than they used to.

Prospects—Fishing goes up and down, and sometimes there are good opportunities and sometimes not. Right now the market is such that captains can pick and choose their crew because the economy here in Rhode Island is quite depressed. When the economy is good, the cream of the crop find good jobs, so employers sometimes have to take crewmen who aren't the most competent. Success boils down to the individual and his desire and determination to succeed. If you're persistent, it's hard to miss.

Benefits—A lot of people say that they value the way of life a lot more than the income, but generally the income is pretty good, frequently better than average. Even a crewman on one of these boats makes a better income than the guy who works in a supermarket or mows lawns or whatever.

Being your own boss and doing what you want to do is nice. It's not a nine-to-five job; you don't have set hours. It's an exciting and challenging lifestyle. There's always the possibility of a good trip and good money, and that way of life appeals to many people.

Pay—The pay scale runs the whole gamut. It ranges from a very meager living to owner/operators who probably make two or three times what their crewmen make. Let's say we're talking about the draggers (trawl netters) that I represent. I would say that the average share right now on those vessels is in the $40,000 range. My crewmen make around $40,000 annually. The owner/operator, if he's astute, can make more than that. It just depends on the individual and what he's willing to put into it.

Negatives—The fisherman is away from home a good bit of time. Some think that's great, but others are not happy about being away from their families. As any anthropologist will tell you, there's a lot of divorce and difficulty because of the irregular hours. The wives differ in opinion as much as the fishermen.

It's a dangerous occupation, and fishermen always make light of it, but the fact is it's not easy. It's a very demanding occupation. A lot of times you fish around the clock, day and night, nearly to the point of exhaustion. I don't think there's anyone who can say he appreciates being thrown around out of his bunk when rough weather hits.

The future—I think it will depend on management more than anything else. There's a lot of controversy here in the east about "limited entry." I believe that if you leave the fishermen alone, things will straighten out on their own. I do have to concede, though, that with today's technology it's much easier to devastate a stock of fish, and economically that could be catastrophic. But I think there's been a lot of haste and over-management. There are those who believe that the fisheries should be tightly managed. They are the bureaucrats and environmentalists who teach that fishermen are rapists of our resources. If that continues, I do think there will be limited access to the fisheries. Given what we've seen recently, it would be rather naive to think that the government and environmentalists are going to butt out and leave fishermen alone.

Career Case Study

Nat Bingham, California
Nat Bingham has worked on the Pacific Coast as a commercial fisherman for 30 years, fishing primarily for salmon and crab. He owns his own boat, and was president of the Pacific Coast Federation of Fishermen's Association for nine years. He is an active advocate of fishery habitat protection. He is married, has two children, and lives in Mendocino, California.

Requirements—Attitude ranks top. The economics are marginal, and you have to have a very positive attitude to be successful. This is not an easy profession to succeed in, and if you maintain a negative outlook, you're going to be very depressed, and poor. You need a wide range of mechanical skills: plumbing, hydraulics, diesel mechanics, and traditional knots and ties that fishermen use. You must be knowledgeable about the specific gear types you utilize. For example, a crab fisherman would have to know all about the crab pots he uses, and have skills, for instance, in welding.

A lot of those skills can be transferred from the construction or timber industry because the tools and methods are very similar. Navigational skills are very important—being able to know where you are on the ocean. Local knowledge of the area you're fishing is another major component.

With the vastly increased participation of the government in recent years, it's also become more and more important that fishermen decipher and understand the complex regulatory issues that constantly come down from various government agencies. Many fishermen are hiring fisheries specialists who act as interpreters and mitigators for them to get them through the necessary hoops.

The fisheries specialist field is very embryonic at this point, but for someone who's looking to get into the commercial fishing industry, it's quite a viable option. For someone who's trained in biology and law, there are numerous potential opportunities.

Prospects—Only when a fishery is in an expanding phase do new people get an opportunity to come in. It's a difficult market for newcomers. The way most get in is by knowing someone who is in the industry. Another option is to start out as a deckhand and work your way up through the ranks. I think that's the best route to take because you learn all aspects of the business first-hand. You also don't need to come in with too much capital; if you're physically fit, bright and capable, it's fairly easy.

But if you want to be a fisherman, the only way to break in, other than becoming a deckhand, is to come up with the investment capital and get your own boat. That is very expensive to do. If someone wanted to fish in Alaska, for instance, they'd have to get a transferable permit, which, depending on the permit, can range from $30,000 to $250,000 just for the piece of paper that says you can fish. You have to look at it on a regional basis. The situation is different in different parts of the country.

One thing to consider is that there are few women in this industry. The ones who have tried have had some horrific experiences. There is a lot of harassment and abuse. A woman will be stuck out there with one guy, in living quarters the size of a phone booth, and he tells her to put out or get off the boat. You see it many times, and I don't like it, but I have to say it's true. Fortunately, there are women who are working to change the situation, but I think it will be a long time coming.

Benefits—Basically it's a very satisfying, rewarding way of life. You're independent; you're your own boss. The biggest advantage to me is the satisfaction of knowing that, much like a farmer, you're producing food for the public, which is emotionally rewarding. You can make a decent living.

It's unlike salaried professions; it partakes of the nature of gambling, which is exciting. There are winners and losers. You can struggle and make practically nothing for years, then hit a bonanza year and be rolling in it. There's tremendous emotional satisfaction in being a "highliner" as they call you when you've had a successful trip. You're the hero; everybody loves you.

There's a great deal of triumph and tragedy—it's very stimulating. The industry by nature attracts adventurous individuals, people who probably wouldn't do well in other fields because they'd be considered misfits.

Pay—It's hard to generalize a pay scale because fisheries vary so widely. Someone working as a deckhand on a factory trawler could make anywhere from $15,000 to $30,000. I know that typical deckhands here on the west coast make about $15,000 to $20,000, and successful skippers double that.

You have to remember that many of these fisheries are cyclical. You can go for many poor years, but if you hang in there, you are there for the bonanza years that pop up. Then you have a big boom of income. I know that in the last crab bonanza, five boats made over a quarter of a million dollars each. That sounds like a lot of money, but it has to be contrasted with the bad years. The fishermen who are successful are the ones who hang in there and participate in more than one fishery, who have all the right permits and are able to move within different fisheries so that they can jump right in when the bonanza hits.

Negatives—There is a certain amount of physical risk: the possibility of losing the vessel, of sinking, drowning or getting hurt. Insurance costs are very high, and many fishermen choose to avoid that by not carrying insurance. Luckily, the majority of fishermen are safe operators.

It's very difficult to have a stable family life, because you're gone so much. The wife is in charge when her husband's gone, and then he wants to come home and take over. It can cause some interesting problems.

Weather is a factor, of course. You're totally dependent on the conditions. You can get everything ready to go and be set to fish, then end up not being able to go out because of the weather.

The future—I feel that the industry is going through a period of transition right now. Like many sectors of the economy, we've been in a recession in the early '90s. We didn't really participate in the boom era of the '80s. The salmon fishery went flat in the 1970s and continued to be flat until the late 1980s. Supply and demand doesn't really work the way you might think in fishing. If you can't provide a constant supply, you're the one who suffers. Things may be very different in the next decade.

References

The National Fisherman, PO Box 7438, Portland, ME 04112-7438; (207) 842-5600 or fax (207) 842-5603.

National Fisheries Institute, 1901 North Fort Myer Drive, Ste 700, Arlington, VA 22209; (703) 524-8880 or fax (703) 524-4619.

Marine Technology Institute, 1828 L Street NW, Ste 906, Washington, D.C. 20036-5104; (202) 775-5966 or fax (202) 429-9417. E-mail: mtspubs@aol.com.

Conservation Corps

Dreams—Imagine spending every day in the great outdoors. Why it's heaven itself, earning a living while helping repair nature's scars, creating homes for fish and wildlife. No desk job for you, no way. This is just what you wanted: physical work in wild settings, far, far away from the city.

Nightmares—You love the outdoors, but all the time? Your boss won't cut you slack whether it's a rainstorm or 100 degrees, and it never seems to be anything else. The work is more physically demanding than you expected, you're exhausted every night, and it's a good thing because you're not making enough money to have a night life.

Realities—You're out there all right, but that's what you wanted, solving environmental challenges with physical work, with long days in all kinds of weather. The pay is fair, and it stretches farther in rural areas. The bottom line is that you are a giver in this world, not a taker, and there's much to be said for that.

What it's all about—The value of your life is never determined by the wonders you have achieved for yourself. It is measured instead by the wonders you have achieved for others.

It is like the difference between the basketball player who passes the ball so deftly that everyone on the court is affected by his play, and the player who merely hogs the ball and shoots, affecting only himself. The passer is well-loved by his teammates, respected by even the opposition. The ball-hog shooter, on the other hand, is often disliked by even his own teammates.

For success in the conservation corps field of play, you need to bring with you the ethic of the passer, not the shooter. The primary motive behind every action of a conservation corps employee is to make the world a better place; if you succeed at that, you will profit in the process. It doesn't matter what level you work on, from an entry-level grunt to a field leader or even a staff director. You need the same outlook. If you have it, you will sleep better than practically anybody you will meet.

That is because you go to bed knowing you have just spent the day improving the world. You also go to bed tired, because this job often involves hard physical work and long days, at times in arduous weather. But conservation corps employees do this in the wildlands of America, out amid the streams, forests, meadows, prairies, and canyons. They are responsible for many wildlife and fishery success stories.

If you want the ultimate outdoor job, this is it, because you are out there all the time. The opportunities are quite good for newcomers who want to try it out for awhile, decent for college-educated field directors, and fair enough for regional managers. Each job is different, especially in pay and responsibilities.

For newcomers, you are expected to be the arms, legs and strength of the system. The work, tools and problems are presented, and you do the physical work with your mates to solve them. The work ranges wide: chainsawing out a large tree that has fallen across a river and blocked the migratory spawning run of salmon, planting trees on a steep erosion-damaged slope in a remote forest, repairing a high mountain trail in a fragile meadow, taking a stand against a forest fire, or building a new culvert to keep silt out of a stream. You get the idea. Anything that helps nature is apt to fall your way.

The pay for entry-level positions is only fair, ranging from minimum wage to $10 per hour. Regardless, corps members relish their work and joke about the financial rewards. In California, their motto is, "Hard work, low pay, and more!" It is regarded as an exceptional job for a young person, age 18 to 23, who has bypassed college for the time being and wants to be in the great outdoors and get paid for it.

In order to secure the higher-paying job of a field director, where you lead a group of grunts, you need at least a college degree with a specialty. A master's degree works out better. Why? Well, consider a common challenge in the northern tier states—erosion in heavily logged forests. A field team from the conservation corps moves in, having been assigned to stop the erosion. A field director with a master's in soil science will be in demand, because a soil specialist will be able to identify the erosion problem, then direct the crew as to how to repair it.

That is exactly why college training in a specialty can pay off. For starters, specialists are needed in soil science, hydrology, aquatic biology, marine biology, wildlife biology (very competitive), and fire science. Most field directors top out at around $40,000, and that kind of money goes a long way when you are living in a rural area where costs are vastly lower than in a city.

The best way to advance is to be willing to take a job change regardless of where it is, rather than grinding out a career with only one agency, waiting for openings to become available. The top position of this field is a regional manager—the policy maker. In that position, you select all field operations, coordinate the people and equipment for them, run a budget, inspire the troops on the inside, then promote the program on the outside. It takes a unique, multi-faceted personality to pull it off, one who is not only detail-oriented with numbers, but public relations-oriented with the media. Not many people can handle it.

If you can, you are well rewarded, being paid anywhere from $45,000 on up to $60,000, sometimes more. But even as a regional manager, the focus is never on you, but rather the work that needs completing, the projects to be undertaken that will make the world a better place. People who work for a conservation corps tend to be at peace with the world. After all, nobody who takes, takes and takes from this planet gets much happiness. Those who give back, on the other hand . . . well, just remember the story about the basketball player.

Career Case Study

Chris Goetzke, California

Chris Goetzke has worked as a conservationist/crew supervisor for ten years for the California Conservation Corps, and is also a career development specialist for Sierra College. His work experience includes working for the U.S. Forest Service, San Diego County Outdoor Education and in construction. He enjoys geology and plants, which he'll "teach to anyone who is unfortunate enough to go on a hike with me." He lives in Grass Valley, California.

Requirements—Number one, you must be familiar with physical work. I'd say the job is moderately to heavily demanding, physically. Our corps members do a great deal of outdoor work—digging with shovels and yanking trees out of drain channels. If you work with a forest agency, you'll be hoisting, lifting, chopping, and doing chainsaw work.

In terms of formal education, an associate's degree is the minimum to get solidly into the field. A bachelor's degree would allow more opportunities to develop as a specialist, for instance, a fisheries manager or silt-culture specialist.

I've found it very helpful to suck up as much information and knowledge as you can, inside and outside of the job, in regard to conservation, ecology, botany and various earth sciences. Many of my projects have been improved by the knowledge I had of the environments and elements I was working with. The greater depth of understanding a person has of his or her environment and how things work, the more he or she will be able to bring to projects.

You must be able to plan and organize if you want to stay in the field. If you're just working for the summer or in a one-year program, your duties are pretty limited and straightforward. But if you want to move up, you need to develop an ability to organize and plan out jobs, to master and familiarize yourself with each task. It's comparable to building a house; you have to figure out when you're going to put in the plumbing, when you're going to order the concrete, when the wiring should be done.

It's important to recognize the value of teamwork and motivation. If you can encourage and inspire a group that you're working with, everyone in the group will benefit, including you.

Prospects—I think it's certainly competitive everywhere right now. I do think that there are significant opportunities for women and minorities in the conservation industry, especially in government agencies such as the U.S. Forest Service. They have some good affirmative action programs. Region 5 of the Forest Service currently has two or three women rangers; ten years ago, women rangers were essentially unheard of.

There's new thinking encroaching upon the timber industry. Economic analyses have shown that there are better ways to manage timber than clear cutting. A lot of companies are rethinking what they're doing, and job opportunities will result.

A good way to start out is to find out about the summer

programs offered by various organizations. They're often eight- to ten-week stints that don't offer more than a small stipend, but they provide room and board, and it's a good way to get experience over summer break. There are also some excellent training opportunities available, where you can learn basic skills like how to build trails.

I do think that someone who is willing to compete, willing to travel and make an aggressive job search can break in. A person may have to go to Wyoming to get in and relocate to Texas to move up. You have to be willing to be a gypsy for a while if you want to advance.

Benefits—I like the variety of the work I do. I've built bridges for state parks, acted as a wilderness guard, built trails, performed some surveying, and worked on erosion control and habitat improvement, just to name a few. And I've been able to do these things in all kinds of different places. I can go visit these places on vacation and see the work that I've contributed to.

I appreciate my connection to the earth and I'm amazed at the variety of wonders it has to offer. In the course of my work I've found things like dinosaur bones and plants that haven't been catalogued, or at least aren't published in any current literature, and these little bits of wonder that are thrown at me by the earth bring me great pleasure.

I like working outside, learning new skills and passing these skills on to other people. I like being able to show the kids I work with that there's nothing wrong with physical labor and learning craftsman-like work. We've contributed to very important pieces of work; for instance, the building of barrier-free trails for the disabled and the restoration of historic sites, and we take pride in our achievements.

Pay—An entry-level position pays around $8 to $10 an hour, and those type of positions usually involve a specific duty, like firefighting. In most of the summer seasonal positions, there are varying amounts of overtime, and with that comes a larger paycheck. If you are in a professional class, a specialist, you'll make more money, and that is largely dependent on your level of education. If you are going to hold a position at the bachelor's level and try to bump up your pay based on time and experience, your pay increase will probably be rather measured. But if you're at a master's level, your income opportunities are more open.

Right now I'm making something in the neighborhood of $35,000, and I have about ten years of experience. But not all of that experience is with the organization I'm with now; I've changed jobs for the sake of variety and challenge, so I've lost a little ground.

Negatives—It's very physically demanding. Some days it's brutally hot. You might have to work on a fire and end up with a 16-hour shift. Being a slave to political winds is sometimes frustrating. In the Forest Service, when determining how many trees are going to be logged in a specific area, politics often play a bigger role than the people who are directly involved. What's best in the conservation sense isn't always what's best in the political sense, and politics almost always win. People on the ground don't always get listened to.

The future—Conservation is an area that I see a fair amount of growth in. The new ecologically-aware focus is going to stimulate growth in all areas of conservation. The questions of forest management, the expanded use of state parks and public lands, clean water, and clean land all are poised and ready for growth, but the monies that are available to take in new employees are limited right now. That's a political issue, and I do think that we will be seeing growth in that area as well. The action just hasn't started yet. There's certainly a lot of work to be done.

Career Case Study

Mike Hughes, Missouri

Mike Hughes is the director of Kansas City Urban Youth Corps. Before taking that job, he worked for the Full Employment Council in Kansas City as a counselor and project coordinator. His work experience includes more than 10 years in construction, a stint as a research analyst for the State of Missouri, and four years in the Air Force. He enjoys reading and bass fishing, has two sons, and lives in Kansas City.

Requirements—Everyone on the staff has some degree of experience with, knowledge of, and concern for youth. I helped design and put together the main elements of this program and I manage the activities. In order to do that, I had to have some knowledge of government and business and some writing and communication skills. Good leadership skills and the ability to work with others is also required. At all levels of corps staff, it's important to have enthusiasm and a strong sense of values, because that's what we're passing on to the youth we're trying to help. It would be helpful to have some experience in construction and/or a conservation-related field. I happened to have been a contractor and community service-oriented person before I came here, and I've found that those experiences have been tremendous assets.

In terms of formal education, a bachelor's degree is required for all management or supervisor level positions. We've never specified what type of degree one must have. However, an education counselor or instructor, for example, should have a degree in education.

Prospects—I was one of 75 people who applied for this job in 1990. I'm sure that there would be even more competition now, with the double-digit unemployment rate we're dealing with. The economy is tight right now, and because of that we have a limited staff, so we require everyone to be multi-disciplined in their roles and duties.

When we advertise, we get a lot of people who apply, but often people don't realize the depth of what they're applying for until the interview. They sometimes decline the potential job offer during the interview.

Benefits—Having been a contractor and an employer who was once very reticent about hiring young people, I appreciate having been given the opportunity to manage young people and realize they can be great. I found that they can be easily trained, motivated and professional. They can be very productive and can make valuable contributions to society. Today's youth are resilient, and even though they've been beaten up by the media, the fact is that they really do want to be successful citizens.

I've grown and gained enrichment myself with this job and working with "at-risk" youth, and it's really motivated me when times are tough. I like the fact that you can see tangible results in terms of lives. When you see ex-gang members, ex-drug sellers, and high school drop-outs start to believe in themselves and acquire self-esteem, it's extremely rewarding. I see them realizing that they can be successful and make a difference in this environment as a good citizen rather than an outlaw. They begin to believe in the theory of helping others and not just themselves. That carries over to their families, friends and the community.

I feel fortunate that I have a job where I can help my community and the youth in this age group. My biggest concern is helping build lives, not parking lots and buildings.

Pay—Anyone working in the social service field can always use an extra dollar or two, however, money is not our motivator. Most people who work in this movement are not in it for the money only; we're in it for the people we serve. Directors and staff members who work within the "Corps Movement" work for the vision of helping others and making this world a better place to live in.

Negatives—Once you get involved, you begin to feel frustrated that you can't help more of the youth in the community. I often feel that more people in this particular age group—18 to 23—need time in programs like this. Although this is a twelve-month program, it can be rough to change a life around after 17 years of neglect. You have to be a Mother Superior to help some and a drill instructor in the Marines to help others. The youth are the ones who turn themselves around; once they're out of the program you just have to hope that what they've learned stays with them.

I feel that we don't have enough money to make our programs more comprehensive. My staff needs more resources and a wider range of employment opportunities for youth that graduate. We want to help a wider range of youth from a diversity standpoint: more females, more Hispanics and more whites. There are a lot of people out there who need this service, but there's just no way to help everybody.

The future—Youth service is a way to improve our cities and this country. I look at this movement as a very optimistically-driven activity, committed to helping America. Hopefully Congress will begin to put more money into programs such as these so we can afford to add to the program services. There is definitely a burning need for conservation corps all over the country and it all comes down to priorities for our government leadership.

References

National Association of Service and Conservation Corps (NASCC), 666 11th Street NW, Ste 500, Washington, D.C. 20001; (202) 737-6272.

Corporation for National Service (Americorp), 1201 New York Avenue NW, Washington, D.C. 20525; (202) 606-5000 or fax (202) 565-2794.

Student Conservation Association, Inc., PO Box 550, Charlestown, NH 03603; (603) 543-1700.

Careers in Ecology, from the Center for Environmental Studies, Arizona State University, Tempe, AZ 85287; (602) 965-2975.

National Parks & Conservation Association, 1776 Massachusetts Avenue NW, Washington, D.C. 20036; (202) 223-6722.

Environmental Job Opportunities Bulletin, from Institute for Environmental Studies, University of Wisconsin-Madison, 555 North Park Street, 15 Science Hall, Madison, WI 53706; (608)263-3185.

Greater Miami Service Corps, 810 NW 28th Street, Miami, FLA 33127; (305)638-4672.

Also call the U.S. Forest Service, state departments of fish and game, and state forest agencies.

Conservation Organization Director

Dreams—As director of a conservation organization, you know how lucky the world is that you are here to save it. You meet with the governor, maybe the president, and get pictured in newspapers and interviewed on TV as a hero. All the while you are scheduling your meetings with the heavies afield to have fun, and then when all is done, you get paid more than $100,000.

Nightmares—Nobody pays any attention to you, not the governor, not the newspapers, not even your mother. You never seem to have enough members, so you make less money than you anticipated. Because there is so much to do, you are in a perpetual state of panic and die of a heart attack before anything gets done. The End.

Realities—Absolute organization skills are a must, and so is discipline in sticking to your agenda and not letting scattered energy from the outside waste your time. For the special people who can do that, you can earn a good salary, often $40,000 to $65,000, sometimes more, and make the world a better place, but it usually means living in a population center and enjoying the outdoors when you can schedule meetings there.

What it's all about—Oh what a tight rope you tip-toe as a director of a conservation organization. If you fall off on one side, you end up an over-zealous workaholic crusading to save the world from all its problems. In the process you create a giant problem for yourself: "I never have enough time," and maybe have a heart attack. And if you fall off the other side of that tight rope, you become the self-anointed protector of the common people—ego-driven, money-hungry and star-crazed. "By the way, I met with the governor yesterday," you tell everyone. Eventually you become miserable with the puerile victories won for yourself over those of your pledged environmental cause.

Then there are the people who actually walk that tight rope. Not only that, but they manage to balance themselves easily and are actually quite comfortable in such a high place, never even thinking to look down and discover that there is no net to catch them.

The finest directors of conservation organizations all have this ability, and they share several other traits: They keep from falling off the tight rope to the side of workaholic crusader by developing the ability to set an agenda and stick to it; they are incorrigible list makers, and they stick to that list no matter what. They pick their chief concerns, and then make sure they win at them, rather than hopping from issue to issue like a lightweight political gadfly. They don't become a prisoner of incoming phone calls. Whether they win or lose, they learn "Don't take it personally," the hardest lesson of all. But what the heck, it keeps them from having heart problems.

Good directors of conservation organizations keep from falling off that tight rope to the other side—into the pit of egomania— by realizing they are not working for glory, but for spirit, for the pureness nature intended for land and water. They realize the governor is probably less qualified than they are to make an environmental decision, and the only thing special about meeting with him is the chance to enlighten and instruct him so he doesn't screw up too badly.

As for money, there's no sense in worrying about it. You will be paid very well—$45,000 is the minimum salary, with $75,000 not unusual, and six figures not so rare either for the larger organizations.

Any way you go, as director of a conservation organization, you can schedule yourself field time, maybe a little "research," which can consist of just about anything you please. A director of a wetlands conservation group, for instance, can schedule meetings at dawn in a duck blind; in fact, it's the best way to do business. A director of a fishing group can take the politicos fishing. Get the picture? If you play your cards right, you can get it all—regular outings, connections with the heavies, and most importantly, the conservation victories your supporters are paying you for.

It can be easy to start such a job, and the future prospects for doing so are excellent. All you have to do is pick an issue that isn't going to go away, like clean water; pick a name, like "Americans for Clean Water;" get a letterhead and you're in business. To get paid, all you need are members. The more members, the more you get paid. Even organizations with just 3,000 members pay their directors $40,000 to $50,000. Of course, you need excellent communication skills and you also need to be a good office manager.

Like many careers, it is best to get on-the-job training working for a well-established organization before taking one on personally. That's because it can be difficult to walk that tight rope. The most common predicament directors find themselves in is having too much to do and no time to do it.

It happens like this: You start the day happy as can be, working on solving problems A, B and C, then get phone calls alerting you about new problems D and E. Meanwhile, you remember you have four letters to get out, adding problems F, G, H and I, and in addition, there is an upcoming fund-raising banquet, J, and you need to obtain raffle items, K. Right then, a newspaper columnist friendly to the cause calls for an interview, L, and while talking, tips you off on M, N, O and P. Because N and O are urgent, you call your subordinates in for a meeting, P, and after a 15-minute discussion, they bring up three new issues, Q, R and S, and then your secretary comes in to tell you that there is an urgent phone call, T. You take the call, U, which turns out to be irrelevant, but the guy won't shut up anyway. Then you remember your lunch date with three government bureaucrats, V, W and X, and before you get to dessert, they tell you they can't do what they promised last month, creating a new problem, Y, that you thought already had been solved. Then somehow, you confront Z, the fact that you need to act nice to the buffoons who double-crossed you, and then get the hell out of Dodge.

It can all be worth the trouble. Sometimes, believe it or not, things actually work out right.

Career Case Study

Sharon Rushton, Arkansas

Sharon Rushton is the Executive Director of the Future Fisherman Foundation and the Director of Education for the American Fishing Tackle Manufacturers Association. For the past 20 years, she has combined writing, broadcasting, speaking and management skills to communicate issues and develop education programs

*in the outdoors field. Sharon currently lives in Fort
Smith, Arkansas, where she enjoys fishing, photography,
hunting and skiing.*

Requirements—Good communication and leadership skills
are important, as well as a strong background in conservation.
Marketing and administration skills help, too. A bachelor's degree
would be minimal; most positions I know of require a master's
degree. It would depend on the type of organization, of course. A
director of an organization is an upper-level position and requires
years of experience in the conservation field. They're not going to
choose someone just out of college. Working on the staff of a non-
profit organization, with a fish and wildlife agency, parks and
recreation department, U.S. Forest Service or any similar position
can provide some of the experience needed. A position such as an
environmentalist for an oil or other private company is another
example.

Prospects—The National Wildlife Federation's Conservation Directory lists conservation organizations around the country;
that's a good place to start. Historically, directors of organizations
hold their positions for a long time, so it's a matter of having the
qualifications and waiting for a position to open. If being a director
of an organization is your goal, you need to stay flexible and
consider several organizations, not just one. You might want to
consider state conservation organizations before moving on to a
national level.

Benefits—The primary benefit to running an organization is
the ability to make a contribution back to society. Through the
Future Fisherman Foundation and our "Hooked on Fishing—Not
on Drugs" program, we're able not only to have an impact on the
environment, but to help lead our youth to a drug-free, wholesome
lifestyle. Being a part of that is a reward in itself.

Pay—Pay for non-profit conservation organization directors
is quite varied, depending on the size of the organization. Some state
organizations may pay $20,000 per year, others may pay more.
Even on the national level pay scales can range substantially
depending on the organization. Low-end on a national scale may
start around $30,000 and go up to over $100,000.

Negatives—Heading up a national organization usually requires substantial travel. This can be a negative for some people. Personally, I like to travel, but often I have to stay on the road even more than I'd like to.

Most directors have to constantly develop funding sources for the organization. That's part of working for a non-profit organization. It's not so much a negative as a frustration—having so many projects that could do so much good and not having enough money to do them.

Career Case Study

Jack Lorenz, Virginia

Jack Lorenz has been the executive director of the Izaak Walton League since 1974. The Izaak Walton League is the national leader in promoting ethical behavior for outdoor participants. In 1992, he took a new job with the League as a specialty writer.

Requirements—You have to believe in your cause, and be imaginative and persistent as hell, pursuing whatever your goal might be. I got into it because of my love of the outdoors. It just happened that I was at the right place at the right time. I was a public relations man for a brewery, and in 1970, I convinced the management that they should have an environmental program, so they put me in charge of it. About two years later, my supervisor told me that the following year's budget would not include the environmental program; the money had been spent on one 30-second TV commercial to be aired during the Superbowl.

I realized right away that the company apparently did not have the environmental commitment I was looking for, so I accepted, after much deliberation, the job of magazine editor for the Izaak Walton League. It was one of those opportunities that turned out to be much more than I expected; in May of 1974 I was appointed executive director.

My advice to someone who wants to work in conservation is to get a National Wildlife Federation Conservation Directory, which lists hundreds of conservation agencies. Read the profiles, see what sounds good to you, and plan your strategy from there. Be careful of what you study in school, too. When I'm interviewing people, I don't only ask for their resumes, I ask for copies of their business letters. The way they are written is a good indication of the person's communication skills and level of dedication to the job at hand; for instance, if they use two pages for what should be a two-paragraph memo, that says to me that they're not using their time efficiently. They're not going to be able to move through six or seven things a day; they're going to do six or seven things a year.

Prospects—There are over 18,000 current environmental organizations, ranging from small local groups to national giants with millions of members. They seem to spring up daily because there's always a new threat to the environment.

The important thing to remember is that you can't start out in conservation just because you want a job. If I were speaking to a young person today, I would suggest that they volunteer. Don't just do something to get paid. Get in there and get established; sell yourself by doing a good job. That works.

Be creative: If you're applying for a job and there are other candidates, offer to work for free for a month. That way you've given them an offer they will have a hard time refusing, and you'll have a chance to prove yourself. Once you've proven yourself, you're in to stay.

It really takes intense devotion to your cause. If you want to do something badly enough, you've got be willing to sacrifice and work 24 hours a day to prove yourself.

Benefits—The biggest reward is seeing a river saved or a wildlife area protected and knowing it will last for generations. You know you've played a role in that, and it's very gratifying.

The job has allowed me to see firsthand a lot of territory; I've been able to fish in every state except Hawaii, even if only for 15 minutes or half an hour. It's rewarding to be able to enjoy the areas you're fighting for.

I've had some wonderful experiences. Once on a plane trip I sat next to a farmer from West Virginia, and we got to talking about some of the thoughts we had about wildlife protection and conservation in general. It was a very nice conversation, and when we landed I gave him my card, and that was the end of that. Then, several years later, we suddenly received a check in the mail for $71,000; the farmer had died and left the Izaak Walton League one-third of his estate. As the League's chief fundraiser, I've heard hundreds of "no's." The memory of one man's generosity makes all those turndowns less painful.

Negatives—For me, it was placing all the things I personally care about—my family, my recreation time, my health—on absolutely the furthest back burner, always intending to take care of them and never quite getting around to it. It's sad, and I regret not spending more time with my boys and my wife. Years and years of self-neglect resulted last year in quintuple bypass surgery and two angioplasties. That's why I've decided to move myself up a notch in my priority list; I'll be occupying a new position with the Izaak Walton League, an American Land Ethic Writing Chair. I'll be able to be active in the things that I care about without the stress of fund raising. That's my big albatross, the one aspect of my job that I've found most unforgiving. Being told "no" eats me up; I have a real problem with it.

The never-ending promotion of the organization, the fundraising and the lack of personal time are the things that lead to burnout in this business. There's no such thing as an eight-hour day, and it's almost always seven days a week.

Pay—Again, this depends on the location and size of the organization you're involved with, so I'll quote scales for fairly large organizations. Someone working as a receptionist or secretary for an organization may be paid around $15,000 to $20,000 a year. When you reach a mid-level management position, you can make $25,000 to $35,000. Upper-level policy managers, people who deal with critical issues, can make between $35,000 and $75,000 a year, sometimes more. These are the most significant people; they not only do their jobs but attract new financial resources as well. I can't emphasize that skill enough. Their ability to help the overall operation determines how they're paid in the long run.

But if money is your greatest priority, stick with the private sector. These days, in the Washington community, a CEO can make anywhere from $65,000 on up. There are directors who make over $100,000 a year, but that's rare. In those instances, they're managing $50 million to $100 million budgets.

The future—It's absolutely dynamite. Since we don't treat the earth very kindly, conservation and environmentalism are growth markets. There are so many people who care deeply about the fate of the earth and want to be involved. It's a buyer's market. We recently put one ad in the Washington Post for an accountant, and received over 300 applications in the first week. People want to be a part of a movement that's making a difference.

Environmental challenges are being created all the time. There are more than 250,000 new mouths to feed every day! Too many businesses keep getting bigger at the expense of the environment. Once they have the natural resources pinpointed, they want to exploit them quickly, and often environmental considerations get short shrift.

I think the thing that has to be realized is that the people running conservation organizations should never stop pushing, not just to improve the organization but to make sure that every dollar that comes in is put to work for the mission rather than into the administration of the organization.

References

The National Wildlife Federation Directory lists all organizations in the conservation business; (301) 897-9770 or fax (301) 530-2471.

Environmental Job Opportunities Bulletin, from Institute for Environmental Studies, University of Wisconsin-Madison, 550 North Park Street, 15 Science Hall, Madison, WI 53706; (608) 263-3185 or fax (608) 262-0014.

National Ecological Conservation Opportunities Institute, PO Box 511, Helena, MT 59624; (406) 442-0214.

Also contact land management and fish and game agencies.

Firefighter
—Year Round

Dreams—You are one of the chosen, a firefighter, a rare breed who lives every day dealing the cards of life face up, out there on the edge in a life of exhilaration. You take the challenge and provide the answers, then are rewarded financially. You're a hero to those around you, and a savior to the forests.

Nightmares—The danger cannot be understated. Fires can chase you, trap you, suck the oxygen out of the air, and barbecue you. You get so tired that you can go to sleep standing up. If you have a family, don't plan on spending much time with them in the summer. During the downtime, waiting for a fire to start can drive you nuts.

Realities—This is life in its primal form. You work long hours in hot, dry, dirty, and dangerous conditions, but you get big pay for time in a war zone, as well as a special comradeship from your workmates and a chance to live and feel the earth on its own terms. It's a special reward that few know.

What it's all about—Some people like living way out there on the edge. They discover it's an electrifying place to be for wild adventure, facing the unpredictable, and when it comes to fighting fires, good pay. Stick around for awhile and you will discover that being a forest firefighter is like getting grabbed by the hair on your head and lifted right off the ground.

This job is about the closest thing there is to being in a war. There are times when you are constantly losing ground to the enemy (a big fire), get no rest (fires never sleep), are dirty to the bone (like a junkyard dog), and can suddenly have your life placed in jeopardy (dangerous fires make their own rules).

But you are paid to win this war, and paid well. Nobody complains. After all, you are a firefighter, like a Marine, one of the chosen, and this battle out on the edge of danger against an awesome adversary is just something that comes with the territory. It is not a job for the mousy, but rather for the aggressive. That means action-oriented people who want in on the gut-level passions of life and know what it means to hear the earth's heartbeat.

Of course, every job has its irony. As a firefighter, you face a strange scenario where you can sit around with little to do for weeks, waiting for disaster to strike somewhere. Then when it does, usually in the form of a lightning strike in a dry forest, you may not rest for weeks. It is like two different worlds, one where you do nothing and have all the time in the world to rhapsodize about life, another where you do everything and scarcely have time to brush your teeth. After all, there's a fire out there.

Get one thing clear: Fighting fires is dangerous. Almost every firefighter has at least one story where they tell you how they barely eluded death, and they aren't speaking with forked tongues. "The fire jumped the line, headed straight for us, and we all jumped under a Caterpillar tractor. When the fire went over the top of us, it burned up all the oxygen, and we nearly suffocated to death"..."A crew of us got isolated digging a fire line, then the wind shifted and the sucker came right for us and jumped the line. If it had been 40 yards in the other direction, we would have been fried."

This danger is why firefighters are paid so well, often doubling their base salaries with overtime pay. Like all government jobs, the base pay scales vary according to experience and classifications, from $22,000 to $40,000. But there are times when you will work 100 hours over a span of 12 or 13 straight days, and that creates huge paychecks. Plus, because you are working so much, you won't have time to spend it. Many full-time, career firefighters make $40,000 to $50,000 per year. Some make more, and they deserve every penny of it.

The future for this career is very promising. The forests of America, both on public and private land, are considered one of the country's most valuable natural resources. The money is there to protect them, to keep a lightning strike and small fire from turning into an inferno that might burn 500,000 acres. In addition, there is growing knowledge on how to use small, low-heat fires as a management tool to burn out brush accumulations and reduce the long-term risk of holocausts. Because of this, there will be new openings created for fire science experts.

While you need no college education to get a job on the lines, you will need great physical stamina. For the higher-paying decision-making positions, a degree as a forester is essential. There are many jobs available within the context of firefighting, however, including weather expert, pilot, cook and bulldozer operator. But the best prospects for starting out are as a front-line grunt, a firefighter who is out there in the war.

As a long-term career, there are some unique negatives. The worst is being away from your family for weeks on end during the fire season in the summer and early fall. The working conditions are bad—always hot, dry, dirty and dangerous. There are times a crew of 12 would be willing to pony up their summer's wages to buy a rainstorm. And then there is the waiting, when there are no fires and you busy yourself with organizational tasks. For many, the waiting is the worst part of the job. For others, it's coming home to a nagging mate who wants you to find another line of work.

But most firefighters wouldn't think of such a thing. After all, they know what it's like to be out there on the edge where life and death is often balancing on a precipice. Once you've experienced this stirring sensation, how could you trade it in for a desk job? The answer for most is that they can't. After all, they are firefighters. They are not only out on the front line of a fire, but out in the vortex of life itself.

Career Case Study

Neil Eldridge, Washington

Neil Eldridge started firefighting in 1969 and later became a smokejumper. He suffered a tragic accident in which his parachute caught on a tree limb, the limb broke, and he fell more than 140 feet and broke his back in several places. After a protracted recovery, he is a testimonial to the power of spirit. He now works in timber sales with the Bureau of Indian Affairs. He also enjoys fishing, hunting and boating, and coaches team sports. He lives with his family in Battle Ground, Washington.

Requirements—The basic firefighter just starting out can be hired without any experience in firefighting at all. When I first started, I had no experience whatsoever. The new people usually are put on what's called "Type 2" or pickup teams. They are trained in basic firefighting, must pass a basic physical test, and then are eligible to become a crew member. At that point they're qualified to use a shovel or other hand tool required in firefighting. Established crews that fight fires all over the US, called "hotshots" or Type 1 crews, are filled with people who have one or more years of experience.

I'm somewhat of a gung-ho type person, and I think that helps. Anyone who wants to do well has to be aggressive. Enthusiasm combined with reason and common sense is the ideal attitude to have. In many cases, you need to be able to get in and attack the fire as soon as possible, and if you can attack right at the flame, you can keep it from spreading to hundreds of acres. But sometimes it's not safe or practical to be that close, and you need to know when you shouldn't be in there as well as when you should.

People in permanent positions are the ones who have experience, training, and in many cases, formal education. You can get up to mid-level jobs with no formal education, but if you want to go higher, you have to have a forest technician or professional forester degree. A forester degree requires four years, but you can get a technician degree in two years at many community colleges.

There are probably a thousand different jobs within the title of firefighter. Not everybody is right there on the flames. A lot of people think of us as the people who just throw dirt or water on the flames, but there are a lot of people behind the scenes, and they have to be trained for every job. There are people who locate the lines, people who work with the bulldozers, cooks, pilots, medics, lookout people, fire camp workers, weather researchers, fire behavior specialists, transportation workers, etc.

Prospects—Since about 1985, conditions have been very dry due to the drought situation in the Pacific Northwest. Trees and brush are basically running out of water, and that has caused extreme fire danger. Since so many people have been needed, most workers in the field have become qualified for a wide range of jobs, from crew person to boss. If we were to get one or two wet years in a row and firefighters weren't in such demand, there wouldn't be many opportunities because so many people are qualified. But if things continue to be dry, opportunities will be limitless. Job availability is very dependent on what happens in the summers.

Benefits—Money. That's why a lot of people are in this field. You get a lot of overtime, and you can make a lot of money in a short period. It's exciting, sometimes more exciting than you bargained for, like when lighting is striking around your feet, or when flames are shooting fifty feet in the air.

You get to be outside, which is a definite plus. Even though the work is physically demanding, it's great to be able to be outdoors. And the people you work with are a lot of fun. Generally, in any kind of crew situation, there's a strong sense of camaraderie. Especially the hotshot crews, they really know how to have a good time.

Pay—For permanent positions, the government pays by the GS rating system. A firefighter starting out at GS 3 will make $14,100 a year, and the scale goes up to GS 12, which is about $39,000 a year. That's your base salary, for eight hours a day. But firefighters get a lot of overtime, which is all paid as time and a half. One hundred hours of overtime in a two-week period is not uncommon. You can easily double your salary during the summer months.

There are other kinds of bonus pay too, such as night deferential pay and hazard pay, and that is all in addition to your regular salary. It's all dependent on the fire situation and how many people are working on the fire.

Negatives—The hours are long. It's common to work 12- to 18-hour days. It's also common to work different shifts, which is tough on your mind and body. You can work two or three night shifts in a row, and then you go to a day shift and your sleeping and eating patterns get all messed up.

Your working conditions in a fire are dirty, hot and dry. There are definite dangers and the constant possibility of death or injury. Being transported to and from the fire can actually be one of the most dangerous aspects. The people driving the personnel carriers are often working long hours on dusty roads, and sometimes they fall asleep or they get carried away and drive too fast and wreck. Often when there's a death in a fire, it's one of those guys, or a passenger. Some years I worked there were more deaths caused by transportation accidents than anything else.

Being away from your family is difficult. Many firefighters have families and/or significant others, and when you're gone for days, weeks, or even months at a time, it can be rough.

The future—The jobs will always be here. Fires will always be started by nature or man. In addition, people in the timber industry are starting to seriously consider using fire more as a management tool. For example, some of our timber types are changing. Instead of all the nice big ponderosa pine we used to have, there are lots of firs packed together, and they're getting diseases and insects, which basically renders them useless, and an extreme fire danger. Something will have to be done with these timber types, and more people with the appropriate knowledge and technical expertise are going to be needed to help.

Career Case Study

Steve Upton, West Virginia
Steve Upton is the District Forest Ranger for the West Virginia Division of Forestry, and has worked in fire management since 1968. He enjoys sports, hunting, fishing and playing the guitar. He is married, has two children, and lives in Hurricane, West Virginia.

Requirements—You need to start out with at least an associate's degree. All employees have to go through a basic firefighting course, which consists of a week of intense training on fire suppression and prevention techniques. It covers everything from first aid to weather to fire behavior. After that initial training, there are other kinds of on-the-job training, such as chainsaw use, equipment operation, things like that. We deal with a certain amount of public awareness; we work a lot with the media and schools. We may be on a fire today and giving a lecture to the Kiwanis Club tomorrow. We're also required to teach firefighting techniques to other members of the forestry field, such as loggers.

Naturally you have to like the outdoors in this job, and be in good shape. There is a lot of physical and mental exertion, and a great deal of stamina is involved. The women on the crews seem to deal with that a lot better than the men, for some reason.

Prospects—The job market is better than it has been, but it's still tight. Most of our employees here in West Virginia come from the eastern and northeastern areas, where a lot of our forestry schools are located. There is a lot of rivalry between those graduates. The U.S. Forest Service has the best pay scale and work conditions, so there's a lot of competition for jobs; they generally get the pick of the crop. Over the past few years, we've hired more people out of the technical two-year schools. They have a lot more hands-on experience and they know pretty much what we want them to know by the time they get here. We don't have that many jobs open in this area, although I'm sure that differs from state to state. Some states have much bigger organizations than ours. We have 100 full-time employees, and about five to ten job openings every year. The competition is tough.

Benefits—Firefighters are kind of like circus people; you get the sawdust in your blood, or the fire in your blood, and it's there to stay. There's a lot of satisfaction in knowing when you've controlled and put out a fire that you've overcome tremendous physical and mental odds. You can look back and say, "I've done something today."

You don't have somebody standing over you supervising. You're pretty much on your own as far as how decisions are made, and you organize it, you do it, and the results are yours.

Pay—An entry level position pays between $16,000 and $17,000 a year. The scale goes up to about $25,000, but that takes eons. I've been working for 25 years, and I'm just at $27,000. Overtime is not as lucrative in this area as it is in other states; our system is arranged on a sliding scale, so we're paid time and a half over 40 hours, but our men end up only earning about $3 extra per hour. The more you work, the less you end up getting paid. Eighty or ninety hours a week is not uncommon, and compensation for that is basically nonexistent. Again, that varies depending on your location. Some states have great overtime compensation; some have unions which negotiate these things.

Negatives—A lot of guys around here like to hunt and fish, and the prime hunting and fishing time is when we have our fire season. When everyone is out on the stream or out in the woods, we're out on the fire line.

It can be difficult on your family life; if you're lucky you've got an understanding family. I've got an 18-year-old who just went off to college, and while he was growing up, I was out on the fire line. The job keeps you tied down; you can't leave for vacations because you've got to be available if you're needed.

Physically, it takes it's toll. There are guys with bad knees and bad kidneys from being rocked around the truck so much. It wears you out over the years. You're working long hours in rough working conditions on a continual basis. When you're on a fire, you may get a few hours of sleep in a truck or on somebody's front porch.

The future—The future, as far as forest firefighting goes, is wide open for people who want to get in, particularly in the eastern part of the country. Our third and second growth generation of forest out here is maturing, and it's developing into a pretty big industry. Our goal is to manage it, and with foresters working with owners and firemen keeping fire out of it, it can be harvested and utilized for recreation and a multitude of uses.

References

Society of American Foresters, 515 SW 5th Street, Suite 518, Portland, OR 97201; (503) 222-7456.

Boise Inner Agency Fire Center, 3833 South Development Avenue, Boise, ID 83705-5354; (208)387-5512.(The Center coordinates firefighting for the entire United States.)

International Association of Firefighters, 1750 New York Avenue NW, 3rd Floor, Washington, D.C. 20006; (202) 737-8484 or fax (202) 737-8418.

US Forestry Service, 740 Simms Street, Golden, CO 80401; (303) 275-5350 or fax (303) 275-5671.

Also contact local branches of the National Park Service, U.S. Forest Service, Bureau of Land Management, Bureau of Indian Affairs, state forestry offices, and local fire stations.

Firefighter—Seasonal

Dreams—You champion the cause of Man vs. Nature, or you vs. the forest fire, and win. You live the essence of life, getting dirty, rowdy, and tempting danger, and then get paid better than any of your friends in other jobs. Other people remember their memories; you, on the other hand, are out making them.

Nightmares—You have barely slept for days, your eyes feel like they're being disintegrated by the smoke, and hey, you'd pay a million dollars for a cold drink and a cheeseburger. After a week in a forest fire, you feel like the reincarnation of Cro-Magnon man. Maybe you are. And to think at the beginning of summer you actually wanted to do this.

Realities—The conditions and long hours during a forest fire can be the physical test of a lifetime, but like winning any war, the victory stays with you forever. No experience is necessary, just a tuned body and good attitude, and you will be well rewarded for a summer's work. No whiners need apply. After a summer of this, you will feel good about yourself for years.

What it's all about—The best job in the world is as a seasonal forest fire fighter. Unfortunately, the worst job in the world is also as a seasonal forest fire fighter. There is very little in between. Some people love it. Some hate it. Most manage to do both at the same time.

It's attractive to young people for many reasons. It is exciting and dangerous, and the pay is excellent for a seasonal job. You build a sense of comradeship with your fellow workers, your time is spent in the woods far from cities, you can literally see the results of your success, the work will harden your body, and because it is a seasonal position, you don't feel the long-term sense of accountability that can burden young people in a career.

Right, it may be the best seasonal job in the world. But it also may be the worst. The conditions near a forest fire are terrible, hot, smoky, dusty, and you can be ordered to work like a Titan in that crap for 15 or 16 hours straight. You will be so tired that you may learn how to sleep standing up, which is quite a trick. Actually, it can be difficult to close your eyes because they sting so badly from the smoke. You can also develop something like a smoker's hack from the bad air, and you will get so many layers of dirt on you that it will practically take a Caterpillar tractor to scrape it off.

At the other end of the spectrum, a foible of the job is boredom, believe it or not, because there are times when you literally just sit around for days on end waiting for a fire to start somewhere.

The reason the pay is so good for a seasonal job is because of the long hours and the overtime that accumulates. The base pay for an entry-level position is $1,500 per month, plus $200 in guaranteed overtime (40 extra hours per month). Any additional time for an entry-level position is paid at $7.50 per hour. So a newcomer to firefighting might work long hours, but they can earn close to $2,000 per month.

If you have more experience, you get paid more. After about five years, you can expect to be earning a straight-time salary of $2,000 per month, $500 in guaranteed overtime, and $10 an hour for overtime exceeding 40 hours per month. When working a big fire, the paycheck can get crazy, with over $2,000 in overtime hours alone.

If it is a busy fire season, you can expect hard work, long hours and high pay. For a young person who wants to grunt now, pack some money away, then sit on the beach later, it is one of the best ways to fly.

But fire crews are like a machine and the staff chief won't stand for any squealing in the gears. There is a definite macho attitude that comes with the territory, which means that when you get down in the trenches and start fighting the fire, you pare things down to the base, gut-level elements of performance. Nothing else counts. While the crews are comprised of many intelligent, clever and funny individuals, when the fire starts, everybody becomes an unpolished chunk of coal. All fire fighters know it, share it and love it.

It is important to know that because there are three key matters with this job: whining, endurance, getting along. You can't whine ever, you must endure always, and you have to get along with your mates. If you are physically and mentally prepared, that can take care of the whining and endurance. Remember that the only difference between hardship and adventure is whether or not you have the spirit for it. As for getting along, that is up to you.

How to get hired? This is how: States that are vulnerable to forest fires have departments (often called the "State Department of Forestry") that are set up to hire, coordinate and pay fire crews. The best opportunities are in the more heavily wooded regions, of course. Prospects should make contact in the off-season, gather as much information as possible, get the names of supervisors, and arrange an interview. Get your leg work done by spring. By summer, when the fires start, all the positions are often filled.

No experience is necessary to get hired. That is because you will not only be trained, but directed to accomplish specific tasks by your crew chief. The crew boss is the brains, the crew members are the arms and legs. That is why you will need to be in excellent physical shape, with good stamina and an attitude to match. This is what crew chiefs are looking for. You do not need to be the second coming of Adonis; just in tuned condition, with the ability to work within a group.

A strange phenomenon comes with this job. A forest fire can be like hell, an inferno that can burn your eyes, smoke out your lungs, and torment your ears with the sound of burning, crackling leaves. There you are, though, digging out a fire line with your mates, sweating, dirty, tired, and choking from the smoke. It is the worst day of your life. Then one week later, you describe the affair to somebody, and for some strange reason, instead it sounds like the best day of your life. Years later, perhaps while sitting at a desk job somewhere, you discover that maybe it was.

Career Case Study

Steve Wopschall, California
Steve Wopschall has worked as a seasonal firefighter
since 1987. He attends college in the winter months. He
enjoys skydiving, scuba diving, hiking, swimming, and
all adventures. He lives in Redding, California.

Requirements—Officially, you have to be 18, a high school graduate, and capable of arduous, strenuous work. I'll re-emphasize the need to be very physically fit; you're constantly in situations that require strength and stamina. During the 40-hour firefighter class you're required to take, there are certain standardized tests that you must pass. You have to be able to wear full firefighter gear, extend 200 feet of hose, then break it down and return it to the engine within ten minutes. Some people have trouble with that. You have to be very responsible and flexible, able to handle pressure and think on your feet. People's lives often depend on your decisions. You have to be able to work somewhat unsupervised and use wise judgment. You have to be able to get along with your crew very well because you're with them day in and day out for long periods of time.

Prospects—There's a lot of competition. When I applied in 1987, when there were a lot of fires here in Northern California, there were 10 positions available at this station and about 200 people applied. I think this year there were 22 positions, with between 200 and 300 applicants. It used to be that if you wanted to be a fireman, you just basically had to be big, dumb and kind of brave, but it's become so competitive that people are doing everything they can to stay on top of things: they're taking vocational education classes, attending seminars, getting four-year degrees. And even then it's very difficult to advance.

I'm very frustrated right now. This is my sixth season. I have an associate's degree in social psychology and an associate's degree in general education, and I'm finding it very difficult to advance to a permanent position. Competition for advanced non-entry level positions is very keen, and there are a lot of people being moved around within the department since all the cutbacks.

We respond to a lot more medical calls than we used to, so any previous medical skills, such as CPR, emergency medical training, or First Response training is going to give someone a key edge. It helps to have a clean driving record, too, because employees are sent out on errands a lot. That may not sound like a big deal, but you'd be surprised at how rare it is. Any formal fire training, such as experience at a volunteer fire department, will help a lot.

There are a lot more women in the field than when I first started. I think there were two women working during my first season, and now it's about 50-50.

Benefits—The number one benefit is the caliber of people that you work with. There's no one here in the station that I would not trust with my life. I've been in several situations where my life depended on the actions and decisions of the people I work with, and they always come through. Firefighters are generally trustworthy by nature; you don't have to worry about things disappearing or someone taking advantage of you.

The salary and benefits are quite good. That's why a lot of people get into this. At this station we work four days straight, then get three days off, but that's more than most stations. It's standard to have ten to eleven actual days of work per month, which isn't bad.

I like being in a non-routine job, being outside. Before I started fighting fires, I was going to school to be a computer programmer, and I decided after my first season that I would rather be out fighting fires than sitting in a cubicle, typing in front of a computer all day. I like the adrenaline rush that comes with the job. I think most of the people who stay with it do.

I like being in a public service position. I feel much better about being out in the world doing something that's affecting lives, that's going to count to somebody, than I would about trying to make a new gadget to sell or something.

Pay—In six years, I'm making, with guaranteed overtime, about $2,000 a month plus benefits. An entry-level job right now pays around $1,500 a month base salary, plus about $200 of guaranteed overtime. In 1987, when we were unusually busy, I had one $2,000 overtime check. Some of the people who live here year-round are making $1,200 to $1,500 a month consistently. Overtime pay is where the big money is, and it's beneficial to the employers as well as to the employees, because it's cheaper to pay us overtime than it is to hire more firefighters.

Negatives—We work 24 hours a day for four days. I come in on Wednesday morning and leave Sunday night at 8 PM. We have no time off to run personal errands, even little things like going home to check our mail. When you're on duty you live in a co-ed barrack situation, and there's a certain lack of flexibility and privacy. The working conditions can be absolutely miserable. I know a lot of people who got into this with the sole intention of making a lot of money for school, and when we're out there sweating and dirty and we haven't eaten a good meal in 12 hours, people say, "This sure isn't a desk job."

Recently we were working out in a lightning storm, and we had a 2,000-foot altitude climb with a full pack and chainsaws and all our gear, and then we got rained on, so we were out there trying to stay warm in the pouring rain with lightning striking all around us. It was quite an adventure, but that's part of the job.

The future—Firefighting is one of the few jobs I don't see how they can eliminate. There's no way to replace people with machines in this case. With timber becoming more and more of a precious resource, we're becoming more aggressive in protecting it. We deal not only with forest fires, but with structure fires, medical fires and medical calls, and unfortunately people will always need that service. Fire prevention can do so much, but there's always the human factor. I think once you get past the entry level stage, it's one of the most secure professions to be in.

Career Case Study

Avery McGee, South Carolina
Avery McGee has worked as a seasonal firefighter since 1989. He has worked with the Cherokee Fire Dancers in Oklahoma and in the Plumas National Forest in California. He currently holds a permanent position with the Savannah River Site in South Carolina. Avery lives in Aiken, South Carolina, where he enjoys hunting, fishing and restoring furniture.

Requirements—A seasonal firefighter is required to have basic training in safety and firefighting techniques. That includes basic first aid training, too. You can get advanced-level medical training, but it's not required. There are no educational requirements. You have to be self-disciplined and have a good personality. You have to get along with and interact with other crew members. You also have to be very flexible; in our situation, people live in different areas, and most work elsewhere at full-time jobs. They have to be ready to go if they're called.

Prospects—The program that we had at The Cherokee Nation in Oklahoma was a good one, and it is expanding, so there are a lot of people who want to join. They can only accept so many at a time.

Basically, you don't work unless they call you.

Benefits—The travel is a benefit. You get to go to a lot of places you'd probably never see otherwise, and the people you meet out on the fire are really interesting. It's pretty fast money, too, which is why a lot of people get into it.

Pay—Entry level for a seasonal worker is around $6 to $7, and it doesn't go up much until you become a squad boss or crew boss. We can amass a lot of hours, but in my case we get paid straight, with no extra for overtime. That's different in different states.

Negatives—Being away for two to three weeks at a time can be hard. You have to sleep on the ground, and if there are shower facilities where you are, you usually have to stand in line for two or three hours. It's really hot out there, even more so with the fires going on. It can be dangerous, too. One time when I was working in California, the fire jumped the fire line, and we almost got run over. Everyone had to get out of there fast, and it was pretty scary.

The future—It's been growing fast in the last few years. Fire management is a good area to get into if you're looking for a career, which is usually the goal of seasonal firefighters. The forests are a national natural resource, and they will always need protection.

References

Society of American Foresters, 515 SW 5th Street, Suite 518, Portland, OR 97201; (503) 222-7456.

Boise Inner Agency Fire Center, 3833 South Development Avenue, Boise, ID 83705-5354; (208) 387-5512. (This center coordinates firefighting for the entire United States.)

US Forestry Service, 740 Simms Street, Golden, CO 80401; (303) 275-5350 or fax (303) 275-5671.

Also contact local branches of the National Park Service, U.S. Forest Service, Bureau of Land Management, Bureau of Indian Affairs, state forestry offices, and local fire stations.

Fish Hatchery
Specialist

Dreams—You are special, someone who actually creates life and adds to the joy of anglers and profits of commercial fishermen. Every day, you have the power of life in your hands. The joy from that pays a great reward, not to mention a tolerable salary. Every day is fascinating, with new puzzles to solve, and the proof of your success is right there in the water.

Nightmares—There so many details, it's like putting shoes on a multi-legged monster. If you blow the deal, thousands of fish will die, which is devastating. You never seem to get any time off, either from the demands of the fish, or the demands of bureaucrats. Right when you sit down for dinner, Joe Politician shows up for a hatchery tour.

Realities—The satisfaction is genuine from parenting thousands and thousands of fish, but so is the sense of always being at work, worrying about the little buggers. The pay is not bad, but considering the education requirements, should be better. Hatchery specialists either love their job as patriarch of the outdoors, or hate it, saying it's "hard work, low pay."

What it's all about—"So what do you do for a living?" comes the inevitable question from strangers. "I am the mom and dad of millions of fish," you can answer as a fish hatchery specialist, "the great creator for the outdoors." Know what? You'll be telling the truth.

Fish hatchery specialists are responsible for playing the role of Divine Being for 40 hours a week, sometimes a bit more. They spawn out adult fish, incubate the eggs, sit on the nest (so to speak) until the progeny hatch, then mother the young until the fish are large enough to stock in public waters. The entire process, from start to finish, is a challenge that takes knowledge, wisdom and time— and provides a special satisfaction in seeing life start and directly improving the lives of recreational anglers or commercial fishermen.

This may sound like a job for the supernatural, but actually a unique outlook with a strong educational background is enough. Unique because most people can be split into two groups—people who like to design a project and people who like to build it. A fish hatchery specialist does both, and is in charge from the concept to the moment of fulfillment. A strong education is required, usually a master's in marine biology with the emphasis on hatchery work. It is possible to get a job at a hatchery with a bachelor's degree, but only with several years of on-site experience, and even then, the long-term prospects are only fair because of the scientific expertise required.

There are so many variables in the hatchery process that this career demands precise thinking and a solid science background. So many things can go wrong—water temperatures, oxygen levels, pH levels, disease control, spawn survival, fish crowding, feeding, 24-hour surveillance, burglary of large brood stock fish, survival in transport. It is up to you to make sure it works out. Unfortunately, the public doesn't want to hear about the labor pains, they just want to see the baby.

It is a great sensation to successfully spawn fish, then see their young hatch. You get another sense of triumph when the fish are stocked, survive, and turn the days of many recreational and professional fishermen into happy ones. Being the caretaker of a hatchery provides some satisfaction as well. Like the head steward at a brewery, you're always assuring that conditions are just right.

For this, the pay should be better, but it is not. Considering the educational demand and exacting standards of the job, a fish hatchery specialist should be paid higher than other government jobs that require less of both. They don't. You get the standard, regimented pay scale, ranging from $21,000 (ouch!) a year in a low-rung start-up job, then topping out at $45,000 after 20 or 30 years. Salaries for biologists are much higher in private industry, often double that, including overtime.

Another fair gripe is the amount of extra time you have to put in, often without fair compensation. Those little fish are living things, and like any baby, you can't always time when they need burping according to your work schedule. Because of this, many hatchery managers live on the hatchery premises. That creates another problem, in which government nabobs always seem to show up and want a tour right when you are sitting down to dinner. They never apologize, either. After all, they're excited about getting a tour; shouldn't you be, too? That's how these yahoos think.

On the other hand, the job security at a government fish hatchery is undeniable. Once established in a position at a hatchery, you are likely to stay there until it becomes a second home. The demand for hatchery-raised fish is always growing, since environmental degradation has hurt natural spawning in so many areas. Hatcheries are well funded in order to help provide what nature can't always get done on its own. In California alone, there are more than 22 state-run hatcheries. In South Carolina, a giant striped bass plant hatches some 60 million larvae a year. There are hatcheries in virtually every part of North America.

There is also an undeniable pleasure in caring for live critters, those little fish you helped create with your own hands. The light in the eyes of hatchery specialists is the inner glow they feel over how they spend their time. If you can't imagine that feeling over a tubful of tiny fish, then this is not the job for you. But if you can . . . then get a good education, maybe a part-time or seasonal job as an assistant at a hatchery, and enjoy caring for these little guys. After awhile you might even feel as if you are both their mom and dad.

Career Case Study

Tom Curtis, South Carolina—Tom Curtis has worked as a fish hatchery specialist since 1970 at Dennis Wildlife Center, the largest striped bass hatchery in the world. He is currently chief of the center. While he attended college, he gained experience by working summers for the North Carolina Department of Wildlife. He enjoys sailing and painting. He is married, has one son, and lives in Bonneau, South Carolina.

Requirements—There are two basic employment levels within the hatchery: biologists, who are supervisors, and technicians, who work for us. For biologist positions, the basic requirement is a master's degree. We do occasionally accept a bachelor's degree with three years experience. This is an entry level position; you can go in straight from college. You start out at the Biologist 1 level, then work your way up to Biologist 4.

Prospects—There are a very limited number of hatcheries and there's not a lot of turnover, but at the same time there's a great deal of interest in environmental studies at the moment, and the universities are turning out hundreds of qualified people. When hiring, we place a lot of weight on previous experience in related fields; anyone who has worked on a fish farm or in a wildlife department before will have an edge.

Some hatchery specialists work on a contract basis, which can often be more lucrative than a permanent position. They'll be hired to do a specific thing, such as research, for a specific amount of time. The market is better for those types of workers because they're more in demand; they save the government agencies money. Because they're hired as contractors, the government doesn't have to supply the benefits that they supply to their permanent employees, so they're saving money. And the contractor gets the opportunity for experience and exposure.

Benefits—I enjoy working with a variety of activities. It's a multi-disciplined program. You have to have the knowledge and skill to keep fish alive and all the basics that go along with that, but you also have to have knowledge of other seemingly unrelated things, such as plumbing. What we do is highly specialized, so we often have to create our own tools and facilities. We do a lot of carpentry, plumbing and electrical work. We also work with electronics, like sonar for fish counting. It's rewarding just to be working in the environmental field, working for fishermen. We provide recreation and resources for the fishermen and the state, and that's a good feeling. Another upside is job security. It's very stable, and that's a big help these days.

Pay—The money you make is very little considering the level of education that's required. When you start out in a Biologist 1 position, you can make about $21,000; after about 25 years of experience, you can expect to be making $45,000. We are not compensated for overtime; I have a friend who works for a power company who said that if he put in the amount of overtime I do, he could make an additional $10,000 a year, on top of his regular salary. It's difficult to advance financially. I haven't had a raise of any type in the last three years; raises are generally very sporadic.

One benefit that the state provides is a house and free utilities. That is standard at all state and federal hatcheries; at least the manager and sometimes one assistant is given a house.

Negatives—The major drawback is that the salaries are very poor, comparatively speaking. A biologist working for a private company would make 30 to 50 percent more than I do. Biologists tend to be somewhat discriminated against. One reason for that is because what we do is so difficult to quantify. An engineer can tell you exactly how much stress it takes to bend steel, but we can't tell how much pollution it takes in a body of water before fish are killed. So we're not always taken as seriously as we should be.

Generally we have long working hours. When we spawn fish, for example, we work 14 to 16 hours a day, seven days a week, for eight weeks straight. It's very difficult on my family life. The disadvantage of free housing, too, is that the house is on the hatchery site, and it always seems to be right when you're sitting down for Sunday dinner that a politician drives up and wants a tour of the hatchery. You end up working late hours and weekends a lot.

By nature, the job tends to damper your enthusiasm about fishing. I have always loved to fish, but the more you work with fish the less avid you become about catching them.

The future—I hope that as people become more environmentally conscious, we will be appreciated more. I think the future looks good, not as financially lucrative as other positions, but I predict that there will be more opportunities opening up. As far as salaries are concerned, we're hoping that the economy will change. I think more hatcheries will be opening and there will be more study and emphasis on aquaculture and related research. As the demand for seafood increases, more hatcheries and specialists will be needed.

Career Case Study

Mike Grover, Oregon

Mike Grover is the assistant manager at Marion Forks Hatchery in Idanha, Oregon. He has worked for various hatcheries throughout Oregon since 1976. Mike lives at the hatchery site, and enjoys snow skiing in the winter and water skiing, power boat racing, hiking, and fishing in the summer.

Requirements—Mainly you need an associate's or bachelor's degree in fisheries or any associated field, such as biology or oceanography. The level of required experience varies from hatchery to hatchery. Any experience in state or private industry is considered an asset, but the minimum is usually two years. Many people start out in a seasonal position, working part time during the summer, and just keep applying until something permanent comes up.

Prospects—There is a lot of competition. Colleges are graduating a good number of qualified people every year, so there is some degree of rivalry. It seems that a lot of people are going into private industry; there is a lot more development of private aquaculture right now, and that area seems to be a bit more stable than the state and federal level.

Benefits—I enjoy the work. It's not mundane, eight-to-five, day-to-day type work. You're changing your routine every day. It's routine on a yearly basis, as far as spawning and all the cycles we go through, but within that we do other things. For example we recently backpacked fish into several high-country lakes because our helicoptor budget was cut, which made the national news. We get to be outside, involved with wildlife, which is one of the reasons people get into this field, I think. You certainly get to live out in some pretty country in most cases. If you enjoy the outdoors, as most everyone around here does, you have the advantage of having recreation right outside your back door. And it's rewarding to see other people make use of the things you're working on; it makes you feel good to see the fish returning, to see people enjoying the recreation. It's a nice feeling to know you're contributing to an important natural resource.

Most hatchery employees live on the hatchery site, and inexpensive housing is provided. There are good medical and retirement benefits also.

Pay—There are seven pay levels, going up about every two years. A bottom-scale entry level position pays just under $1,400 a month. Most people come in with some experience, and start out at a mid-range level, right around $1,500 to $1,600 a month. The top of the manager list is a little over $3,400, and that would be for the manager of a large hatchery. A manager at a smaller hatchery would top out at about $2,900. We usually expect a two to three percent cost of living increase about every two years.

Negatives—Isolation. Most hatcheries are out in the boonies, so to speak, and there isn't much around. A lot of the facilities are old buildings, so there's a lot of upkeep. The hours can vary; we sometimes work 10- to 14-hour days. The weather, especially in the mountains or on the coast, can be a deterrent too. And the pay is not the greatest. I'd say it's very low considering what we have to do.

The future—I think the field is definitely going to increase. There is a need to produce more and do more. There are more people to feed and more uses of the resource for recreation. We've got to continue to improve on what we're doing, and I think manpower will increase as usage grows.

References

American Fisheries Society, 5410 Grosvenor Lane, Suite 110, Bethesda, MD 20814; (301) 897-8616.

National Fish & Wildlife Foundation, 1120 Connecticut Avenue NW, Suite 900, Washington, DC 20036; (202) 857-0166 or fax (202) 857-0162.

US Fish & Wildlife Service, 2625 Parkmont Road, Building A, Olympia, WA 98502; (360) 753-9460.

Note: Most states have their own fish and wildlife departments that operate fish hatcheries.

Fishing Bait Shop Owner/Distributor

*"Your self-image is either your life handicap
or your autopilot for winning."—Dr. Denis Waitley*

Dreams—You have what fishermen want—live bait that will catch them more fish. They are willing to pay a lot for it, enough for you to clear more than $100,000 per year and live the good life, and also hire a few employees to do the hard stuff. Selling bait? Why it's more like selling pure gold.

Nightmares—You get all ready for a three-day weekend, supplying dozens of shops with $10,000 worth of live bait, but a huge storm comes in and nobody goes fishing, eliminating sales. Then your bait traps come up empty, your stock dies at the holding tanks in your garage, and at the stores, the bait goes belly up because the owners forgot about the oxygen pumps.

Realities—There is some big money in this game, but you must play by the rules—some hard, fast ones, about keeping live creatures in perfect condition from the traps to the holding tanks to the stores. Do that and fishermen will buy. Expect large fluctuations in sales and 90-hour weeks during peak season. It can take significant overhead to get an operation set up, but a well-run system can turn into a money machine.

What it's all about—Don't let your pride fool you. Remember it's the cattle that counts, not how big the cowboy hat is. That goes double when it comes to selling fish bait.

A lot of people forget this, then spend a good deal of time extracting their Red Wings out of their mouths. At one evening get-together at a friend's house, I remember watching this entry-level computer programmer spend the evening digesting his boots.

"Well, what do you do for a living?" Mr. Computer said to a stranger.

"I sell fish bait," the stranger answered.

Mr. Computer smiled a bit, perhaps in disbelief, perhaps because he couldn't believe anybody actually did such a thing.

"You're kidding, right?" said Mr. Computer. "Fish bait? Ah, ha, ha, I get it, you're going fishing tomorrow and you have so much extra bait that you want to sell me some. It's a joke. Ha. Well I'm into computers. I like the big hard drives, like 120 megabytes, talk about power, and the new programs to drive them...Listen to this, today I was working on a board when I..."

The stranger just stared at the guy for a moment, then walked away. You see, it was no joke. The guy really did sell fish bait.

And when he left the party, he drove off with his beautiful wife in his restored 1937 Cadillac to his $500,000 home. Meanwhile, the computer programmer's old Chevy Nova wouldn't start, and when the host of the party offered a jump start, that classic Cadillac drove right on by, humming like a 120-megabyte hard drive.

"Who is that guy?" asked Mr. Computer.

"He sells fish bait," was the simple answer.

"Oh." Mr. Computer looked mighty funny the next few days, walking around with his boots jammed in his mouth.

Meanwhile, the bait man just cooled his jets. It was his little secret.

But the secret is getting out. You see, done right, there is a lot of money to be made selling bait. But it's not as simple as opening a small store, putting out a sign that says "Bait Shop," then waiting for the flood of cash-providing customers to come pouring through the door. It doesn't work like that.

What does work is obtaining specialty baits that are in demand by anglers, then distributing them to a network of bait and tackle shops. The baits that sell for the highest price are live baits of all varieties, especially small live baitfish. The species in demand varies from region to region across the country, of course. On the Columbia River corridor in the Pacific Northwest, it's live ghost shrimp for sturgeon. Across much of the south for big bass and catfish, it's live crawdads. In the Midwest, it's quality live minnows, and in some cases, nightcrawlers. In San Francisco Bay, there is such a demand for live bait (grass shrimp, mud shrimp, shiner perch) that there are times when anglers make bait reservations for their weekend trips.

It isn't difficult to find out what fishermen want. Just start asking around at the bait shops. You'll find out. Then ask if they ever run out of a particular specialty item, such as golden shiners at the lakes in Southern California, for instance. If they do, you have a prime opening.

The best approach involves a three-step system: 1) Acquiring live bait. 2) Having holding facilities to keep the live bait healthy. 3) Setting up a distribution network to sell the live bait. To do it right and maximize profits during peak season can require non-stop work—up to 90 hours per week (gulp!).

You can add to your income by having your own bait shop at a dock in a marina. This is particularly helpful because you can submerge holding screens for your bait, which solves a space problem you might have if you try to use your garage at home. But you can go two ways in this business: You can own a single bait shop operation, or become a bait distributor and sell to other bait shop owners.

To be able to distribute, you must first acquire the bait. There are many ways to accomplish this, and it varies according to what bait is in demand. For live fish, from minnows to crawdads to shiners, bait distributors will usually run a network of trapping operations. They (or an employee) will set traps at likely locations, then after a period of time, make the rounds and "work the traps." In some cases, they will use seines to net schools of baitfish, such as minnows and threadfin shad. (State permits and a commercial fishing license are often required for these operations. Always check with state fishery headquarters.) In the case of nightcrawlers, bait sellers will often create a nightcrawler farm. Occasionally, such as with mud shrimp, the bait is imported from out of the area by jet express. There is enough profit in many areas to make it worth the expense.

Once the live bait has been obtained, you must have a way to keep it in perfect condition. This does not always involve a large setup, but often a 500-square-foot garage with several tanks. If you arrange to run your own bait shop at a dock in a marina, then you can put screened holding traps in the water next to the shop, and keep the bait there. In any case, you must get it right.

After all, these are living things we're talking about, and they must be cared for from start to finish. Otherwise, an angler might as well buy a frozen pack of squid or anchovies. What you are offering is quality, and of course, anglers pay for that quality.

That is why you must also work with each shop to make sure their respective bait holding tanks are set up properly. Mortality from live bait transfers can skim the cream right off the top of your earnings. By helping each shop set up tanks, you are making sure survival rates are high. In addition, you are developing a good working relationship with a long-term client. One option here is to supply the shops with tanks, then make an agreement that the tanks will only be used for bait that you personally supply. That can give you a corner of a particular market.

Anglers buy quality live bait because of one reason: They have a better chance of catching fish. As long as the quality is there, they will pay high prices. Once established, bait sellers can make $100,000 per year, some less, and some a lot more. During a year, earnings often fluctuate from mountain tops to deep canyons because of seasons, fish migrations, populations and weather, all factors that are out of your control.

This is a career where the right approach can pay off. It takes careful planning and execution. But done right, you can be rewarded. Just remember the story about the computer programmer and the bait man with the '37 Cadillac.

Career Case Study

Keith Fraser, California

Keith Fraser has been the co-owner of Loch Lomond Live Bait and Tackle since 1972. Prior to that, he taught high school English and journalism for 20 years, and is still a high school baseball coach. He is an avid conservationist and the founding president of United Anglers of California. He is considered the guru of California sturgeon fishing, attracting large crowds to his seminars. He is married and lives in San Rafael, California.

Requirements—To get started, you need three things: capital, prospective customers, and a supply of various kinds of bait. The amount of capital depends on the type of operation. You have to decide on the vehicle you want to transport your merchandise in, which usually ends up being a refrigerated truck, and you have to decide whether you need to hire someone to work for you or to do it all yourself.

You can acquire customers when you purchase the business, steal them from another poor soul in the business, or go out on your own and talk someone into selling your product. Entrepreneurial skills come in handy there.

There are two methods for procuring bait: You can either catch it yourself, with nets, traps, or hook and line, or you can purchase it from other purveyors of bait. The most lucrative way, of course, is to catch it yourself, but a lot of people deal primarily in frozen bait. They buy it from a fisherman who has caught and packaged it, then they mark it up and sell it. Most bait distributors are simply middle men.

Prospects—This is like any other type of business. When things are going well, when the fishing is good and the economy is stable, there are a lot of people trying to cash in on what they see as easy bucks. But during bleak times, bait salespeople are not jumping out of the bushes. It completely depends on the state of the economy and how the fishing is.

Benefits—Personally, I'm in a business that I'm interested in and enjoy. I like getting up and going to work in the morning. I'm right here on the water, on the bay, and if 9 o'clock rolls around and I feel like going out for a swim or going skiing, I can put up a sign that says I'll be back in half an hour and I go.

I share a common interest with the angler and am treated well by my customers. They look at me as the guy who can lead them to the promised land. They think, "Be nice to him, maybe he'll give us some tips." Which I do. And in turn, they let me know how things are going. I want to know how they did, what bait worked best, what the weather was like, where they were. I get to meet all kinds of people, ranging from millionaires to guys who want 50 cents worth of shrimp and count their change out 15 times.

Pay—It's a business of peaks and valleys. I know people who are lucky to make $15,000 to $20,000 a year, and I know some who make upwards of $200,000. There are many variables: location, the availability of fish, whether the fish are biting or have lockjaw, how the weather and tides are. Publicity is another factor. If it's broadcasted that the fishing is lousy, that's going to hurt us tremendously.

The most important tip I can give is to be honest with your customers. If you give them a line of bull, they'll come in once or twice, but after a while they'll catch on and lose confidence, and they'll stop coming in. If the fishing is bad, you've got to say so.

Negatives—The hours can be long. I get calls at home on Christmas Day from people wondering when we're going to open. And if you trap your own bait, it can be very hard work, physically. You have to get up early, too; we open at 6 a.m., but some shops open as early as 4 a.m.

You're dealing with a fluctuating revenue. There can be many months in a row when it's time to open a can and share dinner with the dog, and other times it can be very lucrative. It's extremely inconsistent.

Sometimes the bait is hard to get. We get some of our bait flown in from Oregon and Washington, and if they can't get the prescribed bait because the wind is blowing 90 miles an hour, we're out of luck. People get mad at you and think it's all your fault.

The future—All marine businesses are currently down. There are still excellent periods, but there has been a general decline of natural resources.

One of the obvious current culprits is the economy, but there are other factors: There are more environmental problems, more people fishing and less fish. Man is such a greedy creature. Here in the Bay Area, we're battling with Southern California, which wants all the northern water for farming and such, and that raises havoc with the fisheries. There are similar situations occurring all over the country, even around the world, and I don't see that changing. The almighty dollar is going to be what dictates the future.

I'm still happy to be in this business and I've made good money in it. But projecting the financial scenario for the future is like predicting how many fish you're going to catch on your next trip.

Career Case Study

Dale Mennick, Florida
Dale Mennick and his wife have owned Dolphin Marine since 1987. They also own Coastal Sports, a company which manufactures a light used for crabbing and floundering. Dale worked as a divisional manager for K-Mart for 14 years before getting into the bait and tackle business. He enjoys fishing, water sports, camping, and hunting. The Mennicks have two children and live in Pensacola, Florida.

Requirements—Basically, the most important factor is local knowledge. Anyone can start carrying live bait, but he has to know what to carry and when. For example, I know that shrimp get soft and shed their skin on a full moon, so I don't make a big order at those times. You have to know about the timing—when the fish migrate. As far as in-depth business skills, I think a lot of people make things sound more complicated than they really are. Bait and tackle businesses are for the most part pretty simple operations, and as long as you have some good basic skills, you'll be able to do it. Local knowledge and timing are much more important.

Prospects—It's highly competitive, at least here in Florida. There are a lot of shops out here. Shops that rely on bait alone, unless they've been around for 20 years, will probably never be able to open their doors. A shop owner today needs to have a little bit of everything. When a guy walks in he wants to be able to find everything he needs in one place, and if he can't, he'll go somewhere else. Selling tackle and running charters or renting boats gives you some other options for sales. As far as bait goes, having your own bait boats instead of buying bait from the suppliers is ideal. That way you'll always have bait whether the big guys come through or not.

Benefits—I don't know what else a man would want to do other than run a bait and tackle shop. If you like to fish, it's the best job in the world. It's fun teaching people how to fish and seeing them bring their catches in to be weighed. I think that's why most get into it. I know there's no one around here who did it just to make money. For most of us it's just like seeing the sun rise.

Pay—We've been open for five years and we're just now making a profit. It takes some time. The average markup on merchandise is about 30 percent. So if you do $100,000 in business, you'll get about $30,000, and once you pay all your overhead you could end up with nothing. We initially sunk $62,000 into this business, and this year we'll probably have an income of about $20,000 or $25,000. That's for a small store. There are stores in town doing $2,000,000 in business, but they've been around for 25 years. I think a small shop could get started for around $20,000; that's just for renting a building and putting in enough merchandise and bait to attract customers. If you're talking about owning a building, it's going to be quite a bit more.

Negatives—Long hours. You have to open at six and stay open until the people stop coming in. You have to do quite a bit of volume in order to make any money, which can be tough, and as in any business, you have to make a pretty substantial investment in it.

The future—I think it's pretty good. I think there's a movement away from the big companies, the K-Marts and Wal-Marts, back to smaller shops. The big companies have completely lost that personal touch. If a guy wants to order something in particular, the big stores can't get it for him unless it's in their computer. That's where we have the advantage.

Reference

International Sportsmen's Exposition, PO Box 2569, Vancouver, WA 98668; (800) 545-6100 or (360) 693-3700.

National Fisheries Institute, 1901 North Fort Myer Drive, Ste 700, Arlington, VA 22209; (703) 524-8880 or fax (703) 524-4619.

National Retail Federation, 325 7th Street NW, Washington, D.C. 20004; (202) 783-7971.

Fishing Tackle Shop Owner

Dreams—With all your fishing goodies, you're like a kid in a candy store. People flock to your store just to gaze at all the fun toys, then buy them, setting you up as a wealthy fish bum who fishes whenever you want. Faithful clients would never betray you by shopping at a discount house.

Nightmares—The investment to get started has you living on a shoestring. Then you not only buy the wrong tackle, but a nearby K-Mart is killing you on prices. Your store location turns out to be a stinker. An employee robs you blind, the electricity goes off and all your bait dies, and soon it is "adios, muchachos."

Realities—You need big bucks to get started, a prize location, then quality inventory that sets your shop apart from any other. You need local fishing know-how, business smarts to make the right buys, and the wisdom not to let the flash of a six-figure income get in the way of your fishing time.

What it's all about—If you want a job where you are a combination fortune teller, riverboat gambler and accountant, this is it. If you can do those three things well, you can make a small fortune, have the satisfaction of running your own business, and fish a lot in the bargain. Some shop owners keep a fishing boat at a prize slot at a nearby marina, sometimes within 20 seconds walking distance of their tackle shops—so when the bite is on, off they go.

But if you just like to fish a lot and figure you can parlay your special angling expertise into a successful enterprise, well, you might want to sit out this dance. This is a very unique venture and requires a very unique, multi-faceted individual to make a successful run at it.

The thing to remember is that a tackle shop is like an adult toy store. Anglers like to have lots of toys to gaze at and dream about, maybe even buy. To get lots of buyer traffic, you need a lot of toys to look at. That makes the risks in getting started quite high. Most shops have at least $100,000 in inventory, the larger stores a lot more than that. You will need an additional $40,000 for shop rent or lease, shop decor, and employee overhead to get started. There are no short cuts here.

That is why every fishing tackle shop owner tries to be a fortune teller. When you fill your racks and shelves, you are predicting the future: What will your customers need, want and most importantly, buy? For some dealers, the crystal ball can look pretty cloudy. Others who have a more clear vision get a nice payback. That is where being a riverboat gambler comes in. You are gambling when you buy inventory—price, quantity, models—and if you guess wrong too often you'll be hitch-hiking your way home from the Mississippi.

To make sure you are making the right decision, you have to have the razor-sharp mind of an accountant to know exactly what you have in stock, what it cost you, and what you can sell it for. You have to know exactly what products move in your market and what do not, and then aggressively buy in large quantities for low prices and then try to sell in large quantities at competitive prices. You have to have employees with know-how, the kind that are not available at K-Mart. These things don't come easy.

But the rewards are exceptional for the entrepreneur who can pull it off. For instance, the owner of a relatively small tackle shop in an excellent location can clear $150,000 per year, have a nice boat and a personal parking space at a marina, and in general live a fantasy life. It happens more than you might think.

Most anglers know that fishing teaches success through logic, persistence and experience. Tackle shop owners need the same exact approach, from start to finish.

The first key is choosing the location of your shop. The ideal location is next to a popular boat ramp, or an easy-to-reach location where high numbers of anglers must drive past in order to reach a prize destination—with no other tackle shop in the area, or heaven forbid, a K-Mart. If your location stinks, so will your sales. It's that simple.

Once your location is established, then you can start envisioning what kind of tackle anglers will want when they walk into your store. You must know precisely what they want, then provide it. You must know your local waters, the fisheries, seasonal cycles, and be on top of sudden trends. In other words, you must be a specialty shop, offering something compelling that anglers will not be able to find anywhere else. Your biggest competition is mail-order outfits and the huge chain stores. You can only beat them by providing exactly what anglers want, having employees who have graduated from the University of Fishing, and then having your store in a perfect location.

You might be surprised at profit margins. The best money is in outdoor apparel, sunglasses and shoes, which offer a 50 percent and higher mark-up, and many successful shops are 50 percent clothing because of it. Tackle generally runs 15 to 25 percent mark-up, though you can make more if you make large quantity buys (but that can be risky). The sales of rod-and-reel combinations are another winner, especially if you have them all set up with line, so all the customer has to do is tie on a lure.

There are many ways to spice up sales: mailers, specials on items as traffic-builders, demo shows, seminars, daily recorded fishing reports, locally-recorded videos, exceptional displays, spot advertising, and becoming known as the best regional shop for a specific style of fishing, say ultra-light, fly or marine.

Because the financial risk is significant, the lure of money can outshine the lure of angling. This can cause some tackle shop owners to work all the time, even seven days a week when the fishing is good, and pound that cash away. In the process, however, they completely miss the reason they got in the business to begin with: They love to fish. Some tackle shop owners combat this by scheduling a day of fishing a week just like they schedule their days of working, otherwise they rarely go.

If you can put it all together—afford the start-up, get an ideal location, get good prices on your inventory and qualified sales-people to pitch it—well, you can get the world by the ol' tail.

Career Case Study

Dave Navarro, Florida
Dave Navarro owns and operates World Class Angler,
a small tackle store in Marathon, Florida. Dave, an avid

fisherman himself, is dedicated to providing the highest
in quality for his fellow anglers.

Requirements—Basically you need a great deal of knowledge and experience with the equipment; what it is, how it works, why you use it, when and where. I've been a guide for 18 years, working with every item of tackle you can imagine, and that background has proven to be indispensable.

You need at least a high school education. College is not required, but you must have a basic understanding of bookkeeping, budgeting and marketing, as with any business. This is a seasonal business, and you have to learn to pre-plan, to forecast your year and know your economics. It's similar to the retail clothing business. You have to sell things that are hot, items that people are going to want to buy. If you go with what's hot at that moment, it's going to be worthless in six weeks. The public has gotten smart—they're tired of gimmicks. You have to read constantly to keep up with trends.

You have to be very outgoing and open to everyone. You can't judge people or have the attitude that a guy's a bum because of the way he looks. Many times the ones who look like bums are the ones who buy $20,000 worth of tackle. I like to joke with people; it breaks the ice. For example, the other day Michael Keaton was in here, and I was joking around with him and giving him a hard time. His wife told me, "No one talks to him like that." But he loved it.

Prospects—It is an extremely competitive business. Most areas are saturated with stores. In the area I live there are about 8,000 people and 14 tackle stores. Location is the key. If you're in central Kansas, there probably aren't going to be a lot of tackle stores, but if you're in a major coastal area, you've got to have an edge to succeed. I just read an article on a survey which stated that 78 percent of all fishermen are freshwater fishermen. The majority of the people live at least 50 miles inland, but they take an average of at least two saltwater trips a year.

The key is money. If you have money, you can do anything you want, but if you don't, you've got to have an awful lot of business sense, specifically in the tackle industry. You have to know what your market is and what they want. My advantage is that I specialize in quality. I sell the highest quality tackle, not the cheap stuff that you can find anywhere. The stores that carry that kind of merchandise are the ones that have to compete with the big chain stores, like K-Mart.

Benefits—I have the biggest tackle box in town; everything I could ever want is at my fingertips. I like being independent. When you own your own business, you can do it your way; you can set your own hours, incorporate your own ideals and ideas, and deal with the people you want to deal with. Best of all, you're not working your butt off to make someone else rich.

Pay—I would say that you'd need a minimum of $250,000 to start out. By the time you're done with start-up fees, taxes and inventory, that will be gone. My shop is 700 square feet and I have a $180,000 inventory.

It's comparable to starting an unplanned young family. All these crises you've never imagined in your wildest dreams occur. There's always a gap, something that's gonna pop up and get you. You have to buy diapers, pay the pediatrician, then the car breaks down and on top of everything, you have to go to the dentist and get your teeth fixed. You're broke, working 25 hours a day, and you just learn as you go along. But it's very lucrative if you stick with it. Once you get established, you can expect to make $100,000 to $200,000 a year, depending on how well your store does.

Negatives—It's a very high risk business; it's difficult to predict what will sell. If you project wrong and buy inventory that people don't want, you're stuck with it. It's unlike a specialty shop, which offers unique products; a tackle store is a tackle store. It's also a seasonal business, and you've got to build up enough income to carry you through the off-season.

There is very little consumer loyalty anymore. It used to be if the local store charged 15 cents more than the big stores, the customer would buy it anyway, but with today's economy every penny counts, so now if the big stores sell it for less, that's where they'll buy it. We back up our products for 20 years; that used to mean something. It can be very sporadic. Some days you're swamped, some days you're empty. Selling live bait is difficult; one thing can happen and boom, you're out $2,000.

The future—The fishing industry is immense. Forty-one percent of all humans fish, according to the surveys, and the sportfishing element is increasing rapidly. The "go out and kill all you can" attitude is going away. More people believe in catch-and-release fishing, and I believe it is the way of the future. That bodes well for the future of the sport.

It's one of the least expensive sports to participate in, which is important to people these days. It's growing at a rapid rate, and I think that trend will continue.

Career Case Study

Allen Hardy, Tennessee
Allen Hardy of Nashville, Tennessee, has owned Bill Clay Sporting Goods since 1986, and before that, worked there for many years. When he's not working in the store, Bill enjoys fishing and hunting in exotic locales such as South America and Mexico.

Requirements—I don't think that a college education is a necessary requirement. I took a few classes, and then went back for some accounting courses later, but I never received a degree. In today's world, I think that in order to understand the high-tech facets of business, education is important, but not absolutely required.

If I were talking to someone who wanted to start a store, I would definitely recommend that they work for someone else first, so they can see what they're really getting into. I started out when I was ten years old as the janitor; I'd go get coffee, throw out the trash, run errands. I ended up staying with the business, and Bill Clay, who then owned the store, had no children, so he basically adopted me. I slowly worked my way up in management, and then I bought him out in 1986. I learned everything about the business from the inside out. I think that's the only way to get a really good idea of whether this is something you really want to do.

Too many people think that because they love to hunt and fish, having a sporting goods store would be the greatest thing around. But what many don't realize is that when the fishing's good and the hunting season starts, they'll have to be in the store working. And when they finally get a day off, the fishing is lousy. It's not the bed of roses that everyone thinks it is; it's just another way to make a living.

Prospects—The market is tough, real tough. If a person is going to open his own store, he is generally going to be going up against established stores such as Wal Mart and K-Mart, as well as all the large chains of sporting goods stores.

The angle that those stores use in marketing is low prices, and you have to compete with that by offering something else, such as professional service. In the mega-chain stores, most of the employees are only there for a part-time job. Our store specializes in offering the advice of knowledgeable salespeople. People appreciate that, and in the long run we save them money.

Basically, you have to figure out what your market needs and what's not being offered, and then you have to fill that niche. For instance, our store has an archery department where there are full-time employees who can do repair work, give advice or order special items. The big stores don't offer specialized services like that.

Benefits—Being your own boss is the biggest advantage. With that comes the satisfaction of your own success, seeing your dream come true. You have the ability and the opportunity to make whatever you want happen. You're not dependent on the direction of others, and you benefit from the rewards, both mentally and financially.

I think it's a fun business. It attracts people who are all interested in the same things; the mood is enjoyable, and it is a very pleasant atmosphere to work in.

Pay—How much you make depends on what level you're going into. If you're opening a small bait shop, you're obviously going to make less than if you were to open a large sports store.

I think stores can be opened at most any level with a reasonable amount of capital. I'd estimate the start-up capital for a hunting or fishing store with an adequate line of goods at roughly $100,000 or more. Beyond that, your income is governed by sales, and that varies. I would say in a store that's doing one million dollars a year, the owner could expect an income of about $50,000. That figure starts to go up fast when the store goes over a million; it becomes pure profit because your overhead doesn't increase much.

Negatives—The hours are extremely long. We've been having a big tent sale for the past week, and I think I've been home for a total of about six hours, literally. I've got a tent set up out back, and I've been sleeping there. I go home for an hour a day to take a shower. There have been times I've gone for three months without a day off.

There's a lot of pressure to meet your obligations. These days, people want to shop at their convenience, and if you're not open, they'll go to someone else, so the public pretty much dictates store hours.

The future—I think it's going to continue to be real tough for new stores. Specialty stores will survive as long as they give good service; those are the ones who will succeed. I think that we're going to be seeing more small stores and fewer large independents as in the past. The chain stores are overshadowing that market.

The advantage that specialty stores have is that they are better able to react immediately to changes; if we've been receiving calls about a new product, the people in each department have the authority to pick up the phone and order it right away. We can have the product in a matter of days, and the larger stores, who have to go through many channels in the ordering process, may not get it for six months. That gives us the edge.

References

The National Sporting Goods Association (NSGA) offers a book called *The Cost of Doing Business*, which is considered the bible of the sporting goods industry. Write to 1699 Wall Street, Mount Prospect, IL 60056, or phone (847) 439-4000.

National Retail Federation, 325 7th Street NW, Washington, D.C. 20004; (202) 783-7971.

American Sportfishing Association, 1033 North Fairfax Street, Ste 200, Alexandria, VA 22314; (703) 519-9691.

Fishing Guide

"Life is like riding a bicycle. You don't fall off unless you stop pedaling."
—U.S. Congressman Claude Pepper

Dreams—As a fishing guide, you get to fish every darn day, and are in demand by the rich and famous who can't catch anything without you. Your greatness will be acclaimed on TV outdoors shows and in *Field and Stream*, and what the heck, if you play your cards right, you might even make six figures, plus get product endorsements.

Nightmares—The pressure to deliver can kill you off, and so can the flow of wacky customers. And what if the weather turns bad? It can skim the cream right off your cupcake, not that it was a very thick layer anyway. By the way, hope you like waking up in the middle of the night.

Realities—An extremely high percentage of guides don't make much money, although a few do score big time. However, all guides fish constantly, bringing a lot of adventure and happiness into people's lives. They also see the best that nature has to offer. Egomaniacs won't last a season.

What it's all about—Ever notice how an expert mechanic tightens a bolt just right? Not too tight, not too loose, but rather with just the right touch? A fishing guide has to have the same approach to his job from start to finish: promoting, booking, running the boat (or hiking in a stream), teaching the craft, helping customers hook and land fish, then getting them home with an attitude that will have them booking a return trip.

Always remember the mechanic. Just the right touch. Screw that bolt down too tight and your customers will be smothered by your dominance. Screw that bolt down too loose and they're liable to fall out of the boat (maybe even literally).

In this field, if you hang a shingle outside your door that says "Fishing Guide," it's a given that you know how to catch fish. That comes with the territory. If you have yet to master the craft, that is the first order of business. Most guides start out specializing in a certain type of fishing, usually on a seasonal or weekend basis. As they develop a clientele base, they will branch out to other species of fish and angling styles to cover the times of the year when their specialty is not in season.

Another approach is to master a specific region (often saltwater), then adjust your techniques for the changes in season and different fish available. Either way, you must know your craft. Your customers will expect it. Of course, you will be licensed and bonded, as is required by your state.

They will also expect that your equipment be nothing short of first-class. As you become established, some manufacturers may supply you with free tackle in exchange for putting their decal on your boat. Regardless, quality is expected, including boat, rods, reels, line, and if you include lunch and beverages, well, the food better be good and the drinks ice-cold. But all that is easy enough. After all, these elements are under your complete control.

What you cannot control are the fish. Watch. Right when you feel the most pressure to deliver, sure enough, you will need a Jaws of Life to get their mouths to open. Hey, skunks happen to everybody, and even though most anglers understand that, it can put a terrible stress on the guide. The best way to alleviate that is to offer a "skunk-free guarantee," where customers who get skunked get a free return trip. The benefits are not just for the customers, but for the guide too.

With that safety valve in place, the guide won't feel a daily intense burden to perform like the late Gaddabout Gaddis, America's legendary angler of the 20th century. The guide's attention can then shift toward focusing on the pleasure of the day for the customers.

That's something else you can't control—the customers. They come in all ages, shapes and sizes, all levels of ability and experience, and their expectations and personality quirks will vary just as much. You have to figure out how to catch fish and show a good time regardless of their respective foibles. How do you do it?

Remember the mechanic. Not too tight. Share your knowledge of the outdoors, point out the uniqueness of the area you are fishing, provide a few fishing tips (but not too many), compliment them on their skills, and most importantly, Let Them Do The Talking. That may sound easy, but believe me, many guides are so intrigued by being in control that they monopolize every moment of the day with an unending series of non sequiturs. After a few hours of it, a lot of customers can feel like screaming "Let me outta here!"

Not too tight, but not too loose. Other guides say absolutely nothing. Maybe an occasional, "We oughta be getting a bite pretty soon," but that's it. They don't explain the wonders of nature surrounding them, and city-types who know nothing of the rhythms of natural forces can completely miss seeing the beauty of the great outdoors, or heaven forbid, may even get bored. Or fall out of the boat.

Location is critical to having a successful guiding service. You need to be in demand. To do that, you have to offer a quality experience that anglers can't get on their own. If anybody can just drive to your spot, get out, stand on a rock and start catching fish right next to you, why would they pay you for the privilege? Answer: They won't. That is why most successful guides are working in areas where a boat is required.

The money? This is a crazy area for guides. The ugly truth is that most full-time guides earn less than $20,000 per year. That's ugly. That's why a lot of guides just work weekends, making $5,000 to $8,000 for a summer's or winter's worth of weekends, about twenty of them. That ain't too shabby. In the West, a favored approach is to guide in Alaska full-time in the summer for $7,000 to $8,000, then spend the winter guiding in the Northwest, making $8,000 to $12,000 if you're lucky. The bank account gets slim, but think about what you're doing: fishing in Alaska for trout, then fishing the Northwest for steelhead.

If you want to make the big bucks, you need a completely different approach. The best bet is offering custom saltwater guide service with a 24-foot boat, taking four to six customers a trip, charging $400 to $550 a trip. Only a handful of people have figured this out, and they're making a fortune, grossing well over $100,000 each year, and fishing 200 to 250 days a year.

But what you find with all of the successful guides, regardless of their income, is a similar approach. They all have it. Just like that expert mechanic you know.

Career Case Study

John Dyrssen, Florida
John Dyrssen is a full-time fishing guide based in
Jacksonville Beach, Florida.

Requirements—Obviously, you have to have some experience on your own hook, so to speak. You know how to work the local waters where you intend to guide. You have to have good equipment, of course, and you have to have an attitude that you're going to go out and provide a service that is needed. I've always looked at it this way: I try to give the ride the same quality of service as if I were fishing by myself, trying to catch as many fish as I could.

Any education that you have is going to be beneficial, because you're going to be fishing with all walks of life. I've had celebrities; I've had truck drivers. You certainly want to be able to talk to them if not on an equal level, then on an intelligent level.

Prospects—If the area allows it, sometimes there are places that provide guide services. You might want to talk to them first, because they could have some bookings for you. It's very difficult to start out cold and pick up bookings without doing extensive advertising. With a guide service, you'd have ready-made bookings with the agents that take a percentage of the daily charter. If later on you felt that you had built up enough of a clientele, you could consider going out on your own, or you might like the security of not having to worry about bookings. It can be either side of the street on this one.

Benefits—I kind of backed into guiding, really. I retired a little bit early and I was fishing almost every day. I knew people who would say, "My brother-in-law is coming to town—would you mind taking him fishing?" I looked at my book one week and I was fishing three different days with three different people who I didn't even know. So I told people that I was going to become a real guide. Primarily it was just to discourage them, but it worked out just the opposite—they said, "That's great, we need a service like that." In my particular area, there had been no one doing in-shore guiding, and since I had a larger boat and a captain's license, I decided to guide in-shore, and I started doing charters.

Pay—That's a difficult question. I read an article one time written by a fellow who I have a lot of regard for, a well-known marlin fisherman down in the Virgin Islands. He made the statement that if you want to get rich, get into the guide service, and you will become rich not in money, but in friendships.

You have to love what you're doing. You can't be in it for monetary reasons. There's nothing fixed about the income; you're paid by the day, and if you hit bad weather, you're out of luck. Until you establish a clientele, work can be real inconsistent. But if you're good, you will establish a clientele. The pay definitely isn't great, though. In all candor, it's certainly going to be on the low end. I charge $150 a day, and that's for three people, everything included.

If you want a comparison, you could equate the work of guiding with that of an insurance man. Until you establish clientele, you have to prove yourself. You had better have a steady income from another source before you get into it full-time. It can be unstable—there have been times when I haven't taken a charter out for three weeks because of bad weather. In the winter, especially, you lose a lot of charters.

There are extras, too. Quite often there will be extra fish; sometimes you'll take out clients who don't want to keep their fish, and in certain areas you're allowed to sell them. And there are gratuities, of course. It's rare that a client won't tip. Sometimes it's small, and sometimes it's double the fee.

Negatives—The negatives are what the customers don't see—getting up sometimes at 4 o'clock in the morning and having to get your bait beforehand, all the preparation, the cleaning of the boat, things of that nature. The engine can break down, and you have to make arrangements to get it fixed to save a charter—it's very time-consuming. The customers see us going fishing and my job looks romantic and they say, boy, this is what I'd like to do! But they don't see the downside of it. There's bad weather and late cancellations … I'm not knocking it, because if I didn't like it I wouldn't do it. That's the downside, but the upside outweighs it by far.

The future—Once you have your captain's license, there are other options, like taking home buyers to go look at houses on the waterfront, or taking people on tours. The longer you're in an area, the better you can build a reputation, and from that you build your clientele. Then bookings aren't really a problem. You can get

corporate bookings, which are three to five boats a day. If you're the
one handling the bookings, you can get the fee on all the boats.

Career Case Study

Roger Raynal, California

*Roger Raynal has fourteen years of professional guiding
experience and a bachelor's and a master's degree
from Humboldt State University. He has worked as a
wilderness mule packer, a big game hunting guide, a
cowboy and a rafting guide. He is the owner and
operator of North Rivers Guide Service, and a full-
time fishing guide on the Klamath River in Northern
California, specializing in drift boat and jet boat trips.*

Requirements—A guide is only as good as his attitude. You
can be the best fisherman in the world, but if you don't know how
to deal with people you won't be successful. People hire guides so
they can go out on the river in a relaxed state of mind and enjoy
themselves. It's important for a guide to remember that, and make
sure that everything is taken care of to retain that peace of mind.

A successful day on the river does not necessarily mean
catching a lot of fish. There is a lot to be learned about nature and
the river that can be just as satisfying. I've known guides who have
gone out and caught tons of fish with their customers, and the clients
were still not pleased because of the quality of the overall experience.

Guides have to watch their egos; there are some guides who
maintain that they are the absolute best at what they do, and they
take advantage of their clients' ignorance to boost their own egos.
It's important to be sympathetic to the needs of each person and to
relate to them individually as equals, to be open to their background
and their perceptions, and really get a sense of who they are.

A guide can benefit from training in the natural sciences,
education and communications. A guide's ability to communicate
is essential. However, academic experience is not always necessary
in a formal sense. I've trained guides who have virtually no higher
education and they're great guides. What's important is the ability
to interpret the environment as well as the people.

Get to know the outdoors. Get to know the patterns in nature and the way natural forces work together: air temperature, water temperature, water flow, the history and timing of runs, insect cycles, and environmental impacts, such as the effect of logging on watersheds. In other words, understand the way nature works from the basics up.

All good guides are essentially teachers, and it's the guide's job to try to steer the customers in a direction where they see the outdoors from an ecological perspective. Then they can begin to see the difference between the forest and the tree or the water and the river. However, it's not good to "preach." Understanding the outdoors from an ecological viewpoint allows the client a much broader understanding of his/her sport, which can increase fishing skills and enjoyment.

When you're guiding, you have to get over the impulse to fish for yourself. You have to look at it from a professional point of view. You're being paid to show someone else the ropes, and that's where your attention has to be.

Prospects—The most important key to being successful in your own guiding establishment is to have basic common sense in relation to business. You should target a specific area and make sure that a market for what you want to offer exists there. I've reached a point now, after experiencing all aspects of guiding, where I'm specializing in fly fishing, and because I offer a unique service in this area, I've got a leg up on the competition.

I'd say that it's very beneficial for a beginning guide to apprentice with an established guide. There's no other way to learn the business. There's so much more to it than just being on the river. That's hard for some people to understand, especially those who have never been self-employed. You do a lot of legwork all day long: tying flies, contacting associates, talking on the phone, scouting the river, maintaining equipment.

Benefits—You're your own boss, and you can take a lot of pride in what you do. Whether you break it or make it depends on you. If you love the outdoors, you learn to develop a sense of humility. You realize that you're just a small cog in nature's wheel. You learn to become part of your environment and work with it, and you're able to teach that to other people. Most people aren't familiar with that kind of environment at all; they're insulated from day to day in the cities. I've had people—kids and adults both—who have been caught in huge storms. For people unaccustomed to experiencing the physical discomforts and incredible power that nature can unleash, a storm can be an enlightening and memorable experience. When you're out in the wilderness, you learn to be humble and appreciate the world for all its complexities and frailties.

Pay—A client will pay anywhere from $95-$125 a day, per person, or $185-$200 for two. That's comparatively inexpensive. When you first start guiding for an established outfit, you can expect to earn about $125 per day. And since hired guides have no overhead, their profit margin is higher than that of an outfitter.

I'd estimate that for one season, a beginning guide would make $2500 to $3000 in three months. That's low for guiding, but as a beginning guide, you're paying for your education, learning about the business. As you gain seniority your income will increase. If I make $8,000 or $9,000 in a season on the Snake River, I've done extremely well.

Negatives—The romance can wear off very quickly, especially when business or fishing is difficult and slow. My grandfather said, "Don't ever make your passion your work, because it will become work," meaning labor.

First, it is not financially rewarding, no matter who you are or how big you are. There is a large overhead. It is sometimes more lucrative for someone to be employed by an outfitter than to have their own business.

It's become harder to manage the bureaucratic and administrative aspects of the business these days. There are so many avenues you have to go through. You have to get your guide license, fishing license, insurance, security bond and a river use permit. If you want to use a power boat, you have to have a master's license from the Coast Guard. All vessels have to be registered, usually by multiple agencies. All this makes it very costly, and the margin of profit is smaller.

Environmental factors, such as droughts, can really hurt. You are completely dependent on nature. People are not stupid; they're becoming educated shoppers. They know when the fish are around and when they are not. People never call up and say, "You're a guide; I want to fish; let's go."

Second, if someone starts in this business when they're young and single, it's great, because it's a seasonal job so you have to move and travel. It's rare to stay and guide in one place year round. Years ago, I was moving to three or four places a year. But as you get older, and you slow down a bit and someone comes into your life, priorities change. My wife's career is every bit as important to her as mine is to me, so I can't ask her to move around. Unless your partner wants to travel with you and lead an unsettled lifestyle, you have to address your priorities and make some decisions.

The future—There's a growth industry going on in eco-tourism. I think that's where the focus is going to be. Also, I'm realizing that if I want to maintain my profession, I have to promote conservation, and pay attention to environmental concerns that affect our fisheries, including logging.

You have to be a lot more politically astute now. If we're going to maintain our resources, we have to be educators—sort of bio-politicians. We have to be involved, and that's one thing that will separate good guides from others.

The outdoors will always attract people, and as the pace of life increases, people's desire to get outdoors will increase. In many cases, however, people are unable to take the time to fully enjoy their sport and learn first-hand about the outdoors. This is where guides come in as teachers. We have to make our clients understand the demands which we as sportsmen put on resources. The educational approach is really important. We have to be an interpreter for nature, because we may be the only link our customers have to fishing and nature.

References

American Sportfishing Association, 1033 North Fairfax Street, Ste 200, Alexandria, VA 22314; (703) 519-9691.

Montana Outfitters & Guides Association, Box 9070, Helena, MT 59624; (406) 449-3578.

America Outdoors, PO Box 10847, Knoxville, TN 37939; (423) 558-1812 or (423) 558-1815.

Contact your state's fisheries department for state requirements. Local chambers of commerce can help determine what the area competition is like. Local sportsmen's newspapers also often provide listings.

Forester

Dreams—As a forester, you spend your time in the woods, loving the forest and protecting it. You have tremendous power, dictating terms to timber operations, preventing areas from being butchered by loggers, then leading the restoration process at areas already cut. You are a self-made savior of the wild.

Nightmares—You find out quick: No logging, no job. Your proposals to restrict timber operations get rejected, and then you watch the forest you love get clear-cut. As you lay in bed, the sounds of trees hitting the ground gives you genuine nightmares. You might even cry.

Realities—Logging comes with the territory. Your job is to design a management plan that will protect the forest you love, yet allow a sustainable yield timber harvest. You also get an opportunity to restore many areas. That attitude will get you far, and the money, while not great, still stretches pretty far in rural areas.

What it's all about—When some people inhale a deep breath of mountain air filled with the essence of pines, firs and cedars, it's like this alpine aroma fills their lungs and is sent to every red blood cell pumping through their heart. The smell of conifers keeps some people alive. Take it away and a part of them will die. That is how it is for a forester. They've got to have it. And they get it, nearly every day. If you have this compelling desire to be in the woods, to love it, to protect it, to keep damage to a minimum during a timber operation and then restore it—and always, to smell it—then this is the job for you.

Most foresters have a resolute love for what they do. They walk around and "feel good." The exceptions are the ones who have an avowed aversion to logging. In a nutshell, a forester manages the forest. That includes managing logging operations so they have minimum impact on forest recovery and watersheds. It also includes protecting particularly fragile areas from getting cut, and also bringing damaged areas back to life. That's why foresters feel good. They keep the world a nice place.

The future is very promising for this career. Public awareness, government laws and court rulings are making proper forest management a necessity on both public and private lands. It has become virtually impossible to log anywhere without an environmental document to address the operation. That means there are jobs in this line of work, whether they are for the U.S. Forest Service or Champion International, or even for Joe Q. Public who owns a 10-acre plot in the forest and wants to take a few trees out for lumber to build a cabin. A forester's job, then, is working with logging operations, and not just from start to finish. Rather it's from way before start to well after finish.

It usually starts with a proposal by a company to log a specific amount of board feet of timber off a specified area of land. The forester walks every piece of that land and assesses all impacts, including those to drainages, wildlife, fish, top soil and plants. Then he or she formulates a plan to minimize that damage. Once the agreement is made, the timber operation must follow that plan to the letter, and then after that, complete the planting and restoration work as mandated by the forester.

One of the big changes in forest management is using the restoration process to recreate a diverse forest ecosystem. Even in recent years, the emphasis has been more on growing and cutting trees like a crop. There was little conscience involved. That has changed, both in order to protect wildlife and to ensure that timber operations won't overcut their way into ecological oblivion.

When logging is conducted properly, there is virtually no long-term damage. Laws in most areas now mandate that the level of growing matches the level of cutting, ensuring a long-term supply of lumber. If North America's forests as a collective had been managed like this for the past 150 years instead of the past five, the mountains would still be vibrant with a seeming unending number of giant trees. But because this awareness on a large-scale is a new phenomenon, that is not what exists. In most forests that are not in parks or wilderness, it is difficult to find a tree that is as large as one of the surrounding stumps.

That gets to the heart of the main conflict for foresters. The timber companies still want to cut as many trees as possible; after all, the more they cut, the more money they make. Tremendous political pressure can be exerted on foresters to allow these big time cuts, even though the forester knows that doing so would be bypassing long-term protection.

If a forester has a slam-dunk objection to logging, then the job becomes a very painful one. Right or wrong, part of the job is watching forests get cut down, and that will traumatize the romantic. In addition, you will find your objections being subverted at the political executive levels in both government and corporations. Knowing that can keep you awake some nights.

A more effective approach is to become a good scientist, take time in your laboratory (the woods) to gather data, then come up with a plan that will protect an area for the long term, and allow quick reforestation in the short term. This approach allows negotiation with a timber operation. To flat-out oppose all logging gets you nowhere, and no scientist with a preconceived agenda will get far, particularly in this career.

The key to remember is this: How will you spend your time? It won't be in a traffic jam commuting, in an office in a city, or wearing a tie. It will be in the woods, and your job will be to protect them. Just take a deep breath and smell the trees. You'll know right then if this is the job for you.

Career Case Study

Tom Walz, California

Tom Walz has worked for Sierra Pacific Industries, the largest privately owned timberland company in the state of California, since 1980. He lives in Weaverville, California with his wife and two daughters.

Requirements—Basically, what a forester does is manage timberlands for timber production, wildlife protection and water quality. If you want to be a forester, you have to be someone who enjoys working outdoors. If you don't like being around mosquitoes, snakes and chiggers, this is probably not the job for you.

Educationally, you'll need a four-year bachelor of science degree. It's possible to find positions with a two-year degree, but those are generally limited to work in the field. If you want a decision-making position, a four-year degree from an accredited university is standard.

You can obtain a position right out of college, but having some summer experience working in the field will give you an edge, especially if your summer work has been under the supervision of a professional.

Prospects—The market right now is extremely good. When I graduated from college in 1976, it was almost unheard of to find a permanent position in either the public or private sector. But the field has evolved, and now, with the tightening of regulations and rules, professional, licensed, registered foresters are the only ones who can legally manage a forest, and there is an increasing need for that service.

Benefits—There is a good balance between working outdoors with a renewable resource and dealing with people. You get to be outside working, but you're also in the office, writing management plans. You don't have a day-in, day-out monotony. Being a forester is very reliable, dependable work. You don't find many foresters who switch jobs. If you meet the grade, it's very steady.

Negatives—I think the greatest disadvantage is the uncertainty of land management activities. Because of the increasing regulatory climate, land managers are finding their hands tied for various reasons. There's a lot of pushing and struggling and lawsuits occurring; it's very frustrating at times.

A forestry career takes a lot of time. Generally professional foresters are paid on a salary basis, and every forester works ten to twelve hours a day with no overtime. You do whatever it takes to get the job done. Quite often that means working on Saturdays, and sometimes even on Sundays. It's not uncommon to work 14 days without a day off.

Pay—For someone with a four-year degree, a starting position with a private company will range from $27,000 to $29,000 a year. It doesn't really go up in a straight line from there; it depends on your value to the company and your level of responsibility. Someone who's working exclusively in the field won't have as great an increase in salary as someone who's involved in a decision-making position. As your decision-making authority increases, your salary potential is much greater.

The future—I think this profession is going to become a broader-scope profession. Instead of concentrating on growing and managing forests primarily for timber production, foresters will be the people who deal with wildlife, water and people management. The field is open for tremendous growth. Even though specialists are still going to be needed, companies are going to seek generally knowledgeable people with the ability to be trained. I also predict that as the value of timber keeps increasing, many more private landowners are going to realize that they own a renewable resource and will pursue professional advice, which will in turn offer more opportunities for foresters.

Career Case Study

John Wylie, Texas
John Wylie has worked as a professional forester for
Champion International Corporation since 1974. He
lives in Huntsville, Texas with his wife and daughter,
and enjoys golfing and duck hunting.

Requirements—A forester essentially acts as a manager for all the resources associated with the forest: clean air, water, wildlife, timber. The minimum educational requirement is a four-year degree in some forest management-related study from an accredited school; for example, a bachelor of science degree in industrial forestry. The area of emphasis would depend on the position you want. Business administration courses are beneficial for almost all positions.

You've got to have a positive outlook and be long-sighted. Forestry is not unlike farming in that it's a rotated crop over a long period of time; you won't have immediate results.

Prospects—The market is very competitive. We recently hired four foresters for this company, and we searched literally every college in the south to find the best. Prior to then, we hadn't hired anyone for eight years. From what I've seen, there are a lot of people studying subjects related to forestry right now; they're more interested than ever in environmental management and wildlife.

Benefits—I love outdoor work, which is what attracts most people to the position. It's a very interesting, very diversified job; it's rarely mundane or repetitious. There are always many different things happening. I have a great deal of freedom to do what I think is best and right, and I've found that to be very rewarding.

Negatives—A lot of things are out of your control. The work is very weather-related, and extreme conditions can create havoc sometimes. That can be very frustrating. The job is designed for an eight- to ten-hour day, but at times it's longer. If inventories at mills are low, you may have to work weekends sporadically.

Also, fires don't just occur on weekdays—you never know when they're going to occur and they have to be dealt with. In terms of job placement, the higher up the ladder you are, the more you'll experience long hours.

Pay—An entry-level position will pay between $25,000 and $35,000 per year, depending on your qualifications. It also depends on whether you're working for a government agency or a private business. Within the private sector, it differs from one company to another. In most cases, there are both annual increases and promotional increases. Typically a rating system is used, like the government's grade scale, where each advancement would entail at least one grade change, and each one of those might bring with it a 10 to 15 percent increase.

The future—I think forestry is going to become much more technology-oriented, and I certainly hope that it will continue to grow. Regardless of whether it grows or stays where it is, the fact remains that people will always require wood and paper products, and foresters will always be essential to the management of the land.

References

So You Want to be in Forestry, from Society of American Foresters, 5400 Grosvenor Lane, Bethesda, MD 20814-2198; (301) 897-8720 or fax (301) 897-3690.

National Woodland Owners Association, 374 Maple Avenue East, Suite 210, Vienna, VA 22180; (703) 255-2300.

American Forest & Paper Association, 1111 19th Street NW, Ste 800, Washington, D.C. 20036; (800) 878-8878.

American Forestry Association, 2101 E Street NW, Washington, D.C. 20037; (202) 293-3806 or fax (202) 647-0265. E-mail: Assa@ms3644wpo.US-State.gov.

US Department of Agriculture, Forestry Service, PO Box 9690, Washington, D.C. 20013-6090; (202) 205-8333. (Ask for *A Job with the Forest Service: A Guide to Career Opportunities in Technical Support Positions* and/or *Professional & Administrative Careers in the Forest Service.*

Contact state forestry associations, forestry programs at universities, privately-owned forestry consulting businesses, and federal and state agencies such as the U.S. Forest Service and state parks and recreation departments. A good place to get experience is at a youth conservation corps.

Game Warden

Dreams—You live out in a cabin in the country, spending your days cruising on patrol and staking out the best fishing and hunting spots, busting poachers and sending them to jail, helping others, being supplied with first-class equipment and vehicles, and getting paid enough to live the good life.

Nightmares—You are assigned to work the docks, where everybody hates you, and worse, it's in a city with all the problems that come with it. The gun on your hip is no Christmas ornament, either. You get buried in paperwork, don't seem to have much time for patrol work, and some of the equipment doesn't work right. For this, you earn barely enough to pay rent on a humble flat.

Realities—Game wardens are the best trained of all police officers, well prepared in enforcement, environment and communication. Start-up jobs are usually in poor areas; it takes seniority to fill an opening in a premium rural area. Complaints are many, but so is a lifetime of satisfaction as the guardian of all natural resources.

What it's all about—You couldn't pry a game warden out of his job with a Jaws of Life. Once someone puts the badge on, it's usually for life, and perhaps afterlife. Wardens have unfeigned gusto for each day, as well as a zest to protect the great outdoors, and those two qualities go together perfectly on the job.
But they are also bonded by another quirk: You may never meet a bigger bunch of complainers anywhere on the planet. Wardens, you see, haven't figured out yet that life is not perfect, and

are always pointing out the shortcomings, both to lawbreakers in the form of citations and to their friends in the form of complaints about their job.

Game wardens can seem like walking contradictions, but the bottom line is always to judge someone by what they do, not what they say. And what they do is stay on the job until someone has to pry their rigor mortis-locked fingers off that badge.

There are many reasons for this behavior. For starters, seniority counts big in this game, which means that openings for newcomers are almost always in terrible regions, like Long Beach (California) or New York Harbor. They are terrible because the crime rates are high, the cost of living is out there orbiting with Pluto, traffic is all plugged up (hey, it's the big city), paperwork and other non-patrol work get in the way of your job, and support from the public, district attorney and courts is just plain lousy.

So right off, you have lots to complain about. Very soon you will start asking, "What's so great about being a game warden?" The answer, which you will discover if you stick at it long enough, is plenty. As positions open up out in rural areas, out there in the great outdoors, they are filled by existing wardens who want a change of habitat and have seniority to rate the switch. It might take up to five years, rarely a bit more, but your time will come. When that happens, jump on and hold on tight. You're on for a hell of a ride for the rest of your life.

Game wardens in rural areas often will have an entire county to themselves, patrolling lakes and streams, woods and wetlands. Your salary (topping out around $42,000) stretches twice as far, because rural housing costs are often half that of the city. You get support everywhere, from the concerned public (who often provide tips), from the district attorney (who will prosecute your cases), and even from judges (who will punish convicted poachers). Out in rural areas, far away from the pressure-cooker panic of traffic jams and concrete, there is great satisfaction in protecting fish, birds, wildlife, and their habitat (because you can see the difference). A bonus is that after awhile, a game warden will get to know every fishing and hunting spot there is within a 100-mile radius (after all, "It's my job, heh, heh, heh.")

The problem is that by the time you get such an ideal position, you have already learned about complaining from working in urban or city areas for a few years. And the complaining continues, even when on the threshold of heaven. It's habit that for some becomes an addiction: "Too much paper work, the boss is out of touch, always working weekends and holidays, try dealing with arresting lowlifes all the time, no overtime pay, too many dead animals, the guiltiest are always whining, the laws are too complicated, and try explaining to your neighbors all the time where you are always going in the middle of the night."

After all these complaints, however, the game warden remains a game warden. They all love it. The only way you could vanquish game wardens, any of them, would be to take their badges away— and some literally go to the grave with their badges on. Even though the last words out of their mouths might be a complaint about the patrol radio that doesn't work right.

The best way to get hired is to complete a bachelor's degree with emphasis on police work, wildlife (or environmental studies), and communications. You must be an expert at all three: Police work comes with the territory, wildlife because you are their appointed guardian, and communication because you will be constantly meeting with the public and writing reports. Some individuals get hired without a complete college education, but why whittle down the odds when competition can be severe? Instead, use college to gain an advantage, and get yourself educated as well as possible. You will be paid back in kind.

Then do everything possible to get enrolled in a cadet academy. Two of the best are in Texas and California, and many states and provinces operate schools across North America. One other note: You must always be in superb physical condition. Remember that.

As a first job, be willing to accept anything, anywhere. Then the first time a transfer is available, take it. This is how you move up, and more importantly, out, that is, out of the city and into the country. By the time you are living in a rural area, you will understand why many top game wardens in the country refuse promotions, because that would mean moving back to a city.

As a game warden, you are an appointed guardian of natural resources. You are one of the few people who can make an active difference in the quality of living on this planet, not only for people, but for all the little critters that you will be acting on behalf of. Of all the missions in life, that of a game warden is not only one of the most honorable, it is one of the most satisfying, complaints and all.

Career Case Study

Larry Kring, New York
Larry Kring is the supervising environmental conservation officer for the New York State Department of Environmental Conservation. He has worked for the department since 1973. His previous experience includes participating in forestry research at Syracuse University. Larry enjoys hunting, fishing and woodworking. He is married, has three children, and lives in Heuvelton, New York.

Requirements—Most states require at least two years of college education and some kind of academy training. It varies greatly from state to state. Here in New York, an environmental conservation officer—which is what they're called now—has to have two years of college in a related field, such as forestry, fish and wildlife, or law enforcement. The applicant is then eligible to take the required officer's exam, and if he passes successfully, he may be hired. Officers are then sent to recruit school, which is between 18 and 24 weeks long, and after that's completed, they're assigned a field position.

Our people work alone, so out of necessity, they need a fair amount of common sense and self-motivation. If you can't work without supervision, you'll be very unhappy in this position. An officer has to be able to think on his feet and get along well with people. A lot of the public has this image that wardens are always working with animals, trees and flowers, but we really work with people.

Prospects—There are about 230 positions statewide in New York, and turnover is not great. For one of our last exams, there were 30 positions, and about 9,000 applicants. I would say that's pretty standard. None of the states have a real preponderance of conservation officers; there are a limited number of positions. We actually hire a number of officers from other agencies, such as state police. The pay is competitive and the work conditions are more enjoyable.

Benefits—Working with people. You spend a fair amount of time with people who enjoy the outdoors. You associate with the same crowd. There is no drug task force; we associate with people who use the outdoors rather than drugs.

Game Warden   113

You're not overly supervised, like local police officers or city cops where you have station people breathing down your neck. You set your own hours, work your own time.

Pay—An entry level job pays about $26,000. The next step is basically just an upscale of the same position, and the salary goes up to around $27,500. Once you become an environmental conservation officer, you'll make about $30,000. There's a negotiated salary scale, which goes up by designated yearly amounts.

There generally isn't a large breakdown in supervision. We go from conservation officer to lieutenant, and the salary difference isn't that great. The majority start out as environmental conservation officers and retire as environmental conservation officers. We also have fairly good vision, health, and retirement benefits, comparable to most state worker plans.

Negatives—You work alone a lot, so there is a danger factor. You're not going to get any backup. If you do have to call for help, there's going to be a considerable amount of time before anyone gets there. One thing that occurs often, especially in smaller areas, is that you tend to be "the game warden," so when you go to buy groceries or go out to dinner or go to the county fair, people are always coming up and asking you questions about the job and things that are happening.

You never have any privacy. We have state phones at home, and we take calls day or night, so we get people calling all the time. Some have legitimate questions, but some have ridiculous questions, like when somebody calls from a bar at 2 AM and asks me to settle a bet about the limit of brook trout. Our busiest hours tend to be when the general public aren't working, so there are a lot of night, weekend and holiday work hours. Our officers get to choose their own shifts, but if they get a call after their shift, they have to go back out.

The future—I think the future for conservation officers is great and they're going to be more and more in demand. In just about every state, the traditional warden duty is spreading into environmental conservation, so we're not only protecting wildlife, we're enforcing environmental laws as well, and environmental enforcement is not going to go away. The longevity security is definitely there.

Career Case Study

Steve Pritchett, Texas—Steve Pritchett has worked as a game warden since 1978, and was promoted to captain in 1991 as a special programs coordinator. His work experience includes working as a schoolteacher for nine years. He likes to hunt and fish, and also enjoys track, photography and tinkering with his computer. He is married, has three children, and lives in Austin, Texas.

Requirements—Requirements may differ from state to state, but generally these are standard. You have to be a minimum of 21 years of age, in good physical condition, with no chronic illnesses or disease. You're required to pass both a physical and psychological/emotional examination. Conviction of various degrees of criminal offenses within certain periods of time would totally disqualify an individual, as would a dishonorable discharge from the military. A bachelor's degree from an accredited university is required. You must pass vision standards and have a valid drivers license. You have to be willing to take an assignment anywhere in the state, and be willing to work odd hours and weekends.

We're looking for a gregarious person, someone who is well-rounded and gets along well with the public. It's a people-oriented job. We are law enforcers, and we're most often dealing with individuals rather than the biological angle. We have the full authority of a police officer.

Prospects—Opportunities fluctuate according to current legislative trends. One year we'll have 40 job vacancies; the next year we may have only 20. There are better than 1,800 applicants for every class of 30 to 40 people accepted into the academy. I started in 1978 and competed with 2,071 applicants for 30 positions in our class. It basically works by process of elimination. After all the applications are submitted, each one is evaluated, and the applicants are given a basic test which is then graded. Certain individuals are chosen to continue, and after verification of their personal information, 200 or 300 interview in front of the board. The selection process is very deliberate and intense, and the level of competition is high.

Benefits—Here in Texas, the size of the state and the diversity of the systems and cultures make the job very interesting. Besides enforcing laws and dealing with resources, we deal with disaster relief and assist other enforcement agencies. Our efforts also include educating the public through various programs and written material. We have a lot of interaction with the public, and it's very rewarding and fulfilling, knowing that you're performing a worthwhile service.

The independence is a nice factor. We have a great deal of freedom to do our job in the manner we see fit. We also have the advantage of variety; our assignments may vary when manpower is needed in a certain location. Seasonal trends allow us to work different hours according to what's currently in progress. We can adjust our schedules individually to meet certain needs, and that requires a great deal of flexibility.

Pay—There is tremendous opportunity for advancement, and your pay increases accordingly. A warden cadet, while in the academy, makes $1,930 per month. After the successful completion of academy training, you're a Game Warden I, making $2,040, and after six months that goes up to $2,193. After one year it's $2409. The next step is Warden II, attained after four years, where you make $2,588, and then Warden III, after eight years, at $2,767. The highest warden level is IV, which is achieved 12 years after graduation from the academy, and there you make $2,945. After that you can be promoted to sergeant, lieutenant, captain or major, and the salaries there range from $36,000 to $50,000.

Negatives—It's sometimes difficult to get things done within an eight-hour time frame. It's easy to feel pressured. Weather can also be frustrating, especially here in Texas.

A big liability is danger. Part of being an officer, whether you're a police officer or a game warden, is dealing with the criminal element. As a whole, wildlife conservation officers are more subject to assault than officers in any other field, due to the remoteness of our workplace combined with the fact that the people we deal with are usually armed.

The future—I think it offers excellent opportunities for individuals who are looking for a rewarding career. With the emphasis on environmental issues, more specific efforts are being directed toward the protection of wildlife resource habitats.

References

North American Wildlife Enforcement Officers Association, Secretary-Treasurer, Rural Route 2, Whycocomagh, Nova Scotia, Canada B033MO; (902) 756-2584.

National Fish & Wildlife Foundation, 1120 Connecticut Avenue NW, Suite 900, Washington, D.C. 20036; (202) 857-0166.

International Association of Fish & Wildlife Agencies, 444 North Capitol Street NW, Ste 534, Washington, D.C. 20001; (202) 624-7890.

US Fish & Wildlife Service, 2625 Parkmont Road, Building A, Olympia, WA 98502; (360) 753-9460.

Note: Most states have their own fish and wildlife departments which have a game warden patrol force. Phone for the *National Wildlife Federation Directory,* (301) 897-9770.

Guide for the Physically Challenged

Dreams—As a guide for the physically challenged, you are the richest person in the world, because you have the gift of love, both giving and receiving. You also are working in the outdoors with people who really listen, and want to succeed. The memories are golden.

Nightmares—Instead of golden memories, sometimes you might want some real gold, which you'll never get in this job. Then if you have difficulty tuning in to your students, you can get burned out, and be broke besides. There is also the chance of a serious accident, in which you "thought" the person could do something, and they could not.

Realities—Guiding work requires that you know your craft, have expert communication skills and a profound ability to empathize without sympathizing. The rewards are genuine and go right to the heart, and will last a lot longer than a fat check, which you won't get.

What it's all about—Comes a time for every person when they realize the transient qualities of money, power and prestige, and how easily gold-plated trophies can become covered with rust.

That is when you suddenly think of the things that matter, and you may remember how you helped somebody in dire need, or perhaps how somebody helped you. At that point, you become aware that the things that last through time are not money, power and prestige, but rather the primary feelings between people, good deeds done just because they were the right thing to do.

An outdoor guide for the disabled doesn't have a Day of Reckoning when these truths about the human condition suddenly become self-evident. That's because a guide for the disabled lives this gospel every day.

Right there is the great reward in working with people who are physically challenged. You are constantly in connection with the vital energy of giving and receiving. Some guides who specialize in working with physically challenged people seem always to have a glow about them. They are often buoyant. So they don't make much money—so what? They have something much greater: a heart bonded with others who appreciate the ultimate gift—lending a helping hand.

A new perspective on the physically challenged makes the future look promising for this career: Nobody considers anybody in a wheelchair "handicapped" anymore. That is because they aren't. It has been proven time and time again that individuals with a physical impairment can do just about anything, from climbing Half Dome in Yosemite to competing in the Boston Marathon. Of course, the level of impairments can vary, and with it, the amount of help people need to get going.

That is where you come in. You provide that help. It varies with each person. That is why in this job, you are not only a guide, but also a psychologist and a therapist.

Your level of expertise should be unquestioned, of course. Don't think that because you are instructing the physically challenged that you can get away with knowing less than would otherwise be necessary. You'll never get away with it, and the arrogance of that assumption will turn people off. The best guides in this field usually have solid outdoors skills in many areas. The spectrum can include rafting, kayaking, fishing, camping, photography, skiing . . . even hunting. In Oregon, for instance, forest roads in some areas are closed to vehicles in order to allow access to wheelchair hunters. You are limited only by what is desired and your expertise in offering it.

To do that, you need to be able to communicate your thoughts clearly, and do it with an attitude that will inspire, not frighten or anger. This is a test for all instructors, of course, but more so when working with the physically challenged because it requires more empathy than any other position. Most guides call their jobs "98 percent heartwarming, 2 percent frustrating."

If your personality is such that a sense of frustration starts creeping over you easily, then you are headed for trouble, and maybe downright defeat. While this is rare for people in the field— most go in knowing what they're in for—it still happens. So before making a commitment to this job, take a gut check and make sure your heart is in the right place. If it is, the rewards come in the smiles you get. Stay in touch with that, see with your heart, and you will be repaid in kind.

That's good, because you are unlikely to be repaid in cash. Most guides for the physically challenged don't make much, just $12,000 to $15,000, usually on a part-time or seasonal basis. A more prosperous route is working within a well-established company in an area where the weather allows year-round work. If you can help manage the company (perhaps directing a certain program) and also guide, pay in the $25,000 range is fair.

Directors can make double that, but then again, they spend most of their time in the office with so much detail work that they miss out on the heart-to-heart connections that make this field so compelling.

Career Case Study

Diane Poslosky, California

Diane Poslosky is the director of ETC (Environmental Traveling Companions), a non-profit organization that offers outdoor adventure trips for the physically challenged and disadvantaged youth. Along with her many duties as director, Diane actively participates in guiding whenever she can. Her previous job experience includes teaching and environmental education.

Requirements—The job specifications really depend on which aspect of the field you want to concentrate on. I am the executive director of Environmental Traveling Companions, a non-profit organization that offers guided outdoor adventures for people with special needs. These are people who are physically or developmentally disabled, hearing or vision impaired, "at-risk" or disadvantaged children, teens with cancer, and people with AIDS and other illnesses. In other words, people who might not otherwise have the opportunity to experience the challenge and beauty of wilderness adventures.

With my title of director comes a variety of responsibilities: staff management, fundraising, program development and planning, guide training, and actual guiding.

If you want to work as a guide, you need to be savvy in wilderness skills. You must be competent in and comfortable enough with whatever activity you are leading so that you can forget about yourself and concentrate on the needs of the other participants.

People skills are extremely important. When you're working with people who have special needs, you have to have a heightened sensitivity. You need to have an adaptive mind and the ability to problem solve. I often look at it as a jigsaw puzzle. For example, when you're getting a quadriplegic person into a sea kayak, you have to make sure they're physically, mentally and emotionally comfortable. You have to ask questions and work as a team to figure out the best way to do those things.

Formal training in working with people with special needs is not specifically required. Some of our guides are therapists or teachers, but a lot of them are carpenters, lawyers, computer programmers, etc. My feeling is that anyone who loves the outdoors, is energetic and willing to learn can do it. The key is to be able to relate person to person, not person to disability. Many people tend to focus on the wheelchair, cane or whatever rather than the person. It's important to realize that the wheelchair is just that person's instrument for getting around.

Here at ETC we offer disability awareness training as part of our initial training. If someone is going to guide blind people on sea kayaking trips, we have them kayak and cook blindfolded.

As for a career beyond guiding, I know for me it was just a natural evolution. I had been involved in the organization as a whitewater rafting and cross-country ski guide for six years before I became the director, and I think it was having the hands-on experience in the field and knowing it inside and out that led me here. As the director, I have to have some specific talents: I have to be able to write grant proposals, be a good spokesperson, and be a really strong, enthusiastic advocate for my cause. I believe in our mission 100 percent.

I also have a teaching credential and my degree was in environmental studies, which was a good background. I think it's an advantage in any aspect of outdoor recreation to have some naturalist or environmental education.

Prospects—There probably aren't tons of positions as directors of outdoor adventure programs, but I believe that if someone is focused and really has this as a goal, anything's possible. The Association for Experiential Education puts out a publication every two months listing jobs.

I think that the best way to start out is to do an internship with an organization or guide for a company. That will you give you a basic background, and then you can become a trip leader, and if you want to continue moving up, you can go for a program manager position and then on to a director's position. It's rare to jump right into a management position, so you should be willing to let your career evolve.

Benefits—The overall greatest reward for me is the opportunity to enable people to get out there and challenge themselves and enjoy something that impacts their life—to assist them in doing something that they didn't think was possible for them. What that does for their self-esteem is incredible. That reward is vicarious, in some ways. I'm sure that if I took one hundred trips out to Angel Island by myself, I'd get bored, but seeing it through the eyes of another person brings back the freshness and excitement. It's wonderful to give people the opportunity to embrace the natural world and challenge themselves and succeed.

The adventures really bring out the best in people. Two years ago we were training a group of 14- to 18-year-old kids to become whitewater rafting guides. There was one kid who had just been fired from his job for stealing, was kicked out of his home and was definitely "at risk." He had many problems in his life in the city, but when he got into the raft, he was a natural—he was just great. The leader and responsible human being in him emerged. He phoned me the next spring and asked if he could come back and teach other kids to guide. So here was this inner city kid from Oakland who had become a role model. It's incredibly fulfilling to see that potential surface.

The kind of people who are attracted to this field are generally fun, sensitive and terrific people. It's a wonderful community. You become very close to the people you work with. Here, we refer to the group of guides and staff as the ETC family.

The flexibility is a real benefit. I don't have to dress up except when I am meeting with a foundation or going to a function. And it's not the old punch-the-clock routine. The hours vary constantly. At times I go crazy with all the different hats I have to wear, but generally I love the diversity.

Pay—If you want to work in this field, there are trade-offs, and salary is one of them. It depends on the level you're working at. Guides make approximately $60 to $120 a day, depending on whether they're a head guide or not. In terms of administrative positions, a program manager can expect an income of $18,000 to $28,000 a year, and a director's salary will usually range from $25,000 to $50,000.

Negatives—There's definitely a burnout factor, especially for guides. You really need to take care of yourself and monitor your stress level. That's true with a lot of human service work. There are some careers where you go to work, come home and you're done for the day. But careers such as this one tend to seep into your personal life. There are times when I can't get away from it.

It's a huge responsibility. Ultimately, we take people's lives in our hands. When I sit down and think about that, it feels a little stunning. The risk factor is always there; it's a pivotal point. When you manage risk well and you succeed, it's always rewarding. But if you have a close call, you're on the teetering edge. We've never had a major incident or a liability claim. If we had a lot of close calls, I probably wouldn't be doing this job. It would just be too stressful.

The future—There is a definite need for therapeutic/outdoor adventure programs such as ETC's. As long as the funding is generated, the field will continue to grow. ETC was the first organization of its kind, and there still aren't many out there that offer the same diversity of service. But there are quite a few groups that specialize; they offer specific programs, such as teaching blind people to ski. There's enormous potential there.

I think that the recently passed Americans with Disabilities Act (ADA), which requires that all public places be accessible to everyone, is a huge step into mainstreaming people with disabilities. In the mid-1970s, many people with disabilities were institutionalized, and that's changed dramatically. At this point we serve about 1800 people a year, and I'd love to see that expand. I'd love to see chapters of ETC established.

Career Case Study

John Galland, Minnesota
John Galland has worked in the field of outdoor
adventure for several years, primarily with Outward
Bound programs. John is an avid outdoorsman himself,
and enjoys all facets of wilderness adventure. He lives
in Minneapolis, Minnesota.

Requirements—My primary interest in the outdoors is access to human-powered wilderness, and I use the term "access" because I use a wheelchair. Because of that fact, anything I do outdoors is considered therapeutic, so I guess you'd say I am in the therapeutic recreation business. I'm probably unique in terms of the niche I take up in the outdoor arena.

One of the things working in the business requires is an evaluation of why you want to do it. You have to ask yourself if you want to do it for yourself, for the people with disabilities, or for the sake of doing God's work, because you will burn out eventually and your original motivation has still got to be there.

You need a lot of experience in dealing with people with disabilities and human nature in general. The more experience you have, the better idea you'll have of all the things that can go wrong, and you'll be better prepared to have an alternative plan in a heartbeat.

You have to have the right attitude and the ability to communicate. Here's an example: there's a technique in skiing called sit-skiing. If the novice or beginner doesn't feel comfortable doing it alone, they can have someone secured to them, acting as an anchor. This person needs to be a good skier, of course, but also needs to be a good communicator. There has to be a trusting and open relationship there, so the student will feel comfortable and secure. You can't be a sports jock who's got all the answers and is going to push it down their throats.

Prospects—It's tough. It's a real hard network to figure out at times. I'd say that there are about two or three excellent organizations per state, but there's really no good networking system; you don't hear about them. If you want to work in the experiential field, you have to really know what you're doing in terms of hard and soft skills, and you have to get out there and get people to notice your credibility. You have to have a good resume to take around.

If you have a disability yourself, you have an advantage in terms of perspective. You understand firsthand what the ramifications of having a disability are. That's a plus when you're out there and someone's pissed off and frustrated; a lot of times they'll say, "You don't know what this is like." But if you have a disability, you do.

Apprenticeships and internships are the best way to go. You're working in most cases for nothing, but you get the experience you need. There are a lot of good training programs out there.

Benefits—One of the biggest advantages is that you get to be outside. It's a wonderful process, being out there and seeing people evolve and become enlightened, especially on river trips. I find that around the second or third day, they stop looking at their watches, they stop thinking about what they left at home and what they're doing when they get back. It brings out qualities in people that I think they forget about. I love the process of awareness. People start looking at stars and planets and asking questions about what's going on.

Pay—This business leads to a hand-to-mouth existence. When you start out as an intern, you'll be lucky to get a stipend; often it's just food and a place to stay. When you begin as a professional, you'll generally start out at a little more than minimum wage.

Unless you're doing something that requires a great deal of skill or special certification, like skiing, you won't make a lot of money. You might make $20,000 a year if you do it constantly. The most I've ever made guiding is $15,000. It depends on where you go and what you specialize in.

Negatives—You definitely get the human services burnout. When you try to clock out, you can't unplug. There comes a time with every person who works in human services when they just have to go away. You tend to get too involved, and you have to be careful not to let your world become too small.

Being out on the trail is not always good for relationships, and that can be kind of unsettling. You get job offers and suddenly you're taking off for a month, and that can lead to a lot of resentment. It's not at all conducive to long-term relationships or communities.

The future—I think the field will continue to grow. I think it went through its real growth spurt in the '70s and '80s, but I think there will always be room for good people and there will be more opportunities. You just have to go out and decide what it is you want to do.

References

Association for Experiential Education (AEE), 2305 Canyon Boulevard, Ste 100, Boulder, CO 80302-5651; (303) 440-8844.

Environmental Traveling Companions, Fort Mason Center, Landmark Building C, San Francisco, CA 94123; (415) 474-7662.

Montana Outfitters & Guides Association, Box 9070, Helena, MT 59624; (406) 449-3578.

Other opportunities can be explored through therapeutic recreation programs at universities and internship programs at local organizations.

Hunting Guide

Dreams—A hunting guide is the second coming of Jim Bridger, getting lucrative fees to lead people on fantastic hunts, always exploring awesome wildlife areas, being paid and treated by clients as a king. Who knows, maybe you will be featured in *Field & Stream* magazine.

Nightmares—Putting a trip together can be like putting hiking boots on a giant centipede, but it can get worse. What if the clients can't hack the wilderness, you can't find any game, your cooking is terrible, the tent leaks, and the horses run away? Right, it's a disaster, and not only that, the clients want a refund.

Realities—You spend your days in the wild and your nights in a sleeping bag, sharing a passionate experience with strangers. The money is decent, long-term prospects are good, and the likable, detail-oriented woodsman who can put city folks on game has got a great deal going for a seasonal job.

What it's all about—Hunters have more passion for their sport than the participants of any other outdoor activity. You see that not only in surveys on the outdoors, but also in the eyes of a hunter. When he spots his prey, a hunter's eyes look like a pair of laser beams. Hear those cannons? It's just his heart beating.

That passion is both the best and worst feature for a hunting guide. The best because it guarantees clients who have enthusiasm for the adventure, people who are often delighted to do anything the guide says because they always believe they are on the hunt of their life. Alas, if the results don't match those expectations, that same ardor can boomerang into disappointment, and worse, if there are a few foul-ups on your part along the way, intense anger.

But if you like being out in the wild, really out there in booger country, have the skills of woodsmanship, and get along with all types of people, being a hunting guide can be quite satisfying. The type of people who excel at it tend to have a little of the blarney in them or a good knowledge of outdoor lore or history, which they use to entertain their guests during down time. The bottom line, though, is the ability to run a mistake-free camp, be a good cook, and get your clients reasonable shots at the quarry. Do that consistently and word will get out, and you'll make some good money every fall for years.

Many guides use horses, and during the non-hunting summer season, you can parlay that into day-trip adventure rides or camping/fishing trips for tourists. It can add some cash to your business, although maintaining horses adds overhead.

A bonus is that the future looks quite promising. Many people are working long hours and have less free time available, a trend that is likely to continue well into the future. Because of that, when an overworked hunter with a decent bankroll finally gets some vacation time, he is willing to find a guide and pay him well to take care of everything and get him some good shots. The more exotic the hunt, the more expensive the trip, and the fees are paid without a whimper.

The best way to learn the business is to work under another outfitter for a few seasons. At one point or another, you should try to do every part of the job, and do them all until you're sick of them. If you still like being a hunting guide at that point, you have the ideal aptitude to make it a career.

Every state has its own set of requirements for licensing guides. Alaska is the most strict; before you take a client out by yourself in Alaska, you must have three years experience as an assistant guide under an outfitter, pass a written test, pass a CPR and first-aid course, have hunted two of the past five years, and be recommended by another guide. That is why guides in Alaska are held in esteem throughout the world. In contrast, some states require almost nothing. California is an example, where you plunk down $25 for a hunting license, $62 for a guide's license, about $70 for a bond, and then you can guide for anything. No experience of any kind is required. Guides in California also have difficulty getting clients or getting paid well.

Organization is a key to this job, of course. The best guides always use extensive check lists in planning a hunt. Quality gear is mandatory, so the start-up price can be higher than first projected. You need to know how to fix equipment with few tools to do the job. And, of course, you must have the physical conditioning to handle the job, especially the endurance needed for packing game out of the wilderness, and the outlook of a detective to be able to find game consistently. In addition, you must not only be skilled at every level of woodsmanship, but you also must be likable. Hunters consider their sport something sacred, and as a result, many hunters develop a bond with a guide that makes for a lifetime friendship. You have to be open to that.

Some hunting guides are excellent shots, and have a habit of allowing their clients one shot, and if it misses, they quickly shoot the game themselves. This can outrage some people, and prior to heading afield with clients, all ground rules need to be agreed upon 100 percent. Most hunters who hire guides have very strong personal ethics and are quite successful. They would no more want to take home an animal shot by a guide than be handed a welfare check.

The bottom line is that being a hunting guide is an excellent seasonal job for a likable woodsman who can get by with guile and a gun. If you like waking up before dawn in a sleeping bag out in the middle of nowhere, where the air is clean and crisp and the only thoughts are of the day's coming adventure, then this is the job for you.

Career Case Study

Jack Atcheson, Sr., Montana

Jack Atcheson, Sr. runs Jack Atcheson & Sons, Inc., an international hunting, fishing and photographic consulting and outfitting firm. He has worked in the industry since childhood, and has traveled and hunted extensively throughout North America, Africa, Europe and Asia. He lives in Butte, Montana with his wife, Mary Claire.

Requirements—You have to have an interest in what you're doing. You have to want to pursue this type of work because you like to hunt and fish and see new places. And you have to have ambition, because to do these things, you have to have the strength to continue where other people will want to quit. Most people lack this. Only a small percentage can fall down, shake themselves off, and try again without whining.

You must have the ability, both physically and mentally, to do it. No formal education is required, but the better educated you are, the more likely you are to succeed in dealing with people. If I was going to school, I would take classes in public speaking, to learn to be able to communicate and get my message across—that's very important. Most of the people you deal with are going to be successful and educated, and if you can't communicate on their level, you're not going to succeed to any degree. It's very important to be able to relate to each person, to get your idea across and take them where you want them to go, recognizing that many of them are overweight and in poor physical condition.

You have to be a master baby-sitter. People have been presented with this image of what an outdoor hunting expedition is supposed to be like, and when they actually experience it, many can't handle it. The difference between expectation and reality is enormous. The majority of the people are shocked at how primitive the experience is—even though that's what they came for—and they need an awful lot of care.

You have to be a jack-of-all-trades—you need experience with mechanical work, because there are always things that need fixing: lanterns, flat tires, vehicles. You ought to know about horses, weather, first aid, and most of all, people. Expect bad luck, because it's guaranteed that bad luck will find you, and find a way to turn it around. The very best guides make good things happen out of the very worst. A person who can succeed at that is much in demand. The guide who is ill-equipped will fail right off.

That's the guide aspect. As far as management goes, you will usually start out as a guide or secretary, working for someone else. You really have to work down with everyone else so you can understand all aspects of the business. You can't be a master chef until you learn how to cook and scrub some pans. You have to understand all levels. One important concept that you have to grasp is how to manage money. That's a biggie. You're in charge, and you're on a limited budget, so you have figure out how much to spend, how much to buy, and when to buy it.

Prospects—Your job prospects depend on how much you know and how good you are, the same as any other position. The more knowledgeable you are in the field you want to work in, the more likely you are to be hired.

There are two types of positions: permanent, where you work consistently for one outfit in one area, and migratory, where you move on a regular basis. Permanent positions are scarce. In order to get one, you truly have to be a jack-of-all-trades, you have to be polished, and you have to stand out. For a migratory-type position, you have to follow the market, and that can mean following it from one end of Montana to the other, or from New York to Mexico, depending on where you want to go.

The more you travel, the more you'll come into contact with wealthy and successful people, people above your level, which is a good way to become educated. Everything hinges on you—your success will depend on your ability to understand opportunities when they present themselves.

Benefits—Most obviously, you're doing what you like and want to do. People get into this business because they like hunting and fishing, and they're actually out there giving it a try. People are generally more successful when they get to try what they've always really wanted to do.

It's great to be your own boss. You're working away from management and you're in a responsible position. And it's always a learning experience; you learn more about people and life every time you go out.

Pay—When you're starting out as a guide, the lowest pay would be around $35 to $50 per day, which includes room and board. On the upper scale, it can go up to $100 to $150 per day. When you get into management, I'd say that you're going to make about $150 per day, $200 at the absolute maximum, unless you're getting commissions on sales. In that case it depends, of course, on the individual. And management is a different game; in most cases, you're no longer in the field—you're in the office.

Negatives—Having a job where you move around a lot means that you're not going to have a lot of "regular" friends. If you're married, your spouse may not want to move around a lot with you, and that can cause problems.

You're dealing with people who are sometimes unhappy, and you always have to put on a happy face. If you're not a person who can take stress, you're not going to make it. You also work very long hours with very low pay.

The future—The long-term prospects are probably better than the immediate. It's been predicted that by the year 2000, recreation is going to be the biggest business around, and there always will be a need for people to show other people around. The recreational field is going to become far more diversified; it's expanding all the time. The opportunities are going to be there.

Career Case Study

Ted Epley, Idaho

Ted Epley is owner and operator of Epley's Idaho Outdoor Adventures, a horse and river operation in McCall & Riggins, Idaho. Epley is the President of North American Outfitters and is on the board of the Idaho Outfitter & Guides Association and the National Forest Recreation Association. Epley has been an outfitter and guide for over thirty years. He enjoys hunting, fishing and writing poetry in McCall, Idaho, where he lives with his wife, Karen, and children.

Requirements—I'd say that the most important requisite is the desire to work. I don't feel that you have to have a college education. I didn't, and I've been at it for 30 years. Basically, if you have a knowledge of some type of management, know how to balance a checkbook, and can handle a budget and work with expenses, you can do it.

You must be able to maintain your resources, so you become a conservationist to a degree. You must be knowledgeable about big game, their habitats and species, and knowledgeable about livestock if you're using horses and mules. You have to have equipment: tents, cooking utensils, things of that nature. Wilderness versus non-wilderness camping is quite different—wilderness camping means packing everything in, while you can think a little more elaborately for a developed area.

To own an outfitting operation, the first thing to do would be to find an established outfitter who was interested in selling. You would have to look at the area, see what kind of equipment came with it, and agree upon a price with the seller. Then the buyer and seller would go to the appropriate agencies and get the necessary applications and permits. The requirements for outfitters vary from state to state. Idaho has one of the most detailed requirement systems. Other states are less restrictive, and don't employ what I would consider the most desirable method of protecting and serving the public. We're really concerned that the public is taken care of by qualified outfitters and guides.

Prospects—It's not difficult to find sellers. What is difficult is to find a good business at a fair price. There are limited opportunities to buy really good outfitting businesses. Often you just have to wait until someone retires, or until there's a death or a divorce in the family. There are lots of businesses that change hands every two years because they don't turn many dollars. Some people come in with this glamorous idea—they want to enjoy the life of running a big game hunting operation, but they may not realize the drawbacks of the particular area, like limited wildlife, hard work, or seasonal income, so they give up and move on.

Benefits—It's the love of life for me. I like the outdoors, horses, being on the river, and being in the mountains. I like to be involved in every aspect of my business. I especially like being my own boss. A person who can do something that he enjoys and make a living at it is a lucky person.

Sharing with my family is a big benefit for me—we've had a lot of opportunities to be together. Through my affiliation with other outfitters, my family and I have been able to go on and guide trips that we may never have experienced otherwise. My wife, oldest son and oldest daughter have all been licensed guides. It's been a good life.

Pay—Guides average between $35 and $65 per day, plus room and board. Some outfitters pay monthly, and that can range from $300 to $1200 a month, depending on experience. A study was done on the income of outfitters in Idaho, and the outcome was that the average outfitter nets about 4.5 percent of his gross income. So an outfitter who took in $100,000 would make about $4,500 profit. That varies, of course; some people are better money managers than others, but I'd consider it an accurate figure.

Negatives—It's difficult to work in a resource situation where you're not actually in control. The Forest Service, who controls our area, has a pretty rigid set of rules to follow. There can be a lot of frustration. Everyone doesn't always agree on how things should happen, and there can be some very negative feelings. Some outfitters might feel that federal agencies aren't willing to cooperate.

One of the most difficult aspects is that it's a seasonal business. You have to be a good money manager and know how to carry over when you need to. You also have to be willing to work at other things to make a living.

The future—You've heard the expression: The sky is the limit. If you want to excel, all you have to do is work at it. I think the future looks great for the outfitting business. I started with six head of horses and a car, and today our horse operation consists of 20 head of horses and one team of Belgians. Our river operation includes a large shop, guides' quarters, four buses, and three vans to carry all of our clients. We have a second home near our river operation.

People who really want to get involved and have the financial backing have lots of opportunities. We're seeing lots of people expanding their horizons as far as activities; they're doing cross-country skiing and snowmobiling in the winter, things like that. If you are anywhere near a population center, it's great. We've been seeing more people cater exclusively to the handicapped recently. That seems to be an up-and-coming trend. And qualified guides and leaders are always needed.

References

North American Outfitters, Inc., P.O. Box 505, Boise, ID 83701; (208) 342-1438. They can provide a list of addresses and phone numbers for the Guide and Outfitter's Association in each state.

Montana Outfitters & Guides Association, Box 9070, Helena, MT 59601; (406) 449-3578.

International Sportsmen's Exposition, PO Box 2569, Vancouver, WA 98668; (800) 545-6100 or (300) 693-3700.

US Fish & Wildlife Service, 2625 Parkmont Road, Building A, Olympia, WA 98502; (300) 753-9460.

Hydrologist

Dreams—A hydrologist keeps North America's purest waters untouched and pristine, and saves others that have been violated by despoilers. The pay is decent, as is the personal satisfaction, and you get tremendous respect from both your peers and the public.

Nightmares—You quickly discover that the job focuses on areas that have been damaged, and that you can get smothered by bureaucracy in attempts at environmental repair. What if nobody listens to you? Corporations that damage waterways might be willing to pay you a large salary to represent them in a good light, but it can amount to a bribe.

Realities—You have to love the science of water. If you do, job availability is good, and if you can deal with the government spider web, so is the satisfaction. The pay is enough to float your boat, especially if you live in a rural area. A great side benefit is the great camaraderie with other hydrologists.

What it's all about—Hydrologists, who make studying water a life's passion, always get great pleasure from sitting on a rock watching a river run by. It doesn't matter if they have been in the business of studying water for 40 minutes or 40 years. Hydrologists all share this one common trait: They just plain love to watch that pure water run free.

As they sit there watching that water, it is as if the blood of the earth is running through their bodies and infusing them with both energy and serenity. This is not a metaphysical outlook on the philosophic power of nature; for a hydrologist, these feelings are as real as the hammer strikes for a carpenter putting a nail into wood.

If you have this passion for wild, pure water, as well as a pragmatic approach to science, you can parlay the two into a resplendent career as a hydrologist. It is a job that can be inherently satisfying, where you get the chance to make the world a better place. After all, clean water, along with clear air and a clean earth, are among this planet's basic necessities. Because of that, there are jobs available in a wide array of government agencies and private corporations.

The money in the public sector is decent—$30,000 to $45,000 a year with a few years experience—and that usually includes living in rural areas where your dollar can buy a lot more house. In the private sector, a first-class consultant with ten years of experience can make $60,000 to $75,000, and in some cases a lot more, although this can mean working with the very corporations that despoil North America's clean water. It also usually means living in a metropolitan area.

At the minimum, you need a bachelor's degree with a focus on science. That, along with a summer internship with a government agency like the Forest Service, can lead to a job. But for the long run, you are better off with a master's degree, which will give you the opportunity to specialize in a chosen area of study and make you quite valuable wherever that expertise is needed. If you want to make the really big bucks with the private corporations, a Ph.D. is required.

There are many examples that show how the world needs you in this job: Hydrologists with an emphasis on acid rain are in demand in the northeast; hydrologists with an emphasis on soil erosion are in demand in the northwest and where there has been extensive logging; hydrologists with an emphasis on pesticides are in demand in the farm country; hydrologists with an emphasis on ground water are in demand wherever there are wells; hydrologists with an emphasis in toxics are in demand everywhere (like near Chernobyl).

A growing specialty is a cross between fisheries biology and hydrology. It's called "instream flow hydrology," where specialists determine how much water a stream requires to keep aquatic life healthy. This approach is becoming important wherever water has been diverted out of a stream for other uses, such as farming, and in the process has harmed fisheries.

Right there is one of the big problems a hydrologist faces. You get involved in this career because you love something—pure, free-flowing water. Then you discover your primary demand is in areas where this resource has been defiled, either by pollution, soil erosion, pesticides, pumping or diversions. If your personal attempt to revive a degraded waterway is met by bureaucratic resistance from other agencies—a common problem—you can get frustrated, pessimistic and eventually become a very bitter person.

The best response is to identify and address a problem, do everything possible to fix it, and then move on to another problem. It is impossible for one hydrologist to fix everything at once. This is what scientists call the "Save-The-World-Approach." It is not impossible, however, for a hydrologist to fix a series of problems, taking on each one separately. In time, these solutions as a collective will have an impact in making the world a better place. It is the hydrologist with this approach who is effective, respected and happiest.

The job can be varied and bring a lot of adventure with it. It always means being close to the source—water—whether it is a major river flowing to sea, a rain gauge set deep in the forest, a remote wilderness lake, or leveed canals in farm country. A new-comer to the Forest Service, for instance, might be expected to hike five miles into the wilderness, collect a water sample (to be tested later for residue of aerial pesticide spraying), and then hike out. A great way to spend a day, right? No lie. And along the way on that hike, you can bet that the hydrologist will find a nice rock to sit on and spend a few minutes just watching a river flow by. You see, they just can't help it.

Career Case Study

Michael Furniss, California

Michael Furniss works as a hydrologist for Six Rivers National Forest. He graduated from UC Berkeley with a master's degree in soil science and has worked as a hydrologist since 1978. He was employed by the State Department of Forestry in Sacramento for several years and has worked in various northern California locations. Michael is the editor of the Watershed Management Council Newsletter, has been published in several publications, and teaches part time at Humboldt State University. He lives with his family in Arcata, California.

Requirements—It takes a college degree in hydrology, watershed management or a related field, such as wildland resources science. Some experience is required for most positions, but the demand is high and you can go into an entry-level position straight out of college. If you have a special interest, you should get a master's degree in it. Mine is in soil science.

A big part of this business is communication: on the phone, in the mail, talking face to face. You have to know how to communicate. You need to be good at understanding how landscapes function, but you must also know how to say what you see.

Prospects—It's fairly competitive, although not as much as wildlife biology. More people aspire to working with warm furry things than with water and soil.

There are different types of hydrology that you can get into. There is urban hydrology, which is rooted in civil engineering, and there is wildland hydrology, which is rooted in soil science, biology and geology. There are two types of employers: government and environmental consulting firms. Government employers range all the way from counties to water utilities to the federal government. Private employers include firms that specialize in a specific area of hydrology all the way to firms that do all kinds of environmental work.

Each area of the country has unique problems with water. A lot of my time is spent consulting to make sure that when land disturbance occurs, the effects on water and soil are minor and short-term; this is very challenging sometimes. There's also monitoring and research, to determine the conditions, the trends and what the relationships are between people and water. Restoring damaged watersheds is another major area of work, and the funding for this has increased greatly in the last few years.

Benefits—You get to be outside a lot. You get to spend time trying to understand how nature works. You're involved in a great diversity of situations. You get to do something that feels like it's worthwhile, and feel like you can make a difference, which I think is important to a lot of people going into outdoor careers. Whenever it rains, your mind goes into a state of delight because you understand that the landscape is alive and the rain is its blood. So much happens when it rains.

Pay—Starting pay is around $25,000, topping out at about $55,000. It can go up, but that is more likely to happen when you get into administration or business management.

Negatives—If you're looking to make a lot of money, this isn't the business to go into. You can make a fine living, but it's not a career for pursuing big bucks. There is a tendency for salaries to top out quickly. You get to the top level, and there's nowhere else to go and still do hydrology. You can move to higher-paying jobs, but you really are going into another line of work. You're still called a hydrologist, but you're more of an administrator or planner than a natural scientist.

The future—As a society, Americans are increasingly concerned with both solving environmental problems and keeping clean areas clean. Water is right at the top of the list. If you don't have clean water, you have nothing. This insures that the field of hydrology will become increasingly important in the future. There are a lot of problems with water quality in different parts of North America that are just now being addressed with the idea of fixing them. That will give hydrologists many great opportunities. Most of the people who do this work really love it, and so do I.

Career Case Study

Alan Clingenpeel, Arkansas

Alan Clingenpeel has worked as a hydrologist since 1982, first for the Missouri Department of Conservation and then for the U.S. Forest Service. Alan currently works extensively with universities, research groups and local organizations in order to build and increase our awareness of the aquatic ecosystem. He lives in Hot Springs, Arkansas, where he spends his free hours camping, hiking and fishing.

Requirements—For a hydrologist position in the U.S. Forest Service, you have to meet specific qualifications: You must have six hours of calculus, six hours of physics, and 30 hours of a combination of physical and biological science. That's standard within the federal government. In terms of college education, you can concentrate on any one of several areas: ecology, forestry, geography, geology and biology.

You have to have a desire to learn and discover. If you want to learn accounting, it's a fairly rigid process. There is one specific set of rules and one specific goal. In science, there are a variety of avenues that you can follow. Some hydrologists are interested in processes on land, others get into water chemistry. Another hydrologist might be into the biological aspects. But each one will have the desire to apply himself or herself.

Prospects—It's a pretty wide-open arena. I would say that availability in the market is good right now, especially for entry level positions, and especially for diversity candidates (minority groups).

There are positions available in several agencies and organizations: the U.S. Forest Service, state pollution control agencies, consulting firms, the U.S. Geological Survey (which may be one of the largest hirers), the EPA, and universities.

Benefits—You make a sufficient wage. I'll never be rich, but I'll be comfortable. Health benefits are good, and retirement benefits are excellent. It's a tremendous learning atmosphere. You get to be outdoors, applying yourself in many different ways. Sometimes you'll go out and look at land and soil; sometimes you'll be studying bugs in the water. The day-to-day operations are enjoyable.

Pay—The federal government bases pay on a grade scale number system, starting at GS 5 and going up in increments of two until GS 11, then it goes up in increments of one. A hydrologist in an entry-level position can expect a level of GS 5, earning $17,000 to $21,000 per year. Within a year you can easily move up to level GS 9, and the income there elevates to $30,000 to $40,000. You still get pay increases within levels, so it can vary. I've had ten years of experience, and I'm at GS 12, in the $42,000 range per year. I expect to get up to the $50,000 level.

Negatives—Working with the Forest Service can be demanding. Sometimes I have to work on Saturdays, which takes time away from my family, and I don't necessarily get reimbursed for it. It can take a lot of time from your family.

In terms of politics, you can get some wild shifts. There are problems with funding and times of crisis management where we lose our focus. These are all stressful and negative, but they are eventually overcome.

The future—For the U.S. Forest Service, this is a wonderful time. In the past, the Forest Service has been focused on timber as their most valuable resource, and now they're getting more into the ecological aspect, which opens up possibilities for more positions. When we go through rediscovery, we're learning, and now we're starting to learn more about our ecosystem and how it all fits together. When we're in that learning mode, we're stretching our minds, trying new takes, and it is exciting. That's going to continue to escalate.

References

American Water Works Association, 6666 West Quincy Avenue, Denver, CO 80235; (303) 794-7711.

JOBSource (computerized data bank). Contact: Computerized Employment Systems, Inc; 1720 West Mulberry Unit B9, Fort Collins, CO 80521; (970) 493-1779.

Environmental Job Opportunities Bulletin, from Institute for Environmental Studies, University of Wisconsin-Madison, 550 North Park Street, 15 Science Hall, Madison, WI 53706; (608) 263-3185 or fax (608) 262-0014.

National Ecological & Conservation Opportunities Institute, PO Box 511, Helena, MT 59624; (406) 442-0214.

For information about the U.S. Forest Service, phone a local office and ask to speak to a hydrologist.

Interpretive
Center Director

Dreams—You live in a national park, and what more pristine surroundings could you ask for? None, and not only that, but you are also surrounded by wide-eyed pupils of all ages, visitors to your park who look to you as teacher, hero and mentor. Everybody is awed by your vast knowledge of nature.

Nightmares—Nobody cares about what you know; after all, they're on vacation. It makes you mad when they don't listen, irate when they interrupt, and furious when they go out and do just the opposite of what you directed, like giving the bear a peanut. What's wrong with these people?

Realities—You must have the temperament to get along with anybody, and the teaching skills to inspire visitors rather than have them turn against you. Living in a park is unique—sure, it's divine—but you never get to leave work. The pay can be OK, but it takes shifting positions from park to park to move up quickly.

What it's all about—America has one heck of a problem: 80 percent of the country's population is living in 5 percent of the available area. That means that millions and millions of folks are squeezed together in cities and urban areas and that their day-to-day experience is often distanced from nature, wildlife and wild areas. That is why 50 percent of the respondents in a survey at Yosemite

National Park answered that they thought an iguana is an insect. That is why some youngsters think the only wild animals left are in zoos and Yellowstone Park. That is why so many people have no concept of the skills of woodsmanship, outdoor ethics and nature's ways.

That is also why the late Bill Mott, the director of the National Park Service in the 1980s, phased in interpretive centers at all national parks. It was the start of something good. It was an idea that worked, and there are now interpretive centers at all levels of parks—local, county, regional, state and national, including in Canada. They are considered vital, something as important as picnic tables at campsites.

The reason is because so many people with no outdoor experience will treat camping in wildlands like a trip to a theme park. Some people blame the National Park Service for creating this atmosphere at its more popular parks. While there is some validity to this, the bigger problem is the mindset of the visitors, people who are disconnected from the wild and bring their urban agenda with them when they go camping at a park.

That is where you come in. As an interpretive director, it is your assignment to help visitors to your park make that connection. It is no easy charge, and there are many ways to go about it: passing out informational leaflets to each park visitor, setting up displays at headquarters, campfire talks, self-guided nature trails with signs posted at noted flora, explanatory signs at unique geologic formations, impromptu visits to campers for discussions about dealing with animals (like bears). That is your mission.

To complete it, you enlist the aid of rangers, seasonal aides, volunteers (often seniors in retirement), and the support of the park superintendent. In any case, you need a fleet of people to help get the word out. In smaller parks, rangers can double as interpretive directors.

To enjoy this job, you need to savor the art of teaching, especially with people who have little background in the subject. The latter is both a blessing and a curse. With children and women, it is often a blessing, because they are apt to listen and try to learn the lesson you are bringing to them. Talk about bears, for instance, and you will get their complete, focused attention. With adult males, on the other hand, it's often a curse because they tend to dislike being taught anything, especially about something (the outdoors) that has its roots in America's heritage. Talk about bears, for instance, and a guy will typically interrupt and try to take over the discussion: "There I was, me and a bear, and one of us was going to have to back off or fight. Then I looked at the bear and he..." It happens every day. It will drive you nuts.

That is why another strategy is passing out informational leaflets, making sure each park visitor gets them upon entry. Then when you provide a brochure, such as "Bears and You," the same guy who would have interrupted you in a personal discussion instead becomes absorbed in the information, which he does not see as a direct threat to his masculinity. He ends up getting the message.

Alas, if the visitors have poor reading skills—or poor attention spans—the leaflets don't do the job. And you end up still making personal appearances, or scheduling rangers to do it for you, whether it is a campfire talk, leading a walk, or routing out a hike for a self-guided nature trail. One way or another, it is your job to communicate the park experience to these temporarily dislocated city-types.

The best way to get started is as a seasonal or part-time resource aide at a national park, or as a volunteer where you at least get room and board covered. As a full-timer, you need a four-year degree, preferably in environmental education and park management. A person who has worked summers as a resource aide in a park, then gets a degree in environmental education with a minor in park management, has a good opportunity to get hired.

Most newcomers are paid about $24,000, but like all government jobs, the pays goes up in specified increments according to years on the job, experience and position advancement. A bonus is that a full-time job at a park usually includes lodging. This position tops out in the $37,000 to $42,000 range, for the most part. You can get paid more, but usually only if you are also doing another job at the same time, perhaps as a chief ranger or even superintendent.

A real key in moving up the ranks quickly and getting paid better is mobility—being willing to work at any park where you can improve your position. In the first 10 years, you might work at five to eight parks, for instance, in order to take advantage of opportunities for personal advancement. If you would rather work a lifetime at one park, on the other hand, advancement tends to be quite slow.

An advantage to working at one park, however, is that you will not have to continually uproot your home, and you will have a better chance of maintaining long-term friendships. The advantages are for you to weigh. Most park workers end up in the middle, switching parks four to six times in their first 10 years, then settling down in one park where they feel at home.

Parks can be a magnificent place to live, especially in the off-season. They are among the most pristine places on earth, protected forever from logging, mining and hydro projects. That is what makes them so attractive to city folks, half of whom apparently think an iguana is what just squashed on their windshield. Good luck in your mission to explain to them differently.

Career Case Study

Richard Fedorchak, Utah

Richard Fedorchak is the Assistant Chief Naturalist at Zion National Park. He has worked as a park ranger/ naturalist at several parks, including Glacier National Park, Mount Rainier and Carlsbad Caverns. His prior experience includes working as a law enforcement ranger at Lassen Volcanic National Park, for the U.S. Corps of Engineers, and the U.S. Forest Service. He enjoys hiking, photography, playing the guitar, and computers. He is married to a fellow park ranger, and lives at Zion National Park in Springdale, Utah.

Requirements—I'm speaking specifically from a National Park Service point of view, although I believe that other government agency requirements are similar. Theoretically there's no degree required, but you probably won't have a chance of getting hired, even for a seasonal position, without one. Having the degree itself is more important than what the degree is actually in. Many people on our staff have degrees in biological or earth sciences; a history degree is beneficial if you're working in one of the more historic parks. I have an associate's degree in park management and a bachelor's degree in environmental education.

My job in particular takes both an educational and a biological background, since I have to be knowledgeable about my subject and also understand how to communicate ideas to people. You have to understand the ways people learn. I am the program manager for the park, and that means that I mostly facilitate the front line interpreters. Front line interpreters are the rangers you see taking people on hikes and giving nighttime presentations. My job is to encourage the front line rangers to do the best job they can in interpreting. I like to use the analogy that I am sort of a stagehand; I make sure the stage looks good and all the props are there for the actors and actresses. I look at slide programs and displays in visitor centers and try to think of new ones.

I also assist with the interpretive information signs you see on hiking trails. For instance, we have three natural pools here called Emerald Pools, and people like to swim in them. The problem with that is that with so many people and kids in them all the time, they start to get murky, and the delicate biological life in there is threatened. So we have to put up a sign that tells people nicely not to swim in the pools, and the reason why.

Prospects—It's pretty competitive: 63 people applied for my job here at Zion. I do think that the park service is going to go through some changes. Technically, I am a park ranger/naturalist; the title of park ranger is so generic right now. Rangers take care of just about every facet of the park, and in time I think job descriptions are going to become more distinctive and job requirements will become more specific. It's a good idea to start early and get a variety of experiences. You can go directly to a park or agency and talk to the chief naturalist about what's required and how to go about it; you can talk to recruiters at job fairs on college campuses. One excellent avenue is through the Student Conservation Association. Anyone 18 or older can apply for a position as a resource aide, which lets you do basically everything a park ranger does but with a different uniform and title. It's a great way to get a foot in the door and get experience.

Another option is to volunteer at a park. You don't make any money; you usually get free housing and a stipend. I encourage people to get experience in various areas; for example, I went in as a naturalist, but did extra work in resources management and law enforcement, among other things.

Don't be afraid to dabble in different areas. If you apply for a job and the only position open is fee collecting, take the position. It may not be the most glorious job, but it will get you known, and chances are you will be moved up to a preferable position. Varied experience will make you much more employable.

It also helps to be fairly mobile early on. This is my seventh park in nine years. Some people find that it's really hard to get in where they want to be and they quit, but if you're flexible and willing to move around, you have the opportunity to gain a much wider scope of experience.

Benefits—The people aspect is probably my favorite part of this job. When you're dealing with the human element, there's never a dull moment. You're coming across a totally different group of people every moment, and something completely new always seems to come up. People seem to give us a lot of credit simply for the uniform we wear, and it's great to see someone smile and appreciate you. It's fun, because you're in a vacation atmosphere, and people are there to have a good time.

It's a real challenge to communicate a story to a person who may not have any idea about what's going on. I enjoy challenging my creative powers, thinking of different ways to tell a story so that everyone will relate to it. It's rewarding to think that I might make a difference, that I could possibly turn someone on to something and make them think a little more about the environment and preserving what's around them, even if it's just in their home town. We get cards and letters from all over the world from people who tell us how much they were affected by our programs.

Pay—The National Park Service pays on the government grade scale. Where I am, employees on a GS 5 level can make about $17,000 a year, even less if they're seasonal employees. Most seasonal positions are GS 5. There's a woman on my staff who started in March and will work through September, and she's making $14,000. It goes up with experience. In 1986 I started at GS 4, then I was at GS 5 for three years, then GS 7 for a while, and I just got promoted to GS 9 a few months ago. I'm making somewhere in the neighborhood of $26,000 a year. GS 9 is considered about mid-level. Most folks in my position are at GS 9 or 11, and you don't make a lot of money, but that's not why we're in this field. You also get some health and retirement benefits if you're a permanent employee.

Negatives—The pay. For those who are starting off season-ally and have a family, it's tough. Seasonal employees make very little money and they don't get any benefits. I don't think people realize how much work is involved. I'd say that 98 percent of all park employees average 10- to 12-hour days. Some people assume that we're government workers, which tends to have a negative connotation in itself, so we're often victims of guilt by association. It's understandable, when people see the corruption that occurs in other branches of the government, but that really has nothing to do with us, and it can be difficult to be lumped into the government category.

The future—I foresee some changes happening. Some 60 years ago, rangers and park employees were people who had a background in the outdoors, being in the woods, rather than a formal education. Now that the field is becoming so much more competitive and educational requirements are becoming stiffer, I think we're going to have to pay them a decent wage to get people of necessary caliber on board. We as rangers are going through a little identity crisis as well. We had our own myth of what a park ranger does, and the reality is that the myth is myth—we're suddenly being asked for all these credentials and we're getting paid very little. A solution has to be found that is fair to both ourselves and the public.

Career Case Study

Cindy Neilsen, Montana
Cindy Neilsen is the Chief of Interpretation at Glacier National Park. She has worked for the National Park Service since 1972, at several parks, including Death Valley, Channel Islands and Grand Tetons. She also worked for the Forest Service as a writer/editor. She enjoys hiking and scuba diving. She lives in West Glacier, Montana.

Requirements—The actual legal requirements are relatively low, but in all practicality, the job requires at least a college degree. My degree was in natural science, and I happen to have a master's as well, but neither of those are actual requisites. However, when you get to the level that I'm at, the job practically demands a degree in natural or earth sciences. Archaeology or history are beneficial if you're in one of the historical parks. Another way to go is to get a degree in some sort of communications field, but that's not the traditional path. I do think we'll see that more in the future as interpretive programs continue to improve technologically. Basically, you should have a strong background in communication and an understanding of how to convey the concepts and ideas indigenous to the area you're in.

Prospects—Within the federal government there are 25 people who hold the position of Chief of Interpretation at large national parks such as Everglades, Great Smoky Mountain, Yellowstone, and Glacier. Smaller parks typically have an interpretive specialist, but they would be working at a lower grade than I work at. It's a highly competitive field, because there aren't many positions and it's a very coveted job.

Benefits—One of the things I enjoy the most is dealing with all kinds of people. If you don't, you're simply not cut out for this line of work. No matter what your previous training is, it boils down to the fact that you're communicating information about your park to other people. You find out pretty early on whether that's something you like doing or not. As you move up in the ranks, you will find yourself spending less time out in the field, but compared to other mid-level management jobs, this is still a pretty wonderful place to work. One of the really rewarding aspects is having the opportunity to help others grow in their careers, to maximize your staff and resources to deliver quality education. Seeing your own personal growth is gratifying as well.

Pay—I make just over $40,000 a year. Entry level positions don't pay much, about $18,000. When I worked seasonally, I made even less than that. One of the big challenges for the parks is the fact that there's a need for a large number of employees most of the year, and that decreases dramatically in the winter and early spring months. In order to maximize the park budget, seasonal employees outnumber permanent two to one. In terms of establishing a career, that's certainly one of the biggest hurdles to get over. You're looking at a minimum of three to five years of seasonal work, so you have to be willing to pay your dues before you see a significant increase in income.

Negatives—One of the most difficult factors in government service right now is that there just isn't enough money to achieve optimum programs. We have aging facilities and old exhibits and we're understaffed. We have all the typical budget complaints. You really have to learn how to maximize your resources. The job is certainly challenging; it disciplines you to think clearly and be tough about priorities. I'm constantly answering questions about what's most important. That can be difficult if you're not a leadership-oriented person.

The future—We are seeing changing patterns in both visitors and visitation within the national park system. Visitation has certainly grown in my four years here, and it is continuing to grow nationwide. There is a lot more fall travel than there used to be. The summer season used to end on Labor Day; now we go well into October. Another thing we're seeing is an interest in eco-tourism. Today's visitors not only want to learn about ecological history and make sure they do no harm to the resources, but they want to participate in taking pro-active steps to protect them. There is an increasing need for financial partnerships between the public sector and the private sector. There needs to be more funding, grants and volunteers participating in the improvement of our parks.

References

National Association of Interpretation, P.O. Box 1892, Fort Collins, CO 80522; (970) 491-6434. (Call for bi-weekly national listing of careers in interpretation, including internships and seasonal opportunities.)

National Parks and Conservation Association, 1776 Massachusetts Avenue NW, Washington, D.C. 20036; (202) 223-6722.

National Park Service: Careers and *Seasonal Employment: The National Parks* from US Department of the Interior, National Park Service, PO Box 37127, Washington, D.C. 20013-7127; (202) 208-4649.

Lifeguard

Dreams—There you are, sitting on your perch as king of the beach, bronzed and tanned, getting invited out on dates with a different partner every day of the week. For this you get paid? Oh yeah, now and then you save somebody's life. You are a superstar, likely to make the 10 o'clock news.

Nightmares—Instead of bronzing you, the sun is burning you alive. Instead of new dates, it's chili and hot dogs in front of the TV again. Considering the responsibility, the pay is rotten. As for that poor guy you tried to save the other day, when the ambulance arrived they had to send him to ECU—the Eternal Care Unit.

Realities—This job is like a long fuse to a stick of dynamite, with long waits to flashpoint and an emergency. You must maintain alertness, then react quickly and correctly. You might get a few extra dates, but don't bet the bank on the prospects. The pay is low, the public trust is high, and the reward of saving somebody's life is infinite.

What it's all about—In the space of just 10 or 20 seconds, the value of a lifeguard can be hammered home like a railman pounding a spike with a sledgehammer. Once you see it, you don't forget it. I remember taking a hike on a beach with a pal, Kelly Lynn, and my dog, Rebel, along the tidal line, just watching the scenery. About 20 or 30 people were playing in a mild surf, another 125 or 150 were laying on blankets, some reading, some watching, most just passing the time, hoping to catch a hint of an ocean breeze to cool off.

Suddenly, without warning, Kelly started trotting, then sprinted into the ocean, grabbed an innertube from a youngster who was playing in the shallows, and swam through the light surf. On the back side of the surf line, Kelly reached a fellow who had seemed to be just out for a nice swim. But the way the guy grabbed onto that innertube showed that it was no "nice swim." Then with each of them holding on to the innertube, they caught the next wave and made it in to the beach. "You saved my life," the stranger told Kelly. "I was just out for a swim but I got out too far, and I couldn't get back in. I'm a strong swimmer, but the undertow kept taking me out."

Of the 150 people on the beach, the only one who noticed that the guy was in trouble was Kelly Lynn, a lifeguard. The reason he noticed is because lifeguards are trained to notice the most subtle signs of problems, and develop an acute sense about people and their habits. In the space of just 10 or 20 seconds, a disaster was averted. Nobody else on the beach (no official lifeguard was posted) was even aware of what had transpired, that a life had almost been lost.

It's fairly typical, you discover. The collective public lacks awareness. It becomes your job as a lifeguard to give them a wake-up call. That is the bottom line.

Lifeguard jobs are available during the summer months at popular beaches on the coast, city-operated swimming pools, and private swim and tennis clubs. To qualify for a position does not mean looking like Mr. Golden Bear, USA. Rather it means being a strong swimmer and having passed a course in lifesaving. At some areas, particularly along the southern coasts, there is an additional orientation course that must be passed.

Most newcomers are competitive swimmers who are looking for a way to make some cash while staying close to the water. But it doesn't take many episodes before a lifeguard will become quite serious about this business of lifesaving. After saving somebody's life, some lifeguards define their lives according to this talent, and then go on to careers in some kind of emergency response field, perhaps as a paramedic, fireman or police officer.

The pay per hour may sound high for a summer job, up to $15 per hour. But the top dollar goes to lifeguards working in coastal urban areas, where the money does not stretch as far. In fact, it is a fair gripe that the pay does not match the responsibility, probably the biggest disparity of any outdoor job. In one summer, for instance, Kelly Lynn saved dozens of people from drowning and got paid something like $12 an hour and a lot of handshakes for it. None of the incidents made the newspaper; nobody else on the beach probably even knew about them. To some, being a lifeguard may sound glamorous, but there is actually no hoopla about it.

Of course, there are a few exceptions. Some lifeguards are just beach bums, using their days to perfect their tan and try to get a new date for the night. One lifeguard I heard about bought a luxurious camper for a pick-up truck, then lived at the beach parking lot. Much of his summer consisted of seeing how many women he could get into that camper. As the story goes, he didn't fare so well. Then near the end of the summer, he suddenly met a young woman he really liked, started dating her, then ended up marrying her. Reality strikes again.

So your reason for becoming a lifeguard needs to be focused on the job, not the illusory glamour you may imagine accompanies it. The reality is that instead of exciting, the job can be tedious. You are like a sentinel, always scanning, watching for trouble. You can go days, sometimes weeks without an incident. Persistence with spirit is a requirement in order to maintain your enthusiasm. Then when something happens, you must respond immediately, and do the exact right thing. That takes a unique personality. Good lifeguards have it.

Another problem is the sun. It doesn't go away. Some lifeguards become either so dark or so burned that they take to wearing terry-cloth robes to protect their skin. Doctors have proven that day after day of exposure to intense, bright sunlight can dry out the outer layer of skin. In worst case scenarios, it can cause your skin to develop the texture of leather, as well as become vulnerable to skin cancer.

But most people don't remain a lifeguard long enough for those problems to manifest. After all, this is a summer job. Enjoy it while you're at it. In the meantime, think of the lives that you might save. Remember that most of the incidents take just 10 or 20 seconds. All it takes is being involved in one and the experience will forever change your perspective on the delicate nature of life.

Career Case Study

Bob Buchanan, California

Bob Buchanan has been a lifeguard since 1966, a full-timer since 1972, and is now Captain of Lifeguards and Training Officer for 700 lifeguards in Los Angeles. He enjoys diving and swimming in the summer, snow skiing in the winter. He is married and lives in Malibu, California.

Requirements—In lifeguard work there is a broad range of careers available, from private and public pools to ocean beach areas to lakes and rivers. Each has different requirements. Here in Los Angeles County, a person has to be 18 years of age, have a valid California driver's license, and 20/30 uncorrected vision in each eye. The job is considered physically arduous, so we initially hold a competitive 1,000-meter ocean swim to help determine physical ability. Other things we look for are skills in first aid or CPR, reading and writing, verbal communication, memory, manual dexterity, and abilities to function in hazardous conditions such as cold weather and/or high winds. Our lifeguards are required to successfully complete 60 hours of rookie school before they're hired. In rookie school we try to hone the skills that each person has, and enhance those in which the candidate displays a weakness.

We find that most of the people who try out really take the job seriously and enjoy it, although some are surprised to find out that it has very little in common with the media image of a lifeguard. There is a high degree of responsibility involved, because life and death decisions are going to have to be made, and they have to be able to respond in a very short period of time. If they don't, a life may be lost.

Prospects—We have a very good competition program which brings a lot of people to L.A. County. We usually have about 40 spots available each season, and about 200 people will enter the initial swimming competition. We take the top 100 swimmers and conduct oral interviews with them, then select about 40 people to take a physical exam and participate in our 60 hours of rookie school.

Here in L.A. County we're responsible for 31 miles of public beach. We have about 110 permanent and 600 seasonal lifeguards. There are 150 lifeguard towers, 55 rescue vehicles and a nine-vessel rescue boat fleet. Our lifeguards perform a variety of duties: operate an underwater recovery unit, offer water safety courses in sailing and surfing, staff a junior lifeguard program, and provide youth educational services. The majority of the work is done by our seasonal recurrent lifeguards, supervised by the permanent staff.

Although the competition here is very fierce, I have heard of other locations having trouble finding lifeguards. I think it depends on where you are and the type of program you become involved in.

Benefits—The high pay is a benefit. Lifeguards are able to have a good-paying job in the summer and go to school in the winter. It's outdoors, in a healthy environment with healthy co-workers. Just about everyone at the beach has a love of the ocean and outdoors in common.

The idea of saving a life is a very rewarding one. We make approximately 10,000 rescues a year here, with up to 40 rescues at one tower on a hard day. When you look back on a day's work and think about the fact that you made 10 or 20 rescues, it's very rewarding. It's also gratifying to participate in public education and work with children. A lot of lifeguards end up with skills they didn't have when they came aboard as a rookie.

Pay—An ocean lifeguard here makes $14.15 an hour starting pay. If they were to have an Emergency Medical Technician certification, they would start at $15. There are five pay steps, with 200-hour increments. You top out at $17.53. The Lifeguard Association negotiates the pay for lifeguards, so they are usually compensated fairly. Your location and level of responsibility have a lot to do with it, too. In Tucson, Arizona, lifeguards start at $5.59 an hour. We're at the top of the ladder.

Our lifeguards also accrue sick time. They receive eight hours of sick time credit for every 176 hours they work. They're provided with uniforms, and if they work 180 full days in a year they're provided with equipment, wetsuits and full uniforms.

Negatives—It's weekend and holiday work, primarily. If you have a lot of social activity, it might not be the job you want. The hours are long, overtime is common, and you're dealing with very large crowds of people. You're working when everyone else is playing. We do not recommend doing a lot of socializing on the job, because a lifeguard's job is to watch what's going on in the water at all times.

Lifeguards do get a lot of sun exposure, although they are provided with hats and sun protection. Fair-skinned people could have a problem. There's also the possibility of exposure to communicable diseases with so many people around, and at times environmental conditions, such as high winds, rocks or cold water can be hazardous.

The future—I think that in the U.S., the loss of life by drowning is considered a highly preventable occurrence, and if lifeguards are present, it can be prevented. They're not a mandated service like policemen, and it's possible that lifeguard services could eventually be hit with curtailment, but in an area with warm temperatures and a beachgoing public, I would think that the market would remain fairly stable.

Career Case Study

Mark Williams, Arizona

Mark Williams has been a lifeguard since 1968. He is the pool manager at Cactus Park Pool in Phoenix, Arizona in the summer, and a biology teacher in the winter months. Mark enjoys camping, raising snakes, and collecting sports cards. He lives with his wife and three children in Peoria, Arizona.

Requirements—The requirements vary from place to place, but at a minimum you have to have certification in life-guard training, standard first aid skills, and CPR training. It's a physically demanding job, so you need to be in reasonably good shape and continue to stay in shape, but you don't have to be a bodybuilder or marathon runner. You also need to have reasonably decent writing skills, because if an incident should occur, you have to be able to record and describe it clearly and accurately.

You need to be very people-oriented. You need to be polite, yet assertive enough to get your point across when necessary. You basically need to be a one-person public relations program. You want people to come to your pool, but you want to emphasize the safety factor as well. Lifeguards are looked at by the public as suntanned blonds leaning back in their chairs, having a good time. But in reality it's a very high-stress job. You carry a high level of responsibility, because lives may be lost if you don't do your job.

Prospects—It depends on the area you're in and the type of pool program it has. There is also quite a difference between beach lifeguarding and pool lifeguarding. Here in the Phoenix area, we cannot even get close to the supply of lifeguards for the demand we have. Our season runs from May through September, and since we generally tend to employ students, we start losing people around the beginning of August, just before school starts. It's really hard to keep them. This is an excellent job for young people, and the opportunities are there for the taking in a lot of places.

Benefits—It's a chance to work with really good, active, energetic young people. There's a lot of reward in being able to maintain your skills and do your job well. Teaching swim lessons, which a lot of lifeguards do, is extremely rewarding. I teach three- and four-year-old kids, and when I see them get to a point where they can get out of the pool themselves, it's a real thrill.

It is a good job if you like being outside in the sun. And you're dealing with a recreation program, so most of the people around you are in a positive mood.

Pay—Private lifeguards make well over minimum wage. Here in Phoenix, a beginning lifeguard makes $7.11 per hour. That's not bad for a high school kid. Once they get to the point where they can teach swim lessons, they make $7.42. A management position, which takes about two years to achieve, pays $8.51, and a pool manager makes $9.75.

Negatives—There is a certain lack of respect from the public. Lifeguards are not mindless blond hunks who sit in a chair. There's a big responsibility to this job, and there is a lot of stress involved. You can get really burned out if you're in a busy location. Skin cancer is a possibility; you always have to wear sunscreen. You also have to be very conscious healthwise; little kids do cut themselves at pools and you have to be aware of the dangers of hepatitis, AIDS, and other diseases. We have gloves, masks, the whole deal. That didn't used to be a factor at all, but it's a big problem now.

The future—I think it's only going to get better. Recreation is continuing to go up, and lifeguarding as a whole is becoming more professional and standardized. The level of quality has risen substantially. Twenty-five years ago it was, quite honestly, a mindless-stud-type of profession, but now lifeguards are required to be well-trained, well-qualified people. I think it's being taken more seriously, and instruction is becoming more a part of the job than it used to be, which opens up new realms.

Reference

American Red Cross, Health and Safety Services, 8111 Gatehouse Road, Falls Church, VA 22042; (703) 206-7180.

YWCA-USA, 726 Broadway Avenue, New York, NY 10003; (212) 614-2700.

Lodge Owner

Dreams—What a vision: an idyllic setting along a lake, log cabins with wood stoves, a nearby dock with boats, a lodge with a rock fireplace, tackle shop, and a long dinner table loaded with savory delights every meal. You get a summer-long vacation directing it all, telling yarns at night, guiding by day, with your family or employees doing all the work.

Nightmares—You tried to cut costs, but all you got is a cook that turns out chili, a family that works all the time and is ready to mutiny over it, cabins that are cold, boats that leak, and engines that don't start. Plus, your guests expect you to fix everything, and worse, blame you when they don't catch big fish. Then your mate asks, "How come we're not making all that money you predicted?"

Realities—Planning is everything. No minutia is too small. Projections for costs are critical, and so is an eye for quality at every juncture. The ideal owner is a handyman, an accountant, a travel planner and a guide, and has a mate who can cook or who knows how to hire a good one. Do that and you make $40,000 to $50,000 and more in a four or five-month season—usually in a dream-like setting.

What it's all about—Lodge owners have a saying among themselves that vacationers never hear: "People want to be stupid on vacations." Your job, as lodge owner, is to allow them to be.

You see, there are two ways to take a vacation: A) Do it yourself. B) Pay someone else to do it for you. When someone books a vacation at a lodge, they are opting for Plan B. Lodge owners provide everything, sometimes do everything, and are paid well in the bargain. They allow vacationers to be stupid, or in other words, to never have to think about anything. For many people, particularly those that work and think smart all the time, that is what a real vacation is all about. To be stupid. How wonderful.

So from start to finish, from door-to-door, you do all the thinking for them. The primary duties include providing a comfortable place to sleep, all meals, equipment, licenses, and if necessary, boats, motors, airplanes (such as a float plane trip to a remote destination) and guides.

The duties can also include arranging airline tickets, though some lodge owners shy away from this because it can balloon the overall price of a trip package and scare away prospects. Others figure including airline tickets is a way to add some bonus profit, since some airlines are willing to provide reduced ticket prices to lodge owners who arrange for blocks of tickets, week after week, for a summer.

So that's the job. Simple enough, eh? Position your lodge on the edge of a beautiful lake or stream in a remote location where the fishing and hunting is the best in the world, then hire maids to take care of the rooms, a cook for the meals, a travel agent for the flight tickets, a repair specialist for the boat motors, maybe a fishing and hunting expert to set up a small in-house tackle shop, a gardener to keep up the appearance of the place, and you're in business, right? Well, that's the vision that never quite comes around.

The reason, you find out soon enough, is that employees are like money siphons. Most operations aren't big enough to handle many siphons before emptying the money well. So in response, you—and your family—start doing things yourself. These are the operations that work best. The way it often works out is that the wife is the cook, the husband is the chief guide, repair specialist and travel agent. The daughter is the maid. The son runs the tackle shop and is the gardener. This is the best way to start out. If you go the other route, hiring a team of seasonal employees, you better be a wizard at figures and accounting, because a high overhead makes for a fine line between profit and loss.

Of course, your location must be in a preeminent setting, and ideally, one that is not too expensive to reach. That is why Canadian lodges often do better than those in Alaska, because the price of a trip to Canada is often only one-quarter of what a similar trip to Alaska costs, because of the differences in travel and lodge expenses. But you must be able to offer first-class fishing and hunting, with an option for other adventures, such as hiking, canoeing or exploring unique natural attractions, such as waterfalls or glacial or geologic formations.

Always remember your motto, "People want to be stupid on vacations." That means you not only lead them by the hand, but that everything is quality. The bedsheets should always be clean, the food always sumptuous, abundant and varied, the boat motors should always start on the first pull, and all the lodge employees should be nice people, willing to listen to the vacationers brag about themselves. Smiling and nodding can work wonders.

To get in to this business, you are best off buying an existing operation. A seasonal lodge that can handle about 10 people per week, is set in a remote area, and comes equipped with boats, costs in the $250,000 to $350,000 range. The cost goes up appropriately according to size of operation, number of outbuildings (cabins, repair shops) and potential earnings. Most lodge owners make about $40,000 to $60,000 per year over a relatively short summer season, usually spanning from June though September.

During that period, they will work every day with very long hours (the sun is often up for 16 to 20 hours in the far north), but usually be surrounded by family, and if they double as a guide, fish and hunt whenever they want. In the winter, lodge owners always work the big sports shows in cities in order to attract guests for the summer, and these shows are a real grind.

The other route is the do-it-yourself approach. That is where you buy a patch of land along a lake, build a lodge, some log cabins, an ice house, smoke house, pumphouse and woodshed, then outfit it with boats, tackle, and the works, and hire employees to work it. If this sounds good, well, you had better be a carpenter and an accountant—a carpenter to construct the buildings, because otherwise it will cost you a fortune to hire a foreman, and an accountant because you will need to know where every nickel is going, and there will be a lot of nickels.

The concept of owning a lodge is very attractive, however, particularly for someone who has already made it in another venture and has some side money to sink into a lodge. It can provide a great vacation getaway for yourself as well as for your customers, a tax write-off, and a unique way of life for a few months of every year, a profitable one at that. It is not a retirement job, however, unless you are willing to hire a full-time general manager (and there goes most of the profit). Another bonus is that many lodge owners will trade trips with other lodges—"a week for two at my lodge in Canada in exchange for a week for two at your lodge in Costa Rica."

In addition, the future looks very bright for lodges. That's because there are more and more people living in cities who work very hard most of the year, earning very good money in the process. They work so hard—and miss out on so much adventure—that they are willing to pay high amounts for a quality trip with good fishing in a pristine location where everything is done for them. The group of people who desire this is growing every year. All they want, you will discover, is to be stupid for a week.

Career Case Study

Richard Haavik, Canada—Richard Haavik and his family have owned Rainbow Lodge at Nimpo Lake, British Columbia, since 1972. Richard and wife Coleen have run the business since the late 1970s. His prior experience includes working as a guide for various lodges and on charter boats of the coast of Canada. He enjoys hunting and fishing, hiking, bird watching and flower identification. Richard and Coleen and their two children live at the lodge during the season.

Requirements—Before getting into a business like this, you should work for someone else. If you haven't grown up with a family in the business, take the time to work at a couple of different lodges. You'll have the opportunity to learn the pros and cons of each business, the drawbacks and advantages to smaller versus larger businesses. You should get some guide experience as well.

Education is a negotiable point. Any education is going to be advantageous. You have to consider your clients' level of education as well as yours. The more you know, the easier it's going to be to communicate with them. If you have no or limited education, your business may be limited because you'll have a hard time relating to your clients. You'll reach a point of stagnation. On the other hand, a guy who's from the bush will entertain his clients simply with his personality and character. It's not black and white; it just depends on the individual and situation.

It is important to have a basic knowledge of accounting and business communication. For instance, it looks much more professional to send a letter that's been typed up and printed on a computer than one that's scrawled all over a piece of paper. The biggest mistake I see people make is that they don't start out with enough capital. It's pretty tough to start up right out of the blue, and it takes a few years to get settled. If you're not prepared for all the costs that come up—building, buying equipment, repairs, advertising—it's very likely that you'll fail.

If you're married, you need to make sure that you and your spouse both want to live the lifestyle. If one of you loves the wilderness and the other one is a city person, you're both going to be miserable.

Prospects—In some areas there's lots of competition, and in some areas there's none. It depends on where you are and how remote you want to be. Remember that if you're in a remote area, your start-up capital and your overhead are going to be extremely high because of the difficulty in reaching your location. You should definitely explore the area you're looking at—find a need and fill it. You don't want to start a business where no one's interested in fishing.

The market really fluctuates. It can go for years, when the economy's booming, where every place is filled all season long. Then there are times when money is tight and people are doing other things. It's really dependent on the economy. When you're just starting out, you have to have an off-season job to support yourself.

Benefits—The rewards are in being your own boss and experiencing the self-satisfaction of seeing the concrete results of your labor. If you're successful, the reward is not just financial. You're able to spend a lot of time with your spouse and family. You may not always have a lot of time to actually be with them during the day, but they're always around. During the winter, you have a lot of time off.

Pay—Your profit depends on the size of your operation. We usually sell package deals, which are $1,275 per person for six days, including air fare, lodging, meals, boat and motor, everything. The standard lodge rate is $100 per person per day. If we had 12 people here on the lake every day, we could make a lot of money. You have to decide whether you want to run that kind of business and if you can get the clients. At an average family-run lodge, a couple can make an income in the $50,000 range. Some do much better; some people wish they could do that much—there are many variables. But you can't really look at it in terms of money. It's a way of life.

The business provides for your home, your vehicles and your food. If you have a year-round operation, your living expenses are taken care of all year. All you need is fun money. It's comparable to farming—you don't make a lot of money, but how do you put a monetary value on living what you like to do?

Negatives—You have to be willing to work seven days a week, 15 or 16 hours a day, and be suited to working 100 or 120 days without a day off. Where we are, it is 200 miles to the nearest town, and there's no air service, so the only way to get there is by driving on a long dirt road. You have to like being in a remote location, because typically, even lodges located close to cities can only be reached by boat or plane.

You're dealing with many different types of people, and they can sometimes get on your nerves. They're there day in, day out, and that's something you have to deal with in your family as well.

The future—I think the future looks excellent. There's definitely a market out there; people have more leisure time, they're healthier, and they're starting to reap the benefits of their early retirement plans. They're looking for new places to go. A lot of people have been to Hawaii and the other resort-type places, and we offer a more rustic atmosphere.

People are interested in the wilderness, in natural beauty and history, and businesses who cater to that, who offer a variety of activities, are going to attract a more diverse clientele and be more successful. Another success tool that a lot of lodges take advantage of is the package deals like the ones we offer. We package everything for them so they don't have to worry about getting plane reservations or renting a car. People who are busy don't want to have to worry about anything when they're on vacation. They want to have a brainless trip.

Career Case Study

Kirsten Dixon, Alaska—Kirsten Dixon and her husband Carl have owned River Song Lodge in Alaska since 1982. She is an accomplished chef and the author of "River Song Lodge Cookbook." Kirsten, her husband and their two daughters live at the lodge in a remote area near Anchorage, Alaska.

Requirements—The first is location, which has to be very well thought out. You have to consider how expensive it is, how remote it is, and how many bad weather days you are looking at. There might be fog 30 out of 40 days, which makes it difficult if you rely on airplanes for transportation. It's important to look at the long-term integrity of your plan.

It's also important to look at the competition. You have to determine whether the area can survive the addition of another lodge. Decide on your niche—what's going to make your lodge special in comparison to your competition. You're usually dealing with a high-end clientele, and it's very competitive. You have to figure out your personal strength and capitalize on that. If you hate to cook and garden and you focus on offering service that's dependent on it, you're going to be miserable. I don't like to hunt, so we don't offer any hunting services at all. But I do love to cook, so we specialize in serving great food.

An owner/operator-type lodge is different from one that's run by a corporation. It's so labor-intensive that someone who really cares has got to be there in order to make it work well.

Prospects—Somebody who is looking at this as a career is probably going to start on the small side. I think one of the best tips I could give is to learn something about business. And have a clear goal; even when we were a very tiny operation with only four guests at a time, we envisioned where we wanted to be and acted as such. For example, I joined the World Trade Center, which my husband teased me about. But we got a lot of business from that. You can glean small pearls from organizations like that.

I think it is important to decide what kind of lodge you want to be and outline that clearly from the start. The worldwide fishing community is very large, but there are probably only a handful of real quality fishing lodges around. Fishermen tend to make only a few trips a year, so most lodges concentrate on being competitive, and the competition is very stiff.

We didn't know anything when we started out, and I think that naivete actually really helped us. We didn't worry about the competition; we just went with what seemed to be the best move at the time. In our scenario, my husband is extremely personable, and I like to cook, so we gained a reputation for being a friendly lodge with great food. I think that's the key—to find one specialized aspect that you can excel at and concentrate on it. One of our competitors focuses on flyfishing, another focuses on natural history. I personally think that good food is a good way to go because you can control it, unlike weather and fishing.

Benefits—Certainly being in business for yourself is a great freedom. When we bought this business, we bought time. I used to work as a nurse, and I'd go to work at 6 a.m. and come home after 7 p.m., and I just didn't love the job enough to make it worth it. What I do now is so enjoyable to me that it's hardly like work. It's the way I live my life and it's never a hardship. We meet people from all over the world, and since we're in such close quarters, we get to know them and befriend them. It's a very enriching opportunity.

Pay—The money can fluctuate wildly depending on location and personal management style. The potential is unlimited. We have a gross profit of about 30 percent of our business per year, but I'm sure if we were running the same business outside of Los Angeles or somewhere, growth would be much different. I'm sure people in Iowa don't have the same tourism situation that we do. As owners and managers of our business, we don't take actual salaries. We pay our expenses and put our profits back into the business. Our employees, however, average about $1,000 a month, plus room and board. If someone were to work solely as a manager, I would expect they'd make a salary of $2,000 a month and up, plus benefits and maybe profit sharing.

Negatives—One drawback is that most great lodges have a location that makes access physically difficult. We have to fly in our guests and our supplies; there are no stores nearby, so we have to be much more responsible for ourselves as far as planning goes. When guests stay with us, our operation becomes very labor-intensive; our guests are constantly here because there is simply nowhere else to go.

A lot of lodge owners think that's a nightmare because of the demand on their time, but that depends on your perspective, I guess. One piece of advice I would give is to hire as many employees as you can afford in order to avoid burnout.

The future—Any business that is dependent on a natural resource that is potentially threatened is risky; that is a reality that won't go away. You just have to look at that optimistically. People say, "The fishing in Alaska was so much better 50 years ago," but we keep the attitude that we're going to take what we have now and do the best that we can. As the world becomes a busier, more crowded place, more people will look for activities that take them closer to the outdoors. As long as there are people who are willing to do their part to keep the integrity in the business, the business will continue to grow.

References

High Country Tourist Association, 1490 #2 Pearson Place, Kamloops, BC Canada V1S1J9; (604) 372-7770. This organization can supply listings for many fishing camps and resorts.

International Sportsmen's Exposition, P.O. Box 2569, Vancouver, WA 98668-2569; (206) 693-3700.

Lodge Seasonal Employee

Dreams—The vision is of superlative sunsets and a soft workload (after all, everybody here is on a joy ride). You're generally having the time of your life. You laugh as you envision your friends back home making tacos. Not you—you just sit on the deck of your cabin, sip your Pepsi, and figure, "After a few hours of cleaning up around here, maybe I'll go out skinny dipping in the afternoon with that new cook."

Nightmares—Your boss is on your case, then when you say "Cool out, dude," you're assigned toilet cleaning detail. Seems like the boss wants a lot for the low pay, like working all day, working weekends and general perfection. "What's with all the work? When does the fun start?" You'd never admit it to anybody, but you're actually homesick.

Realities—This is a job, not a vacation, but the employees who work hard and get their tasks completed as requested will have enough down time to play a bit. The base pay is poor, but at the more exotic lodges, the tips make up for it. The natural splendor of the locations is virtually unmatched.

What it's all about—Work is a summer curse for many young adults. If the question, "What are you going to do for the summer?" doesn't echo around the back of your mind all spring, it will instead rattle off the walls of where you live—out of the mouths of your parents.
    Considering how much time is spent at a job, even a part-time

job, it's hard to believe how little time is spent preparing and searching for one. This is especially the case with young adults, who often fall into summer employment by complete accident and some luck, rather than choice.

Well, there is another way, and it beats the heck out of flipping burgers or making tacos. There are thousands of lodges and resorts in magnificent settings across North America that have the need for seasonal help to perform a wide variety of tasks. Consider the options: They need people to clean the rooms, change the sheets, do the laundry, mow the lawn, trim the hedges, get the boats gassed and readied, serve dinner, clean dishes, sweep out the lodge, buy supplies, clean the windows, sell gifts, arrange the fishing tackle, clean fish, box fish, smoke fish, get the ice, clean the boats, pick up litter, and run to town because somebody forget something. Get the picture?

All the things it takes to both run a home and go on vacation, it takes to run a lodge. If you make it known that you can fill these needs, you can end up with a job where the view is of a beautiful lake, seashore or mountain range instead of a thickly-greased metal grill filled with frozen burger patties.

A seasonal worker for a lodge faces many pluses and minuses, of course. On the plus side, it is much less difficult to get a position working for a lodge than it is for a national or state park. (Park jobs are always in demand as glamour jobs.) Since all lodges are set at vacation destinations, you will live in a beautiful setting. In addition, there is likely to be a wide variety of recreational outlets available during your off-time.

Most lodges also have enough employees so that a special spirit of comradeship develops among the summer crew, and close friendships are often made in the process. Finally, working at a lodge provides a chance for young adults to be away from home, making their own way for a while. For many it is the first chance in their lives at complete autonomy.

The down side is shorter. Start with the pay. Though it is better than what your local burger flipper makes, it usually ranges from just $5 to $6 per hour. It can be more if tips are available. You almost always work weekends. Because you are away from home, it can be more difficult to quit a lodge job than a job near home, because mom and dad won't be around to pick up the pieces. So if you don't like the job you've been assigned, too bad—you have to grind it out as best possible.

There can also be a paradox about the getting-away-from-home compulsion that strikes some young adults. Many young people chomp at the bit to leave the homefront, like a race horse making a bolt out of the starting gate, then when finally away, they get so homesick they're like lonely doggies howling at the moon.

So the pluses outweigh the minuses, and compared to a more typical summer job at a grill, a lodge is a land of enchantment. There are two good ways to get on the inside track of one of these jobs.

One under-utilized strategy is to attend the winter sports shows in one of America's large cities, the big shows where hundreds of lodge owners will rent booths to provide displays, brochures and videos in order to attract vacationers for the summer season. As a prospective employee, you can shop your way through dozens of potential jobs at lodges in a few hours, often meeting directly with the owners. By the end of a day or two, you might have several good job offers, and have your pick of the best. With this approach, you have the best chance of garnering a position at one of the world-class lodges where vacationers pay $4,000 a week to visit. That means your summer will be at a location of unmatched beauty, and there will be the opportunity for bonus pay in the form of large tips from each week's stable of wealthy visitors.

Another approach is to select a lodge closer to where you live. Regardless of the proximity, it still takes the personal approach to get hired. The best way to start your search is with a chamber of commerce, which can provide a list of all resorts in a general area. You will then need to phone the lodge, ask if any positions are available, mail off your resume and photo, and follow that up with another phone call to arrange a personal visit and interview. If that sounds like too much trouble compared to getting a job as a burger flipper, well, then you might just be bound to end up as a burger flipper—and someone else will be sitting on a deck at some fabulous resort, watching the sun set each night.

The extra effort is always rewarded. You always get paid back, even though it might not be apparent immediately. What does not work is mailing off a crude, hand-written letter to some distant lodge and saying, "I'd like a job if one is around." You may not even get an answer to a presentation like that. It also doesn't work to call a lodge in the blind and say something like, "Got anything for me to do?"

Hey, you must give them a good reason to want you. A clean appearance and courteous manner count for plenty—why do you think Disneyland is such a success? Providing a brief resume of your education, any past jobs, and interests shows you are serious in your mission. Don't beg, whine or drag your tail, but at some time during the interview, look the lodge owner directly in the eye and say, "I really like your lodge and I want to work for you this summer." Those are magic words to the owner of a lodge.

Follow this prescription and you are apt to spend the summer working in one of North America's glorious retreats, get paid for it, have many great adventures, make new close friends, and happily know that it is your ambition, approach and follow-through that kept you from making tacos all summer.

Career Case Study

Melissa Dietrick, California   *Melissa Dietrick has worked at Lakeview Terrace Lodge as a seasonal cabin cleaner since April of 1992. She is married and has two children, and she enjoys horseback riding and spending time with her family. She lives in Lewiston, California.*

Requirements—For my job, there aren't many requirements besides a knowledge of basic housecleaning. The job is pretty simple; I clean the lodge's cabins, offices and restrooms. Even though this is a fairly big operation for this area—there are 17 cabins as well as a large area for RV hookups—there are not many employees. My only duties are cleaning; I rarely have to deal with guests at all.

Prospects—It's not really competitive around here because we're in such a small community. Most of the people hired for seasonal jobs like these are high school kids on summer vacation. It's a good job to have to earn extra money, and the work is pretty basic.

I got the job by answering an ad in the newspaper. I'd say if you want to work at a resort like this, just find an area you like and start calling lodges to see if they're hiring. There are lots of these places around.

Benefits—I love the area I work in. The cabins overlook the lake, and often you can see the deer outside feeding. The people I work for are good people, too; they're very enjoyable to be around. I come in the morning, pick up my supplies and see what needs to be done, and I go do it. I can do my own thing at my own pace; there's nobody breathing down my neck. There are a lot of interesting people who stay at the lodge, too. Quite a few of them come back every year and you get to know them pretty well after a while.

Pay—Most lodges pay anywhere from minimum wage to $5 an hour. I started out at $5 three months ago and I've had two raises since then. I think if you do a good job and do what's expected of you, you can make a good wage, considering the work you're doing, but I don't think you'd want to try to raise a family on it. I usually only work between eight to ten hours a week. The most I've ever worked in a three-week period was 38 hours.

Negatives—Sometimes I have to work on Saturdays and Sundays, which isn't much fun. I'd rather have my weekends off to spend with my husband and kids. It's hard to look out the window and see everybody down at the lake having a good time when you're stuck inside cleaning. When it's hot, you get tired out fast. Half of the cabins are bigger than my house, and sweeping for an hour straight can get very tiring.

The future—I have noticed a lot more people coming up here on fishing trips before the summer season really starts than in past years, and there are definitely more people here in the summer than there used to be. We fill up fast. I think there should be more places like this available.

Career Case Study

Shiloh MacCabe, Alaska

Shiloh MacCabe works seasonally at Chelatna Lake Lodge in Alaska. She has worked at other lodges in Alaska, including one at Katmai National Monument, while attending the University of Alaska in Anchorage. Shiloh enjoys reading, writing, flying, music, and all outdoor activities.

Requirements—You don't really need any kind of formal education. We're all pretty versatile in our abilities, and it's mostly manual labor. We take turns loading planes and cooking and cleaning. We serve meals to the guests and crew, do laundry, make beds, clean, split wood, haul fuel, clean fish, do maintenance and repair work. Being physically fit is pretty much required. You live here as well as work here, so you have to be tolerant of people, the people you work with as well as the guests. In the real world, you can go to work and go home at night, but here it's all intertwined. A love for the outdoors is good to have because you're exposed to it all the time. Some lodges are in town, but a lot of them, especially here in Alaska, are way out in the boonies. You have to be able to appreciate your surroundings.

Prospects—That really depends on where you are. Some lodges have a lot of turnover and some have a staff that comes back every year. Most lodges have a lot of return staff, especially if they're small operations.

You have to apply yourself if you want a job. You can't just go in to someone's office and say, "I want to work for you." They want to talk to you and find out what kind of qualifications you have. It's always good to be qualified in CPR or other medical training. That will definitely be looked upon as an asset. You'll also probably have a better chance if you're from the area. It can be kind of hard to get a position out of state, although some people are hired through the mail. This job is optimum for college students; it starts in June and ends around the end of September. It's a great way to earn some money to get through the winter.

Benefits—I love this job because I love the outdoors. I love to fish, and I get to fish at least once a week, and there are all kinds of things to do: swimming, canoeing, hiking.

I really like to meet people from all walks of life. We get people who have saved and scrimped for months because they really wanted to go to Alaska, and this is their dream trip. And then you get the rich corporate guys who bring their company buddies and tear up the place. It's really good to be able to offer such personalized service, because we get to know the people who stay here better.

Pay—Again, it depends on the lodge and its location, but I would say the beginning wage for an inexperienced person who had never been in a lodge would be between $1,000 to $1,100 a month, plus tips. Each summer you return you'll make about $50 to $100 more. Tips are usually pretty good. We suggest five to fifteen percent at this lodge, but that varies. I remember one group that stayed three days at a lodge I used to work at, and they tipped each of us $400. But that doesn't happen very often.

Here we split the tips between all the employees, except for personal tips. A lot of the fishing guides and pilots are tipped personally for going the extra mile, like paying special attention and helping someone on the river or flying over an area one more time so people can take pictures of a moose.

Negatives—It gets a little tough and stressful and lonely, especially if you're a single person. You lose contact with the people in town and you can feel really isolated sometimes. A lot of lodges hire couples to avoid people who want to go back and forth to see their mate. We do run into difficult guests sometimes. There are people who expect you to wait on them hand and foot and be there just to serve them, and they can be really rude. Some people really get loose with their tongues. The only thing you can do is smile and accommodate them to the best of your ability. Some people bring their children with them, and they're almost always rowdy, obnoxious, and have no manners. It can be a real pain when you're trying to serve dinner and they're bouncing all over the walls and getting their hands all over the windows.

The future—I think this field will be around for a while. It's a good recreation option, and people seem to want to do more things that are related to the outdoors. As long as those people are around, lodges will be around.

References

High Country Tourist Association, 1490 #2 Pearson Place, Kamloops, BC Canada V1S1J9; (604) 372-7770. This organization can supply listings for many fishing camps and resorts.

International Sportsmen's Exposition, P.O. Box 2569, Vancouver, WA 98668-2569; (360) 693-3700 or (800) 545-6100.

Lookout Tower Spotter

Dreams—A lookout tower spotter has a life of ease and grace in a wilderness setting, living in complete peace—nobody around at all to bug them—while they watch for forest fires and enjoy nature. In their spare time, they can write books, play music, maybe paint, or just enjoy watching the days pass by.

Nightmares—If you have a touch of Jack Nicholson in you, a lookout tower is not the place to discover it. If you get a position where you are completely isolated from other human contact for weeks, you might go stark-raving mad. You say you're an artist? Well, you are more likely to turn into a nut case than a Rembrandt.

Realities—For the self-starter, it is a rare two-for-one offer. You do the primary job, pinpointing where lightning strikes start forest fires, but in the meantime have time for any creative outlets. But for someone who needs a jumpstart to get going, such a position can be a disaster. The loneliness can cut right to the heart, and after a month or so, you'll realize why few spotters last more than a summer or two.

What it's all about—You better like yourself plenty before you agree to set up shop in a lookout tower, because there are long sieges when there will be no one else around. Not just hours, mind you, and not just days, but sometimes weeks with just a scarce few visitors, and perhaps a rare food drop from a helicopter.

Some people go loony with that kind of isolation, regardless of the beauty of the surroundings or the challenge of the duties. But if you like the company—yourself—this job as a spotter can be easy, fun, rewarding, and provide the time for creative work, perhaps to write a novel, poetry, songs, or work on paintings. But that goes only if you draw your inspiration from within. Because if you need outside stimulus to jumpstart your creative passions, you might be ready for a frontal lobotomy, not a book contract, after a few weeks of solitude in a lookout tower.

Yet the job is absolutely vital and carries with it great responsibility. Lookout towers are positioned in forest country on mountain tops, from which a spotter can view a vast array of wildlands. It is up to the spotter to survey the surrounding forest for fires (usually caused by lightning strikes), pinpoint the exact coordinates of the fire, then radio those coordinates to headquarters, which dispatches a firefighting team. The faster the team is on top of the fire, the less chance there is of a lightning strike evolving into a devastating forest inferno. The key person in the entire chain is the spotter.

Most of the active lookout towers are located in the northwestern United States and southwest Canada, while many of the towers in the mountain country of the east have been converted over to tourist attractions. At these towers, volunteers work as hosts to greet visitors attracted by the chance of a memorable vista. At the active towers, spotters are paid, but not paid much, often minimum wage. But with the free time available, the creative can parlay the time and a special interest into projects.

The people who you most often find in this job are women hoping for a career in forestry or writing (using the spare time to work on personal projects), or retired people who like the idea of watching the days pass by slowly.

The lookout tower itself is usually a square structure on stilts, with the tower set up with huge windows for walls. In the center of the tower is a device called a fire locator. You can determine precise coordinates of a fire by pointing one end of the locator at the fire, then looking through the sights to scope it in just right. It works like a range finder. After some practice (there is plenty of time for that), you get to where you can determine locations with razor-sharp precision, as well as learning the area's respective geography in extraordinary detail.

In a summer of blue skies, there can be unbelievable hours of down time. Then when a cumulus suddenly builds on a warm afternoon, a dry thunderstorm can send lightning bolts harpooning into trees, and start many small fires in a matter of minutes. When this occurs, it is mayhem for the spotter—and for the fire crews. Flight squadrons usually arrive first, and in the case of a potential holocaust, they are quickly followed by ground teams. It is the spotter who sets everything in motion.

In some situations, the spotter will live at the lookout tower, getting food drops via helicopter transport. In others, the spotter may be able to live in the nearest town, though that might require a long, slow drive of an hour or more over rough roads. If you get lonely, the drive is well worth it to have contact with another humanoid form.

Sometimes there is no choice. The spotter must live at the tower, and that can create unique scenarios. One story that is a legend among a small circle of foresters is a tale about an ambitious male helicopter pilot who was flying supplies to lookout towers. The guy would land his helicopter at each tower, then get out and deliver a week's worth of stocks to the spotter. In this particular route, all the spotters were young women, and after having not seen another person for a week, they would invite the pilot in to talk for awhile. Maybe about lightning.

The pilot lasted six weeks on the job and then quit to join the army, of all things. When he turned in his letter of resignation, he had lost 15 pounds, had deep, dark circles under his eyes and looked pale and drained, the picture of complete physical deterioration.

"What happened to him?" asked the district ranger.

"I don't know," answered a fire specialist, "but he said something about problems with the spotters at the lookout towers."

Career Case Study

Bonnie Seidel, California—Bonnie Seidel has worked at the U.S. Forest Service Black Fox Mountain lookout tower since 1988. She previously worked as a nurse's aide at a convalescent hospital. Bonnie, her husband and two children live in Redding, California. She enjoys photography, fishing and outdoor activities.

Requirements—The U.S. Forest Service requires you to have a practical knowledge of forestry procedures and the ability to operate the equipment in the tower. You have to be able to read a fire finder, which is a device that helps you figure out how to pinpoint the location of a fire. During a fire, you have to report information by radio: the conditions, wind changes, change in fire color, etc. You have to record and report daily weather readings and maintain the tower. You also have to greet and act as host to visitors who come by.

Prospects—Right now, due to the fact that there are so many cutbacks occurring in state and government agencies, many towers are being shut down. When job openings do occur, the first people who are offered them are the people who have been doing this for years, the ones with seniority. You never know from year to year if your tower is going to remain open.

I'd say most of the lookouts, at least the ones in northern California, are retired folks, although I know one woman who did it for 25 years before she retired. Quite often couples will be hired, so there's more than one person up there. It's mainly a summer job.

Benefits—It's so peaceful there, way up on the mountain. It's a seasonal job, usually from mid-May to October, and when my family and I aren't up there we live a very hectic life at home. We look forward every year to packing up and heading for the hills; it's almost like a vacation. We watch the birds and all the wildlife that comes through. We put out a salt block for the deer and go on nature walks; we go stargazing at night. The sunrises and sunsets are awesome. That's why we're there; it's not for the pay. It's also rewarding to know that you're helping to save the forest, and possibly lives and valuable property.

Pay—The pay isn't much. We're paid on the government grade scale; I think the highest you can go is GS 4, which ends up being around $7 an hour. We work 10 days on, then have 10 days off, which eliminates any overtime or Sunday deferential pay. Being a seasonal position, there are no benefits, but I think it's decent money for what you're required to do.

Negatives—I have two kids, so I don't get bored, but I'm sure that could set in if you were up here all alone. It can be really scary when lightning comes in. The tower is grounded on all four sides, luckily, but the trees right next to us were hit pretty hard one time. When a fire comes through, you sometimes have to work around the clock, and it can be exhausting.

The future—There's been quite a bit of controversy over the question of whether the towers are even necessary anymore. They've replaced a lot of them with these new automated weather stations and satellite cameras, but the argument is that automated weather stations can't spot fires as quickly as a person, and they can't save lives or property. The little piece of paper that the machine spits out doesn't tell you when the lightning strikes hit and the flames start. The government justifies the cutbacks with the excuse that they're trying to save money, but when you look at the sacrifices that are being made, they really don't appear to be saving anything. I really feel that the towers will be phased out, that they will be eliminated in the future.

Career Case Study

Roxy Metzler, Oregon—Roxy Metzler has worked as a part-time fire lookout off and on since 1962. During the fall and winter months she teaches high school English. Roxy enjoys art, music, reading, birdwatching, and painting china and porcelain. She is also active in environmental causes. She is married, has two children and two stepdaughters, and lives in Springfield, Oregon.

Requirements—Good eyesight is number one. You have to have the ability to read and understand certain mathematical information, and you need to have an understanding of weather and some knowledge of fire behavior, although extensive knowledge usually isn't required. There are some physical requirements; you have to be in general good health. I used to work at a station that required a mile's walk to reach, so I had to keep myself in fairly good condition.

You have to be able to deal well with being alone for long periods of time and have the ability to become self-directed. The job by nature forces you to be self-reliant and self-sufficient.

Prospects—Essentially, there are many more people who would like to have these jobs than there are jobs out there. But if a person really wanted to do it, they could. It might mean that they would have to volunteer for some time, earning only a stipend, which I think is about $15 a day. But that's the way a lot of lookouts are staffed, with volunteers. Some experience in forestry might help when looking for a job. A lot of lookouts are staffed by people who work in other areas of the Forest Service in the winter.

Benefits—I like the privacy, the peace and quiet, and being alone. I am a school teacher the rest of the year, and this is a complete and total change from my other career. I have the opportunity to enjoy the scenery, the fresh air, the wildlife. I love the woods, I always have, and this gives me the opportunity to enjoy them in a way that I never could otherwise. One of the advantages is being self-sufficient. In your own little way you're strictly your own boss. You have a certain schedule, with an itinerary and duties you're responsible for, but you get to do everything at your own pace. I get to do things that are very different from my activities the rest of year, like working on the building, and it provides a nice balance.

Pay—I think the going rate now is about $7 an hour. Depending on the national forest, some people are employees of the Forest Service and others are hired on a contract basis. The contract workers tend to make pretty good money. Within the Forest Service, you're limited to the government grade scale system.

The money you make at a lookout is probably better than a typical part-time job. I'm 50 years old, and this is something that I can do that deals with the outdoors and makes a little money. Other Forest Service positions pay more, of course, but I make more than a lot of part-timers.

Negatives—Personally, due to the seasonal schedules of my careers, I basically have no vacation. I go from teaching straight to the lookout, then right back to school in the fall. You're kind of stuck there. I can hike to the river, go for walks in the evenings, and go down to the lake, but I really can't get away to do some of the things I'd like to do. I'm fairly confined to this area. It can be frustrating; for instance, there's an art show that I've been wanting to see all summer, but I haven't been able to get there. I can't attend any of the cultural events that I would normally go to because I'm obligated to stay at the lookout.

It can be lonely, depending on what's happening in your life at the time. You really miss your family. I have a daughter that I haven't seen all summer, and two sisters that I never seem to be able to get together with. Unless they come to see you, you don't get to see or be with your friends and family much.

The future—I think the market is probably going to stay the way it is. I can't tell you what the rest of the nation is like, but lookouts are definitely not being phased out in northwestern Oregon. The number of staffed lookouts here has actually increased because they're so cheap to run. The salary they pay us is a small pittance compared to what they have to pay for airplanes and other types of detection devices.

I think that may not be as accurate in the east, where they don't have the large areas of unpopulated realm that we do. Timber is a very high-value resource here in the west, and its protection is critical. Although I think they're through phasing out lookouts in most areas, it's still an extremely limited field. There just aren't a large number of positions available. But I think that, as with just about any career, if a person is absolutely determined to do it, they could.

References

The National Historic Lookout Register, sponsored by the American Resources Group, 374 Maple Avenue East, Suite 210, Vienna, VA 22180; (703) 255-2700.

California Department of Forestry & Fire Protection, 1416 9th Street, PO Box 944246, Sacramento, CA 94244-2460; (916) 653-7772.

Massachusetts Division of Forest & Parks, 100 Cambridge Street, Boston, MA 02202; (617) 727-3180.

US Forest Service, 740 Simms Street, Golden, CO 80401; (303) 275-5350 for fax (303) 275-5671.

Marine Patrol

Dreams—You get to catch the bad guys. Whoo-ya! What a job, with plenty of time on the water, protecting resources and using your smarts for detective work and seamanship. The job is one of the most independent of any government position, providing a rare combination of autonomy and secure pay.

Nightmares—The bad guys get away, and nothing matches that for a zero. Except when you catch them and the court system throws them back on the water as if they were too small a fish. Then there are equipment and support problems: The boat leaks, the motor doesn't start, your boss doesn't seem to care and won't pay any overtime to help you catch the fish pirates.

Realities—This job requires the best you can offer, including brain power, physical strength, and plenty of psychology. In return, you get the independence the comes from patrolling the sea, plus excitement from detective work and satisfaction from nailing the guilty. Insider's tip: There is a lot of competition, so you must be well prepared to get hired.

What it's all about—At 10 knots aboard the patrol boat, you pilot an invisible course through fog, watching the little green blip on the radar screen. "There it is," you announce, staring into the scope. "That's the boat! About 200 yards away."

You cut the throttle of the patrol boat, slowing and gliding quietly through the ocean swells, approaching with complete stealth. Suddenly, just 40 feet in front of your bow, the outline of a boat appears in the fog. "Take over the controls," you order a mate. Then you run to the bow, and when the boats touch, you jump aboard, ready to draw your gun. Just in case.

"Everybody freeze!" you shout. "This is the Department of Fisheries! You are under arrest for gillnetting in a protected area! Nobody move! You are completely surrounded!"

The suspects comply. They are handcuffed and formally arrested, and then with your fellow marine patrol wardens, you search the boat and find illegal nets, several tons of illegally-caught fish, two automatic rifles, and a small amount of drugs. Everything is confiscated, including the boat, and taken to port. The suspects are booked in county jail.

This is the life of a marine patrol warden, the guardian of the coast, a unique individual who is part police officer, part sea wolf, and part of the collective public's conscience. It is a career that is exciting, fulfilling, confidence-inspiring, and can make heroes out of good stock. Every day is different, with a touch of danger adding a perpetual edge.

There are also intellectual and psychological challenges. Intellectual because you must be completely versed in fisheries and environmental law, seamanship and safety; psychological because you need just the right touch in dealing with your superiors (most of them bureaucrats), the public, and of course, suspected lawbreakers—all of whom are carrying knives or guns. The ability to write short reports is also a requisite, since every arrest includes a police-style account of the incident.

Of these elements, which do you think is the most important? The answer: None of them. There is another component which is much more important: Successful marine patrol wardens are linked by their passion for life. Of all the qualities you need, that is the most important. You either have it or you aren't suited for the job.

Everything else can be learned. You start the learning process by going to college and getting trained in law enforcement and marine biology or resources conservation. At the same time, you should study boating safety and navigation on your own and become proficient in both. It is also imperative that you be in good physical condition, and it is advisable to take physical fitness courses, such as running or weight training.

If it sounds like there are many requirements, you are right. This is a very attractive job, and if you are to land one, you must be at the top of your game in each of the categories: physical, intellectual and psychological. If you put it all together, you are presenting yourself as a prepared candidate who is difficult to turn down. Persistence and know-how can pay off.

Once established, marine patrol wardens top out near $40,000 per year, including overtime. They start closer to $24,000, then go up the ladder from there. The money is typical for most government professionals. What is not typical are the experiences you will get. After all, you will be on the water, on patrol, checking commercial fishing vessels, sport anglers, and keeping an eye on marine species of all types. You are the guardian of the sea, the heart behind the badge.

Of course, every job has its Grand Canyons, this one included. Most of these canyons have to do with politics, and the fact that the bureaucrats in decision-making positions are usually political appointees who have no concept of what you do or need on the job. As a result, there are times you don't get special equipment (like night scopes), overtime money (requisite for big busts), operating expenses for boats (they break), and office support in court (district attorneys often must be pressured to take your cases).

When you don't get backing from your superiors in these types of circumstances, this job can turn mighty lonely. When you bust somebody after a day of detective work and a five-hour stakeout, then watch the case get mishandled by a district attorney, the sense of futility is unbelievable.

While that happens, it is not the typical experience. For the most part, your work is honored and respected by both the public and your peers. Your days are spent on the sea, loving and protecting all of its many creatures. On days off, when somebody asks you what you do for a living, you answer, "I'm a marine patrol warden" and it makes you feel good inside. You should. For individuals with the passion for it, this is a great life.

Career Case Study

Bob Wright, California
Bob Wright has worked as a game warden since 1972, and since 1983 as a marine patrol specialist based in Monterey, California. He has a bachelor's degree from Chico State University. He enjoys hunting and catch-and-release saltwater fishing, scuba diving, waterskiing, basketball and softball. He is married, has a four-year-old son, and lives in Pleasant Hill, California.

Requirements—You must have at least 60 semester hours (two years) of college, with a major in biological science, police science, law enforcement, national resources conservation, ecology, or some related field. It really helps to have a four-year degree; that's what they're going to look for when you're being evaluated. You can technically take the required written test with a two-year degree, but then you have to go through an oral exam. Being able to tell them that you have a bachelor's degree shows that you've followed through and finished something. We have a new director now who's pushing for a four-year degree requisite, so I wouldn't be surprised if it is soon required.

As far as attitude is concerned, you have to be really good with people; you should be an outgoing person who can converse with people of all levels, from the very intelligent to those who are just getting by. You have to be easy-going as well as outgoing, and able to make people feel comfortable in your presence. You have to have the ability to handle yourself evenly in all types of situations, and be prepared for lots of ups and downs.

It's really important to stay in good physical condition. There's a lot of physical labor involved in marine patrol: you move nets and crab pots, pull in lines, seize heavy equipment. You're often moving from boat to boat, and that requires agility. It's very easy to be injured. I've seen a lot of careers ended by injuries. And as you get older you have to keep it up. Also, more women have been coming into the department, and they have to work really hard on the physical training in the academy, which is extremely rigorous and demanding, even for the most fit person.

Prospects—It's very competitive. When you apply, you take a written test, which is either pass or fail, and then you have an oral interview, where they rate you on a point system. Your scores are combined, and then you are placed on an eligibility list. Where you are on the list depends on how well you did.

I really want to emphasize here that any little extra thing you might know, any little bit of experience, can work in your favor. If you have a basic police officer standards and training certificate, a diving certificate, a first aid card, or are certified in CPR, if you've taken a basic law enforcement class at the local junior college, put it down. It might not seem very relevant at the time, but with such tight competition, one half or one point more can make the difference between you and a competitor. I would also emphasize the importance of hanging in there if you really want a job. Even when it seems hopeless, like you'll never make it, don't give up. I was on the eligibility list for two and a half years before I got in, and I never gave up, I always had hope.

The Fish and Game Department now has its own academy, and if you qualify and are accepted to it, putting yourself through could give you an edge in competition for a very limited number of jobs.

I would say the market, although competitive, is good right now for women. Fish and Game is looking for good, qualified women, and they have a good chance of getting in if they meet the qualifications. One thing to consider if you're an ambitious person is that there isn't much opportunity for advancement in this field. You can go up to patrol lieutenant, then to patrol captain, then to chief of patrol, but those positions don't open up very often. Someone who's a high achiever and wants to get to the top should realize that there's not much room. If you do get promoted, you most likely are going to have to relocate.

Benefits—The number one benefit for me is that I'm working in an environment that I love. The things that I'm checking out are things that I really enjoy and care about and have had a personal interest in my whole life. I consider the ocean the last frontier; there are still things in the ocean that haven't been damaged or exploited, and we can hold on to them and protect them. I take that very personally, and it's rewarding to be a part of that. I really like working alone. I get to make my own cases and I don't have a supervisor right over my back. You initiate a lot of your own work plans; you have a designated area to patrol, and you figure out how to work it. You don't have someone handing you a memo telling you what to do. It's rewarding to be independent.

Pay—After you take your tests, you technically start out as a cadet, and you'll make $2,075 to $2,469 per month. You're a cadet until you get through the academy, which lasts 20 weeks. You have to pass and graduate, and then you become a Range A warden, making $2,223 to $2,669. Next you go through a ten-week field training program, which is three four-week periods, and you have to pass each period with a different Field Training Officer (FTO). At that point you're a Range B warden, at $2,661 to $3,206.

After completing a year and a half of work, you can start a

physical maintenance program, where you are tested on physical agility once a year, and you can earn up to an extra $65 per month merit pay. There are other financial compensations. If you become certified with Fish and Game as a diver, you get $9 an hour dive pay above your salary. And under special circumstances, we do get overtime; money from special funds will occasionally be used to pay us overtime when we're concentrating on certain causes.

Negatives—You had better have a good, understanding relationship with your wife or husband, because you're on call 24 hours a day, seven days a week, even on your days off. You have to work a lot of unusual hours. We always work weekends and holidays, because that's when high volume activity occurs. The majority of my marine work is performed under the guise of darkness or fog. You're at the mercy of nature a lot of the time—you'll have to wait for a certain tide or certain conditions, early morning before the wind blows, for example. And it can take many, many hours to achieve your goals—anywhere from weeks to months to years to catch some of the guys. They're professionals, and they're good at what they do.

As wardens, we're basically specialized police officers. We have to know everything a police officer has to know and more. When enforcing the law, we run into other criminal activities besides wildlife-related offenses, and we often get into situations that you wouldn't imagine a Fish and Game warden would be dealing with. One time I boarded a boat to check things out and found ten and a half tons of marijuana. It's in situations like that where all your training comes up. There is a high degree of danger, and you have to combine your people skills with all the technical and physical skills you have.

The training you receive at the Fish and Game Academy is excellent, and you'd better learn it, because you will have occasion to use it, and one mistake can be the end. You have to be alert and professional at all times.

The future—I hate to say it, but I believe that our job description is going to change dramatically. I predict that a lot of the resources that we're working with today are not going to be as abundant in the years to come.

We're putting a lot of emphasis on pollution, environmental permits, regulation enforcement, etc. It's becoming less hands-on work and more paperwork. I see wardens becoming more of a human processor than a wildlife processor. I've noticed that at busy times, such as openers, we really have to patrol from a human aspect, covering huge areas containing large amounts of people. We're becoming environmental specialists and criminal law enforcers rather than wildlife protectors. The old image of what a Fish and Game warden does is just about gone; the real world is coming in slowly but surely.

Career Case Study

Sandy Dares, Louisiana—Sandy Dares is a captain in the enforcement division of the Louisiana Department of Wildlife and Fisheries, and has been with the department since 1981. He holds a BS degree in civil engineering, and his past work experience includes working as a civil engineer. He enjoys hunting, fishing, boating, camping and playing basketball. He is married, has two daughters, and lives in New Orleans, Louisiana.

Requirements—In Louisiana, all that's required is a driver's license and 60 hours of college credit. The college credit can be substituted with two years of full-time law enforcement work. You apply through the Louisiana Department of Civil Service.

You have to be a person who loves to be outdoors. Although we do have to handle paperwork, it's more of a patrol situation, and we're outside a good deal of the time. You have to be self-motivated, because you're not closely supervised. You're usually out in the middle of nowhere. If you take advantage of that and lay around, you're not going to be successful. There has to be a willingness to take responsibility, and most people with that quality are inherently independent and self-reliant. Overall, you just have to have a deep concern for and commitment to what you're doing.

Prospects—I think the job market is fairly stable. Most states haven't increased their forces recently, with the possible exception of Texas and Florida.

Here in Louisiana we've traditionally had a pretty high turnover rate. Over the past 10 years we've probably replaced about 50 percent of our men. There's a lot of competition. But a lot of guys who think they'd love the job because they love to hunt and fish are disillusioned. On opening day they're not out there hunting and fishing, they're patrolling. A lot of people, too, aren't cut out for law enforcement. They don't like giving tickets.

We've been getting a lot of very qualified applicants, particularly with the job market being on the decline. We look for a certain attitude more than experience, though. Some of our best agents are former outlaws, guys who took it as a challenge to break the laws and then were reformed. If those guys can turn around, they can be incredibly successful agents. They know all the tricks and they know their way around because they used to be on the side of the guys they're going after.

Benefits—The personal benefit is the satisfaction of outsmarting offenders, especially the guys who are serious about their violating, who are commercializing it and supplementing their income with it. You get a strong sense of accomplishment, knowing that you're preserving resources that will be there for future generations. And you're out in the outdoors. It's very rewarding to have a lot of freedom and flexibility, particularly on the coast, where you can work 20 days a month and do something different every day. We have decent retirement and insurance benefits. We are also provided with almost all the gear we need: uniforms, body armor, a vehicle or boat, camera, binoculars. It's also a pretty stable field, so you don't have to worry about job security.

Pay—Starting pay for an entry-level position is around $18,000 a year. After one year you're bumped up to about $19,000, and then, at the end of eighteen months, a senior agent position can move you up to around $21,000. The next position is sergeant, making $23,000 to $24,000, then lieutenant, at around $25,000, then captain, at $28,000 to $29,000.

Negatives—It all depends on how you look at it. You work most weekends and holidays, and lots of nights, but I see that as an advantage, because I'm out there when no one else is. I hunt and fish on my days off during the week. You've got to have a very flexible schedule, which a lot of the new guys don't like. We have to change our schedules as calls come in and so forth. There are times when you're taking your wife out to dinner and you get a call; that can be hard on your family life. There's a certain amount of stress that your wife and kids go through. You sometimes have to miss important events, like a kid's birthday party.

A lot of guys get discouraged because they take their job very seriously and are dedicated to enforcing the law, but they begin to find that not everybody else is so committed, particularly in the court systems. When the judges are dealing with murders and rapes and such, they don't always take wildlife offense cases too seriously. People don't often go to jail for wildlife violations, and that can be discouraging when you catch the same guys over and over. It's really discouraging to spend weeks or months going after a guy and then see him get nothing but a slap on the wrist, but you have to accept that it's not always going to go according to the way you think it should.

The future—I think the field has a strong future, because as long as there are a lot of fishing and boating activities around, the resources will need protection. And that shows no sign of slowing down.

There seems to be more of a trend toward marine patrol agents investigating accidents and participating in boat safety. These days, anyone with $8,000 or $10,000 can get a boat that can go 60 miles per hour and there are basically no regulations restricting them. I think more emphasis is going to be placed on that. I also think that a lot of states are going to start separating their water patrol forces and make them more specialized. They'll have teams of guys who only do boating safety work and they'll have strike forces and teams of covert people.

References

National Fish & Wildlife Foundation, 1120 Connecticut Avenue NW, Suite 900, Washington, D.C. 20036; (202) 857-0166.

National Marine Fisheries, 1315 East-West Highway, Silver Springs, MD 20910; (301) 713-2239.

California Maritime Academy, PO Box 1392, Vallejo, CA 94590; (707) 648-4222 or fax (707) 649-4773. E-mail: enroll@prop.csum.edu.

Mountain Climbing Guide

Dreams—There you are, on the peak of the mountain again with a team of adoring clients you have led to another successful ascent. You create "once-in-a-lifetime" memories every day of the climbing season, then get paid for it. You are an example of how to live life on the edge and beyond.

Nightmares—You hurt your knee, lightning bolts are striking all around you, a client falls into a crevice, and it starts raining. Nobody in the group likes your cooking or your jokes, so they mutiny and go home.

Realities—You must know your mountain, your craft and your clients, and that done, can make safe, exciting ascents and clear $100 a day or so. The greatest reward is savoring the climbing experience—all of it, not just the last few steps to the summit.

What it's all about—There's no faking it in the high country. You either know your stuff or you get squashed. After all, mountains wait for you to make a mistake, then accept no excuse.

This basic truth is always in the forefront for mountain climbing guides. They know this truth well, seeing it and living it on a daily basis, and it is their primary job to make sure their clients have a similar comprehension. That isn't always so simple. In fact, it can be more difficult than reaching a mountain peak.

Every climber knows that every mountain has its own personality. Every guide knows that every climber has his or her own personality. You have to manage to put the two together. For instance, some mountains require patience; that means toning down the over-aggressive climber. Some mountains require an assault;

that means hyping up the cautious. Some mountains require a simple, long grind; that means inspiring the weak of conviction. Just as a mountain is more difficult to climb than it is to look at, it is more difficult to lead your charges than it is to think you can.

In other words, just as you must become an expert of mountains, you must also become an expert of the behavior of mountain climbers. Every seasoned guide calls it the most difficult part of the job.

Most mountain climbing guides work either part-time (usually weekends), or on a seasonal full-time basis. Because weather is the most common "stopper" on a climb, mountaineers are a prisoner of the seasons. That greatly reduces the chance for a decent annual income; most guides make little over $100 per day. You can do better by leading small groups, then charging a group rate of $300 to $400 or more, depending on the number of days afield. But group trips can be difficult to put together. Since climbing is an extremely personal experience, strangers will rarely choose to climb with each other.

All mountain climbing guides have a remarkable passion for the mountain. It's what keeps them going. When they get tired of the job of guiding, that basic passion for the mountain comes to the rescue. It underlies everything. It is why they are so cheerful when they put together their gear for a trip, plan the meals, scan the maps. If you don't have a zest for adventure, then find another line of work.

Most trips start with a meeting between the guide and climbers. The guide will trace the route of the climb on a map, then review details of the route and any difficulties that may be encountered. Special attention is given to any area where safety may be an issue. By the end of the meeting, the climbers will have a realistic outlook as to what challenges are ahead, how difficult areas will be addressed, and what is the guide's style of communication. Done right, a pre-trip orientation meeting can smooth over the entire trip.

Done wrong, and it can cause perpetual problems. For instance, to inspire a positive attitude, you tell someone that a particular part of the ascent is "no sweat—you'll fly right through it," but it turns out to be a terrible gut-whipper. That can devastate the confidence of an individual in himself, and when he discovers you have been less than truthful, in you.

If an area is going to be difficult, don't gloss it over by saying, "Heck, I've done it dozens of times." Instead say, "It's difficult but do-able." Then plan the route carefully, explain any special techniques that will be required, each person's placement and role in the climb, and a time reference as to what is typical. If a guide comes to a meeting of the minds with clients, everything has a way of working out for the better. It's a matter of the clients always having realistic expectations.

In addition, there is nothing more important than being fully trained in safety, first-aid and rescue. Contact the American Mountain Guides Association and get an outline of their beginner's course. All guides should briefly explain their safety qualifications so the clients will know that they are with a trained, responsible person.

And, of course, you must know everything about your mountain. Everything. Slides, glaciers, rock falls, easy spots and tough spots, where you can get water and where you cannot. You must know how different clouds signify different weather patterns; for instance, lenticular means winds on top, and a sudden vertical development of a cumulonimbus means a short, violent thunderstorm. Your gear must be perfect; your health and stamina must be strong. For this, you get maybe $100 or so a day. No problem. After all, you are on the mountain.

Career Case Study

Michael Zanger, California   *Michael Zanger is the director of Shasta Mountain Guides in Mt. Shasta, California. He has lived and climbed in the Mt. Shasta area for the past 24 years, and his travels include expeditions throughout North America, Alaska, Canada, Europe, Africa and the Himalayas. He has also taught mountaineering at a local junior college and led special outdoor programs for high-risk youth and the physically challenged.*

Requirements—Let me begin by telling you a little joke. Two mountain guides, one young and one old, put money into the lottery for several years. Finally, they won. The young guide asked the old one, "What are you going to do with the money?"

The old guide answered, "Well, I'm going to pay off the house, put the kids through college, buy a Corvette and take the wife on a cruise. How about you?"

The young guide replied, "Oh, I think I'll just keep guiding until the money runs out."

It's almost a Catch-22. It takes a great deal of mountain experience—a very extensive knowledge of mountaineering, climbing, weather, geography, the whole alpine experience—in order to prepare yourself with the skills necessary to guide professionally. You have to really get along well with people. You have to be a psychologist, a baby-sitter, a cook, and a maitre d'. You have to know a lot of jokes and have a great sense of humor. You have to have clear judgment and problem-solving skills. Good communication skills are a necessity, and you must always be willing to improve on the development of those skills.

Prospects—The best thing to do is check out possible apprenticeship programs with established guide companies. You can sometimes apprentice with one of them; there are many different ones, some big, some small. That's one way to go, and probably the best way. You can also go through the American Mountain Guides Association; they are preparing to offer a beginner's course so that people can get some kind of background before they really get into it.

Benefits—You're outdoors, you're in the mountains. The mountains tend to bring out the best or the worst in people, usually the best, and you get the chance to know many interesting people in that kind of environment. And you have the chance to put forth the importance of environmental ethics and care to people.

Pay—It really varies. Some apprenticeship programs pay minimally; once you're guiding professionally you can sometimes make around $100-$150 a day.

Negatives—There's always the objective danger factor that comes from the mountains: falling rocks, bad weather, things like that. You have to take it seriously—after all, folks' lives are often at stake while climbing. It's not always consistent. You often have to set your schedule according to your clients' schedules, and you have to learn to be very patient and practice empathy for others.

The future—If you're good and if you want to improve your skills, you can keep on doing it indefinitely. You can eventually move on to bigger things, like international guiding.

Career Case Study

Kitty Calhoun-Grissom, Washington

Kitty Calhoun-Grissom began climbing at the age of 18 on rock crags in her native North Carolina. Grissom has climbed the Cassin Ridge on McKinley, the south face of Chacraraju, attempted a new route on Thelay Sagar, and ascended Dhaulagiri alpine-style. Grissom has been a guide for the American Alpine Institute since 1985 and is currently pursuing an MBA degree at the University of Washington. She and her husband live in Seattle, Washington.

Requirements—Guiding involves instructing and climbing with people up different peaks and routes. The most important thing to have is actual experience; you constantly need to draw on your judgement. The more experience you have, the better you'll be able to assess situations.

Technical skills, teaching skills and people skills need to be combined. Basic knowledge of first aid is required, but that's fairly easy to learn. People skills are more of a personal thing. You're with people, strangers, for days at a time, so you really have to be able to relate to anyone.

Prospects—There are two ways to go about guiding: You can be a private guide, or work for a guiding company. It seems to me that in the states, the successful private guides tend to be experienced climbers who are well known, so I would think that you need a pretty extensive background to make it that way. Climbing companies always need good guides, and if you have experience, it's really not too hard to find a position. They really want people who have that special combination of qualifications that experience gives you.

Benefits—A major benefit is being able to make a living at something you like to do. Not everybody gets to do that. Another is that I've ended up traveling and guiding in a lot of places outside of the U.S. that I wouldn't have been able to go to otherwise; I've guided in Peru, Alaska, Bolivia, Argentina and Nepal.

Pay—Again, it depends on whether you're an independent guide or working for a company. Private guides tend to make more money per trip, but they don't have the security that is available with a guide service. Each guide service structures their pay scale differently. At American Alpine Institute, a beginning guide starts at around $55 per day, and each year that goes up about $5 a day, no matter where you work or how many clients you have.

Negatives—The first that comes to mind is that guiding is glorified; people think it's a great job and they don't realize that it's not always great. You take a lot of risks. You're ultimately responsible for your clients' lives, which can be stressful, especially on harder routes. You're risking your own life, too, because you're roped up with these people.

There's a feeling of pressure as well. Often the clients I take are business people who have a lot of money, but not a lot of time. When they take a vacation, it's a big deal to them, and they want to have the most successful trip possible. You're responsible for that, so you're on call 24 hours a day when you're with them.

It's not a nine-to-five sort of job. You don't just come home at night after a day of guiding; you're gone for days or weeks at a time. It can be very hard on relationships.

The future—I think the field is really going to be expanding. Climbing is getting more and more popular; I've noticed one trend in which wealthy clients want to climb each of the highest peaks on every continent, and they're willing to pay a lot for guides. That's becoming very popular. As long as people want to go up mountains, guides will always have jobs.

Reference

American Mountain Guides Association, P.O. Box 2128, Estes Park, CO 80517; (970) 586-0571.

Montana Outfitters & Guides Association, Box 9070, Helena, MT 59624; (406) 449-3578.

International Tour Management Institute (ITMI), 625 Market Street, Ste 610, San Francisco, CA 94102; (415) 957-9489.

Outfitter/Rafting Guide

Dreams—An outfitter spends day after day in the outback, wild and untamed, and is a heroic figure to clients. The pay can be great, with plenty of time to spend it in the winter. There is never any question as to who the boss is. Who? Why you, of course, a modern-day Daniel Boone.

Nightmares—You never have any time to yourself. If you are a numbnut with numbers, the high overhead can kill you. The planning details, phone calls and accounting are endless, and worst of all, if you get mad, everybody will hate you.

Realities—This is an ideal position for a natural leader who likes people and is well-versed in the outdoors, and who also has a mind for detail, money and the realities of others. Self-promotion is a key, and bad moods or sniveling are not allowed. To get use permits in popular areas, working with the government is a requirement.

What it's all about—Were you ever in the Boy Scouts, Girl Scouts, Cub Scouts or Brownies? Remember the trips you went on? Remember the role of the pack leader?
Well, being an outfitter isn't much different from being the pack leader of a troop of scouts for a week. The buck stops here. It doesn't matter if it's a rafting trip, horseback riding trip, backpack outing, a camping/fishing/hunting adventure, or just getting out there and watching the trees grow. It is the outfitter who puts it all together, and you must have the personality for minutia, as well as know everything about your craft. A rafting outfitter, for example, most know how to handle any kind of water in any style of craft.

Where's the mosquito repellent? Where's the lemonade? When do we eat? When do we get there? Aren't you tired? How come it's raining in the middle of summer? Why won't the fish bite? If you can answer these questions with a smile, not a fake smile, but an actual, big, wide grin because you're so happy to be in the outdoors instead of in an office, then maybe you should consider being an outfitter. Maybe you have actually been one of those troop leaders, or perhaps a YMCA director, Little League coach, or were in charge of your company picnic. You need that kind of style.

From start to finish, it is the outfitter who makes an outdoors adventure trip simple and fun for anybody from any background. The outfitter usually selects the destination, provides the food and cooks it, provides the gear and demonstrates it, and answers just about every question conceivable, including "Why is the sky blue?" And they do it with a smile, a real one.

The future prospects are excellent. Ironically, it's because so many people are living in cities. One National Park survey showed that 90 percent of park visitors were from urban areas and had little experience or knowledge about the outdoors. Another poll shows that 75 percent of Americans feel a yearning to enjoy the outdoors, despite their lack of experience. That is where the outfitter comes in. Just like a troop leader, you show the way.

Because so many city people have this need for adventure in a wild place, an outfitter is provided with many opportunities, not only from sheer numbers, but by offering specialized trips. There are many possibilities: A backpacking trip for women only, a fishing trip for the physically disadvantaged, a camping trip for inner-city youth, a pack trip for single parents and their children, a hunting trip for those confined to wheelchairs. Some outfitters are making a killing by focusing on young executive women from big cities, charging them a fortune to go hiking and camping for a week in a national park. You are only limited by what you can think of...

Ironically, the most difficult clientele is not a specialized group with little or no experience; they are willing to listen and learn. Such is not the case with members of the general public who know just enough to think they don't need your help. There are many TV-reared individuals who take for granted that they can change channels by pushing buttons. When they discover that approach doesn't work in the outdoors, that it takes know-how, logic, persistence, and physical resolve, whiners are often born.

Somehow, these whiners have a way of blaming you for the anthill that they decided to put their sleeping bags on.

Most of your clients will be quite enthusiastic and happy, however. You can keep them that way by demonstrating excellent outdoors skills and communicating these skills. Remember, they may not know a grommet from priming paste. You can blow the deal by blabbing incessantly about how wonderful you are, then when it comes to a moment of truth, clamming up with a case of lockjaw. Just remember your days as a scout, and the pack leaders you always liked the best. That's what it takes.

To make money, you also have to have the ability run it as a business, of course. Since a lot of money flows in and out, you have to make sure you crank in a percentage for yourself, at least five percent. Some do better than that. What seems a real key to making good money is attracting clients from major population areas. That can be difficult if you are based in Yellowknife, Great West Territories. But if you can get a use permit with a major park or popular national forest and tap into people from L.A., New York, Chicago, or other big cities, that's when the dough can really start to roll.

The best way to start out is as a guide, working under an experienced outfitter. After a summer, you will see for yourself what makes this job tick, and you will know whether or not you want to walk farther down the road. If the answer is yes, and you have an inheritance, then forget it and move to Costa Rica . . . heh, heh, just kidding. Then the best route is to buy an established company, so you bypass the first struggling years virtually all entrepreneurs face.

The alternative is starting out on your own, usually on a small scale with perhaps one employee (often your mate). If you choose the do-it-yourself route, buying good equipment will put you in the hole to start, and you will discover that it is difficult to attract clients the first few years. That means you also have the additional job of promoter. Attending sports shows in major cities, a royal pain, becomes a must. So is getting listings in club newsletters, local newspapers, and in the columns of large-circulation outdoors writers. Another promotion technique is to join forces with other independent outfitters and hire a public relations specialist to give your businesses a lift.

If it sounds like a nightmare, just remember that when you wake up in the morning, you will be in one of the most beautiful places on earth. Remember that you will be with people who have chosen you to teach them, to lead the way on what may be the most wondrous outdoors experience of their lives. Remember that you are trading traffic jams in the city for a trail where deer are more common than people. Sounds pretty good, eh? To outfitters with the right personality, it is heaven.

Career Case Study

Joe Daly, California—Joe Daly received both his bachelor's and master's degrees from the State University of New York at Albany. He taught for 10 years at the public high schools of New York and California. During that time he traveled to Japan, West Africa, Europe, and throughout much of North America. Along with Dick Linford, Joe co-founded ECHO: The Wilderness Co., which specializes in whitewater rafting trips in Idaho, Oregon and California. Joe and his wife, Sue, reside in Berkeley, California.

Requirements—I don't think you need to have a high degree of formal education, but it is important to have a broad range of skills. River outfitting is a typical small business, and you have to wear many hats. It's not simply knowing how to row a boat. While we all dream of many days on the river, in reality we know we have to spend time in the office: hiring, training, marketing, dealing with the bank, negotiating insurance—all the things that businesses have to take care of.

You have to be attuned to what's going on in the world—be aware, flexible and quick to adjust to trends. We have found that we get caught up in how fast things move. It used to be, "I'll put it in the mail," and now it's "Yes, I can fax you the information." You have to know how to respond to the public's tempo.

For example, I read an article in the Wall Street Journal about how some hotels in San Francisco have made provisions for couples who want to bring their children on business trips, and that got me thinking about our river trips. Soon afterward we started special kids' trips with a "fun director," where the kids can do their own thing but still be within immediate reach of their family. The program has become a great success.

People skills are extremely important. We serve the great

global public, and we have to be aware of the needs and ways of many types of people. We cater to some people from other countries, and it's critical that we're sensitive and alert to their customs.

We also need to know how to effectively deal with the guides we have. It is so important to have good relations with them—they're like family. As a boss, you spend many hours per day with guides for days on end, and if your approach to them is dictator-like, you'll be in trouble fast. You have to demonstrate an understanding of guides' strengths and weaknesses and be able to deal with them productively.

Typically an outfitter is a guide first. That experience can be gained quite quickly. The basic ability to row a boat can be learned in a matter of weeks or months—it's quite easy if you're athletic. Hurdle number two is much more challenging—the broad range of skills that have to be brought to the arrangement. I am very fortunate in having a great business partner. In our case, where I have weaknesses, he has strengths, and vice versa. We've been working together for 21 years now, and we've realized as the years have passed how delicate a partnership is; we've realized that having a common philosophy and an open and honest relationship are rare. We both feel lucky that the partnership has worked so well.

Prospects—It is not as easy as it was in the '70s. There aren't thousands upon thousands of opportunities out there anymore. Almost every river in the West now has a permit system and the government limits the number of outfitters on each river. If you come along and say, "Okay, I want to start a rafting business," you have to buy out an existing company. The government reviews the transaction, and if all is in order, the permit is transferred. But you do have to have some financial resources. If you were working as a guide, operating on a guide's salary, you couldn't walk up to someone and say, "I want to buy your business."

Benefits—First, the pure joy of being out on a river, floating on the water, is a great sensation. Out in the middle of a river, you get a great sense of space. And then you have the whitewater, which gets the adrenaline going. The excitement of running a river well gives you a great sense of achievement.

Second, the crews I work with are extraordinary. Many of them have become my life-long friends, which I don't think can be said often about employers and employees. We have been fortunate to have employed so many fine people.

Additionally, the clients are a lot of fun. Jack Cole once said, "Outfitters don't make money, they make friends." You sit around a campfire and trade stories, and people communicate—they open up. The river experience brings them together. People initially come for the actual rafting experience, but they come back for the social aspect. It's a healthy experience. You're enjoying clean air, quiet settings, beautiful campsites. It's very refreshing and restorative.

I enjoy the variety of things I have to do in a year's cycle. First there's the actual season of running rivers, then an annual review of the season, where you evaluate how everything went. Next comes the planning stage, where you prepare for next season, and finally the promotional period, when you really push advertising and marketing like crazy. Finally, the cycle begins again and it's time to be back on the river. The variety keeps the years from being monotonous.

Pay—Somebody who starts out as a guide—and that's the typical way to begin—would make about $50 a day. When you take on the added responsibilities of a head guide, the pay can go up to about $115 per day.

As an outfitter, I would estimate that most earn an income in the range of $30,000 to $50,000 a year. Nobody's getting rich, but nobody's starving, and it's a good lifestyle. I think about the people who are out on the freeways, driving hard, sitting in an office all day, and I feel very fortunate.

Negatives—I can't see as many negatives as positives, but they are there. First, there's nobody telling you to go home—the hours are long, and you have to stick with it until a project is done. In terms of the office season, there's always one more thing to be taken care of—one more letter to write, one more phone call to make. In the summer, when we're running trips, it's tough on families. We're gone for days at a time. And when we are home, the telephone rings a lot, sometimes late at night, sometimes early in the morning. It can be disruptive to other aspects of your life.

There are uncertainties: weather, water, the economy. January, February and March are the typical months for rain and snow, and if it doesn't come, we start worrying. As rafting outfitters, we need water in our rivers.

The future—I think the job market for guides is here to stay. There seems to be a natural changeover for guides; they work for three to five years, then go on and finish school, start families, and begin their own lives, so there are always positions opening up. But there will always be a limited number of openings in the outfitting business because of the governmental permit system.

River running will continue on certain rivers for generations, because of the exciting whitewater, scenic beauty and tradition. The future looks steady in terms of reliability of job openings. It looks uncertain in terms of the government; the government has great control over this business as far as permits are concerned.

Career Case Study

Steve Lentz, Idaho

Steve Lentz is a seasoned river veteran with 20 years of river experience. He is the owner and operator of Middle Fork River Company, which won Travel and Leisure's Mark of Innovation Award in 1991. Lentz is a member of the Idaho Outfitters & Guides Association, Ducks Unlimited, American Rivers, and several other state and local organizations. He is also the treasurer of America Outdoors.

Requirements—I believe that there needs to be a parallel of interests, that when combined, will make for a very good outfitter. One is being interested in and informed about the technical aspects of rafting: understanding currents, being able to read water, knowledge of river dynamics and what's going on underneath the surface. This training is an absolute necessity to be able to predict what will happen as you're guiding guests.

The second requisite is a love of people; you have to want to serve them and accommodate them in what may be, to them, a very foreign environment. You may have a guy on a trip who's the CEO of a major company, and he may be asking you very basic questions about elemental aspects of rafting. It's your job to make him feel secure and confident, making sure that he understands and is comfortable with what is going on around him. This is where professional guides are important. They are what separates one rafting outfitter from another. If your guides aren't sensitive to the needs of your clients, the essential trust won't be established between them, and that reflects on your company.

Both of these qualities are essential to running a superior outfitting business. You might be a technically perfect person, but if you don't have the desire to serve people, the balance will be off. One can't happen without the other.

Prospects—It's difficult to establish your own business now because most rivers are controlled by the government. You can't just go into your local Forest Service office and get a special permit and start your own rafting company. There are only so many permits available for each drainage, and they are difficult to come by. There are satellite businesses to consider, such as equipment rentals, that offer more opportunities, but those focus away from the actual participation aspect of the field.

Benefits—There is a great reward in watching people's personal growth occur. Often they approach the week to come with a lot of anxiety, and it's really great to see confidence overcome their fear.

This is one of the few businesses around where people look forward to being with you—it's not like a cruise, where you have all kinds of employees around and a different waiter every night. It's one group of people going out with one group of guides, and great friendships often come out of that.

Pay—On the average, a guide will begin working for $25 a day. Professional guides on premier wilderness rivers, such as the Rogue, the Middle Fork and the Colorado will make as much as $100 a day, with tips of approximately 20 percent of the trip fee.

Income possibilities become limited with the control of guest numbers. The Forest Service allows me 24 people at a time, so my earnings are restricted to a point. A company in good standing can expect a profit of about 15 percent of its gross sales. If all the chips land where they should and you're free and clear, that figure can go up, but there are always extra expenses, like equipment that needs to be replaced or repaired. It's very rare to be free and clear.

Negatives—It's actually difficult for me to see any downsides. I look at the unexpected things that sometimes happen as more of a challenge rather than a negative. You're often faced with obstacles such as equipment failure, or having some unforeseen incident happen in the middle of your trip, and you have to deal with it using the resources around you. Being surrounded by 150 square miles of wilderness limits one's resources. But that can be a challenge to me.

Another challenge is securing your clients' trust; they need to be reassured that their needs and expectations are going to be met, and for many people, that's not always a given. The adventure should begin with the first phone conversation, so that by the time the guests arrive, trust has already been established.

The future—I think it's a field that's going to continue to grow. As the cities grow and become more congested, people are going to look more toward getting away and experiencing healthy activities. Outdoor adventures provide a creative outlet for people who love the wilderness, a way to enjoy the magnificent beauty while leaving it unchanged.

These vacations can also give families a learning arena. Long after the thrill is gone, the family bond remains with good strong memories. Outfitting will become instrumental in educating the public about resource protection. Luxury wilderness is not just a way of being cared for, but a way to care for the wilderness.

Technology is also allowing us to move forward. A larger variety of craft is available, which allows us to offer more choices. We're seeing everything from 18 to 20-foot Grand Canyon rigs down to canoes and little inflatable kayaks. With that kind of choice, you can keep the experiences fresh for people. Where people used to come to us for just one trip, now they're coming back four or five times to try different things. Consequently you end up with a business with a very high rate of return.

References

America Outdoors, P.O. Box 10847, Knoxville, TN 37939; (423) 558-1812 or (423) 558-1815.

International Sportsmen's Expositions, PO Box 2569, Vancouver, WA 98668, (360) 693-3700 or (800) 545-6100.

The Paddler Magazine, PO Box 1341, Eagle, ID 83616; (208) 939-4500.

Professional Paddle Sports Association, PO Box 248, Butler, KY 41006; (606) 472-2205.

Other agencies to contact include the state and federal land agencies which issue permits: U.S. Forest Service, Bureau of Land Management, and the U.S. National Park Service.

Pack Trip Guide

Dreams—Every day is heaven. Your surroundings are always so pure and pristine. The air, water, trees, and your clients look at you as if you were Jedediah Smith, and actually pay you, too. You may not see a traffic jam all summer. And hey, you don't even have to carry your gear.

Nightmares—Every day is hell. The horses can know more about the wild than your clients. Then there is the client that won't shut up, and the one that won't let out a peep. It rains, the tent leaks, a bear gets the food, and by the way, where's the map?

Realities—There is plenty of heaven and hell. You get day after day of wilderness, and as long as you don't get homesick, you'll be living in perpetual paradise. Clients can be troublesome— after all, they need your leadership (and pack animals), but you can get used to that. If you own a business, attending sports shows to recruit business is a dry patch of life.

What it's all about—A good wilderness trip is like taking a shower where you wash off accumulated layers of civilization. When you finally get all the city off, you often discover somebody who is a pretty nice person after all.

Pack trip guides know this. They better, because they are working primarily with people from cities, and when they first start out, the cleansing process hasn't taken effect yet. So the first few days on the trail, the pack trip guide learns to grin and bear it, knowing that by the end of the trip, all will fall into place.

The basic job of a pack trip guide is to lead a group of campers off into the wild, usually on horseback, sometimes on llamas, rarely on foot with the gear packed on the backs of donkeys, llamas or even goats, believe it or not. The idea is that you do not have to carry your gear. It is instead packed on the back of an animal, hence the "pack" in pack trip.

Thus the focus for a guide is less on physical demands, and more on the ability to communicate, set up a camp, cook, clean up, know first-aid, and demonstrate skills of woodsmanship. It is one thing to be a good woodsman, you will discover, and another thing entirely to be a good guide.

What seems to happen the first day or two on the trail is that your customers will be split into two personality groups. On one side are the I-can-do-anything variety, who brag of past accomplishments at every opportunity, and often dominate the conversation (i.e. they talk too much). On the other side are the I-don't-know-if-I-can-make-it types, who ask short questions and always follow your lead (and don't say hardly anything).

Over the course of a week's adventure in the wilderness, a phenomena often occurs where the brash get whittled down to size and the timid gain confidence. By the end of the adventure, everyone on the trip usually realizes that they have all shared the same challenges and adventures, and the group can come out of the quest bonded as a unit. All differences are cast aside. The talkers might even start listening (gasp!)

As a pack trip guide, you already know this will occur, even if it seems unlikely on Day 1. Your primary job is to ease this transition for your customers, to try to get the brash to focus, to help inspire the timid onward. A trip into the wilderness is an ideal vehicle for doing so.

Your personal makeup, especially your ability to communicate clearly, becomes the critical facet. A guide can master how to handle horses, load a pack, read a map, and cook a camp dinner, but the ability to communicate in a clear, comfortable manner to anyone is a more difficult personal test. If you get past that key hurdle, then the job is excellent for people who like living in the wilderness. The pay is decent, and as a guide within a company, you can go an entire summer where you virtually never hear a phone ring. You will see more shooting stars than brake lights of cars. You can also get a severe case of homesickness.

If you take it to the next level, owning and managing your own company, it gets a lot more complicated, and fast. The overhead is high—paying for pack animals, equipment, supplies, food, and insurance. You need the detailed mind of an accountant to make sure that there is money left over for you, which usually ranges from 3.5 to 5 percent of gross income. You also have to promote, usually by attending the major sports shows during winter in big cities, which creates a high expense and is a real grind. But that is how most outfitters get their customers.

You also need to know how to hire and train guides. And you have to negotiate with government bureaucracies to obtain permits for some areas, which can be an unbelievable pain in the posterior.

There are two different outlooks for the future of this career. On the one hand, there will be a growing need for pack trip guides. That is because more and more people from the city have a need for them (see the chapter on outfitters). The prospects for quality seasonal employment are most promising. But for a long-term career as a pack trip outfitter, burn-out seems to be a problem. Some guides just get tired—physically tired of going up and down mountains, and emotionally tired from perpetually accommodating the public.

Then there are others who love it so much that during the off-season in the winter, they actually have trouble sleeping in a bed. No problem. They pull out their favorite sleeping bag and lay it on the floor, and then go deep into slumberland, dreaming of summer in the wilderness, of verdant meadows, wildflowers and the crystal-fresh taste of a clear mountain morning.

Career Case Study

Barbara Opdahl, Idaho

Barb Opdahl worked in a variety of fields, including the trucking business and the U.S. Postal Service, before she and her husband, Harlan, got into the pack-trip business. They have owned and operated Triple "O" Outfitters, Inc. since 1980. Barb also serves on the Advisory Board for the State of Idaho Small Business Development Center. Barb and Harlan have four children and seven grandchildren and reside in Pierce, Idaho.

Requirements—To be an outfitter in Idaho, first you have to have what is known as an "area system." An area system is basically a system in which a company guides outfitted trips for compensation, in a specific region for which they have been issued special permits. Idaho is the only state with the area system policy, but other states have similar regulations. In order to get an area system, a company has to be licensed by the state and permitted by the agency which has jurisdiction over the land, such as the Forest Service or the Bureau of Land Management.

You have to have a love of people and animals, because you're with them for five or six days straight. And you have to be willing to be flexible; you can't think that at ten o'clock every day you're going to be at a certain point or doing one certain thing. You have to learn to throw your clock away.

It's important to have a basic knowledge of the outdoors. You need to know elemental things about outdoor survival. One important point is that you must be able to handle isolation. You're out there in the wilderness, and it's kind of "we and thee."

It's true of any business that you need management skills. That's the down side of the business—I've found it to be really hard to deal with. It's definitely a learning experience, so you have to be willing to learn. We've gone to many seminars and workshops for small-business management. We went to one a while ago and the speaker said, "Your business is only as good as the books you keep." We almost fell off our chairs, because that's our weakness—we have a terrible bookkeeping system.

Prospects—I would say that the best way to get into outfitting is to purchase a company. In this market, starting your own business is difficult, if not impossible, and it's easier to find an established business that's looking to sell, although they're expensive to buy.

There are options, too. If you can come up with a unique idea, you may be eligible for a permit for what is called "new opportunity." Permits are handed out on availability, and if you can come up with a service that's not being offered and you can prove that the demand is there, you can get in. Our company came up with the idea of the Lewis & Clark Trail Ride, which we marketed to the Smithsonian Institute in Washington D.C. They use the trip as one of their domestic study tours.

There are lots of things to think about—you have to consider the environmental impact the service will have on the land, for one thing. If the public thinks it will be damaging, they will voice their opinions. It can become sticky. You have to really want to do it, and you have to have a lot of dedication.

Benefits—You get to be outdoors, smelling the fresh air, enjoying the scenery and being away from the hustle and bustle of living. When you're outside, it's very easy to get lost in your surroundings and push the real world out of your mind.

You meet a lot of wonderful people. We have met people from all over the world, and the exciting thing to me is realizing that people are people, no matter what they do or who they are. Whether they have a lot of wealth or power or whatever doesn't matter—we're all the same out there. Every group is like a new family; there's real bonding that happens when you're in the outdoors.

It's great to feel that you don't have to punch a time clock. When it's daylight you get up, when it's dark you go to sleep, and there's somebody to tell you when it's time to eat in between.

Pay—We charge between $600 and $2300 per person per trip, depending on the trip. Our expenses are taken out of that, and those include guides' salaries, equipment, food, advertising, liability insurance, vehicle upkeep . . . and then there are all the other outside services, like motels for certain clients, for example. We also have legal and professional fees to think about. As a business person, I should be able to tell you what our profits are, but I honestly can't. The expenses vary, and we don't have a very efficient bookkeeping system.

Negatives—There's a certain idealism that this business is really glamorous, that you make all this money, but that's not the whole picture. I guess that's the biggest negative, that it's not something you're going to get rich doing. The pay is very low. In Idaho, the average outfitting company's income is 4.5 percent of their gross income. Outfitting is a way of life, like farming. Everything we do revolves around the business and everything comes out of and goes into the business.

It's hard work, physically. You put in lots of long hours and long days. And it's also seasonal. In the winter we do all our bookings and sports shows.

The future—I would say that the long-term possibilities are not very positive. It's a great life and we enjoy it, but as we get older we're saying, "How much longer can we do this, physically?" As the saying goes, the mountains get taller every year. You just can't stand up to it forever. It all depends on what you're willing to sacrifice to make it work.

It could definitely lead to other things. It's a good background for the tourism market. We've gained a lot of knowledge and experience through working with people, and that's great training for anything in the tourism field.

Career Case Study

Steve Biggs, California

Steve Biggs has owned and operated Shasta Llamas, the oldest and largest llama-packing business in North America, since 1979. Prior to working in the pack-trip field, Steve worked for the Office of Economic Opportunity in the 1960s, and taught sociology, community action and institutional change at Lone Mountain College in San Francisco in the 1970s. He currently resides on a 40-acre ranch in Mt. Shasta, California.

Requirements—Most importantly, you need to have some experience or knowledge in the areas of financial management, government regulations, marketing, and tax laws, as well as personnel management and labor laws if you're going to have paid employees. As with any business, you need organizational, planning, administrative and management skills. A college education would be preferable, considering the type of clientele you're dealing with—many of them are well-educated.

It's an outdoor job, and you have to love the mountains and everything in them. You also need at least a fundamental knowledge of natural history, mountaineering, first aid, and search and rescue. It's essential to know the basics, like what kind of equipment you'll need for each particular trip, how to manage and care for your livestock, and the history of the area you're in.

You need group relationship and interpersonal skills. It's important to know how to relate to people—you can't be a recluse if you want to do this type of work. You should love to interact and take care of people. You're constantly answering questions, catering to what they need, comforting them. Leadership skills are necessary; you need to like working with groups of people in the outdoors. You have to remember that you are there in part to teach and to facilitate people's knowledge and skill-building. You need to be physically fit and like physical labor, and be able to deal with routine—day after day of doing the same thing.

Prospects—If someone wants to start their own business, they should first find a location: A beautiful mountain area within a three- to five-hour's drive of a metropolitan area is ideal. The area needs to be attractive to the market you want to reach. The next consideration is finding your start-up capital. Then it's a matter of reaching your clients. Marketing is a critical aspect.

If you were buying somebody out, you'd have to look at the viability of the business as it stands—where they're located, how they're doing. One criteria that many people overlook is that it's very beneficial to be located in an area where there are other attractive vacation opportunities available; for example, bed and breakfast inns, rafting trips, plays, concerts. People often like to combine their packing trips with other things, or at least have the option to do so.

Benefits—I enjoy meeting and interacting with new people. We meet some really wonderful people, and that's an enriching experience.

When you run your own business, you can be creative. You're your own boss. You can make your own hours and give yourself the freedom of flexibility. Being in the outdoors, in the mountains, is really a beautiful experience. Being physically and mentally active is also very rewarding. And you feel a sense of accomplishment from the work that you do, especially if you're doing most of it yourself.

Pay—How much you make depends on whether you do it yourself or hire people, how big your staff is, and what your volume is. If the owner guides and cooks and has a fairly steady clientele, I'd say he or she could make between $10,000 and $20,000 per summer. Of course, he or she could make nothing—there are many variables. If guides and cooks are hired and the volume goes up, I'd say the range is still about the same, because you have increased expenditures with increased volume. If volume doesn't go up, profits will go down if you hire additional help.

Location is important. If there were a greater demand, if we were in an area such as Yosemite National Park, I'm sure we would be doing ten times the business we're doing now.

Negatives—You're liable for your guests. You have to be watching, managing, supervising, and waiting for things to go wrong. And something always goes wrong. You just have to have things covered the best you can. That demand is always on you.

Dealing with the government is not pleasant. They're a pain in the neck. The government is a giant bureaucracy that pumps out paper, and it's a constant hassle and a mess of red tape.

The work is draining—physically, emotionally and psychologically. You get to a point where you never want to open another zip-lock bag again. That's the routine—you're constantly getting in and out of packs. Somebody wants lemonade, someone wants cookies. You've got to be organized. If you run into problems with particular people, a lot of your energy can be taken up. That's rare, though—I've had maybe one and a half "bad" people.

You have to be really careful of the kind of people you hire as guides, too. Guides are everything, and if they can't handle the obstacles that come up in the job, they have the potential to ruin your business. They have to be fresh and ready to go. For clients, this is an exciting new experience, and even though it may be your guide's hundredth trip, he or she has to be up and excited too.

You get paid last. Everyone else has to get paid, and if there's any money left over, you pay yourself.

The future—The field has been expanding, not by leaps and bounds, but there are new businesses started every year. For those who have the skills I've talked about, I think the job prospects are very good. The adventure travel industry is the fastest-growing industry in the country. The recession affected us greatly, but as the economy improves, I predict that the trend will continue growing quickly, particularly for those businesses that cater to families and provide natural history instruction.

As far as guides are concerned, llama packers in particular don't hire very often. Many owners run their businesses as a family venture; they're very small mom-and-pop type outfits. But opportunities can be found if you look for them.

The skills and experience you gain in the packing business can carry over to just about any aspect of adventure travel, if you decide to move on. But if you choose to, you could stay in it for a lifetime. You can gradually phase out of actual guiding and explore different aspects of the business.

References

International Llama Association, 2755 S. Locust Street, Suite 114, Denver, CO 80222; (303) 756-9004.

Adventure Travel Society, Inc., 6551 South Revere Parkway, Suite 160, Englewood, CO 80111; (303) 649-9016.

America Outdoors, P.O. Box 10847, Knoxville, TN 37939' (423) 558-1812 or (423) 558-1815.

California Outdoors, PO Box 67, Angels Camp, CA 95222; (800) 552-3625 or fax (209) 736-2902. E-mail: reservations@oars.com.

Many states also have outfitter and guide associations.

Park Ranger

Dreams—A park ranger lives in heaven, not on earth. He or she is always in a divine natural setting, working to help keep it that way—managing resources, designing trails, leading campfire talks to visitors—then living in a pretty log home in the park, all paid for. Heh, heh, heh. It doesn't get any better.

Nightmares—This is heaven? More like the other place. You do a lot of police work (that's why you're packing a gun), and when you have time, you have to clean up the restrooms, empty the trash cans and take entrance fees. You can't stand all the people, who have no concept that a park isn't supposed to be a theme park. By mid-summer, you'll be howling "Let me outta here!"

Realities—The park you work for will determine the quality of your job and your life. Small state parks in remote settings beat the heck out of big national parks. Rangers who are willing to relocate whenever a better position is available (which is hard on families), end up with the better career. It can be difficult for white males to get that first job, unless they are just too good to pass by or they submit to working in one of the tent cities.

What it's all about—Being a park ranger can be just about the best job in the world. The best! It can also be the worst. The worst! How's that? Well, there are two different styles involved, and they are about as far apart as the North Pole and the South Pole.

The ideal position is to work as a ranger in an obscure state park. Here the state will provide a residence in the park for the ranger, usually a picturesque little log cabin in a beautiful, hidden setting. Because park visitors are not rampant, the ranger spends his time managing the natural resources of the park, occasionally designing new trail routes, happily answering questions to park visitors, perhaps leading campfire circle talks during the evening for campers. In this dream, the ranger doesn't have to pick up litter, clean up bathroom facilities, or sit in a kiosk taking entrance fees. Why? Because seasonal help takes care of those inanities. The pay is great, too, around $38,000 after five years, and that money stretches a long way when your rent and home expenses are already paid for.

Rangers who have a set-up like that are living the dream. It happens. Maybe they don't have the notoriety that comes with being a ranger in a famous national park, but they have the job they want, the peace of mind, and nearly every day can be a joy.

Then there is the South Pole, and the job is so different that you might hardly recognize it. It starts by working at a highly popular national park, say Yellowstone or Yosemite, or perhaps a state or county park set close to a metropolitan area. There are so many park visitors that they become a daily epidemic of trouble, breaking every law imaginable. Soon you become more of a police officer than a ranger, writing up tickets and lecturing on inappropriate behavior, and before long, you start walking around angry at everything. If your seasonal help is cut in order to save money, you find yourself having to clean restrooms, pick up litter at campgrounds, and even sit like a boob taking entrance fees. Because you live off-site, your salary doesn't stretch as far, especially if the park is near a metropolitan area where rents are significantly higher.

That, my friends, is a nightmare. You might as well take the "range" out of ranger because you're never out there. Instead you have become the police and custodian for a tent city. Rangers who end up in a position like this often become very bitter and will curse the sight of every Winnebago they see crossing through the park entrance. And by the way, if you don't like packing a gun, then find another career. It's part of the job, an unfortunate necessity at many parks, something that just comes with the territory.

So the inevitable question is how do you get a job that is the dream instead of the nightmare? The answer is careful planning, patience, spending a few years paying your dues, then being amenable to relocating.

You start by getting a college degree. The best approach is to major is some kind of environmental science and minor in police work. A ranger has to do both, and if you can demonstrate proficiency in both, you will greatly increase your odds of employment. Another suggestion is to work your summers as a seasonal aid in parks, then network with rangers, picking their brains for every little tip on the realities of the job. It also gives you practical experience, which counts for plenty against other college grads who don't have it.

The first job can be very easy to get, or very difficult. If you are willing to work at a metropolitan park, or one of the overpopulated national parks, a well-qualified prospect can get hired. At first, you may not even mind that you are doing police and custodial work. In a while, however, you will, and you will want to leave. That is why openings have a way of popping up. Another approach to getting that first job is to look in the most obscure places possible, where people with families often don't want to live. If you don't mind relocating to the boondocks, this is the best way to get a job in an unpeopled area and actually get to do the work you desire.

The pay usually starts out around $22,000 to $25,000 for a full-time ranger. Because this is a government job, you are set at a pay level according to time on the job, although merit increases are possible. The best way to move up the ladder is to be willing to move around a lot, working at different parks as openings on the next rung become available, rather than grind out a career at one park.

But wait! There are times when spending a career at one park can be extremely desirable, even if it means passing up promotions. That is when you are almost completely happy somewhere. Knowing when you have something good can be difficult, especially if you have nothing to compare it to, but is very important. Never trade a good deal for an unknown one.

Another reality is government hiring practices, where the most qualified people often do not get rewarded. When there is an opening available, bureaucrats will sometimes pass over a highly qualified white male in favor of nearly anybody else. That means two things: Opportunities can be excellent for females and minorities, and if you are a white male, you have to be the absolute best you can be, just too good for a supervisor to let go.

If you prepare yourself in every way possible to become a ranger, things have a way of working out. In this field, you never know where you might wind up. If that doesn't bother you, then onward with your venture!

Career Case Study

Sandy Kogl, Alaska

Sandy Kogl has worked as a full-time park ranger since 1975. She is an ardent outdoorswoman and enjoys kayaking, hiking, gardening, and cross-country skiing. She lives in Alaska near Denali National Park.

Requirements—A bachelor's degree in natural science or park management is considered an asset, but not an absolute requirement. As with many other outdoor-related fields, rangers generally have a compelling desire to help people and facilitate knowledge in a natural environment. We're committed to helping others and have a genuine love for the outdoors. Personally, I feel a need to work for a conservation or preservation-based system; that's very gratifying for me.

Prospects—There aren't many openings for full-time ranger positions; it's very competitive. I think it's fairly amazing that for the amount of publicity that rangers have gotten for being incredibly underpaid and overworked, there are still so many people who are dedicated enough to want to do this.

Most of the people who are hired have worked for many summers as a seasonal employee. The typical ranger first works at several different parks and gains as much experience as possible through seasonal employment. Most park rangers entering the field now have special skills—medical experience, mountaineering training, or experience in structural firefighting. A good number of rangers have been trained in law enforcement.

Benefits—I enjoy that I have a part in preserving the outstanding resources around me, and it is reassuring that there is a percentage of the public that really does appreciate what's being done with taxpayers' dollars.

There's a lot of satisfaction in living in an area that is so incredibly rich in resources and being paid for watching bears and traveling in the backcountry, things that many people never get to experience at all.

I have exceptionally dedicated co-workers. The seasonal staff is always an incredibly gifted group of people. They're so enthused about being here; it gives those of us who are here all year a refreshing perspective on the things we sometimes take for granted.

Pay—National park rangers are paid on the government's grade scale system. A ranger in an entry-level permanent position, starting at GS 7, will make $22,000 a year. In addition, Alaska and a few other selected areas add a 25 percent cost of living increase. The pay goes up considerably with each grade scale increase; a GS 9 will make $26,800; a GS 11 will make $32,400; and a chief ranger, who is at GS 12, will make $38,800.

It's difficult to advance grades and stay in the same park. If you want to get a grade increase, it usually means competing for a transfer to another park.

Negatives—The politics are unpleasant. Management decisions affecting resources are often based on political and commercial concerns rather than what's best for the park, because somebody's trying to make a buck.

There are always some visitors who expect a national park to provide them with all the amenities they left at home. They'll ask, "Where's the cocktail lounge and the golf course?" That can be frustrating.

Rangers are generally paid for an eight-hour workday, and most of us work more than that, uncompensated. We often do things simply for the good of the park, and we do put in a lot of extra time.

Sometimes, as we work more and more behind a desk or in front of a computer, we wonder where we're headed.

The future—The future is very uncertain. There have been various pronouncements that things will get better, that the focus on parks will be directed more toward resources than politics, but I think that will be dictated by election results.

I think that demands upon the park service to provide recreational services will increase as people continue to look toward the outdoors for recreation opportunities.

Career Case Study

Ed Russell, New York—Ed Russell has worked as a forest ranger for the New York State Department of Environmental Conservation since 1986. Previous occupations included being a lifeguard, a paramedic, a youth camp director, a computer programmer and senior computer analyst. Ed is involved in developing local emergency medical services and is active in community efforts. He is married and has three children, with whom he enjoys camping and canoeing.

Requirements—The requirements differ from state to state. I know that the requirements here are very different from federal regulations. In New York state, you have to have at least a two-year degree in some forest-related field such as forest management or forest recreation. An accepted alternative to a degree is five years of documented professional technical experience in something like forest management or forest biology.

There are physical requirements; you have to pass a physical fitness test and meet eyesight and hearing standards. You must also pass the Civil Service exam, a written test that is only given every four years.

The job responsibilities include search and rescue, forest fire management, care of state lands (state forests and forest preserves), public education and environmental law enforcement. I don't know about other states, but in New York forest rangers are now required to carry a gun. Here, a forest ranger is considered a peace officer, which means we can do almost everything a police officer can do.

You should be independent, self-motivated, and able to deal well with all kinds of people. You really have to have a strong respect for both the people who use the land and the land itself. It's important to be able to weigh the two carefully.

Prospects—The last time job openings came up, there were 11 people hired, and something like 300 applicants. There are a total of 102 positions in all of New York state—it's very competitive. You have to be willing to wait, and you must have the resources to do something else while you're waiting. I have a four-year degree and got a 93 on my Civil Service exam, and I had to wait three years before I was hired. That was a little over nine years after I graduated from college. In national polls, forest ranger is the second most desired job in the country. However, most of the people who think they want to do it have no idea what it's really all about.

Benefits—I enjoy taking care of people and helping them out. I like the variety of the job—there are very few things that are consistent. Some people need routine, but I hate doing the same thing all the time. Another advantage is that I'm fairly independent; I schedule my own day and plan my own projects.

I think that because of the image that people have of rangers, we generally receive a lot of respect. We are able to meet a great variety of people—they really run the entire gamut.

Pay—Current base pay for an entry level position is $25,900, which includes a 12 percent premium. We are paid no overtime, so the 12 percent is basically a catch-all for whatever time is used. That is being contested by the Department of Labor right now.

For the first five years, you'll receive yearly raises in increments of approximately $1,100. After that there are longevity increments of $750. The top rate is around $33,000. There are very few chances for advancement. There are a limited number of lieutenant and captain positions, but the turnover is quite infrequent.

Negatives—The people who use the land are not always as conscientious as we would like them to be. There are many hunters and fishermen who have great respect for the land and the animals, and there are others who have none at all. It's the same with hikers and campers. We get people who claim to be experienced outdoorsmen, and we find that they know nothing about low-impact camping or conservation. It can be very frustrating.

Here where I work, the number one responsibility of rangers is search and rescue. That can be very physically challenging because it's so unpredictable; you may have three or four rescues in one week and then none for three months.

In New York, rangers usually work out of their own homes. The state installs a business phone which each ranger is responsible for 24 hours a day. That means that even if it's your day off, if you happen to be near that phone, you're going to have to get out there and do whatever needs to be done. We get a lot of calls at night, and we take a lot of calls for things we aren't normally in charge of, just because we're often the only officials around. Our districts are large, and there isn't a lot of close-by help, so if something unexpected happens, we're it.

We don't have a large resource base to draw from. State funding has been very meager for the last five years, and federal funding has all but disappeared. Rangers have to work with less than modern equipment, and we're taking on more responsibilities than we've had in the past. We have to do a lot more paperwork than ever before. We have a little joke around here that the rangers need two trucks—one for all the paperwork and one for everything else.

The future—I think the demand for rangers is going to increase. A lot more people are using the backwoods areas, and the interest in hiking and climbing is growing rapidly. Whether the ranger title and job description will endure remains to be seen; it's possible that with all the budget cuts, ranger duties will eventually be merged with the duties of other state and federal agencies.

References

The Society of American Foresters, 5400 Grosvenor Lane, Bethesda, MD 20814-2198; (301) 897-8720.

National Parks and Conservation Association, 1776 Massachusetts Avenue NW, Washington, D.C. 20036; (202) 223-6722 or fax (202) 659-0650.

National Park Service: Careers from US Department of the Interior, National Park Service, PO Box 37127, Washington, D.C. 20013-7127; (202) 208-4649.

Massachusetts Division of Forestry & Parks, 100 Cambridge Street, Boston, MA 02202; (617) 727-3180.

National Recreation & Park Association, 2775 South Quincy Street, Ste 300, Arlington, VA 22206; (703) 820-4940.

Academic institutions can often provide information and/or contacts; outstanding programs are offered by both Colorado State University in Fort Collins, Colorado and Humboldt State University in Arcata, California.

Park Seasonal Employee

Dreams—You stroll in to your favorite park, get hired to help a ranger, then are provided lodging, a meal program, and plenty of time off to go hiking, swimming and fishing. The park visitors take a natural liking to you, which is noticed by the park superintendent, who then promises you a full-time job as a park ranger when you graduate from college.

Nightmares—You had to jump through hoops to get the job, then all you do is work, work, work, and what's so fun about cleaning the bathrooms? Even on your days off, you're at work. The pay isn't much, the park visitors are swine, and if you see one more plugged-up toilet you'll be applying at Burger King tomorrow.

Realities—A logical, persistent approach can still get you a summer job at a park, but it will not happen by accident. All parks are in exquisite settings, and lodging is often provided. The jobs are service-oriented and for hard workers, not self-anointed all-stars, although career-minded youth can use them as a stepping stone to something better.

What it's all about—A lot of people can't figure out why it is so difficult to get a seasonal job at a park. But it is, and if you look at the backgrounds of the people getting park jobs these days, you'll discover why fast enough.

The key is that it isn't just high school or college students on summer vacation filling seasonal positions at parks, as was common just 10 years ago. The job has become so attractive—the vision of living and working in the great outdoors—that there are many teachers and other professionals who are now competing for park employment during the summer. There aren't less cookies to go around, just more people reaching into the jar.

This does not mean it is impossible for a high school or college student to get summer employment at a park. After all, there are more than 100,000 park positions available in North America, including some at more than 50 national parks. Because of the popularity of the U.S. park system, as well as the recent commercialization of them, the parks need employees, lots of them. With the proper approach, virtually anyone can still get one of these summer jobs. But without the proper approach . . . well, you might as well sign up for the "Think and Get Rich" seminar, then have a seat in your favorite chair, think about it, and wait for the money to start rolling in.

The employment opportunities are diverse at parks, with summer jobs in all areas: gift shops, stables, food service, rental shops, administration, front desk, maintenance, gardening, camping, housekeeping, tour guides, supplies, transportation, interpretive center, entrance station . . . .What is available varies on a park-by-park basis.

There are also many bonuses, including lodging, meal programs and, of course, the fantastic recreation possibilities when you're not working. The pay is fair, usually around $5.50 to $7 per hour, but what the heck, ya can't beat the view. In addition, once you have secured a job and worked for 90 days, in future summers you will be given priority for rehire, even if it is at a different park.

What it always comes down to is how to get that first job, that first parting of the curtains, that first ray of light. When it comes to parks, especially national parks, the answers are many.

You must be neatly groomed, polite and speak clearly. Easy enough, right? Wrong. A lot of prospects fail at all three, showing up scraggly, rude, and with terrible grammar and diction.

Then in late winter, you must contact prospective parks for employment possibilities, typing a short, direct letter to the park superintendent. Easy enough, right? Wrong. A lot prospects wait until late spring or early summer to make the first contact, when all positions are filled—or they contact only one park, which puts too narrow a limit on the possibilities.

When you learn of potential openings, you immediately send

a professional, typed cover letter explaining why you want a certain job, a resume that details your education, past jobs, interests, and a photo. Easy enough, right? Wrong. Many seasonal job hunters typically don't do anything but fill out an employment form, then wonder why they don't get hired.

Follow up your letter with phone calls to arrange an employment interview. Easy enough, right? Wrong. Many prospects just give up if they employer doesn't call them.

At the interview, explain how a summer job at a park fits into your long-range career plans. Easy enough, right? Wrong. Most job hunters looking for a summer job don't understand the significance of explaining their career goals to an employer.

So you must do all these things right. In addition, there are a few other tips that can get you on the inside track. If you are a student with a focus on one of the environmental sciences, make sure you let the park know. Rangers like hiring students who have chosen the field as a career. They know that a summer job in a park can be like an apprenticeship, and that young people in this capacity often do excellent work. Another note is that interpretive centers at parks always show preferential hiring for high school and college instructors, people who know the subject and are comfortable talking to groups of people about it.

The growing number of visitors to parks insures these jobs will be available well into the future. In a typical summer, some 3.5 million people will visit Yosemite and another 3 million will go to Yellowstone. Even Glen Canyon National Recreational (where there are 44 job categories) gets 3 million visitors a year, six times what the government originally projected for the year 2000.

When that many people are allowed into a relatively small area over the course of a summer, they will need services. That's where you come in. You can't just saunter in to a park and expect a ranger to create a job for you, but with the right approach, you can spend a summer living and working in one of nature's finest showpieces.

Career Case Study

Stephanie Helline, Colorado
Stephanie Helline works as a seasonal public information
assistant at Rocky Mountain National Park. In the off-
season, she works as a consultant for a desktop publishing

firm in Colorado Springs. She enjoys hiking, backpacking, birdwatching, horseback riding, and bicycling.

Requirements—There are a lot of different positions available: law enforcers, interpreters, maintenance crews, trail crews, campground rangers, entrance workers. Different skills are needed for different positions. When you fill out your government application, you rate yourself based on your skills. You tell them what experience and education you have that you think is applicable. Your application is then scored, and you're put on the register. As openings come up, those who are most qualified are selected. A diverse background, such as CPR or medical training, helps a lot.

Prospects—It's really competitive. Flexibility might be an asset to help you get an edge; sometimes you're notified right before season starts. You have to work up a ladder for some positions. For example, if you want to be an interpretive ranger you might not get in your first year, but you can take a different, maybe less desirable job, and try again the next season. You're more likely to get the job if you've already had some experience at the park. There are winter seasonal positions available, but not as many as in summer. A lot of seasonal rangers are teachers or have other full-time jobs in the winter, so there's less competition.

Benefits—The chance to live in a national park is a great advantage. There's a variety of housing available in the park, which makes it convenient, and you get the chance to know the area you're in. You have a much different outlook on the park when you're there all season as opposed to camping for a week. You meet people with similar interests, and often there are a lot of return employees, so it's kind of like a reunion every summer.

Pay—The pay is pretty low, considering the level of responsibility that's required. It's around minimum wage, sometimes a little higher depending on experience and the specific job.

Negatives—It's only seasonal work. You have to be willing to be flexible and mobile because you will most likely work in one place in the summer and move to a warmer climate in the winter. You're constantly moving back and forth.

You don't usually have weekends off; it's your job to be there for visitors' protection seven days a week.

The future—Most people who enjoy the work and stick with it do finally get a permanent position. I think that the park service is going to be faced with decreasing funding as our resources continue to dwindle. With 2.9 million visitors a year (at Rocky Mountain), we're loving the parks to death. I think the next step in limiting visitation may be a reservation system. We have to restrain the number of people that are here at one time in order to preserve parks.

But I believe that even though visitation will continue to increase, the number of park employees will either stay the same or decrease. The park system is on a very tight budget, and there are more and more volunteer workers who are willing to work just for the experience. I can't see any increase in the number of positions unless there's an increase in resources.

Career Case Study

David Roemer, New Mexico

David Roemer is a seasonal ranger for Carlsbad Caverns National Park. He is a graduate student at the University of Montana, majoring in environmental studies. His past work experience includes being a lifeguard and a musician. He enjoys caving, studying bats, water sports and nature-oriented activities. He lives in Carlsbad, New Mexico.

Requirements—There are really no educational requirements. I've had a little bit of schooling—I've taken classes in geology, communications, biology and environmental studies. Many seasonal workers are people who live in the area and need summer jobs, so they apply, get a job, and are trained for whatever position they receive. Usually the people that get hired have backgrounds and interests that relate to the park's resources.

It's getting so that you need experience to break in. If you've worked more than 90 days for the park, you are placed on higher priority for rehire, and there are a lot of people who return summer after summer.

Prospects—There is definitely a lot of competition. It's pretty tough. I didn't just apply and get a job. I spent three or four months working for only forty dollars per week, volunteering through the Student Conservation Association. If you do a good job as a volunteer or an intern, your chances of getting hired are very good. And many people who want to stay in the field can use that experience to move up the ladder; they'll volunteer, then become a seasonal employee, and then move on to other parks.

If you have some good solid experience in an outdoor-related field, it's quite possible the park will go after you. I'm going after my master of science degree in environmental studies, and the park likes that. The park service wants people who know what's going on around them and who can communicate that knowledge effectively.

Benefits—Being in close contact with the caves of the Guadalupe Mountains and the Chihuahuan desert is an intense learning experience for me. Hiking in the backcountry and crawling through underground wilderness has taught me more about those resources than I could learn in any class, and it has enabled me to discover a lot about myself.

Communicating and sharing that experience with others is a fantastic challenge, which I also consider a major benefit. It can be extremely frustrating, especially on busy days when no one has the time to talk with a ranger, but when I get a chance to connect with visitors, I'm reminded of how great this job is. The best part of my job is leading off-trail caving trips for visitors, where they can directly experience the value of an undeveloped cave.

Pay—Many seasonals get hired at the government GS 3 level. I started at level 4, and I make a little above $7 an hour. On Sundays and holidays I get paid deferential pay, which is slightly higher than normal wage. I work 40 hours a week, usually four ten-hour days, but that's great, because that means three-day weekends, and that's one extra day to go out and explore the backcountry, or one extra day to recover from a two-day trip.

There is a mechanism in the system that allows upgrading in salary, but I haven't experienced it yet. This is my second season and I haven't received a raise. Everybody ought to be making a lot more than they do, and that's something the park service will hopefully change. I have a friend who works here who is trained as an emergency medical technician, and she's not getting paid anything extra for those services. If she took that training somewhere else, it would be worth a lot more in salary. In a sense it's kind of nice, because you know that people are working here for the right reasons.

Negatives—Within every government agency there's a certain amount of bureaucracy that gets in the way. I take an active stance against much of what the government does on my behalf, including resource management policies and land use decisions, so working for the government was a little bit of a shock to me. As a seasonal employee, I'm a bit more isolated from the political hassles. I've heard many permanent employees say that when they grow up, they want to be a seasonal worker.

I'm still a student, so I'm used to moving around every three months or so, and stability is not a priority in my life, but I imagine if you have a family it wouldn't be the best career. It's a rather nomadic lifestyle.

The future—The park service has a lot of real problems that they need to confront. One is that we're so overwhelmed with visitors that it's extremely difficult to instill a sense of the importance of the preservation and protection of the park. There are so many people that guided tours just aren't possible, and it's hard to preach biological conservation to people just passing by.

The park service is never going to be hurting for people to do the job that I do. People, especially young people, are always going to be looking for summer employment. I think the park's biggest problem is going to be keeping their permanent employees, people who could make a lot more money in the private sector.

References

National Parks and Conservation Association, 1776 Massachusetts Avenue NW, Suite 200, Washington, D.C. 20036; (202) 223-6722 or fax (202) 659-0650.

National Park Service, P.O Box 37127, Washington, D.C. 20013; (202) 208-4649.

California Department of Fish & Game, Education Branch, 1416 9th Street, Sacramento, CA 95814; (916) 653-8120.

Seasonal Employment: The National Parks, from US Department of the Interior, National Park Service, PO Box 37127, Washington, D.C. 20013-7127; (202) 208-4649.

Party Boat Deckhand

Dreams—What a life, spending every day on the briny blue, getting wages and tips, and for what? To help people catch fish? Sounds like a scam. Everyone loves you: the customers for your expertise, the captain for your brilliant assistance, and hey, if you ever need a date, there are plenty of tourists hanging around the docks when the boat comes in every afternoon.

Nightmares—You knew you shouldn't have gone out with lovely Brunhilda last night, but you did, and now it's 3:30 a.m. and it's time to go to the boat. Arrrrrgh! And for what, a boat-load of seasick greenhorns who might throw up on you? And what about those tips you heard about? Then there's Captain Bligh, who wants to keelhaul you.

Realities—Young people with a passion for the sea, fishing and people will discover an action-packed job with a reward, making $75 to $125 a day (depending on the size of tips). It can make for outstanding seasonal work. You must sacrifice your night life, work many days in a row when the fishing is hot, and most importantly, have a reliable alarm clock.

What it's all about—You must like people. You must like the sea. You must like fishing. You must like waking up early. Still with us? If so, of all the jobs suited for young people, there may be no better work than that as a deckhand of a party boat. You get lots of action, good pay (outstanding at times), the opportunity to be around people at their best (after all, they're fishing), and a life on the open ocean amid the seabirds, sea lions and denizens of the deep. If you have any long-term yearnings to become a party boat skipper, then become a deckhand and discover first hand what the sportfishing business is all about.

The hardest part of the job is hearing the alarm clock go off in the middle of the night every summer morning. If you stayed up much past eight or nine o'clock the night before, then getting yourself out of bed when that alarm clock goes off at 3:45 a.m. can be more tortuous than walking the plank above a school of milling sharks. Most deckhands adapt, cutting short any night life, or will find themselves every morning facing a boss who will closely resemble Captain Bligh.

For deckhands who love fishing, the sea and people, leaving the bed for the boat is as easy as envisioning the coming day's events. The job has plenty of excitement, and it can inspire you to overlook some of the shortcomings. The peaks are netting or gaffing prize fish landed by the customers, meeting fascinating people from diverse backgrounds, and days when the tips outgun the wages. It happens more than you might think.

The day starts with you arriving early (is there any other time?) to prepare the boat for the day's customers. It is the deckhand's job to set up rental tackle and bait, and sometimes account for payment. On the water, the deckhand is then available as a fishing instructor, constantly watching over a boat full of students, helping clean up line tangles, backlashes and tackle set ups. You will often clean the fish, then clean the boat and anything else the captain can think of. If you have the spirit for the sea, that much can be fun.

The pay is good for a seasonal job, usually $50 to $75 a day, plus tips. The latter can really add up, too. A boat load of 20 people might tip you $25 to $50 on the average, sometimes over $100 when the fishing is exceptional and the people are in a state of jubilation. Unlike most seasonal jobs, this one runs every day when the fishing is good; at times you might work 20 or 25 days in a row. When this happens, you can earn $2,500 to $3,500 in a month.

You also get first-class training on running a party boat business. When a skipper takes a liking to you as a deckhand, you will be shown all the little tricks of the trade that it takes to run a successful business. This is of great value.

For this, there are some sacrifices. One is the night life. Just plain forget that. Another is that usually one person per trip ends up being a crackpot, often an inebriated crackpot, and will not only make life miserable for you, but might throw up on you, too. Don't laugh, it happens. You will learn always to stand upwind of someone who looks a little green in the gills. You will also learn to wear a hat and never look up at the seagulls.

In some areas, where the seasons run longer than just the summer months, it can be difficult getting hired for a summer job. Like any boss, most skippers want commitment, and if their fishing season runs April through October, a college student can run into a severe conflict at both the beginning and end of the season. To be considered for the job, you need to be completely proficient in fishing skills, have the ability to communicate those skills, and make a clear commitment that you will be on time.

There are two routes to learn of job availability. One is to hang around the wharfs when the boats come in every afternoon. Skippers take a liking to young, curious "wharf rats" who are always asking questions. Let different skippers know, in person, that you would like to be trained as a deckhand. Skippers network every day on the marine radio, and when someone eventually has an opening, your name will come up. Talk to as many other working deckhands and skippers as possible. Don't be a jerk who won't go away, but rather a persistent prospect looking for a foot in the door. This approach works best for young adults, ages 16 to 22.

For those older or with some experience, a different strategy is more effective. Most regions have associations that skippers join, and as a prospect, you should contact the secretary of the respective association and announce your job availability and qualifications. The secretary, usually a skipper, will then put the word out over the marine radio. More business is conducted by skippers over the radio than many prospects understand.

Most deckhands like their work, and many later pass the Coast Guard captain's test and become a first mate, sometimes even buying their own party boats and starting their own businesses. There are only a few stoppers: showing up late to the boat (do it twice, and you're fired), substance abuse (usually an immediate good-bye), and not getting along with the customers (the Number One lesson is that you're there to show them a good time).

But why blow the bargain? After all, deckhands have a good deal going for them . . . In fact, there is one story about a burdened skipper, buried in debt from boat payments, insurance and rising fuel prices, who muttered, "I should have stayed a deckhand. No risk. Fair pay. Everybody on the boat likes you. When the trip is over, the work is over."

The irony is that in some cases, he is exactly right.

Career Case Study

Tony Broglio, California
Tony Broglio has been a deckhand in the San Francisco
Bay Area since 1981, and has been involved in the
boating industry since high school. He lives in Richmond,
California, and enjoys basketball, baseball and music.

Requirements—You definitely need experience with fishing and boating. It's really tough to train a green person who's never been around boats. You'd have to put them on a boat and let them work for just about nothing to get to know what's going on. You have to have a good personality and be able to deal with long hours and not a lot of money. One of the main jobs of a deckhand is public relations; you have to be good with the public. We've had passengers ranging from students to brain surgeons, and everybody gets treated equally. Every day is different.

Prospects—It's hard for skippers to find good deckhands, because there's not a lot of guaranteed money in it. Some guys come in and only get to work seven days in a month, so they quit. Down the road they might have the chance to work 100 days in a row, but they can't see that. The job depends on the skippers, too. If you apply with one of the older skippers who don't help out that much, they're going to want someone really experienced who can handle a lot of responsibility. But if you get a younger guy who's out there participating, not as much will be required of you.

There are very few female deckhands. I only know of one woman skipper and two female deckhands in the San Francisco Bay Area, where there are more than 50 party boats. There just aren't many women in the industry, period.

It's not a really stable job, unless you want to hustle. When your boat shuts down and your skipper doesn't need you, you just put it out on the radio that you have a day off and you want to work. Your success depends on how hard you work.

Benefits—I love being on the ocean every day. You might be in the same area twice, but never see the same thing. For example, you might be in a particular spot one day and see porpoises, and the next day see a Great White in the same spot.

I like meeting the people, too. Some groups I can't wait to see again. Usually they're really friendly and it's fun talking to them and getting to know them a little.

Pay—I think the average pay for a deckhand is about $50 to $60 a day, plus whatever gratuities you get. It depends on the skipper. Each operator pays his crew what he feels they're worth. Tips really vary; you can have groups that get full limits and don't tip you a buck, and groups who lose everything they had and give you $100.

Negatives—Bad weather can make it tough to work. No one is really enthused about fishing when they're cold and wet, and if the fishing is bad, it can be the worst day of your life. There can be groups that aren't a lot of fun, like a bar group, a bunch of guys who come on the boat after closing down a bar and want to continue trying to close down the bar. I don't know why they'd want to come on a boat just to get drunk and pass out, but they do. They'll lose their fish and blame it all on you.

The future—It's going to be tough. There are fewer charter boats than ever, and if habitat problems keep arising as they are all over the country, there are not going to be too many boats left to work on. The future does not look that great.

Career Case Study

Lee Leffard, Florida
Lee Leffard, a licensed charter boat captain, has worked as a mate in Pensacola, Florida off and on since 1978. He formerly ran a retail/wholesale seafood business. In the winter months, Lee is a full-time "Mr. Mom" to his daughter and a professional musician with the Pensacola Symphony. He also teaches music lessons. He lives with his wife and daughter in Gulf Breeze, Florida.

Requirements—You have to know everything about fishing. The only way to do that is to read magazines associated with the business: sportfishing magazines, saltwater fishing magazines, anything to do with your trade. You have to ask questions and keep your ears open. You have to be willing to change and risk constantly. A friend of mine worked on charters for years; the captain told him exactly what to do and he did it, day in and day out. And they did okay. A good mate will get on a set pattern of how he's going to do things, and if it doesn't work, he's got to adjust and try things that might be totally off the wall. He's got to stick his neck out and risk getting it cut off sometimes.

You have to have a very businesslike attitude. That's your job every day, to go out and try to catch fish for people. A good mate looks at each person when they walk up, and his feeling in the back of his mind is that they don't know anything, they can't even tie their shoes. But you can't judge people as they walk down the dock. Everybody gets equal treatment. You have to be very flexible. When the fishing is slow, you've got to be able to interact with the party, to get things going and keep the morale up, but still do your job.

Prospects—Most of the boats up here in Pensacola have a set mate at the beginning of the season. They have one mate who shows up every day, and he's good or he wouldn't be working. There aren't a lot of jobs for people off the street. When you get into the private boats, like private sportfishing boats, it can be really tough. If the owner doesn't like you, you're gone. If you do one little thing wrong, you're gone. Basically, if you wake up in the morning and look wrong, you're gone.

It's an interesting business. Not everybody can do it. But if you're good at what you do, if you're single and want to move around and travel, you can make a full-time living at it, especially in places like South Florida, Costa Rica and Cozumel. If you're good you can travel all over the world.

We have taken a few people on that had past fishing experience and a good background fishing on private boats, but usually they don't realize how much work is involved with working on a charter and they quit. If we run an eight-hour charter, that means eight hours from the time we leave until the time we come back. That doesn't count the time it takes before and after to get set up and cleaned up. It can turn into an 11- or 12-hour day.

The last person we tried out was applying as a backup mate. The captain told me to really work him, to just sit back and supervise. The guy got on the boat and got a big surprise. He didn't understand that the boat's got to be made ready before you leave: you've got to get the tackle ready, cut the bait, get all the passengers on and through the trip, clean the fish, and clean the boat. At the end of the day he said to me, "Lee, there's a whole lot more to this than fishing." I said, "Paul, fishing is the easy part."

Benefits—I like to see people catch fish. I like to see people who have never been deep sea fishing in their life, who step on the boat and catch a big red snapper and just get overwhelmed by it. That's what I like the most. The kids are great, too. To be quite honest, a small percentage of them are a pain in the neck, but most of them are very well behaved. Yesterday we had a husband and wife and their two kids, and the kids had never seen the Gulf of Mexico or Florida before; they had never been deep sea fishing, and they had a ball.

It's a lot of fun. You get bragging rights, which are nice. If you know you're on a good boat with a good captain, doing the best job you can do, you can feel good about it. My boss and I work perfectly together. We usually don't even talk to each other on trips, but I know what he's doing and he knows what I'm doing and we don't worry about it. There's an old saying that says a good captain and his mate are closer than a good husband and wife, which I believe is true. We have fights just like my wife and I do, but we always resolve everything and get the job done.

Pay—To be quite honest, when people come up to me and say they want to be a mate, I look 'em in the eye and say, "Are you crazy?" They hear stories about the $150 tips, which I do get, but when you average it all out and compare it to the number of hours you have to put in, it's not that great. You've got to love what you're doing in this business.

The pay really depends on what part of the country you're in. I would say, on an average, you could probably gross about $20,000 a year. That's on a boat that fishes all day, 200 days a year.

Negatives—What really bugs me is somebody who charters a boat for a day, gets on after paying $500 or $600 and then thinks, "I own this boat for the day." They start snapping their fingers at the captain and myself.

I don't like people who get on the boat and know everything. They'll start saying, "I've been snapper fishing for years, and I've done this and I've done that," and all they want to do is catch a whole bunch of big fish.

Twenty years ago you could go out and catch snapper and grouper, get back and go down to the market, sell them and make enough to pay for the trip and maybe put a few bucks in your pocket, and still take fish home. You can't do that anymore; the fish just aren't there. But there are some guys who still try, and I don't like them.

The future—It can go either way. Fishing's coming back strong, but it's costing more and more to get into the business, so much that it's almost cost-prohibitive. You're looking at $200,000 or $300,000 just to get into chartering. Something I've noticed about many young kids looking to do this is they're not willing to work, to put in the time to learn, to take care of the boat. Every so often there are one or two who are, but the majority want to step on, put in their eight hours, and step off, no more and no less.

References

National Marine Fisheries Commission, 1315 East-West Highway, Silver Springs, MD 20910; (301) 713-2239.

Maritime Institute, 1310 Rosecrans Street #G, San Diego, CA 92106; (619) 225-1783.

Note: There are many regional organizations of party boat skippers, where information on job openings for deckhands may be available.

Party Boat Skipper

Dreams—Every day is spent on the briny blue, catching big fish, rhapsodizing about Moby Dick. Your customers put their faith and their money in you, and in turn, you reward them day after day. You love watching the sun rise each morning, counting your money, and never have trouble getting to sleep at night. After all, you are living the American dream.

Nightmares—It's dawn and the motor won't start, the boat leaks, and when you finally have enough people for a trip, the fish don't bite. The overhead is ridiculous, the government is perpetuating the decline of fisheries, and on the water, you don't feel like helping the latest loon on the railing unsnarl his line. As for that alarm clock at 3:30 a.m.—shoot it.

Realities—The individual who knows how to promote and account as well as he fishes can do well enough, earning in the $35,000 range, and in a hot year, more than $100,000. Peaks and valleys are the rule. It requires a unique individual who can do a lot of things well, including waking up in the middle of the night. Must-do: Try this out first as a deckhand.

What it's all about—"A long time forgotten are the dreams that just fell by the way . . . " That Waylon Jennings' line goes right to the heart of the careers of many party boat skippers. There may be no other career where the vision and the life that follows spans such a great gulf.
Party boat skippers live a crazy saga of peaks and valleys, often on the precipice of an economic Death Valley. They deal

---

perpetually with skewed fishing regulations, Coast Guard inspections, oblique government fees and preposterous insurance costs that add up to a terrible overhead. For them, waking up in the middle of the night is normal. Getting seasick is career threatening. And on virtually every trip, there will be at least one kook who you would like to feed to the sharks. For this, a party boat skipper usually earns about $30,000 to $35,000 a year.

It's just not worth it, right? As Waylon also says, "Wrong!" There is scarcely a party boat skipper on the planet who would trade life on a boat for a sit-down job. Many become addicted to the sea the same way a truck driver becomes addicted with white-line fever. Why? There are many reasons. One is that with the dawn of each day, you never know what's going to happen next, what you might see, what might be caught. Another are the people, because many of your customers can end up being loyal friends. Then there is the atypical combination of skills that are required; it is one of the most unique jobs in America.

You have to be a master pilot to pass the Coast Guard seaman tests, a detective to find the fish each day, a technician to keep the boat operations running smooth, a teacher to help customers who are new to fishing, an accountant to make sure both ends meet, a promoter to attract customers, a safety expert to handle emergencies, a politician to work with state and federal bureaucrats, and hey, you also need to be a generally nice person so you don't turn off newcomers who board your boat. Quite a lot of requirements.

The way it usually works out is that a party boat skipper can do all these things rather naturally, as if with a six sense. Passing the Coast Guard tests—a check ride and written exam—is usually one of the more difficult barriers for newcomers. For old-timers, it's the accounting and promotional work that often doesn't get done.

Yet right there—accounting and promotion—are the two keys that can determine the financial success of your business as a party boat skipper. Too many skippers forget that it is a business they are in. They don't keep a close, up-to-date account of exactly how many nickels are coming in and how many nickels are going out. They don't promote themselves. They think that when the trip is done, "it's time to go home."

A key difference between the many skippers who make $20,000 and the rare few that top $100,000 is often promotion. After every trip, they call newspapers with their fishing report. They are constantly trying to attract media members to go fishing with them, whether they are from newspapers, magazines, outdoorsmen's tabloids, radio or TV stations. They join sportsmen's organizations. They attend the winter sports shows. They advertise. They give away free trips on radio shows. In other words, they promote: "Come fishing with me and you will have a good time." Succeed and you make big money.

Of course, there is the matter of catching fish. That comes with the territory. With fish populations cycling up and down, usually in direct correlation to habitat conditions, a slow period of fish catching during what should be peak season can really slow down the customer count and put a giant crimp in your wallet. You expect it during the off-season, when weather and seasonal migrations of fish can keep your boat tied up at the dock, but during peak season? A real nightmare. Because of the politicization of resource issues and a number of fishery declines, the party boat skipper ends up hurting the worst.

To get in the business fresh, figure on paying $40,000 to $65,000 for a boat, and an additional $5,000 to $7,000 per year for insurance. These are your largest fixed costs. Gas, boat and engine maintenance, deckhand expenses, boat docking fees, and licenses can add up to a tidy sum that can turn a marginal year into a bad one.

The only way to go is to first work as a deckhand on another boat, working every day until anybody else would be sick of it. If you still like it, then this is the career for you after all. And regardless of how much money you make, hey, at least it's no desk job.

Career Case Study

Tommy Rothery, California

Tommy Rothery got his first job as a deckhand at age 17, and then became a licensed skipper at age 19. He has run the internationally-known Royal Polaris sportsfishing boat since 1975. He likes to hunt, fish, jet ski and snow ski. He is married, has two children, and lives in Spring Valley, California.

Requirements—Someone who comes from another industry, say, a fireman or police officer who likes to fish and wants to become a skipper, usually doesn't have the knowledge or time on the sea to be on the upper end of the fleet. Becoming a skipper means starting at the bottom and working your way up. That usually means getting a job as a deckhand.

When I'm hiring deckhands, I look for guys who have no experience, who are in it not for just a part-time job, but for a career. I want somebody who's willing to hang in there for five or six years, who's good with people and hustles.

Back in the old days, the 1950s, it was standard for people in this industry to have coarse personalities; they just loaded people on the boat and that was that. Now the whole atmosphere has gone from just packing people on to more of a recreation activity. There is a different class of people wanting to get out there and fish, and there's more money at stake. No matter what position you hold on the boat, whether you're a deckhand or captain, you've got to be able to relate to people and make them feel comfortable. You have to have a good rapport with people.

It's even more so for captains. We've gone from being the guy who's up in the wheelhouse all day to someone who really participates in the whole venture. I come down and greet everyone, then give an orientation and a one-on-one seminar on fishing. I want to let them know that I'm a real person; I'm not just up there in my ivory tower. I let them know that they're welcome to come up and see what I do whenever they want, and I try to discourage people from calling me "Captain." You become a lot more equal when you're on a first-name basis.

I also try to learn everyone's name on each trip, so instead of saying, "Excuse me, sir," I can say, "Hey, Bob..." People are really impressed when you take the time to do that.

When you decide that you want to become a captain, you have to get a captain's license. You're required to have 730 days sea time before you can get your basic license, and I would strongly recommend going to a licensing school for that. They really teach you what you need to know for the test and pretty much make sure that everyone passes. Once you've acquired your license, it helps to be in a position where you know there's a future, to be on a boat that runs most the year and where you know that the owner is going to put you out there on the water.

The first few trips are tough, because you haven't been around long enough to get your name known and have people be comfortable with your reputation. For that reason it can be beneficial to get into long-range trips rather than one- and two-day trips. Fishing experience, obviously, is important too. There are a lot of people who think they want to be a captain just because they love to fish, but they may not have the natural knack for thinking like a fish, which you really have to have. You can have the best equipment available, but if you don't know the area you're in and its patterns and quirks, it's not going to do you much good.

Prospects—It's tough, but there is potential out there. The long-range trips are what you want to be in right now. There are opportunities on the one- and two-day boats, but if you're looking to do it as a career, the knowledge you acquire is just not enough to give you a good thorough knowledge of the industry. I've seen one-day captains try to become long-range skippers, and they typically don't do well. On the other hand, when you've started out as a long-range skipper, you can always go back and start doing day trips if you want.

To succeed in this industry, you have to be in the inner circle. If you don't get the right information to help you out, you're going to get dragged down. When people know you as one of them, they'll include you as one of the guys who always knows where everybody is and what they're doing. If you're ten miles out it can be kind of lonely, and without the right contacts you can miss out on some really big stuff.

Benefits—You're working for yourself and you have control of the situation you're in. It's the best feeling in the world, to find a school and get everybody fishing, seeing them smiling and running around. I love to throw a bait out there, hook up, and hand the rod to one of the passengers. They get so excited—it's great. It's a pretty neat high, working toward making people happy. I think I almost enjoy that more than fishing for myself.

Pay—You don't do this to get rich. The average long-range operator can make around $100 a day. Daily operators can make up to $125, but that's also on a seasonal basis.

Negatives—You have to be able to handle being away from home for long periods of time. You run 90 to 120 days without being able to get off the boat except for the time it takes to do your laundry. If you have a family, that can be really difficult. I missed the birth of one of my children by four hours. And once you become a captain you have the responsibility of being there all the time. You can't throw it into someone else's hands.

When you're taking people out with the hope of catching fish, you end up either a hero or a jerk. If you do find fish, everybody loves you, but if you don't, even if people are understanding, you always wonder if they're thinking, "This guy doesn't know what he's doing."

You're responsible for the whole crew; they are going to echo your personality and attitude. As long as I'm up, they're up. So if I'm depressed or in a bad mood, I have to put on a happy face for everybody.

The future—I wouldn't say that the market is good. I don't think there are going to be any huge quantities of openings anytime soon. I know a couple of boats that could use new captains right now, but for someone who is just starting out, that wouldn't do them much good. It's hard to just walk down the deck and ask for a job; you've got to be on the inside to move up. You have to start at the bottom and work up, and be at the right place at the right time. Timing is very important; you have to be there at the right moment.

Career Case Study

Jerry Lastfogel, Maryland

Jerry Lastfogel has been in the fishing industry for 38 years and is known as "Captain Hook." He is an executive with the Maryland Charter Boat Association. His past work experience includes catering and working as a police officer. He lives with his wife, Debbie, in Edgewater, Maryland.

Requirements—Before you can get your Coast Guard license, you have to have at least two year's documented experience on the water, working as a deckhand or bait boy or whatever. That has to be certified by the captains you work for. After you've worked on the boats for the required number of hours, you have to study what they call the "Rules of the Road," sort of like a driver's test but a little more extensive. There are certain rules that you have to be familiar with, universal laws pertaining to water transportation that you should know by heart. There are different rules for different parts of the country.

You have to have a love for the water. Commonly people who get into this business are people who started fishing as children from a rowboat and just aspired to bigger boats.

Prospects—Anyone who has a desire to be in the business can go into it, but it takes a lot of hard work to be successful. The hardest thing is to invest in a serviceable vessel. The average young fellow is going to be paying between $30,000 and $150,000 just for his vessel, unless he comes from a family of boat-builders. That's a lot of capital.

You have to earn your dues. You have to have competitive prices, advertise, and build a book. You have to learn what's going on. But once it's in your blood, it's there to stay. As far as job openings, it's pretty much the same as being a guide—the old guys die off and new guys come in.

More women seem to be taking advantage of opportunities. Five of the 300 members of the Maryland Charter Boat Association are women who are licensed captains. In fact, the winner of our last Memorial Day contest, winning a $2000 prize, was aboard a vessel captained by a woman. I've been around 38 years, and it's just been during the last five that women have gone to the trouble of going through all the rigmarole. The macho captain image is still prevalent, but we know women are there.

Benefits—No matter how bad things are, when I get up and I'm behind the wheel, watching the sun come up over the water on a pretty day, the gratification is beyond description. I have my own twin-engine vessel; it took ten years to pay her off, but she's mine now. It's a labor of love.

Pay—The first few years can be tough. Some guys break even, others who can build a book up and can fish four or five days a week can make a profit. It really varies; it's a very gray area.

The government right now is in the process of adding a lot of user fees and requirements for additional equipment that costs thousands of dollars. I've broken even two years in a row now, made maybe four or five thousand dollars. It's highly competitive business, and you have to realize that when you're a charter boat captain you're a businessman. It's very challenging.

Negatives—You always hope that nothing goes wrong with

your vessel mechanically, especially if you work seasonally. And you don't want a bad weather scene, either. A major hurricane can wipe you out for a season.

Some guys get so wrapped up in fishing that they lose track of reality. If you're not stable, the love for your vessel and what you're doing could conceivably lead you to neglect your responsibilities and obligations on-shore. That can be a real problem if you have a wife and family. I wouldn't say that happens very often, but it is something to be aware of.

The future—There will always be charter boat captains. I've been around for 38 years and I don't see any sign of the business slowing down. There are a good many people who make a living at it. It's a family tradition that is passed down from generation to generation. It's all they know, and it's a heritage to many. I do think it's a lot harder to start out than when I did it years ago. The electronics and things on vessels are a lot more complicated and precise than in the old days, and the regulations are new; now they're part of the Department of Transportation. There are a lot of rules and regulations to adhere to.

Protection and conservation are buzzwords now, and although it's certainly important that our resources be preserved, we don't want to be regulated to death. A good number of us could be regulated right out of business.

References

National Marine Fisheries Commission, 1315 East-West Highway, Silver Springs, MD 20910; (301)713-2239.

Maritime Institute, 1310 Rosecrans Street #G, San Diego, CA 92106; (619)225-1783.

Coast Guard Information Center, 14180 Dallas Parkway, Dallas, TX 75240-9795; (800)424-8883, extension 5003.

Note: There are many regional organizations of party boat skippers.

Peace Corps Volunteer

Dreams—You are treated like royalty by the residents you are helping, live in the best conditions available, and your life is shaped by helping others, not taking from them. The salary may not sound so great, but it stretches a mile out in Zimbabwe. For the rest of your life, when you say, "I worked for the Peace Corps," everyone will be fascinated with your tales.

Nightmares—It's the middle of the night, and some strange bug is sitting on your chest. It's good it woke you up, because you've got a case of diarrhea and you better sprint to the bathroom. Wait a minute, what bathroom? You'd pay all your savings, all hundred dollars of it, to go back home for a pizza and then a night in your own bed.

Realities—It's a two-year commitment in a Third World country that needs your help in some specialty. Expect long hours, low pay in dollars, and high pay in the emotional uplift from helping other humans in need. The experience of living in another culture is unmatched.

What it's all about—"This is the toughest job you'll ever love." That's the outlook for success in the Peace Corps. All the good things you have heard about the Peace Corps are true. Alas, so are all the bad things. But the bottom line is this: See with your heart, and the view will end up just fine.

It can be the ideal alternative for a college graduate who isn't quite ready to join the American work force. Not only are the personal rewards of working for the Peace Corps beyond measure, but when you return to the U.S. and start looking for a job, your experience will set you apart from other candidates. Employers see it as demonstrable proof that your heart is in the right place. That's because it is. The experiences you will have in the Peace Corps will provide a backdrop for the rest of your life.

Signing up for the Peace Corps, however, is not as easy as simply walking into a recruiting station and signing your life away. This ain't the army. For one thing, the Peace Corps accepts mostly college graduates, although extensive specialized experience may be substituted. For another, you have to pass a two-month training program. If you are still on track at that point, then get ready to launch into a new orbit.

It's a two-year adventure in which you will be sent to a Third World country, most likely one on the African continent. It is no vacation. You are there because the Peace Corps is there, helping in education, medical care, agricultural development, or perhaps a craft such as carpentry. Remember, this is for two years. After a year, you can't say, "Well, I've had enough. Now I'd like to go home and have a root beer float." You must fulfill your mission. That is the general picture.

To fine-tune the picture, consider that you will be paid a monthly allowance where the rent for your living quarters will be one-quarter of that salary. So if your salary turns out to be $750 per month, don't get ready to jump into a piranha-infested river—because your rent will only be about $187 per month. It all has a way of working out, and compared to the local residents, you will actually be living like a king, not King Kong.

The local citizenry has a collective understanding that you are there to help. They will give you respect and cooperation despite the cultural and ethnic differences. Just don't start acting out the Ugly American routine. Do that and you might get put in a pot—by your fellow Peace Corps workers. This is a situation where style means as much as substance.

Most volunteers adapt quite well to the settings, regardless of their respective backgrounds. That's because many fresh college graduates have been worn down by interminable studying and are in urgent need for a dramatic change of scenery. In the Peace Corps, they get exactly that. That is why the best parts of the job are experiencing a completely separate culture—and doing something for the benefit of humanity. Other positive factors include the travel opportunities, and that your basic needs are taken care of, including housing, food, medical, and hey, sometimes you get Saturday nights off.

The inside word is that after just a short time, you will discover that there are adventures and articles that can be traded for if you bring the right goods. In big demand in Third World countries are T-shirts, baseball hats, buttons and pins—just make sure they have an American-style logo on them. A New York Yankees baseball hat, a San Francisco 49ers T-shirt, a pin with Madonna's picture on it—these are worth more than gold. Bring all you can arrange. It may sound crazy, but it can really pay off. You can trade them for local goods, a fishing or hunting trip, or perpetual good will.

There are some factors that you just have to learn to deal with. At times the living conditions are not good. After two years in the Peace Corps, you might qualify for a master's degree in entomology after seeing all the little crawly things. In some countries, mosquito nets are standard sleepwear. Language problems can be confounding. If you get homesick and want to phone mom and dad, it can take a week's worth of red tape to get the phone call through. The mail is very slow. And while the pay is sufficient when you're on assignment, don't plan on saving up to buy a Corvette.

A nice touch, however, is that when your two-year stint is up and you are returning home, the Peace Corps will pay you a "readjustment allowance." In other words, you are provided with some money to help you get reestablished in mainstream American society. It can range up to $4,000 or $5,000.

For the most part, your mission will be one of benevolence. What volunteers always remember the best are the faces of the individuals they help—the looks of concern, acknowledgment and gratitude. Only rarely are these feelings of emotional connection verbalized, but they are there, they are real, and it is something you feel and know to be true. That is when you realize the true blessing of the job.

Career Case Study

Julie Huffaker, Washington, D.C.   Julie Huffaker worked for the Peace Corps in Botswana, Africa, where she taught science for one year, then became a coordinator for pre-school programs. She is continuing to work for the Peace Corps in Washington, D.C. as a University Programs Specialist. Julie's prior experience included working on a mental health ward and performing research at Emory Medical School. She lives in Washington, D.C., where she enjoys spending time with the two wild dogs she brought back from Africa.

Requirements—You have to be an American citizen over 18 years of age. Most people are required to have a bachelor's degree, unless you have a great deal of experience in a technical field. The selection is more competitive now, because the demand in the field is not matching the number of applications coming in. Many countries now request that you have a master's degree in education to be a teacher. I kind of snuck in. One of the countries suddenly had a request for 60 science instructors, and I had some experience tutoring, so I got in.

There is a 10-page application that you have to fill out, which is pretty intense. They want to know all about your background, experience, etc., and they ask for six references. You also have an oral interview, which varies from person to person. Mine was pretty rigorous. You have to pass a thorough physical exam as well.

They like you to know some non-English language, but it's not required. I've heard people say that if you can just get through all the bureaucracy and red tape of the application process here in the States, you'll do fine overseas. You have to be really flexible. I found myself re-evaluating my beliefs constantly. You really have to be open and able to accept the fact that it's easier to change yourself than your environment. Sometimes certain things would really get to me, and I had to take a look and ask myself if it was me or just my beliefs. It helps if you're fairly mature.

Prospects—I've heard somewhere that they receive four or five applications for every available position. This year 40,000 people applied for 4,000 or 5,000 positions. It seems that when the job market is down, a lot of people think that they'll just take off for a while and get some experience in the Peace Corps until the economy gets better. Unfortunately the market isn't much better there.

Previous volunteer work or community service work can help give you an advantage. If you've traveled overseas or done any kind of international service work, you'll have a much better chance of being accepted.

Benefits—I learned a lot about myself while I was in Africa. I gained a lot of patience and respect for other cultures that I didn't have before, because I didn't know much about them. It's one thing to sympathize with the poverty of a country from afar, and quite another thing to actually experience it and realize what they have to deal with. I worked with a lot of local administrators during my second year, and I was very impressed by them; they're so motivated to clean up their country and get things going. I met a couple of women lawyers in Botswana who were really passionate about changing conditions for women there, and they were very successful at what they did. It was very inspirational for me. It made me look at our country and think, "If they can do it, why can't we?"

A lot of people get discouraged if they don't see their services resulting in any huge impact, but I learned how to reach people by not trying to change them or preach to them, but by just being me, teaching by example. I had a lot of fun, letting them get to know me as a person rather than as "an American." It was rewarding to me to see the effect my actions had on the students and other teachers. The fact that I came to school every day on time and got things done really impressed them.

Pay—Your allowance depends on the country in which you're assigned. In Botswana they gave the same amount of money to everyone regardless of what part of the country they were in. People in the city could go out and buy fresh vegetables or go to a movie if they wanted, but the people in the desert didn't have too many opportunities to spend their money. The people who lived in the desert tended to have a lot more travel money on vacations.

I think they try to figure your income so you're in the median range. For example, when I was a teacher I made 480 pula. The regular teachers there were paid from 400 to 600 pula, so I was just about in the middle. But Peace Corps volunteers don't pay for housing; that's all provided for you. As a teacher, you are usually set up in a duplex with another teacher, or you're housed with a family—whatever's available.

Negatives—Physically, Botswana was not very pretty. That was just my situation, though; I'm sure it depends on where you go. Everyone got dusty and dehydrated, but medically it was an okay situation. It can be frustrating to adjust; it takes a good six or eight months. You always have to deal with a certain attitude of "What are you Americans doing in our country?" but I think a lot of that is based on ignorance. Americans have a certain reputation in many countries; they see us all as fat and rich, and if we need money we just go to our parents and get it. It takes some time to let them know that we're not all like that.

There is a danger factor. I almost got attacked by a crocodile once, and another time I was charged by a lion. It's easy to forget you're in Africa, because it's so beautiful and peaceful. Sometimes it's hard to realize that over the horizon there are no subdivisions like in the U.S.

The future—My experience in the Peace Corps has helped me tremendously. I would do it again in a minute. The attitudes and ideas that people are bringing back to our country are helping to change the way Americans view the world. A lot of people are returning and seeing what they can offer to underprivileged youth, as teachers or public health workers. There are a lot of opportunities becoming established for returned Peace Corps volunteers. Whether they'll flourish depends on how much support they receive.

Career Case Study

John Teeple, Oregon

John Teeple worked as a Peace Corps volunteer in Morocco, Africa as a beekeeper from 1989 to 1991. His previous experience includes working for Vail Associates in Colorado and Grand Teton National Park in Wyoming. He currently works as an account representative at Direct Mail Projects in Portland, Oregon. John is an avid outdoorsman who enjoys running, mountain biking and mountain climbing. By the way, those are bees on his smiling face.

Requirements—There are no real set requirements, but there are guidelines set by the Peace Corps. They do look for a college degree, but extensive experience can be substituted. Ten years of experience working on a farm will be looked upon as an asset, even if that person has had no formal schooling. Lately there has been a trend toward skills related to teaching English and community development, especially for the eastern block countries. In third world countries, reforestation, agricultural development and other resource-oriented skills are needed as well.

You have to go through a pretty in-depth interview process when you apply. That process seems to discourage a lot of volunteers because it's pretty bureaucratic, which is exactly the mentality that a lot of volunteers want to avoid. Once you get overseas, it's really not as cut-and-dried as the application process. The application process can be disheartening.

A sense of adventure is definitely a requirement. A high level of tolerance, not only of other people but of other cultures, is important, too. When you're in a foreign country, you have to realize that you're going to be looked upon as someone special. There are times when you'll just want to get away and have time to yourself, but every time you walk out the door you're the center of attention, and you have to be diplomatic. If you act nasty to someone, your reputation is going to be shot. You have to have the flexibility to appreciate other cultures and understand that what may be offensive to you may mean nothing to someone else, and vice versa.

Prospects—From what I've seen, competition seems to depend on how you go through the application process. At the university where I applied it was very competitive. As far as I know there are no set quotas for the number of people accepted, but if a recruiter has a lot of people applying at once, he's going to have more freedom to be selective. He's going to make recommendations based on what he sees, and if there are a lot of highly qualified people applying, he's naturally going to be more particular.

Benefits—Personal growth was number one for me. It's a once in a lifetime experience, something I'll never forget. In relation to one's career, it is definitely an exercise in self-motivation. Very few people have a direct supervisor telling them what to do, and for me, that was an opportunity to structure projects and motivate myself. There's no one pushing you, telling you whether you've failed or succeeded, so you have to operate on your own judgement and sense of what to do.

It's an opportunity to travel, to live and work abroad doing something that is pretty widely known and respected. You get the adventure, plus a good plug on your resume. Though experience abroad in the Peace Corps is not directly related to most businesses, it is considered a positive asset, much more than if you went out and toured Europe on your own for a couple of years.

You have a lot of freedom to accomplish the things you want to do. There is no structured, standardized operation guide to follow. You are given your basic job guideline, then they pretty much let you go. That varies, of course; English teachers, for example, have to make daily lesson plans and show up to school every day, which makes it seem more like a traditional job. But there are so many diverse kinds of jobs. I knew of a couple of guys in the Mediterranean whose job was basically to bird watch, scuba dive, and count Monk seals.

Pay—Don't plan on joining to make money, but the Peace Corps does take care of you. We called it "Mother Peace Corps." The medical care was excellent; there was a nurse at our disposal 24 hours a day, and we were provided with everything we needed. Your salary depends on where you are. Where I was, it ended up to be about two times what my rent was. After your Close of Service (COS), they give you a readjustment allowance based on the number of months you served; it's around $200 a month, so you receive about $4,000 to $5,000.

Negatives—Sometimes there's a lot of bureaucracy involved. For example, if your living quarters were set up somewhere other than where you worked and you wanted to move closer, you'd have to go through a lot of red tape. Getting things like that done is not easy. You have to fill out request forms and go through all the channels; basically, it's a real pain. Some people say it's the easiest job you'll ever hate. The whole pace of life over there often moves really slowly. It gets kind of difficult for people who are used to a fast-paced lifestyle, and you really have to learn to slow down and adapt. It is sometimes difficult to get things necessary for your area of expertise, such as tools, transportation or resources.

I didn't have a lot of trouble being away from home, although I'm sure some people get homesick. You tend to get so involved in what you're doing that you don't think about it much.

When I came back, it took me a long time to get back in the swing of things. I remember that I couldn't get away from the TV, especially MTV.

The future—The Peace Corps itself has a five-year limit, so it's not something you can do forever. You can spend three years in a foreign country, and another two with the Washington, D.C. Peace Corps division, but you're pretty limited after that. It is a great point from which to move into other service positions, though, or any sort of international career.

Reference

Peace Corps, 1990 K Street NW, Washington, D.C. 20526; (800) 424-8580.

Office of Returned Volunteer Career Services, 1990 K Street NW, Washington, D.C. 20526; (800) 424-8580, ext 2284.

Photographer

Dreams—Outdoors photographers are paid to visit the most beautiful places in the world, develop a unique appreciation for natural beauty, and can do their work as a part-time hobby to make some fair change, or a full-time job with a chance at $100,000 a year.

Nightmares—They are prisoners of hope without an "off" button, always looking for another picture. High overhead can be a problem, weather can foul up a schedule, and labs can foul up your film. Worst, editors can take months to return slides they'll never use, scratch the ones they do, and then provide little pay until you hit the national markets.

Realities—It is easy to start on a part-time basis, but very difficult to start as a full-timer, requiring more emphasis on hustling your shots than the skill in taking them. If you can do both, this can be a lucrative career filled with exciting trips. The background noise will include constant pressure to produce quality, and your friends will want you to take free pictures at their weddings.

What it's all about—All successful outdoors photographers share one common element: They are graduates of the University of Nature. They have the ability to see the world in its finest terms, then capture it for presentation to those with lesser but appreciative visions. Regardless of equipment, experience and attitude, all have an "eye" for what makes a good photo, and are constantly in a state of mind where all they see becomes visual images to be captured on film. If that sounds like you, well, you have a pretty good chance of success.

It is a good job to participate in on a part-time basis. If you sell enough photos of your weekend adventures, you can write off all your expenses on your taxes, plus make some pin money. Once you have established yourself as a quality contributor with several magazine editors, the doors have a way of opening to new fields of dreams, and in turn, a chance for selling single photos for $500 to $1,500.

The best way to get started is to buy the book *Photography Market,* which details thousands of markets to sell your photos. Just scanning through the book, reading what editors require and pay, can get the brain churning as to all the photos that are waiting to be taken and sold. It will also give you a realistic idea of pay rates. Pretty soon, you will start to envision what is possible.

That passion must carry you through as you learn the technical expertise with your camera, how to hustle your shots with editors, and ultimately, how to compose a photo so it has just the right touch. In the process, you are bound to suffer great humility. Rejections, low pay and problems with equipment and weather come with the territory for the newcomer. Those who have low self-esteem never make it past these obstacles. But if the flame burns, then light the wick, because a great career is possible for those who can self-ignite.

Outdoors photographers make a living at it by having huge inventories of slides, all carefully filed, and are always adding to them. Then when an editor suddenly calls for a specific shot, all the photographer has to do is find it in their personal photo library, then send it in with an appropriate caption. Many photographers also keep hundreds of generic, stock-type photos on file at many magazines or with an agency, so the editor doesn't even need to make a phone call to buy one. This can result in easy sales and a more orderly flow of checks to your mailbox, rather than relying solely on assignments, big-time feature spreads or cover shots.

Options include selling photos for advertisements, book covers, postcards, and even calendars, although the latter is usually a financial disaster if produced independent of a national chain. During the lean times, a photographer might even show up at the local boat ramp and take pictures of fishermen with their fish, then sell them for a quick $25 or $50 apiece. At one time or another, most outdoors photographers will tap into all of these markets.

It is wise to invest in a computer and professional letterhead, and at least occasionally try to write a short story to go with your photos. The computer will allow you to keep a neat, filed record of where every photo is, whether it's in your file or that of a magazine in New York, and also to print quality letters, captions and manuscripts for editors. In addition, you can practice writing with a computer, and even if writing isn't your strength, you may occasionally sell story/photo packages where photos alone won't do the job.

One problem is that the better you get in the business, the less patience you will have with editors who don't pay enough, flop photos, and worse, scratch your slides. Because it takes passion to be a good photographer, that energy can turn and become volcanic-level anger. Rather than get mad at the world, a better approach is to diversify your markets, so you allow no one editor to have power over your well-being.

That done, then hang on for the ride. It's exciting—you will travel to the greatest places on earth, and have periods when you make a lot of money and others when you make none. There will be times when the weather won't clear for a week, others when every picture you snap feels like it will fetch $500.

Even though most photographers take unbelievable numbers of pictures, remember this story about Ansel Adams: At a lecture, he was asked, "Mr. Adams, how many pictures do you need to take to get a really good one?" Ansel Adams just smiled, then said, "One."

Career Case Study

Ron Spomer, Idaho

Ron Spomer is a full-time free-lance photographer/ writer who has been in the photography business since the late 1970s. He became established while working as an information specialist for the South Dakota Game, Fish and Parks Department. His work has since been published in over 70 magazines, including Audubon, National Wildlife and Wildlife Conservation, as well as several books and brochures. He has also won many national awards.

Requirements—You have to be gullible, romantic and stupid. You have to have lots of staying power, lots of gumption. Most of the wildlife photographers I know haven't had any formal schooling—they just picked up a camera and started taking pictures. A few lucky ones find a mentor who can give them a few tips. I would recommend taking a few outdoor photography workshops. I've found those to be more beneficial than the university-type classes, which mostly focus on the artistic side of photography rather than the business side. The most important thing in starting out is to get the right equipment. Too many young photographers start out buying inexpensive stuff, and it really affects the quality of their work.

Prospects—Starting to sell your work is a process of trying to find your strengths as a photographer, then finding your market. Once you find your market, you can write up proposals and start sending your slides to publishers. The other avenue is to send out just a few samples, a variety of slides that show what you can do, and hope that someone needs something in that vein. You can try calling magazine editors and offering your work over the phone, but that can be risky. You'll soon find out who frowns on that and who doesn't. If you bug them too much you'll be blacklisted. Ideally, you will get on editors' "wish lists" and get your work known. You can sell slides to stock houses, too. More and more clients are dealing with stock houses rather than giving photographers assignments. It saves the editors time and money.

Benefits—Once you're established, you have a lot of time to go a lot of places, see all the things you want to see. You get to be outside a lot. It's not a nine-to-five kind of thing. More like midnight to midnight.

Pay—You need at least a year of work before you can start making any money. More often it takes about three years to really get established. When you start out, you need to have another job and keep photography on the side, because it takes a lot of money to start out. You need to finance your own equipment and costs. It's easy to spend $10,000 a year on equipment and film—costs add up fast. But I've found that you can make a good middle-class living. A real hustler can make up to $100,000 a year, but that's someone who's really working at it all the time.

Negatives—Although you do have the opportunity to travel and be outside a lot, your camera is kind of an albatross. You see images in everything, so you're always working. Also, many people don't realize the incredible amount of office time you need to put in. I'd say that less than 50 percent of your time is actually spent out in the field. It seems like I'm always in this office, at the computer or file cabinet or looking at slides.

You have to write up submission forms, keep files, and label and keep track of your slides. You have to edit your slides harshly and be your own worst critic. You send out slides and then have to track them down months later. Sometimes you look in a magazine and find your slides published without your knowledge and you have to go after those guys. Scratched slides are a big problem, too—if they're returned to you scratched, you've lost the slide and there goes any opportunity to ever sell it again. So you have to go through the whole process of trying to get compensated for the loss. It can be a real hassle.

The future—With the technology changing the way it is, everyone's getting a little bit nervous. I've been hearing that magazines are becoming white elephants, almost obsolete, with the video market moving in. Very few photographers are getting assignments because of stock houses, and the pay hasn't gone up in the last ten years. It's like treading water.

Career Case Study

Valentine Atkinson, California

Valentine Atkinson is an internationally respected travel and leisure photographer who specializes in angling and shooting sports worldwide. He has traveled about the world for the last 20 years photographing the fine art of flyfishing. Atkinson's work appears in many publications, including Esquire, Sports Afield, Field & Stream, The New York Times, Newsweek, and Geo.

Requirements—Someone looking to get into photography probably should go to art or photography school. That's not a necessity, but it certainly helps. They should feel a need to work for themselves, and above all, truly love their work.

Prospects—Fifty years ago you could just go out and become a photographer. These days you have to be a lot more creative and willing to work with people. You really have to be alert, especially with new advances in technology and equipment.

Benefits—I grew up in the outdoors and I really love to be out there. You spend a large portion of your day outside, where you love to be, communicating with the outdoors. You have a very flexible schedule; it's not a day-in, day-out, nine-to-five kind of thing, and you often get to travel to places you might not go otherwise.

Pay—There are a lot of companies out there that need to display their products, and you can make $200 to $500 a shot for those. I think that most people who really want to get involved with photography are willing to take what they can get to begin with.

If you can work at another job full-time and freelance on the side for a while, that's ideal. Unless you're extremely well-connected, it's hard to generate enough income to cover your expenses when you start out.

There are three primary marketing channels for outdoor and travel photography: advertising, corporate and editorial. For editorial work you can make anywhere from $40,000 to $100,000, with corporate it's $75,000 to around $150,000, and in advertising it can go up from there. There is definitely money to be made; it depends on your level of commitment, the quality of your work, marketing savvy, and of course the condition of the marketplace.

Negatives—You don't get a steady paycheck; it's either feast or famine. Rejection becomes a daily experience—you need to have an optimistic approach and a thick skin. You get assignments when you can, and hopefully you get paid within 30 days. Sometimes it's more like 60 days. Basically a secure future is uncertain.

Self-employment and sound business management are often tough to negotiate, especially as an artist. Objective help with planning business goals can really make a difference.

The future—A good way to add to a steady income is to get into stock photography. In this day and age, there are a lot fewer dollars available for assignment work, and stock photography is a good option. Working with respected stock agencies and/or having your own stock business is almost a requirement. Employing a representative to increase your marketing opportunities and assist in negotiating is a real advantage. Finding the right "fit" in business philosophy and style is critical.

Career Case Study

James Tallon, Arizona

James Tallon is an independent outdoor photographer who has worked in the field for more than 30 years. He writes a column for Outdoor and Travel magazine, and worked as an editor for Arizona Game & Fish publications in the mid-1960s. He has won several awards for photography and layout.

Requirements—I don't think you need a Ph.D. in photography to make a success of it. With all the new automatic cameras and superior metering systems, you can get by without learning exposure via f/stops and shutter speeds, but you should learn these basics for a better understanding of what's going on.

I think a person can get a jump-start in photography by thoroughly studying his or her camera manual and taking a course in art appreciation. Photographers who make the skip from art to photography always seem to do extremely well. Modern cameras may expose and focus for you, but there's no auto-composition, and composition is everything.

Beginners tend to short themselves on cameras and lenses; composition can be changed drastically by switching to other lenses, perhaps from a so-so shot to an award-winner or a big sale. One shot can pay for a couple of cameras and lenses. A sunset with flying geese got me $1,500 as the dust cover for the Smithsonian's *Fire of Life* book.

Sebastiao Salgardo, an extremely talented photojournalist, said it better than me when he said, "Photography is not a profession; it is a way of life. You can't go home (after shooting) and put it aside." If there's a trade secret to this game, that's it.

Prospects—I sold my first picture story in 1958. At that time, there were fewer photographers and consequently more opportunities. My goal was magazine photography primarily. I found that by connecting a set of photographs with some short copy, I made many more sales. That is still true today, even though some of the publications that used tons of my work are now gone, dead. Now I think the quality demands are much greater, because there are more skilled people, and there is less of a marketplace. That means to succeed, a photographer will likely spend much more time marketing than actually shooting pictures. It seems the last thing you need to know in the "business" of photography is photography itself.

Benefits—The real reward of being a photographer is you get to be a photographer. The camera has taken me places that I would have never been able to afford to go on my own. There are some photographers who beat their brains out at this game and never have any fun. With photography as a lifestyle, you have to have fun as you go. On the other hand, you have people who don't work at photography hard enough, even when it's vital to their livelihood. Outdoors writers rank high among them. Thousands of great pictures have been lost because so many outdoors writers have not disciplined themselves to spend less time with the rod and gun, and more with the camera.

Pay—As I said before, there's no great money in my kind of photography. Now that I'm shooting mainly stock, the pay has improved considerably. Sometimes I'll take low pay to do a job because I know I'll make stock sales down the road from it that will amount to much more than I made for the original job.

It's very dangerous to undercharge. Early in my career, I nearly lost an assignment to the Havasupai Indian Reservation in Grand Canyon because I wanted to go so badly. I drastically underpriced it. The client, who loved the pictures, was kind enough to tell me that because of my low figure, he thought I was an amateur.

One wildlife photographer I know, whose work is so-so, is in the six-figure income bracket because he is so skilled at selling his work. To him, and to me, a computer with a word processor and database has become equally as important as a camera.

The future—"Kid-snappers," photographers who shoot kid portraits, like at school, can make much more than I do. One told me he grosses well over $100,000 a year. But he has never been to Australia, Hawaii, Alaska, Costa Rica or some of the other great places that I have. His type of photography is just another job. He

---

is not in the great outdoors. That is the life that I love.

References

Outdoor Writers of America, 2017 Cato Avenue, Suite 101, State College, PA 16801;(814) 234-1011. OWAA can also provide contacts for regional outdoors writers organizations.

Society for Environmental Journalists, PO Box 27506, Philadelphia, PA 19118; (215) 247-9710.

Professional Photographers of America, Inc, 57 Forsythe Street NW, Ste 1600, Atlanta, GA 30303; (404) 522-8600 or fax (404) 614-6400.

American Society of Media Photographers, Washington Road, Ste 502, Princeton Junction, NJ 08550-1033; (609) 799-8300 or fax (609) 799-2233.

The book *Photographers Market* provides listings, guidelines, contacts and pay rates for hundreds of magazines.

Public Affairs Officer

Dreams—There you are again on the TV news, captivating the viewers. Aren't you wonderful? You just gotta admit it. You are the magic link from your department to the public eye, with such magnetism that dozens of media members treat you like a deity. Well, they should. After all, you know more about the department than your latest politically-appointed boss.

Nightmares—You have to cover the tracks for a superior who is a political lackey, find yourself fumbling for words on a live TV interview, then accidentally make your boss look like a doof. Soon thereafter, you get reassigned to counting chipmunks in the Mojave Desert.

Realities—Good diction, clear thinking and a fresh, attractive presentation is what every public affairs officer must have. Have it and you will get to work on projects afield, leading the way for media of all types, as well as become an insider who will know more about a department's workings than anybody else. The pay is OK, even quite decent if you get positioned in a rural area.

What it's all about—Some people open their mouths now and then just to change feet. If you have this problem, then a career as a public affairs officer is definitely not for you. On the other hand, if you have the ability to keep your feet on the ground, not in your mouth, this career may be worth a hard look.

This is a job for people who can express their thoughts clearly and concisely, with clean diction. If you can do that, this is a field you can excel in. If you also have mastered a topic of interest, are at least semi-attractive, maybe have a touch of humor, can write a bit, and have a degree in public relations or journalism, you can count on getting a good job out there.

When a member of the media has a question, it is the public affairs officer who answers the call. Newspaper writers are notorious for having very little time, and you must be able to answer the questions quickly, often on the spot, and do it in a manner that can be quoted in print. Do that consistently and you will be prized among newspaper writers, radio broadcasters, and TV field reporters—as well as your superiors.

For those with the aptitude, this career has a lot going for it. The energy you expend will not be dead-ended, but cycled out to the public via the media. If you are a good time manager, you will be able to spend time afield on a regular basis, whether researching special projects, hosting media or networking with field employees. The pay is decent, starting around $20,000 and climbing to $40,000, which can stretch a long way in rural areas.

The excitement of the job ranges far. It includes arranging field trips with the media to promote the success of a special project, alerting media to breaking stories, writing, mailing or faxing press releases, and getting an insider's look at how decisions are made in government agencies. A public affairs officer often knows more about the workings of a department than anybody else, including the executive officers.

In some cases, such as working with the National Parks Department or the Forest Service, there are additional duties as a liaison to provide information directly to the public. If a visitor to a national forest wants to know where to camp, where to cut firewood, and any special rules, it is the public affairs officer (often doubling as recreation officer) who provides the information. In other words, your job is communicating. As long as you can keep from chomping on your feet too much, you'll do fine. You'll find they aren't too tasty anyway.

To make it to the top in public affairs, you should master at least one topic, and have the ability to speak adequately about many others. That is why you should minor in a science of some kind (for a specialty) along with majoring in public affairs or journalism. You also need to be at least semi-attractive. Why? Because this work can include live TV interviews, and you need to project the image of the department you are working for. In the long run, nurturing your ability to write can provide a career boost, since you will be able to write press releases about sensitive topics.

Getting that first job is always the hardest, of course. There are three successful routes. The best approach is to work part-time for an agency, perhaps as a seasonal aid, to get your foot in the door. Showing this kind of ambition makes it easier to inspire someone to hire you. Another strategy to the top-paying jobs is to work as a journalist. Then when a desirable public affairs position becomes available, show up with your impressive professional credentials. If they want a professional who can step right in and take over, well, there you are.

Another path is to work for an agency in whatever job you can get into, regardless of the duties, then transfer into public affairs when a position becomes available. It works if you network well with several agencies, keep tuned in to any prospective openings, and also are willing to uproot your home and move to wherever the job is. It may be surprising, but quite a few positions are filled this way, from the inside rather than the outside.

There can be one very disconcerting element to the job. It's the office politics. In a worst-case scenario, it can destroy the spirit of the well-intentioned. The public affairs officer may know of unethical behavior of superiors, behavior that may undermine the ability of the department to carry out their function. You can feel like a real hypocrite when you spend your days extolling the virtues of your department's programs, but know full well that your boss is a politically-appointed creep who could care less, and may actually sabotage the department's success. Unfortunately, this happens more than it should, especially in the case of wildlife departments that get pressured by development interests.

There is only one way to respond and keep your job palatable. Pick an interest you have mastered—your chosen specialty—get to know the experts who are running the programs, and promote the heck out of them. In other words, take something that is good and let the media know just how good it is. With that approach, you will not only like yourself, but you will like your job. And it is the best way known to keep your feet out of your mouth.

Career Case Study

Melissa Carlson, Colorado
Melissa Carlson has worked since 1979 as a public affairs officer with the U.S. Forest Service. Her background is in speech communications and research recreation management. She enjoys photography and collecting antiques, and lives in Fort Collins, Colorado.

Requirements—Getting into public affairs, at least in the U.S. Forest Service, doesn't require a lot of formal education. A college degree isn't actually required, but most people on staff have one. The degrees vary, some are in forestry or journalism. Mine was in drama, so you can see that it's possible to get into the field with a background that's not directly related.

The job does require the kind of formal communication skills that you would acquire in journalism or broadcasting. You need strong writing and public speaking abilities. Experience is more important. If you've had specific media training or experience in any kind of communications field, you'll probably be rated higher.

It's helpful to be outgoing and flexible. You've got to be comfortable talking with a wide variety of people, because that's what you're doing all day long. Interpersonal communication skills are the main key.

Prospects—The job market's pretty narrow right now. Within the Forest Service, there are 35,000 full-time employees, and only 200 of those are public affairs positions. Since there are so few jobs in the system, turnover can be fairly slow. The jobs are hard to come by, so if you really want to get in you've got to have an edge on the competition, have some proven communication skills and combine that with an understanding of natural resources. Again, solid experience is extremely helpful. I've known public affairs workers who were former congressional aides, foresters, wildlife biologists, and broadcasters. It boils down to who has the people skills, who can competently communicate the knowledge at hand.

Benefits—The job has a lot of benefits. It's really fun most of the time. It's great being able to work with a wide variety of people—folks who are out in the woods camping, people who work in trade and technical areas, media people, politicians. You're in contact with a very interesting cross-range of people. The variety is extremely challenging and stimulating. Something new and different is always going on. You never get bored.

It's personally satisfying to help people understand the forest system and how we manage it, to help them comprehend the importance of our resources and how they can have a part in preserving and protecting them.

Pay—There are only a small number of entry level jobs, since many public affairs people start out in other fields. Entry level employees usually start out at the GS 5 level, which pays about $17,600 a year. But most public affairs positions are at GS 11 or 12, which run in the high $30,000 range. It's basically a mid-management level position.

Negatives—It gets frustrating because you juggle so many things that you just can't get everything done when you want to. We have some folks who don't like what the Forest Service is doing, so we often have some conflict resolution to deal with. We're put in the position of explaining the motives behind the actions. From a job standpoint, it's a fairly limited field. There aren't tremendous opportunities to move up, and the competition is fierce.

The future—Within the Forest Service, the market has been growing a little bit. The government is realizing that we need to get the public involved in what we're doing. To do that, they've got to have people representing their ideas and goals and taking messages back in order to understand what the public's interests are. The field is not likely to shrink at all.

Career Case Study

Mardie Lane, Hawaii   Mardie Lane is a public affairs specialist/park ranger in Hawaii Volcanoes National Park. She has a degree in park management and environmental education and is also a registered nurse. Her past experience includes working for state parks in Oregon and Honolulu Zoo in Hawaii. She enjoys horses, swimming, snorkeling, hiking, photography, and observing the wildlife and rare birds in Hawaii. She lives on the island of Hawaii.

Requirements—I think what really helps, in terms of education, is to learn as much as you can about various subjects relating to the field you want to work in. There are degree programs in tourism and public affairs. Combine these areas of emphases with geology, biology and anthropology. In your particular park area, become a specialist in at least one thing, and become a generalist in everything. Develop and refine your skills in public speaking and writing.

You must be able to work with a lot of different people. It's not an isolated position. You work with a whole network of organizations, and you really have to like people. You are part of a team, and you must act as such.

In most parks, public affairs encompasses a number of jobs. You lead tours, help the media with factual information for magazine articles and books, do radio and TV interviews, and help obtain special use permits for motion pictures or commercials. You write the park brochures, help put together signs explaining natural phenomena, and answer questions for the general public. You have to have good speaking skills, and you have to anticipate what people would like to know and combine it with what the park wants them to know.

Prospects—Almost every park will have at least one person assigned as responsible for public affairs. However, there are only 30 titled Public Affairs Specialists out of 14,000 employees in the entire national park system. They are coveted positions, and openings are rare. In most national parks, a staff person assumes the role and function for public information as a part of the job of superintendent, division chief or interpretive specialist.

My advice would be to get a good strong general education, then investigate the area you're interested in, and immerse yourself in a lot of different park activities so that you'll have a solid background and be knowledgeable about the area. Then apply for seasonal positions and work your way through the ranks.

I'm speaking specifically about public affairs people who work in the field. There are regional offices within the system where there are key employees whose specific title is Public Affairs Officer. But in the field, because there's a need for employees with diverse skills, I feel that more people are doing it in addition to other regular duties rather than as a specific position.

Benefits—You get to be one of the people who fights a fire, interprets a natural phenomenon, or deals with some unique situation, and you can turn the experience around and explain it to the public in a way that allows them to learn from it. And you are able to tell it with more accuracy and enthusiasm than someone who heard it secondhand ever could.

Media people, who we deal with constantly, are interesting characters. They're always looking for new angles, challenges, different ways to do things. They're fascinating people to work with.

It's also gratifying to win support for the principles you believe in. You are responsible for communicating to the public the importance of preserving and appreciating our natural resources. It's very exciting to realize that you can take a stand and provide your views for the public's review. Through me, they can understand what it's like to be in the middle of controversial issues and see both sides of the story.

Pay—The pay scale depends on the actual position held. It may range from a part-time duty of a regular ranger at GS level 7, making around $22,000, up to the superintendent level, which is up to $50,000. The superintendent job, of course, is a whole different position in itself. Basically, in government agencies, your pay is going to reflect the government service level that you're at. There are many variables: years of experience, amount of responsibility, diversity of duties.

Negatives—It can be very consuming. Incidents know no time. We are on call on holidays, weekends, all night long. You tend to start feeling like you're always working. I recently went from a major fire to a helicopter crash to a car break-in, with no break in between. I've been at points where I couldn't really remember having my typical two days in a row off. The reality of the position is such that we respond when we have to get the information out, whether that's in the middle of the day or at two o'clock in the morning. We have to see what's happening and then get on the phone.

It's certainly never boring, but sometimes 16 hours fly by and I won't even know it. When incidents do happen, when there is a serious injury or death in the park, it tends to cast a shadow on your way of thinking. You begin to look at your park more in terms of communicating hazards to people rather than enjoying the scenic beauty. Safety is the most important thing in a park. Luckily, incidents of that nature are rare, but when they occur you have to disassociate your own emotions, turn the event around and use it to emphasize the inherent dangers of a wilderness area. It changes your perspective.

The future—I think the job market is going to have to expand. There's more demand than ever for the public use of land and natural resources. Parks are going to have to compete and be front and forward with what they believe and represent, and they will need more people to be out there representing them. I think that we're really fortunate that the public has begun to perceive our parks as a valuable agency. That needs to be promoted, and people dedicated to these causes will be needed.

References

National Parks & Conservation Association, 1776 Massachusetts Avenue NW, Washington, D.C. 20036; (202) 223-6722.

National Parks Service, PO Box 37127, Washington, D.C. 20013; (202) 208-4649.

JOBSource (computerized data bank). Contact: Computerized Employment Systems, Inc., 1720 West Mulberry Unit B9, Fort Collins, CO 805021; (970) 493-1779.

Contact the public affairs department of government agencies in your area and ask them for employment information.

Public Relations

Dreams—A public relations specialist makes a six-figure salary while traveling about the hemisphere first-class, meeting with clients, business executives and media superstars. They always have the best clothes, cars and friends.

Nightmares—It is outright futility to deal with ego-maniacal clients who expect the moon, like "10 minutes with Alan King," or worse, delay paying your fee until you provide increased sales. Then there is the media, including those who won't even return a phone call, much less give a valid product a plug, and high overhead for telephones, postage and meals.

Realities—Most people who settle in at PR for five to ten years make a decent living, earning $45,000 to $60,000, and do get perks such as trips, product samples and friends in high places. They can plan on having to hold the hands of clients, high monthly expenses, and kissing a lot of butt.

What it's all about—Have you ever known a woman who was a natural charmer, yet did not threaten other women? Have you ever known a friendly man who had such enthusiasm that whenever he talked, you felt a sense of magnetism? When you look in the mirror, do you see that you have the capability to be friendly, intelligent, enthusiastic, and concise? Even with strangers?

You do? Then you may have the perfect aptitude for a public relations career, a position that can be prosperous and also provide independence. And if your clients are outdoors-oriented, you will also spend plenty of time out of the office. It's a unique job that takes a unique person, someone who is comfortable in blue jeans or a tailored suit, someone who might drive a Cadillac to a luncheon, then head off with a client to go duck hunting.

These innate personality qualities are the keys to success in PR work. Most public relations specialists are born with them, then learn the other elements of the business, such as networking with media, the cost-effectiveness of advertising, mailers and promotions, how to obtain new clients and how much to charge them, and how to work the phones. These things can be learned. A special zeal for the job, however, starts from the heart.

But when you put both together, you have a chance to make a lot of money, rub shoulders with big-time media and insiders in the business world, and travel and have a lot of fun. And get this: There is always a job available. Sure, there is competition, but if you have those magic intangibles, you can create your own private fiefdom.

This is the way it works. A client has a product, a good product, but can't seem to figure out how to promote and market it. It might be a boat show, a marina at a lake, a hotel at an exotic vacation destination, a computer company that makes boat navigation devices, or a manufacturer of fishing rods. Typically, the client will come to you saying, "I'm just not making as much money as I think I should."

You devise a promotion or marketing scheme, sometimes both, that will help the client make more money, then carry it out to completion. If your plan works, everybody wins. The client makes more money, and is happy to pay you well for promoting their product. If you own your own public relations firm, you are paid a flat fee; as an employee of a firm, you are paid a salary.

Most newcomers will start out with an agency, learn the business, and earn $20,000 to $35,000. Some people are content with that. Others, however, are not. If you become an executive with a company, or form your own agency and can hold clients, the sky is the limit. After 10 years in the business, many PR specialists make more than $60,000, and some top $100,000. The best do better.

At first glance to some, it would appear the job is just a matter of writing press releases, then mailing them to newspapers, radio and TV stations. Sorry folks. A typical newspaper columnist receives about 100 press releases a week and most are not even opened. In fact, some media members will not open any mail that is computer generated, looking for laser-printed labels as a tip-off. Still, every day, bushels of such PR letters are mailed to newspapers and thrown away. If that's your game, you might as well organize a Bigfoot expedition and try to sell it as an NBC "Sunday Night Movie."

The first order of business is always to "break through to the other side," that is, to get to know radio show hosts, columnists and TV personalities. You can do this by feeding them items year around that will spice up their stories. Then when you have something to promote that fits into their agenda, they are more apt to listen. That is why women need to be charmers in this business and men enthusiastic. You have to be able to convince without the "convincee" realizing they are being convinced.

A few rules on dealing with both clients and media: Always be 100 percent honest and never exaggerate; make personal contact (especially prior to sending a press release); arrange field meetings but don't waste anybody's time; promote the positive but never whine about a client; mix business with pleasure; and always take a product as far as it will go.

The idea of what is possible can be fantastic. Consider a PR specialist who is hired by an exotic vacation hotel to promote and increase business. It usually starts with a low-cost or complimentary trip, then spending a few afternoons with the lodge's management planning a promotion campaign. You end up making money and having a great trip. You get the idea. If you have the ability to dream, the outdoor manufacturers' field is unlimited.

The best way to start such a career is to go by the book, getting a college degree in public relations with a minor in business, then working for a reputable agency to learn the ropes. But in the long run, the best way to make a lot of money and have a lot of fun is to throw that same book out the window. Go for broke and start your own agency, find your own clients, work personally with media, and write your own ticket.

There will always be a need for PR. Why? Because every year, someone has a new product or a yearning to improve an old one, and wants to improve sales. A good public relations specialist is often the fastest route to doing that. There is always a need; a public relations specialist simply fills it, and can make a profitable and enjoyable career at it.

Career Case Study

Rob Brown, California   *Rob Brown is the executive vice-president of All-Media Group, which is comprised of a broadcast media company and public relations promotions firm that specializes in recreation. He is the general manager of the firm's broadcast subsidiary, AMI News, which produces ski, camp, and outdoor news reports for over 2,000 radio stations, CNN, the NBC Radio Network, and SportsTicker. He is an avid fisherman and duck hunter and lives in Orinda, California.*

Requirements—A bachelor's degree in business and communications or public relations marketing is a minimum requirement. A lot of schools are starting to offer degrees in PR marketing. We prefer people who have an MBA.

It's a great field for entry level. Experience needed depends on the agency. We like two to three years of experience, but we will hire kids out of school if they have a good solid degree and some work experience, an internship or something like that. We like to see people who have had experience in clerical administration, who have been around all aspects of business.

Prospects—The market is very competitive. There are a lot of opportunities, particularly for women. We're seeing a lot of women getting into this field. It really depends on whether you go with an agency or in-house. I recommend an agency for people just starting out, because you get to learn about everything: selling, marketing, business. You get to work on several accounts at one time. With a large firm, your job security is based on the revenue-building of the firm. In-house is more of a permanent position, and you can end up doing the same thing over and over.

Benefits—I find media people very intelligent. They're very curious, and I like being around those kind of people.

Pay—For an agency, entry level begins at about $17,000 to $18,000 with a degree and some experience. For an account executive, it's usually between $55,000 and $60,000, and when you get into senior management it goes up to $80,000 plus.

Negatives—A negative is the uncertainty—the complete lack of control of publicity work. You can do your best, provide a great story for TV, and you don't even get a second of air time. Your clients can blame you.

The future—At an agency, they're limitless. Opportunities are all predicated on sales. Most kids starting out have not been trained from the practical side. They don't understand that it's a business; we need to make money. The ones who learn that early on and make money for the company are the ones who last.

Career Case Study

Geri Haber, Florida   Geri Haber is the vice-president of Bruce Rubin Associates, a general public relations firm in Florida. Geri's position allows her to travel extensively around the country, and when she's not working, she enjoys exercising, boating, and spending time with her 15- year-old son. She lives in Miami, Florida.

Requirements—I find that most public relations practitioners have an undergraduate degree in journalism, English or public relations. Many have a variety of backgrounds. A lot of people feel that it's important that they have the public relations major, and that is helpful, but personally, I like to see a strong journalistic background as well. Too many people come in with a PR degree, not knowing what public relations really means. People with backgrounds in journalism tend to have a good strong knowledge of what is news and what is not.

Heyman, a research firm that specializes in public relations, conducted a study of 591 public relations people and concluded that 48 percent had been trained in print journalism. Fifty-seven percent did not hold graduate degrees. Of those who did, an MBA was far and away the most popular. The business aspect has become extremely important. I've got a broad range of responsibilities, and having that business background is essential in dealing with each of those.

It's extremely important to have people skills and the ability to adapt to any situation. People fall into the trap of thinking, "I'd be good at this because I like people," but liking people is not enough.

Prospects—The market is exceptionally competitive. And since you're narrowing it down specifically to the outdoors market, the scope is even more confined. There are two divisions within the career: agency, which is outside council; and corporate, which is inside. I think that the competition for the job market right now is very high; these are tough times for everyone. The more senior positions, of course, are the ones that are most competitive.

I've found the outdoor industry to be very male-dominated, but I am definitely seeing more and more women step in, which is a positive trend. When I first started out, I was the only woman in a room full of men, but I see that changing in the field today. What a lot of companies today are doing is combining careers— incorporating marketing, advertising and public relations. The danger in that is that often, too much is assigned to one person to handle. When that happens, many times public relations is the area that doesn't get enough attention.

Benefits—For me, one of the main benefits is the diverse types of people I deal with. I'm able to associate with a variety of people, from major company executives, trade media, and manufacturers, to the media and industry people. I find that there's a special type of bond between people who work in the outdoor business. They're just a nice group of people.

I'm able to see the results of what I do, whether it's a boat show or television program. In the past, PR has been a career that is somewhat minimized in the overall corporate picture, but now public relations practitioners are a much more important factor in the bottom line. In one study, the CEOs of several companies were asked for their estimation of what return they gained on their investment in public relations, and the overall average was 188 percent. That is proof that companies are increasingly listening to PR people. We've proven ourselves to be very cost-effective.

It's a fun profession. I find that for almost every time I have to dress up in my suits and be professional, I have an opportunity to be outside on a boat, wearing sporty clothing and being with a fun crowd of people. I'm constantly thrown into different groups, and that underlying fun aspect is always there.

Pay—Many factors have to be taken into consideration. There are very different pay scales depending on the region. The Heyman study came up with figures that I would consider somewhat high: a range of $30,000 to $150,000 per year. Of course, in metropolitan areas such as New York or Los Angeles, that may be accurate, but these figures sound more accurate to me: For an entry-level position, one could expect around $18,000 to $20,000 per year. Within about five years, at an account executive position, $30,000 to $35,000 is reasonable, and up from there an account supervisor would net between $40,000 and $50,000. A corporate vice-president or an account supervisor with 10 or more years experience can make from $50,000 to $70,000, but those positions aren't common.

Negatives—Long working hours are probably the number one liability. In this business, that's how it has to be. We joke that we work half days—12 hours. We do whatever it takes. This job is extremely deadline-oriented, just like newspapers and magazines, and to get the job done right, you have to work hard. There's a lot of stress involved. If you don't get it right, you're not going to reach the bottom-line result.

The burnout factor tends to set in eventually, but what combats that are positive results, and on top of that, everyone does have a good time. I look at boat shows that we've had for 10 or 15 years, and I see the results of hard work. We're very serious about what we do; we are very successful and proud.

The future—I think the future of the market will get better as the market gets better. Right now, most internal departments are being hit pretty hard, but I predict that as the economy gets better, we'll see this field opening up. Many financial analysts have said that the outdoors industry should be one of the first to bounce back. I particularly see more public relations specialty firms opening up.

This career can very definitely lead to other things. I think that with a little more experience, I could actually switch over to one of the areas that I do PR for. I could manage shows or even run a company. Because we get so involved in all areas of our clients' businesses, we end up learning a great deal about their careers.

The profession is being viewed as more and more indispensable; that will create more opportunities and probably eventually bump up salaries. If this career is taken seriously enough and all the opportunities it has to offer are taken advantage of, I believe that it can lead to a variety of directions.

References

Public Relations Society of America, 33 Irving Place, New York, New York 10033; (212) 995-2230. Each state has its own local affiliates as well; check local directories.

International Association of Business Communications, 1 Halladie Plaza, Suite 600, San Francisco, CA 94102; (415) 433-3400.

Radio Show Host

Dreams—As the host of an outdoors radio show, you can have short hours, high pay, instant celebrity status, and an excellent vehicle to sell other products such as books or videos. Plus, your show will probably be syndicated across the country, making you rich and famous beyond your wildest fantasies.

Nightmares—Nobody, especially program directors, seems to care about your dreams except you. Start-up pay can be zero, and it can be fatal if you get too nervous, stutter or have a case of brainlock on the air. If you have no marketing experience or are lazy, obtaining sponsors can be very difficult.

Realities—A lot of leg work can eventually equal short hours and good pay. A clear, concise voice beats a deep but floundering one, and there is no substitute for knowing the subject. This can be an excellent side job, but just make sure you get paid, right from the start.

What it's all about—Think personal. That's the key right there with a radio show. From getting slotted airtime to arranging a sponsor to pulling off the show, you have to take care of everything personally, and do it in a personable manner.

You see, there are two different worlds for people who try to establish an outdoors radio show. One world is quite lucrative, where you spend just four or five hours a week at it, then pocket $15,000 to $20,000 a year, sometimes more, in addition to promoting other products you may have available. The other world is in a different orbit, where you make very little money, yet worry just the same about the sound of your voice, the content of your show, and how many people might be listening.

The difference between the two worlds is usually simply the approach: meeting personally with program directors at radio stations to cement agreements, taking personal responsibility to obtain sponsors, and making your show personal and compelling so the audience will try to tune in to every segment. Get the keyword: Personal! Your success depends on you, not somebody else, every step of the way. Do that and you can make a lot of money for your time and become something of a celebrity in the process.

However, that is not what often happens. The way it usually works is more like this: After appearing on a radio show as a guest, perhaps because of a special interest you have mastered, you are then invited to try a short live report. It works so well that you are invited to make a regular appearance, usually for free.

In the meantime, you figure the station will try to get you a sponsor, maybe even syndication to radio stations in other regions. Then, after a few months, you suddenly realize you are getting paid very little, or perhaps not getting paid at all. In addition, you realize that the station has done nothing to get you sponsored. That is when the quality in your show starts to slip, and before long, you're gone, either out of choice or from a well-placed boot to your rear end.

Just like that, another promising radio show prospect is out of luck, soured forever on the experience. "They never did anything for me," is the usual complaint. Well, guess what? They never will. You have to take care of it yourself.

For starters, consider how most people try to get a radio show. They do it by sending in sample tapes to a program director, then waiting for a response. You might as well wait near a cactus for a polar bear to amble by. Program directors have huge piles of these tapes, and they don't have time to listen to them, especially for a show that comes without a sponsor.

Think personal. Make personal contact with the program director. Get an interview, then tell the program director personally why your show will make money—for him, for you, and for your sponsors. Define the demographics of the area, explaining how your show will fit into the station's format, attracting new listeners and guaranteeing a large market share. Tell him you will arrange the sponsors, so for the station, it will be like getting free money. If the program director is interested, only then is it time to present sample tapes that are timed and tailored for the station's market.

How do you get a sponsor? This is how. You make personal contacts with local boat shows, regional outdoor chains and national manufacturers. Did you know, for instance, that the Ford F-150 pickup truck that outdoorsmen find so popular is the No. 1 selling vehicle in the world? That's an example of a perfect bigtime sponsor for a outdoors radio show. There are hundreds of others on the national level, listed in the supporting members directory for the Outdoor Writers Association of America, and hundreds more in your own market.

Regardless of how much money changes hands between the sponsor and the radio station, just make sure you get at least $40 to $75 per show if it's a short segment, or for a longer, fully developed program, at least $200 per hour. The ideal format is 90 seconds. That format starts with a 15-second teaser, a break for the sponsor's advertisement, then a 75-second show. Provide seven of those a week and you will not only have the chance to attract a large, daily audience, but also have the opportunity to sell the same shows to markets in other regions. How? The same way. Personal contact. You have to do the leg work yourself. Do it and you can make some decent dough.

The best prospects are 50,000-watt AM radio stations that broadcast sports, country music, or 100 percent news or talk radio. For it to be worthwhile to sponsors, you need to document how many people their messages will reach. With the personal approach, you can develop a job that takes very little time to master, rewards you with good pay, and makes you an instant hero to many listeners. Sound good? It can be. But you must take care of every detail. Personally.

Career Case Study

Bob Hirsch, Arizona
Bob Hirsch is the host of "Escape to the Outdoors," a daily radio show in Arizona that has won many national awards. He has been a freelance writer since 1972 and has written a syndicated outdoors column for the Phoenix Gazette for the past twelve years. He is the founder and editor of "Arizona Roamin'," a small weekly magazine that is distributed at Outdoor Outfitters, a sporting

*goods chain in Arizona. Hirsch has written five books,
and is also a paid speaker at sports shows, seminars and
banquets. He lives with his wife, Mary, in Cave Creek,
Arizona.*

Requirements—To begin with, people worry about their voice. Many people have all kinds of things going on between their ears, but don't have the deep resonant voice they think they need. But that's not all that important. If you've got something to say that people want to hear, that's what counts. Anyone can have a radio show.

Beginners need to realize that when you're writing for radio, you need to write text to speak rather than to read. You do need to write your own stuff, too—when you hear those guys on the radio, they're not ad-libbing. If you ever ad-lib a show on the radio and go back and listen to it later, it can sound pretty embarrassing.

It also helps to have taken some kind of communications classes. Most of life is based on communicating well, and I think it benefits anyone to learn how to do it. But I know a lot of people who had no background when they started out. The best advice is to practice. Pretend you're on the radio. Record yourself. Practice really does make perfect in this case.

Prospects—Most people start out with a fishing report, a two to four-minute deal. You need to start small. Approach a radio station and tell them you're an expert on this place or that place and want to do a short report. Then they'll find you a sponsor, or you can go out and find your own sponsors. Consider doing it for nothing at first, just to get your name known. Another option is to buy an hour of radio time yourself and get enough advertising to pay for it. That's a little trickier, but it can be done. Once you get in, you can eventually build up to a network or syndicated show. That's the ultimate.

Benefits—It's a way to make extra money, which is always nice, but mainly it's fun and it helps my books sell better. One of the things that radio does for you is make you a media darling. Before you get out there you're a nobody, but as soon as they've heard you on the radio or seen you on TV for two minutes, suddenly you're a hero. It helps in other areas of your life. You can make a name for yourself faster. People will be more likely to pick up your book than if they've never heard of you.

Pay—It's tough to make a living just by radio alone. You might make 50 bucks for a two to four-minute fishing report. After you get on for a while, you can make around $300 to $400 a week. The secret here is to get a syndicated show. If you have a show featuring a large area, you could get a two or three-state syndicate, and you'd have around 150 stations buying your show. At about $25 a station, it can add up.

Negatives—By the time you run down an interview, go back and edit and finish it up, sometimes you can waste a lot of time. You can plan a two-minute interview and have the guy talk for twenty minutes, and then you have to go back and sift through it all to find the gems. There's a lot of legwork involved, and it's not worth it sometimes. The pay's not that great either.

The future—Our culture is more interested in the outdoors and environmental issues now, so there are more possibilities and opportunities available. It's not just fishing and hunting; it's camping, bird watching, hiking. Radio is getting stronger; everybody's got their radio on in the car. I run into people who have the radio on at work all day, too.

Career Case Study

Wade Bourne, Tennessee—Wade Bourne is a full-time freelance outdoor broadcaster, writer and photographer. He produces In-Fisherman Radio North, South and Autumn syndications, and has a listening audience of over 1.5 million. Bourne also serves as a senior writer for both Southern Outdoors and Bassmaster magazines. He frequently writes articles for other outdoor publications and is the author of the book, "Fishing Fundamentals." He lives near Clarksville, Tennessee with his wife and children.

Requirements—There are two primary requirements. The first would be a sound working knowledge of the outdoors. I may not consider myself an expert in a particular subject, for instance, but I have to know enough to ask good questions. The second requirement is a general basic grasp of communicative skills, such as proper grammar and clear enunciation. Taking some sort of communication classes can be valuable. I have a degree in journalism, but I probably would have really benefited from a broadcast class. You also have to have a lot of energy.

Prospects—There are two types of shows: the syndicated show and the local show. The local format is the way to start out. The best thing would be to sit down with a station manager at a small station and talk to him about doing a show, assuming they would be interested in an outdoors show. Some stations wouldn't even consider it, like the pop stations. Ask him for some suggestions, and decide if you can design a program around those suggestions. Then you try to convince him to put you on the air for some number of minutes a week.

Many shows pay very little; some don't want to pay anything at all. I would suggest the barter system. Go out and find your own sponsors and give your show to the station for free, with the stipulation that they play the sponsor's advertisements. Everybody comes out a winner that way.

My theory for being successful is to take one piece of information and use it in as many ways as possible. I kind of fell into radio; I started out as a writer. The way it happens is you'll go out to do a magazine story, which can lead to a newspaper feature. I started doing a little photography too, then I branched into television. I spent eight years in TV, then I got into radio. It all starts tying in together.

Benefits—I probably have a million and a half listeners. It helps me to build my stature, and that leads to jobs and calls that probably wouldn't happen otherwise. All freelancers have to be pretty good PR people, not that you have to compromise your morals or cut shady deals, but the better known you are, the more successful you'll be.

Pay—That's really hard to say. It depends on whether you go the syndication route or you're just doing local shows. With a 15-minute talk show in a medium-sized market, with one show on one station, you can make around $50 a show. The only way to make real money is syndication. That's harder to do on a large scale, but the regional syndication idea is still wide open. My shows air on about

650 stations, and for those I work probably eight full days a month. Half of my income comes from radio, and a third of my time goes into it. If you went into syndication on a large scale, you could make a lot of money, but that's doing your own advertising and all that. And you've got to have the capital to finance a project of that size to begin with. I wouldn't recommend that someone who has no radio experience bank his whole income on it.

Negatives—I don't see any negatives right now, to be perfectly honest. If I did it full-time, I would probably see the money as a negative.

The future—I'm an optimist by nature, and I know that if I wanted to do it full-time, I could make a very good living. Whether anyone else could do that, I don't know, because at this point I've got a good corner on the market.

Career Case Study

Charly McTee, Texas—Charly McTee has been a widely-respected radio personality since 1976. He is editor of Wildlife News Network, a weekly half-hour outdoor news program.

Requirements—You should know everything that you can about the outdoors. I would rate it as a moderately difficult thing to get into. The questions you get may cover any outdoor topic, and you have to be prepared to give answers. You have three choices: Answer as best as you can, find an expert, or say "I don't know." What you choose is critical. You need to be able to speak in a straightforward manner, with as few fits and starts and "uhs" and "duhs" as possible. That's probably the hardest thing to learn, because in everyday speech those fits and starts are so easily forgiven. And like any other job, it's a business operation. You have to balance what it costs you to do it.

Prospects—There are probably quite a few jobs available, some of them not even known yet. You have to prove that you have this show that will enrich the station and attract listeners. It basically takes getting in the face of the program manager and saying, "I've got a hot show that I want to do for you, here are the numbers, oh and by the way here are four sponsors who are ready to go." Most outdoor shows are limited to local, country-type stations, and compared with other types of shows, much more knowledge and cooperation is required from the host.

Benefits—There are some very small financial benefits. Very small. You get whatever ego-stroking goes along with it; you're locally acclaimed as an expert and once in a while maybe someone will buy you dinner. That's about it.

Pay—It's not very much. There are a number of different ways you can go about it: The station can pay you per show, or the station will barter with you—they'll sell half the spots and give you the other half to sell yourself. Or you can sell all the spots yourself. Sometimes the station will just give you the time if it's an educational show or something like that. The most lucrative is where the station gives you the spot and you go out and sell it, but that takes knowledge and experience and knowing the right people.

The maximum income is much less than people might imagine. There have been times in the past when I've grossed over $20,000, but I'm making significantly less than that now. A great deal depends on the pay scale and how much work you're willing to do. You're always making your own deal in this, there are no cut-and-dried deals.

In a small station in a local market, you will make maybe five to seven dollars for a 60-second spot. That's a case where you'd have to get more than one spot. If you're lucky you could make around $25 a week. There are a variety of different ways to do it. It really can vary, with a spot ranging from $5 to $100. It's a very negotiable market, and it depends on how much the station wants you there. If they really want you, then they'll make sure you get expenses for coming and going to the station and such.

I think syndication is probably a very good idea. It takes a person who is willing to do the legwork and sell. With syndication, you generate a deeper layer of problems. For one, you have to invoice and bill, and that can be complicated. If you just have one station with four shows at $25 each, that's easy, they just hand you a check for $100. But when you get into percentages and stuff like that, the billing can be quite complicated.

Negatives—It's a great deal of work. You have a lot of people who are depending on you to steer them straight, and if you have the integrity to do so, then you have to see that those people get straight answers. No one remembers when you've done something right, but they sure remember when you've done something wrong.

You wind up doing a lot of work at strange times. You'll end up in a dark little room at 10 o'clock at night, trying to make this show stay within the format, while everyone else is going to bed.

The future—Right now it's in a state of flux. Radio is not like it used to be; much of it now is prerecorded. Material comes on cards and you just plug the cards in. Shows come in a particular length and a particular format. It's become increasingly programmed, which makes it extremely tough for those who need to run longer times. What you leave out is much more important than what you include. There are signs that radio is reverting back to the way it used to be, but no one really knows. If radio fragments and goes to a more open format, there will be more openings for shows.

References

National Association of Broadcasters, 1771 N Street NW, Washington, D.C. 20036; (202) 429-5300.

Outdoor Writers Association of America, 2017 Cato Avenue, Suite 101, State College, PA 16801; (814) 234-1011.

Sailing Instructor

Dreams—The sailing instructor is as free as the wind and always on the water, parading his expertise for reverent pupils. The pay is great, so is the scenery, and you might even wear a captain's hat and get away with it. The comradeship with other instructors is nonpareil.

Nightmares—The wind dies and you have no motor assist, your boat leaks and nobody will bail, so you're basically marooned and taking on water. Then you get seasick and run into a rock, putting a big hole in the bottom of the boat, which then sinks. Of course, the survivors sue you—providing you survived.

Realities—This is a good business prospect in urban areas near large bodies of water, but poor in rural areas. The job requires just the right mix of intellectual sharpness and physical command, with a split between boat time and class time. For those with the qualifications, opportunities are good in many areas of the world.

What it's all about—Boating is one of the last easy ways for someone to gain a true sense of freedom. The major problem with urban America is the traffic. It doesn't take long and it can make you feel all bound-up inside. That is why boating is so popular. There are no stop lights, no traffic jams, no boundaries, and the physical demands are minimal. Sailing is the ultimate expression of this freedom, since no motor is required and you are moving amid the rhythms of the currents. It is also just enough of an intellectual challenge to be attractive.

As traffic gets worse in metropolitan areas, the popularity of sailing is projected to improve at the same rate. That makes the future promising for a sailing instructor, or even better, someone who manages a sailing school. As an entrepreneur, you could even parlay a modest business of selling new and used sailboats to your more wealthy students. Put all three together—instructing on the water, running a class, and occasionally selling a boat—and you're talking about a career that is fun, intellectually stimulating and financially rewarding.

Sailboat instructors make about $15 per hour in urban areas, a decent part-time job. If you run your own school full-time and you aren't making $50,000 a year, you're screwing up somehow. Add in the net profits from selling a few sailboats now and then, and hey, you have a real chance to crack the magic $100,000 level. On another front, a plus for part-time instructors is that if you want to travel, say to Hawaii, the Caribbean, or the Mediterranean, you will likely find a job teaching sailing. That can allow someone with a meager bank account to see the world on a pay-as-you-go basis.

The greatest benefit of sailing, the ability to easily claim a sense of freedom from the metropolitan jungle, is also its greatest drawback. How? This is how: As soon as you leave an urban area, sailing largely loses its appeal, and the ability for you to make money at it declines proportionately. What this means is that the greatest financial opportunities are in big cities located near large bodies of water. So if you are looking for a career to escape the city, this is not it.

But if you are looking for a career to escape the office, well, this can do just fine. To get started, it is mandatory to become certified by both the American Sailing Association and the U.S. Coast Guard, and if you have never taught, you might volunteer with the Coast Guard Auxiliary, which offers introductory classes on weekday evenings to the public. The latter provides a low-risk setting to find out if your aptitude is well-matched for the job.

If it is, you might consider opening up your own sailing school. The best way to attract pupils is to offer free sailboat rides, usually about 30 minutes long, then recruit people who take the free ride. If they get hooked, then they will want to buy a boat. Guess what? Right. If you have your business together, you'll score coming and going.

Getting that first job is always the most difficult, and this field is no exception. To get hired by a sailing company as a sailing instructor, the advice is to make yourself so well qualified that you are considered a "can't-miss hire." Get to know the people in the business. Get certified. Teach some introductory classes with the Auxiliary. Learn to conduct yourself as a professional. You might even volunteer to recruit your own students, guaranteeing a class for your sailing company.

But hey, if you can recruit your own students, then why not start your own business? If you can afford the initial financial shock of insurance and renting a room for instruction, then you will start off from the beginning making the kind of money that is possible. You will be doing what you want with just the right split between time on the water and time in the classroom. Not only that, but your pupils will look up to you, some may even idolize you (seriously), because you will be a master at something (sailboating) that is mysterious, fascinating and even a bit scary for them.

And best of all, out there on the water, as far as you can see there won't be a stop light in sight.

Career Case Study

Anthony Sandberg, California Anthony Sandberg is *the president and founder of Olympic Circle Sailing Club, established in 1978 and rated by the American Sailing Association as one of the top 10 sailing schools in the country. His past work experience includes two years with the Peace Corps in Nepal and Costa Rica, and extensive work with disadvantaged youth. Anthony has sailed all around the world, spending time in the Mediterranean and the Caribbean. He and his wife live in Berkeley, California.*

Requirements—First of all, you need to be very skillful in sailing, with a broad variety of experiences in your background. A summer's experience is adequate if you want to teach at a local lake or instruct kids, but if you want to teach ocean and coastal sailing as well, you have to be very proficient. Ideal qualifications include a Coast Guard license, for which you must have 360 documented days of being on the water and then pass a rigorous test; navigation skills, knowledge of safety procedures, and finally, an evaluation and certification from the American Sailing Association. That certification is respected worldwide. Those are the difficult requirements.

Then there are the soft skills, the interpersonal relationships.

Young, enthusiastic sailors are actually not always the ideal instructors because they're so excited about their knowledge and what they've learned that they concentrate too much on impressing their students. A good instructor has no doubts that he can handle the boat in any circumstance and instead of focusing on himself, he takes pleasure in showing students the necessary tools. He can then teach those skills in a dependable, logical sequence and enjoy watching the students learn.

Prospects—I'd say the market is wide open. For people who have paid their dues, who have all of the qualifications and the experience, there are many openings. The problem with many would-be instructors is that they have Swiss-cheese knowledge. They specialize in one specific area and know a lot about a particular boat or technique, but are illiterate in every other area.

At my company, 25 people apply for every one we can actually hire. But the positions are out there. Right now I have eight positions open, and the same is true for many other sailing companies. A good way to start getting the general knowledge that you need is to practice teaching in small boat programs. Then you have a chance to grow with the sport.

Benefits—You're outdoors, enjoying an activity you love, with fun, enthusiastic, bright people. The people who choose to learn to sail are almost always outgoing and friendly; those are the type of people who are drawn to the sport. There's a great camaraderie between instructors as well. They are, in general, a warm and fun group of people. And there's a great diversity; we have instructors who are doctors, lawyers, teachers, engineers, actors, and television personalities. All of them enjoy augmenting their professional careers with this exciting outdoor activity.

The best way to really learn something is to teach it. Teaching forces you to take everything apart, look at it, and put it back together. Sailing is a timeless worldwide sport, and there's always the chance to travel. There are employment opportunities in thousands of exotic places if you have the right qualifications.

Pay—An instructor who is Coast Guard and ASA-certified can make between $12 and $15 an hour. That goes up with capability. If they have lecturing skills, it's possible to go as high as $20 an hour. That's fairly standard across the country.

How much you work depends on your location. In some places, the season may last around four months; in others, such as California, it lasts eight or nine months. A lot of instructors migrate; they spend the summer in the north and the winter in the Caribbean or South America. If you get to the point of running your own sailing company, it's not unrealistic to expect between $50,000 and $70,000 a year.

Negatives—You have to be careful out in the sun; you should always be aware of skin cancer. There's a burnout factor, too. You can only say, "Here's the bow, here's the stern, and this is how you turn the boat" so many times. And the pay is only a subsistence living.

The future—Today if you want to go camping in Yosemite, you have to go through Ticketron. Many of the standard recreation options are losing their appeal; public parks aren't being taken care of, and the usual vacation spots are becoming saturated. Sailing is about to become a huge boom sport and the employment opportunities will come right along with it.

Sailing has a mysterious, almost genetic lure. It's a natural, peaceful way to feel at one with nature. I think the current green movement will embrace the concept of sailing.

I think that the people who want to participate are surfacing, too. When you're in your early 20s and 30s, you're into challenging solo sports, like Rollerblading, mountain biking and rock climbing. People in their 40s want to concentrate more on doing things with their friends and families, activities that involve less impact. And the message is finally out there that boat ownership is not necessary to go sailing. With that one door opening, sailing no longer has to be an exclusive sport.

I do believe that as the sport becomes more popular, it's likely that there will be more rules and regulations. As soon as it's legislated, instructors will be required to meet certain certification standards and the quality of instruction in general will go up.

Career Case Study

Debby Wiggins, New York

Debby Wiggins and her husband have owned Oyster Bay Sailing School in New York since 1987. She was honored by the American Sailing Association as Outstanding Instructor of the Year in 1991. When school is not in session, Debby enjoys traveling, spending time with her family, and of course, sailing.

Requirements—First of all, you need to be a really good, skilled sailor. You have to know the parts of the boat and understand the language of sailing, and you have to be able to communicate that. Here at my school, we don't touch anything once we're teaching on the boat; we let the students do everything, but the instructor is there to save the day, if necessary. You have to be able to anticipate what students are going to do, so that you can keep them out of trouble. There is some classroom work involved, so you've got to have some speaking skills as well.

Being able to communicate the skills you're teaching is important. If you love sailing and you're enthusiastic, it will show, and students pick up on that. If an instructor is not enthusiastic about the activity, the student is going to start having doubts right away.

Prospects—There's a fair amount of competition. We get a lot of people calling us and coming by our booth at boat shows. One thought to consider is that teaching sailing is pretty much a part-time job. Most lessons are done on the weekends, and while we do hire some full-time instructors during the season, the only people who really make a career of it are the ones who move around with the warm weather to different areas of the country or world. You'd have to make it a lifestyle.

Many of our instructors are retired people who just love to sail, others are college students who work for us during the season. Others deliver boats, work as marine surveyors or do repair work on boats. When I'm interviewing for an instructing position, I look for someone who has many years of sailing experience.

Benefits—You get to be out on the water, teaching others to do something you love to do. If you like people, there's nothing better. What's really nice about the students you meet is that learning to sail isn't a necessary part of their lives; they're there because they want to learn, and they're ready to have fun. When you see them sail by themselves, it's very gratifying.

Pay—I can only speak for our school. On the average an instructor will make $8 to $10 an hour. Some places will pay less, some more; it depends on the individual company. Unless the instructor takes a managerial position in the company, the pay probably won't change much.

Negatives—It's seasonal employment in the Northeast, and unless you're fortunate enough to line up jobs elsewhere, it's hard to make a career out of it. If you can run a sailing school, you can make it a career and the lifestyle is marvelous.

The future—As far as I can see, sailing is here to stay. I don't see any lack of interest in wanting to learn how to sail. It is a social sport, and one of the least expensive to participate in. I think more and more people are interested in adding sailing to their bag of tricks; they like to say, "I can ski, I can play tennis and I can sail."

People who have friends who own boats often come in for lessons. They love to go out on the boat, but they don't know what they're doing, and they want to know how to handle themselves. There's something for everyone in sailing. Some people want to race and compete; other people have enough of that during the week at their regular jobs, and they just want to lay back and sail.

References

American Sailing Association, 13922 Marquesas Way, Marina del Rey, CA 90292; (310) 822-7171 or fax (310)822-4741.

U.S. Sailing Association (racing organization), Box 209, Newport, RI 02840; (401) 849-5200.

California Maritime Academy, 200 Maritime Academy Drive, Vallejo, CA 94590; (707)648-4222 or fax (707)649-4773. HTPP://www.csum.edu.

Ski Instructor

Dreams—As a ski instructor, you get to ski all the time with the best equipment while high-rollers are laying some giant tips on you and attractive pupils want to party with you all night. You dream of snow, and when you get it, you figure you died and went to heaven.

Nightmares—You find you can't stand being around strangers all day long, and while you may be an expert skier, you discover you hate slowing down and actually don't like teaching at all. You like the attractive pupils, but they don't like you. Suddenly it hits you: You're in it for all the wrong reasons. Not only that, but you could break a leg at any moment.

Realities—Face it, this is a decent full-time seasonal job for a young person, or a part-time position for others, as long as you are friendly, clean, and have the ability to communicate the art of skiing. You ski a lot, always with the best equipment, and once established, you can get a job at virtually any ski resort.

What it's all about—What a life, eh? Spending your days skiing and getting paid for it, then off you go, carousing into the night with your pupils. Sound too good to be true? Well, sometimes it almost is.

For ski instructors with the right personality, this is life in the happy lane. You are constantly meeting a wide assortment of people, many who will look upon you as some kind of guru and do their best to please you. Your time is spent in beautiful areas, perhaps at Aspen or Tahoe from November through April, and if you're a full-timer, perhaps Austria or New Zealand from May through October. As an instructor, you get the best of the world of skiing—the best equipment, clothes and respect on the slopes. If you have a knack for business and some ideas to go with it, you may even eventually help manage a ski park.

And, of course, you can't forget that you will be constantly meeting pupils who are attractive and athletic, who might just be free for an evening while on vacation from the city. Sounds good, eh? Well, as it turns out, even the most rakish instructors, male and female alike, discover that having rotating partners each week fractures the psyche. It doesn't take long until many frequently take a pass on the night life.

Which gets us right back to the job, day-in and day-out, as the real attraction. How does it work? Well, you show up, often never knowing what the prospects are for getting work/lessons/money. When snow conditions are poor, it can be a dry piece of life waiting for a student to arrive. Then when someone does sign up for a lesson, you are never allowed to be in a bad mood. For instance, figure it takes 10 to 15 minutes in the chairlift heading up the mountain, and in that time you have to act pleasant with any stranger, no matter what they say, do, or on another front, how they may happen to . . . smell! Any poorly-timed remarks on your part, and wham, there goes your tip.

Nobody makes much money giving ski lessons, about $50 to $60 for a full day. But if you can figure out how to consistently get tips, you can double that. Some ski instructors will select a key moment during the lesson, and then say in a friendly but direct manner: "Ski instructors aren't paid much, you know, so we depend on tips in order to make ends meet." At the end of a lesson, a statement like that has a way of sticking in someone's mind, and can result in a good tip. Instructors who don't mention tips end up being prisoners of hope, then have a way of getting zilched. Before long, they start getting disgruntled about the lousy pay, and it can result in a poor attitude with students. If that happens, it won't be long and it's "adios." Time to find another job.

But it can be an ideal position, providing you have a passion for snow, love to be around all kinds of people, and have expert communication skills. It is especially well-suited for people in their twenties, perhaps as a seasonal full-time job, before they embark on a more financially rewarding career.

Rarely, instructors are plucked to move up the corporate ladder at a ski area. People who shine as instructors, and who also are well organized and show initiative, are occasionally groomed for higher ranking and paying jobs at a ski park. But when you go that route, you discover that you ski less and less, and spend more and more time in an office. One day you will look up and say, "This isn't at all what I had in mind."

The prospects for getting a job as a ski instructor are quite good for a young person who is an advanced skier, athletic, well groomed, friendly, and able to communicate with anybody. In the United States and Canada, there are more than 700 ski areas, and an additional 250 in Europe and New Zealand. Every winter, there are always many openings. The best time to apply for a job in the U.S. is in October. If you're new to the game, don't wait until it starts snowing.

The evolution of the career is such that it can be pretty easy to turn into a ski bum every winter, perhaps moving each year to a different ski park. Some instructors will spend several years at it, combining it with a full-time seasonal position in the summer, perhaps as a rafting guide, forest fire fighter, fishing boat deckhand . . . you get the idea. At age 22, that might sound ideal. At age 42, well, the shoe doesn't always fit so well anymore.

So put it in perspective, wax up your skis, and let it fly down the mountain a few times. You might just have something here that will create some of the best times of your life.

Career Case Study

Dennis Herbel, Colorado

Dennis Herbel has worked as a ski instructor at Keystone Resort in Colorado for the past 13 years. He has also worked as a park ranger at Colorado Grand National Monument. During the off-season, Herbel works as a sailing instructor and runs a charter sailboat. He lives in Dillon, Colorado.

Requirements—Some people think you need to be a certified instructor, but it's not required; in fact, you need to teach for two years before you're even eligible for certification. Certification is difficult. There are three levels; I'm stage three. But in most cases, you just need to have basic skiing skills.

It's also important to have good communication skills. Ski areas look for good communicators, people who have backgrounds in retail sales or who have been schoolteachers, things like that. You need solid people skills. Skiing is actually the last priority. You can be the world's greatest skier, but if you don't work well with people, you won't make it as an instructor.

You tend to become a bartender-like figure—people tell you all their problems. The barrier that's usually there between strangers is broken, and they'll tell you anything. They know they're leaving tomorrow and they want to get out all their troubles and go home the next day.

Lift rides become interesting; you get all kinds of people. A lot of couples come up together, for example, and you get the guy who brings his girlfriend and wants to spend the night with her, but not the day. During the day he wants to do his own thing, so he sticks her in ski school. So I get to hear what a jerk he is. Then there's the old guy who's not real athletic, maybe a little overweight, who's been married for years and wants to tell you all about it, about his nagging wife and all his troubles. You become a lot more than a guide.

Prospects—At a high-volume ski area such as the one I work for, they might need 15 to 20 instructors a day. During the high season we need a hundred or more. The market is pretty wide open. If a person wants to be a ski instructor, it's fairly easy to find a job. The highest rate of turnover is with children's instructors because they tend to be younger.

Most instructors have other jobs in the summer, of course. I run a sailing school and a charter boat. We've got people from all fields: golf pros, construction workers, trail guides and farmers. There are also people who do it year-round. They're here for our winter, then they head over to New Zealand or Austria, sometimes even South America.

Benefits—You never have to grow up. It's not your average, everyday career. You're outside in a beautiful environment, doing something you love. If you have an athletic background, if you grew up with an active lifestyle, you remain an athlete and still make a living.

Pay—On the average, an instructor will make between $6.50 and $16 an hour. The average work day is about five hours long. During the low season, full-time instructors are required to be here four days a week; during high season it's six days a week, and we can work every day if we want to. One disadvantage is that they won't pay overtime, so there's no extra benefit in putting in anything over a forty-hour week. Often you'll teach people of wealth, and quite often they tip pretty well. I've been tipped $700 in one week, but I've gone for two months with no tips at all, too. There's no standard rule like there is in restaurants. There's no sign and no one to advise people about it; it's pretty much up to the individual.

Negatives—There's always the chance that you can get injured. You can get hit by somebody. You can lose a knee. By grooming the runs, the ski areas are taking away anything that will slow people down, like moguls for example, and people tend to ski slightly above their ability. That makes it more dangerous; people start running into each other a lot more.

There's the possibility of getting sick. All kinds of viruses are floating around, and it's very easy to catch flus and colds.

Toward the end of the season, you generally get burned out with being nice. As an instructor, you're always on stage, and you can only be on stage for so long before you get tired of it.

Thirty years ago, this was considered a glamorous job—you know, the guy with the Austrian accent and the suntan—but it's really turned into a duty. You're constantly standing out in the cold, settling fights between families, stopping crime when you have to, dealing with macho man problems. There's often nothing at all glamorous about it.

The future—You start out as a basic ski instructor. If you do a good job of being a human being, your clients will come back, and you can start building a private-lesson clientele. The ski school recognizes return business, and you create that, so that's an opportunity to improve your standing with the school.

As far as moving up into management, if you have good organizational skills you can get into training, assigning lessons, things like that. If you want to keep going, you can eventually become an assistant ski school director or a manager. The truth about being promoted to a position in management, though, is that it boosts your ego but lowers your income. You'll get an increase in salary but your workload increases too, so if you broke it down into an hourly wage, you'd actually be making less.

Career Case Study

Tim Wertz, California

Tim Wertz has been a professional ski instructor at Dodge Ridge for five years. He started skiing when he was twelve, and became a ski instructor at age 17. His other job experience includes working as a carpenter and driving a school bus. He lives in Sonora, California and attends Columbia Junior College.

Requirements—You have to know the basics as far as knowing how to ski. The level of ability all depends on the resort. Dodge Ridge is more of a family-type resort, mostly beginners, so pretty much anyone who knows how to ski can get a job as an instructor. Before the season opens, they have an orientation where they show you how to teach; they show basic techniques like the wedge.

Definitely you have to get along with people. You have to make changes in your attitude to accommodate the people. If your students are having a bad day at the resort, you've got to flip it around and make them feel at ease.

Prospects—There is a big turnover rate. People come in and find out that they don't make a lot of money and they don't get to ski as much as they thought they would, so they quit. It's pretty easy to find a job as a ski instructor. There are a lot of people that come back, though. Some of them go on to other, bigger resorts.

Benefits—You get good deals on skiing. Some resorts will let you ski for free if you're a member of PSIA (Professional Ski Instructors of America). Not all resorts do that, but some of the big ones do. You get good deals on equipment too, through Pro Deal.

Pay—If you're not a member of PSIA, the pay is minimum wage, and if you are a member, it's around $6 an hour. It can go all the way up to $12 an hour for someone who's fully certified. There isn't a lot of money in it, but you can get by. Someone who's fully certified can make maybe $20,000 a year.

Negatives—You get tired of people sometimes. I was getting burned out; I'd been doing it for five years, and you get to the point where you get tired of pleasing people all the time by doing things their way. You're laughing at their stupid jokes and trying to make them have a good time. That's basically what you have to do all the time. I don't know if that would be a minus for everybody, but I know it gets to a lot of people.

There's not a lot of money in it, either. If you don't work one day you get two hours show-up pay, and that's it. It's not a great way to make a living.

The future—If you stay at a certain resort long enough, you can move up. It takes quite a few years and a lot of knowledge. It depends on how hard you want to work for the resort and if you're good with people. That's the most important; if you're not good with people, you're out of there.

References

Professional Ski Instructors of America (PSIA), 133 South Van Gordon Street, Suite 101, Lakewood, CO 80228, (303)987-9390 or fax (303)988-3005. E-mail: natoff@genie.geis.com.

The *White Book of Ski Areas* provides detailed information for every ski area in the United States, Canada and South America. (See page 311.)

National Ski Patrol, Inc., Ste 100, 133 South Van Gordon Street, Lakewood, CO 80228; (303)988-1111 or fax (303)988-3005.

Ski-related magazines, such as *Ski, Skiing,* and *Powder* offer helpful material as well.

Ski Park Seasonal Employee

Dreams—What a scam you've got here. You put in your hours, practically sleepwalking your way through the day, then ski for free whenever you want. With all the new people you meet, you get invited to all kinds of parties. You don't save any money, but so what? The fringe benefits make up for it.

Nightmares—What is this, they actually want you to work? Hey, it's cold out there all day long. A certain percentage of the public is comprised of jerks, and you're supposed to smile? After the tough days, it turns out you're too tired to ski or to party, or do anything but sleep. Hey, when does the fun start?

Realities—This is the ground floor of the ski industry, with openings available for friendly people who know how to serve customers with a smile. You do get to ski for free on your off- time, make enough money to get by, and have a good chance to make plenty of good friends.

What it's all about—Anything to keep from getting a "real" job, eh? Well, sometimes. Sometimes not.
  In the case of the classic ski bum, this job can be a way to do as little as possible, ski as much as possible, and meet lots of new partiers. At least that's the theory. In the case of someone who is simply devoted to skiing and wants to be around it, this can be a

personally rewarding job, even if the pay ain't necessarily the greatest. In reality, rarely do the twain meet.

For one thing, if you are just a ski bum looking for a free ride through winter, it is no easy trick to con the manager of a ski park into hiring you. As for the prospective employee who has more inspiring intentions, devotion alone won't get you there either. A ski park manager wants something far different.

What? Listen close. What the ski park manager wants is somebody who likes to help people. It's that simple. A generally nice person who is helpful to children, kind to strangers and is a lousy skier makes a better employee than any member of a posse of snowboard jumpers who can do a 360-degree flip but doesn't have the magic words "Let me help you" in their vocabulary. The kind of person who makes a good ski park employee is one who gives the last bite of their chocolate chip cookie to a stray dog.

If you are that kind of person, there is a job for you out there. Every ski area requires a wide variety of employees every winter. Most of them involve working with the public: concessions, equipment rentals, snowmaking, snowgrooming, ski school, lifts, equipment repair, maintenance, and for large ski areas, lodging. The jobs don't pay a great deal, usually just $5 or $6 per hour.

But it will get you by for a winter, or even a few winters. In fact, if you like service-oriented positions, you could have quite a time working at a ski park in the winter, then a national park in the summer. The two provide very similar kinds of work. It is respectable enough, while you decide what long-term career direction you want to take.

The best thing you can do in this position is try to serve the customers well. Be friendly and you will be repaid in kind. Be helpful, kind . . . well, you know, kind of like the Boy Scout motto. That will get you hired, keep you employed, and eventually get you a pay raise and maybe a promotion to a section chief.

Never think nobody is watching. That's the attitude of the ski bum who has just conned his way into a job. Well, somebody is always watching. You always get paid back.

Take, for instance, the job of helping people get on and off the chairlifts. It is among the most important at a ski area; an accident and injury due to an attendant's negligence can result in a terrible lawsuit. Regardless, at virtually any ski area, you can see attendants who are practically dozing off in the lift huts, and others who are angry that their utter wonderfulness is not more acclaimed and would happily use cattle prods on the skiers to get them moving more quickly.

General managers of ski areas hate attitude problems. When they interview people for seasonal jobs, that is what they look for to weed out candidates. The first impression you must make in the interview is that you are neither a bum looking for a free ride, nor a self-proclaimed wonder hopping from crisis to crisis.

Not you. "Why, I'm looking for a start in the ski industry, and figure getting in on the ground floor is the right way to go about it. I enjoy helping people and I think you have the best ski park in the industry. Of all the people you might interview, I am the best for the job because of my ability to get along with people. I want this job."

Oddly enough, many ski park managers never hear this speech. They rarely see a prospective employee look them in the eye and say, "I want this job." If you say it, watch out—you might just get it.

For the person who takes this outlook to the interview, the prospects are good. If you get hired and demonstrate that you know how to walk your talk, you can get promoted to a section chief, and possibly get hired year-round. Many ski areas have a corral of year-round employees. One reason is that all improvements at a ski park are made in the summer. Another reason is that many ski areas are opening their lifts for mountain tours during the summer to add a little bonus business.

Working at a ski area requires a bit of mental toughness because of the continual exposure to cold, a variety of customer attitudes, and a sense of pressure from the boss to be nice all the time. The ski park employees who are happiest can handle all of these demands.

Oh yeah, one other thing: Anytime you are not working, you get to ski for free. It's the best deal in town.

Career Case Study

Chad Lewis, Maine—Chad Lewis has worked as a lift operator for Sunday River Ski Resort in Maine for several seasons. When he's not working, he enjoys snowboarding. Chad lives in Bethel, Maine.

Requirements—You've got to have a driving personality where your spirits are up all the time. You're dealing with the public all day long, and if you come across one jerk, you can't let him bring you down.

You have to maintain an upbeat mood. I've found that most people come on vacation to complain and let it all out, and they leave their brains at home. A lot of crazy things happen and you can't let them get to you; you just have to be able to brush them off.

You have to be fit. The majority of ski resort jobs are physically demanding. In a lot of positions, like lift operating or snowmaking, there's no brain work involved; you're just doing manual labor. I sometimes load 1,000 to 2,000 chairs in one day. It's just grunt work—you've got to be willing to do it.

Being in the cold all day is very draining. A lot of days you're standing out there from eight in the morning until four or five in the afternoon. So you really have to like snow and cold weather. You have to be open to the lifestyle in general.

Prospects—The availability of jobs depends on where you are. In places like Utah, where the skiing is really great, it's a lot harder because there's so much competition. There are a lot of people there who want to ski for free. Back East it's a little easier because people aren't into the sport quite as much. I'd say that a good percentage of most East Coast resorts' employees don't even ski; they're just there for the job, to support their families.

Benefits—Most resorts give their employees a free season pass. That's probably the number one benefit. You can ski for free whenever you want.

You run into all kinds of cool people. There is a lot of fun, a lot of good times. The atmosphere is different from the outside world; people are more relaxed, more giving. They're into giving to each other and helping each other out. It's a great environment to live in.

Pay—I work five days a week for $5.50 an hour, and I'm one of the better paid lift operators. Most of the menial jobs here pay around minimum wage.

Many resorts are pretty cheap when it comes to raises, but there is room for advancement. If you have half a brain, and if you have the ambition, you can move up to a foreman or supervisor position, which pays a little better. Not much, though. You'll never be driving a BMW or living in a $300,000 house as long as you're working at a ski area.

Negatives—The pay is not good for the work you're doing. You work really hard and you sometimes don't get any appreciation. I've noticed that at the beginning of the season and the end of the season, people are smiling and happy, but anytime in between they're pretty grumpy. Basically they're pissed that they had to pay 37 bucks, and they're going to dump all over you.

It's not a stable job. You never know if you're going to have money for the next week or when you're going to get laid off. The cold weather is really a physical strain, too; when it's 20 below and I've been out there all day, I burn a lot of calories.

The future—From a recreational perspective, skiing will be popular as long as it's possible. Snowmaking has introduced a whole new wave of skiing possibility—there will always be snow as long as the temperature is low enough.

Snowboarding has created a whole new influx of people, too. It's becoming more and more popular, and the industry is expanding because of that.

Skiing and snowboarding both are a big ego thing. People like to say, "I ski." It's a fashion show, and it's also a soul thing, a brotherhood-type thing, similar to surfing. It's a different, unique way of thinking, and people want to be a part of it.

Career Case Study

Paul Martin, Nevada

Paul Martin is the head of the host and hostess department at Heavenly Valley ski area in Lake Tahoe during the winter, and holds a management position at a local golf course in the summer. He was born and raised in Connecticut and has a bachelor's degree from Colby College. He also teaches golf and is currently working toward PGA membership.

Requirements—I'm the supervisor for the host/hostess department at Heavenly Valley. Hosts and hostesses are basically responsible for general customer service on the mountain. Their main function is general customer service on the hill and that entails a variety of responsibilities. They ski the beginner and intermediate runs, looking for lost and confused skiers, they stand at stationary positions and give directions, and they lead tours to familiarize people with the mountain. To be a host or hostess, you need to be outgoing, very people-oriented, and able to present yourself professionally. You should be a competent skier and enjoy meeting people and speaking publicly, because that's a large part of the job.

When I interview potential employees, I look for certain characteristics: I notice if they look me in the eye or not, if they're fidgeting or tapping their fingers; basically I look for someone who is at ease with themselves and others.

Prospects—There's a lot of competition. The little experience required makes it a popular job. Last season I interviewed over 100 applicants for 12 positions, and many of those who were hired were return employees. The others had special skills, such as being fluent in Spanish or Japanese. It really depends on the resort. Some areas don't even hire outside people; they use only their ski instructors who don't have lessons for hosts. Mammoth Mountain uses a strictly volunteer method, in exchange for free ski passes.

Knowledge of the area will definitely give you an edge. I worked in retail for Heavenly for five years before I moved to this position. I was at the right place at the right time, but I also had a really comprehensive knowledge of the mountain. I think it would be fairly difficult for an outside person, someone unfamiliar with the area, to break in. Local knowledge really helps out, because you have privileged information: from the ins and outs of the mountain and the secret places to ski to the best restaurants and bars in town.

Benefits—It's a low-stress, young, athletic environment. If you enjoy skiing, you're able to share that with other people who also love it. It's a lot of fun and very interesting to meet new people. We get people from all over the country and the world: Texas, Florida, Brazil and Japan. A lot of them come in groups, and often they're professionals who are getting away from their normal routines for the first time. They can be pretty wild people. You're able to be outdoors; your office is 20,000 acres. You get to ski on the job, and when you're off, you ski for free.

Pay—It's really not very good. Here at Heavenly the hosts and hostesses make around $5.45 an hour. That goes up in 25 cent increments each year.

Managerial positions such as mine are paid on a salary basis. A supervisor can expect to make between $1,500 and $1,700 a month.

Negatives—You have to be on the hill when it's 20 below and windy and freezing. Even when no one else seems to want to go out, you have to.

Most of the time the general public is fairly positive, but there's that one percent who are having a bad day, and you're often an easy target. Keeping a smile pasted on 24 hours a day is sometimes very difficult.

The future—I think the ski industry only has room for growth. Because of the shrinking dollar, the industry is getting more and more customer-oriented, and as the resorts concentrate on being more user-friendly, they're going to require an increased number of people to help them. I think that in the host area, they're going to require better, more advanced skiers.

References

White Book of Ski Areas, from Inter-Ski Services, Inc., P.O. Box 9595, Friendship Station, Washington, D.C. 20016; (202) 342-0886.

National Ski Area Association, 133 South Van Gordon Street, Ste 300, Lakewood, CO 80228; (303) 987-1111.

National Ski Patrol, Inc., Ste 100, 133 South Gordon Street, Lakewood, CO 80228; (303) 988-1111 or fax (303) 988-3005.

Several ski magazines, including *Ski, Skiing,* and *Powder,* list job prospects in the back pages.

Ski Park Owner

Dreams—A ski park owner is a symbol of success to everybody, an executive who knows how to make money and how to play. One stays forever young, yet gets respect by presence alone. The words "I own a ski park" can sound like magic, and they are. The annual income is great, and when you sell, you make a fortune.

Nightmares—What if it doesn't snow? Or only snows on weekends? Then you get devastated financially, because nobody shows up. To save money, you try to do too much, get overstressed and start firing everybody. Pretty soon you're a tyrant, your employees hate you, and their attitudes drive skiers away to your competition. Finally, you go bankrupt.

Realities—A good solid financial base, created from several investors, will get you through bad times and establish a lot of padding during the good times. You will become something of a celebrity, and if you use that power to keep employees' attitudes up, you will be repaid well by return business. A sharp mind for number crunching, promotion and improvements is a necessity.

What it's all about—You probably think you need a huge bundle of cash in your bank account to buy a ski park, right? Well, that is one way to go about it, but it is not only the worst way, but the least practiced way as well.

Instead, the way to do it is to have a consortium of private investors put up a fair amount of cash, then borrow the rest from a bank, using the ski park as collateral. You can end up as a majority owner with relatively little personal cash risk. Of course, the more you put up yourself, the easier it is to attract both partners and bank loans.

A fair-sized ski park, say one with seven chairlifts that is located in a non-peak area, is worth about $5 million. The best way to buy such a place is first to become an executive with the ski park. General manager is the ideal position. As a general manager, you will get to know the remarkable peaks and valleys of cash flow of a ski park operation, and exactly what is a reasonable monthly overhead based on projected income. It is different for every location. Then, as an executive, you make your offer. As an insider, it will be viewed as friendly, not hostile.

It is very unusual for someone to enter the picture on his or her own from the outside and bankroll the entire project, even for corporations. The risk is too high, especially with annual improvements expected by skiers. If you spread yourself thin and then there is a bad winter for snow, even a once-wealthy business can get whittled down to size in a hurry.

Like most executive positions, the higher the risk, the bigger the payoff if you score. During a winter when there is lots of snow, yet clear weather on weekends and holidays, you can clear $125,000 to $250,000, or even millions if the ski park location is amid a major tourist hub. That is in about four months' time, from December through March, after all your partners and expenses have been paid off and summer improvements are paid for. You get paid last. In addition, the value of the ski park tends to rise each year, so even if it becomes only a fair profit-maker, you can cash in your chips in five or ten years and still make a killing.

If you choose to be a hands-on owner, you will save money by not hiring a lot of management executives. But the do-it-yourself method can mean long hours, no fun, and can actually hurt your earnings because areas can be overlooked. No one person can do it all. The best advice is to have a small circle of specialists for each area of operation: concessions, rentals, snowmaking, ski school, lifts, equipment repair, maintenance, promotions, and for a large ski area, lodging.

Then if you want to live it up, give yourself a break and hire a general manager to oversee the entire operation, and do whatever you want. That means skiing whenever you want, trouble shooting special concerns, being available for promotions, or just counting your money and being a first-class ski bum. Over time, a ski park owner will usually try all those things.

One absolute key is making sure all the employees are friendly and courteous. At some ski parks, the employees at the chairlifts seem like they would like to use taser guns on skiers, or at the opposite end of the behavior spectrum, would prefer to take a siesta. If those attitudes pervade the energy of a ski park, it can devastate return business and undermine the nucleus of long-term financial solvency, because skiers just won't come back. That is why it is a good idea for a ski park owner to be active—on the slopes, in the cafe, in the rental shop—demonstrating the proper attitude. If a malcontent refuses to get in line, then you have to be able to sit that person down and say, "I don't know how we will make it without you, but starting today we're going to try."

The best examples of how to make it big are entertainment parks such as Disneyland, Disney World, and Marriott's. It's not just the rides. It's the employees. Every single one does everything possible to make the experience a good one for all visitors. It's the same at a ski park. There is some irony in the fact that a multi-million dollar investment can come down to the attitudes of people making $5 an hour, but that's the way it is.

Over time, the weather will treat you good and treat you bad. That evens out. What does not is your management style, your vision of improvements, how much fun you choose to have, how much money it takes to get in, and how much you take to get out. For an executive who can dream, the price is right.

Career Case Study

Frank Helm, California   *Frank M. Helm, Jr. has been the owner and operator of Dodge Ridge Ski Area since 1976. He is the past president of the California Ski Industry Association and continues to be a member of the board of directors. Frank and his wife Sally enjoy bicycling, skiing and travel. Frank also enjoys fly fishing, providing there are "lots of naive fish in the stream and no bushes along the bank."*

Requirements—There are different ways of going about it. To become the owner and general manager of an area, it's often easier to go through the ranks rather than going right in and buying the area. I went to the University of California for four years, then went into business with my father, a Chevrolet dealer. In the end I decided I just didn't like that business, so I went on to other things— I built houses for a while and worked for an employer's council.

Then, in 1975, I heard about Dodge Ridge being for sale. My wife and I were interested in moving to the mountains, so we looked into it, and found a couple of other investors who were thinking about getting in on it. They ended up falling through, but my wife and I were still interested, so I went up there and worked as a lift operator for the first year, and in retail and food service, all those areas, to see if I liked being around it as much as I thought I would. And I did, so we went ahead and put together the deal. I went in as owner/manager, and that year was the second and worst year of the drought in the '70s. Luckily the previous owner, Earl Purdy, stayed on and helped me.

You have to have some capital, or access to capital, if you want to own an area. How much depends on what the seller wants. In our case they wanted all cash, $2.9 million. We put some of our own in, and the remainder we borrowed from the banks. But there are many ways it can be done. The seller might say they want half down, or a quarter down, and so much in improvements made every year. Or you might be dealing with a seller's bank, who might want to be paid off.

Prospects—Ski areas change hands very rarely. It's much easier to become a general manager by just working your way through the ranks than trying to go in and buy an area. It's a hell of a lot cheaper that way, too.

Benefits—I think that the lifestyle is the main benefit. You're in the mountains; you have clear air and earth. I'm an ex-smoker, and I've kind of turned a new leaf—I'm interested in being healthy and living as long as I can. The mountains allow me to ski in the winter and bike in the summer, a lifestyle that I wouldn't have in some place like downtown L.A. There is clean air, no pollution, and less of a problem with crime and drugs.

On the business side, I like the fact that I can call my own shots. I like the fact that I own my own business. By virtue of buying an area, you can have any position you want. I've always looked at my position as just another employee; I have to work just as hard or harder than anyone. But I think that working for anyone else, I would be totally unemployable.

Pay—In my position, it depends on the size of the area. A business can only afford so much, and it has to pay a fair wage to its employees, whether it's me as an owner, or someone in the retail part. It has to pay what the position's worth. I would say from $3,000 a month to $8,000 or $9,000 a month.

Negatives—The volatility of the weather is the biggest negative. If we don't get any snow, that's tough to deal with. It can be real unpredictable. Dealing with personnel can be hard.

You're perhaps more isolated in the mountains. If you want to go to a play or to the symphony, you're not going to be able to do it as easily. But actually, I don't even think about things like that anymore.

The future—Depending on your age and other factors, there are many things that this could lead to. Personally, I don't have any desire to go on and build another ski area or anything like that, but that's certainly a possibility for someone else. If someone was interested in pure business, this could be a perfect training ground for other areas. It's good experience for businesses that change from year to year, and of course, you get a background in dealing with personnel and things like that, all the aspects of any business.

I see myself as continuing to be involved. I don't like the idea of retiring, not completely anyway. I want to be able to work and have an active part for as long as I can.

Career Case Study

> *Tom Corcoran, New Hampshire*   *Tom Corcoran is the president, CEO and founder of Waterville Valley, New Hampshire's largest year-round ski resort. He directed its construction and opening and now oversees all operations.*

Requirements—If you're going to run a ski area successfully, you have to be first and foremost a businessperson. I have an MBA from Harvard, so I had very good business training. An MBA is becoming fairly standard for many corporate positions today; it's an indication of a strong business background. All of the people who hold top management positions in my company have MBAs, as well as extensive and diverse business experience outside of the skiing industry. An MBA doesn't mean that a person is bright or able or has good people skills, but it does mean that he or she has been trained to have a variety of business skills. That experience is particularly helpful in the ski resort industry, because we're essentially running many small businesses simultaneously with a relatively small management staff.

We're a small company, but we have a lot of small, diverse parts. We have two ski areas and a resort operation, and within those we have retail operations, hotels, ski schools, rental and repair services, a golf course, and food service operations. You must bring a number of skills to the position in order to successfully incorporate all facets of the business.

You must be capable of handling the fact that you're dealing with unpredictable weather. You have to prepare for all possibilities mentally, emotionally and financially. Sometimes it doesn't snow; it rains, or there's no favorable weather at all, and you have to pick yourself up and keep going. You've got to have a farmer's mentality. You should also enjoy living in a rural area, and if you're married, have a spouse who can accept that as well. People who are city-oriented and who get cabin fever easily will generally not do well in this business.

Prospects—It's a difficult industry to get a job in, because there are relatively few ski resorts and only a limited number of management positions. There aren't a lot of entry-level positions, and there's not a lot of turnover. The ones who step into positions are the ones who have experience, or happen to be at the right place at the right time. If there's a shifting, it's within the industry. I would caution people who do not work in the ski industry that there aren't a lot of openings for people outside the field. If you don't ski yourself and have a great love of skiing, a good management position will be difficult to find.

Benefits—Obviously, you're your own boss, and with that comes many advantages. I sit in my office and I look out the window at a beautiful mountain that's three minutes away, and my home is two minutes away. It's mentally stimulating; you have to make a lot of decisions and meet a lot of challenges.

It's a team effort. I work with a group of people who are extremely enjoyable to work with. The people who are drawn to this lifestyle are resilient, hardy, independent, and self-confident. They have a great sense of humor, they're bright, and it's fun to be around people like that.

The atmosphere is refreshing. It's environmentally clean, a good place for kids and families. You're providing a release for people. It's very rewarding to see people creating happy memories and going around with big smiles.

Pay—In the last six years, we've invested $15 million into this company, and we're considered a medium-sized area. Of that, $12 million went into the mountain and the remaining $3 million into the valley operations. Our business has increased consistently every year for the past four years, but at the same time, I've seen other ski areas go out of business. It's a very capital-intensive business.

The income of an owner depends on the financial success of the area. For the types of skills you have to bring to the job, the pay is probably less than you might imagine. I've heard that George Gillette, the owner of Vail, has compensation of $1.5 million, but I know of many others who make around $20,000. The range is anywhere in between.

A significant part of the compensation is not monetary. I know that with the skills and experience I have now, I could make a lot more money working outside a ski area than I can here, but I choose to combine my avocation with my vocation.

Negatives—It's a tricky business. Obviously, we're dependent on weather, and sometimes the weather goes against you. This past January it rained almost every weekend. We virtually put the mountain back together every week with snowmaking and slope grooming, and every week we had to watch it wash away. It was an unmitigated disaster, and it was hard to keep smiles on our faces. It's not an easy business. The people who are in it truly love it, but it's not for everyone.

The future—There are two viable kinds of ski areas: small, part-time areas without a lot of competition, and the larger, Vail-class resorts. There is a niche for small areas, but many of them have disappeared. That market has diminished; it has become increasingly hard to support ski areas that depend solely on the winter season. Bigger, diversified places such as this one—resorts which are created for year-round business—are the ones that survive. They're not just into skiing; they offer shopping, dining, entertainment, and a variety of recreational experiences.

The industry is going through a process of shake-out right now due to technological improvement. There's hardly any resemblance to what was available to the public ten years ago. Skiing is here to stay; with all the technological improvements of snowmaking and grooming, we're now able to ensure that there will always be skiing. It's a lifetime activity that takes place in a beautiful outdoor environment, a sport that people can participate in whether they're very young or very old.

References

Ski Industries of America, 8377-B Greensboro Drive, McLean VA 22102; (703) 556-9020; or fax (703) 821-8276. E-mail: siamail@IX@netcom.com.

Sno-engineering, Inc., (provides job placement information); write 34 School Street, Littleton, New Hampshire 03561, or phone (603) 444-4811 or fax (603) 444-0414. E-mail: snoe@snoe.com.

National Ski Area Association, 133 South Van Gordon Street, Ste 300, Lakewood, CO 80228; (303) 987-1111.

Surfing Instructor

Dreams—Being a surfing instructor is a glamorous adventure. You get treated like royalty on the beach, get top pay for having fun, and maybe even get featured on TV, the radio and in the newspapers as an outdoor personality. And by the way, notice how the hard-bodies can't keep their eyes off you?

Nightmares—What if nobody likes you? Or wants a lesson? Or worse, you get students but they don't pay up? Or heaven forbid, what if a student is injured and you don't have insurance or training in first-aid? Then there are those morning lessons after a late-night party. It doesn't get much worse.

Realities—The instructor with the professional approach from start to finish can do quite well. Attitude, good promotion, equipment, insurance, and of course, skill, can result in a steady stream of students, a good living and respect on the beach. For talented females, this can be an especially lucrative job.

What it's all about—If a doctor were to tap in to your veins, would he find blood or sea water pumping through your body? If you plan on being a surfing instructor, he'd better find sea water. Either that, or plan on sprouting a set of gills.

You have to have a passionate love for the sea to become a surfing instructor, because that is where you'll be, day-in and day-out. You have to learn about how tides, wind and weather affect wave conditions. You have to be able to get along and communicate clearly with all types of people, not just surf bums like yourself. And you have to be a professional, certified in advanced first-aid, CPR and life-saving, and get an insurance policy.

That done, this career market is wide open, lucrative, and for males and females alike, holds the opportunity to meet lots of companions. After all, the beach tends to bring out some of America's more attractive physical specimens.

The pay? Because surfing is such a difficult sport, a good instructor can charge $20 to $35 for a single one-hour lesson. You can add to that by having group rates and signing up three or four people at a time. Another option is having a five-step lesson program, where you sign up people for a package deal, taking them from beginner to intermediate level with a weekly lesson over the course of two months. Always get paid in advance, so once you're on the water, the focus is on surfing, not money.

A trick that few think of is bringing along a waterproof camera, taking pictures of your students during their moments of glory, then selling them a framed print for an additional $75 or $100. For a five-step lesson, you could include a certificate of graduation and a framed photo as part of the package. Get the idea? For the ambitious, there is money to be made.

But no jerks need apply for this job. Surfing is very difficult to learn, even more difficult to excel at. If you laugh at a student, deride their abilities, or explain to them how wonderful you are compared to them, you will not only lose that student, but word will get around—"The guy's a jerk"—and you will have a terrible time with the locals or getting anybody to sign up. Before long, you'll just be another surf bum like everybody else, trying to figure out how to buy your next six-pack.

You also will need to provide all equipment and have complete lifeguard training. Insurance is mandatory. Remember, this is a business you are starting, and you need to approach it as a professional. Do so and you will be rewarded.

Alas, the pitfalls for the unprofessional are many, especially for the surfing instructor who likes to party more than teach. Hangovers can really get in the way of pulling off those morning lessons. So can an inability to read a tidebook or weather patterns, a must in scheduling lessons when surf conditions are projected to be at their best. Then there is the business side of it, where you must be able to project earnings and balance them with expenses, so you're making a living at it, month in and month out.

If you sit waiting for the phone to ring, it can be a long sit. You have to be pro-active. There are many ways to promote yourself, and it doesn't take money for advertising, but rather energy and personality. Remember, as a surfing instructor, you will be considered a unique commodity by the media.

Take advantage of that. Present yourself to local newspapers and radio stations as a potential subject for a feature story. Check out your local TV news broadcasts, find out which reporters are in the field looking for features, then contact them and invite them out for a free lesson. TV reporters have giant egos, and they love to have film clips of themselves on the news. In the process, you will get fantastic free publicity that can keep you in students for months.

Other tips are posting professionally crafted notices on public billboards and directly approaching beginner surfers on the water. Of course, you can't make them feel stupid—"Say, I noticed how badly you surf"—but rather make it known that you are there to help with a friendly, non-scary invitation.

One word of caution. This is not a profession to take halfway. You either go all the way with it, doing everything possible to make a career of it, or don't go at all. It's boom or bust. You will be looked at either as a professional (and make some good money) or a surf bum (and make none). How you approach it will decide which one.

Career Case Study

Richard Schmidt, California—Richard Schmidt is known internationally as one of the world's premier big-wave riders. Since the late 1970s, he has traveled the world in search of the biggest and most challenging waves. He currently rides professionally for Team O'Neill International and competes on the California and Hawaii legs of the Association Surfing Professionals World Tour. Each summer he returns to Santa Cruz, California, where he teaches surfing and works as a beach lifeguard.

Requirements—There are no real set requirements, but you should have training in CPR, advanced first aid, and advanced lifesaving. You should be comfortable and knowledgeable about the ocean—a good enough surfer to know what you're doing, to judge weather conditions and things like that. You have to be outgoing and social, and have a lot of patience. It's important to be able to get along with most everybody. People can be intimidated by learning to surf.

Prospects—There still aren't many surfing instructors around. There are more than there were 10 years ago, but that's still not many. Anyone can teach surfing. If you've been surfing for your whole life and decide that you want to teach, all you basically have to do is go out and get your insurance and buy soft surf boards. That's critical—you have to have equipment that people can handle while they're learning.

I started out as a lifeguard. I had been a lifeguard for the city of Santa Cruz for 13 years; a friend of mine was teaching surfing, and he ended up handing it over to me. I worked for the city, and it slowly worked up to me getting a percentage of the fee. Then I started getting into private lessons, and I still do that, as well as running a surf camp.

Benefits—It keeps me healthy and in good shape for my own surfing. There's nowhere I'd rather be than outdoors, in the ocean.

Negatives—Sun damage is always a real danger. I usually wear a hat and lots of sunscreen when I'm teaching. Sometimes I get so busy with lessons that I don't have time for myself. I'm too tired to see, much less surf.

Pay—When I first started, I was getting $8 an hour. Now I make around $35 an hour for a private lesson. You pretty much set your own rates, although you should take into consideration what other people are charging if you have competition. It's usually a gradual thing. Teaching is something that takes a while to learn; every year I run into something new when I'm surfing that I can pass on to others.

The future—I think it's getting more acceptable to teach surfing. Back when I first started, there was maybe one other guy doing it here in Santa Cruz. But it's a growing sport, and like any other sport, you need good instructors. I have definitely noticed an increase in people wanting to learn. A lot of people think that it's just something they should try because they're in California, so they can go back to the Midwest and say, "Yeah, I surf."

People also seem to feel like they should take advantage of their natural resources. I get a wide range of people, about 50 to 60 percent of which are kids, but lots of people around the mid-thirties range, too. For them, surfing is something that they've always wanted to try but thought they missed out on, and when they see that the opportunity is out there, they get really excited. Not everyone sticks with it, because it takes a lot of time and dedication to learn, but a lot of people are willing to try.

Career Case Study

Brett Buchler, Delaware
Brett Buchler runs Surf Sessions, a surfing camp that provides "supervised ocean experiences for confirmed and future wave riders." He has over 15 years of combined experience as a classroom teacher, ski instructor and camp counselor. His ocean experience exceeds 20 years. He has surfed in Hawaii, the Caribbean, the South Pacific, the Mediterranean, Europe, and the east and west coasts of the U.S. Brett works as a schoolteacher during the off-season and lives in Frankford, Delaware with his wife and children.

Requirements—I don't think it requires anything special in the way of experience or education. You need to have a love of the sport and the desire to share what you know with other people. Surfing is often a very individualistic sport; locals can be very territorial and have a bad attitude toward newcomers. I started surfing when I got out of college; I was an inlander, and I knew what it was like not to be a local. So I decided to start a camp for kids who want to learn to surf but may not have the opportunity to live near the beach.

I've taught both skiing and surfing, and I came to realize that you don't need to be the best, in terms of skill, to teach. You mainly have to have a positive attitude, patience and the desire to teach others about an activity that will bring them enjoyment.

Prospects—Right now there's not much competition, especially on the east coast. I think mine is the only camp around this area. There are more private instructors, guys who give a few lessons a day, but there's not much competition even there.

A lot of people go out and try to learn to surf on their own. They don't realize that an instructor can save them hours of frustration. There are some basics that you aren't aware of when you're trying to learn by yourself, simple maneuvers that sometimes seem opposite in principle to what you think you should do. Learning a few fundamental pointers can save a lot of time. Anyone who's fairly athletic can learn to surf, but instructors can supply the shortcuts.

Benefits—It's the best feeling to see someone stand up on a board for the first time, to see how thrilled they are. It's great for anyone's self-esteem. I teach four-year-old kids and people over 50, and almost everyone gets hooked.

Surfing is one of the most physically and mentally challenging sports I know of. You have to combine coordination, timing and the ability to test yourself against nature, and it's incredibly rewarding when you get it right. It's a great way to keep in shape; you use every muscle in your body.

It also keeps you in touch with nature. You're out there in the water watching beautiful waves come in, and you're right there in the middle, challenging them.

Pay—Instructing allows me to live my summers at the beach—that's my profit. I've been doing this for five years and it's basically gotten me a van and 15 surfboards. I work as a schoolteacher for most of the year, and surfing lessons just supplement that income for me. I wouldn't want to depend on it.

I charge $350 a week for the surf camp, and that includes room, board and equipment. I take nine, maybe ten kids at a time; that keeps my overhead low. A half-day private lesson, which consists of about two hours of water time, costs $15. That includes a board. A full day is $30. That's relatively inexpensive; I know that other people charge up to $50 for a comparable lesson. I end up just about breaking even by the time I advertise and consider other costs.

I've tried to keep my rates relatively low. I'm not in this for the money. This is the story I tell the kids: After college, I took a year off to travel, and it turned into about 15 years. I've been all over the world, working as a ski instructor and a guide and seeing lots of places. I have a strong faith in God, and I figure that somebody up there must really be looking out for me to allow me to do all that, so I decided that I was meant to share it with other people. I incorporate that into my camp.

Negatives—Once you get hooked on surfing, your life begins to revolve around the waves. You're always watching for good waves and wind conditions. Sometimes conditions are only good for one or two hours a day, and if you want to surf, you have to be available during that window of time. True surfers are available at all times.

From a teacher's perspective, it can be frustrating to have to stay on the inside of the break with the beginners when the waves are really great. And it can be tiring, too; there are days when you don't even want to go in because the water or wind is so cold.

You have to guard against letting your ego convince you that you're somebody simply because you can perform a sport well. I've observed that in "glamour jobs" such as teaching surfing and skiing, there's a prevailing attitude of superiority, and this can be easy to succumb to. You can begin to identify with the job to a point where you are not quite sure who you are when the snow melts or the waves go flat.

Future—To be honest, I don't think there will ever be a big enough market to support someone full time. Maybe one person per beach town on the coast could survive on private lessons, but there's just not enough demand. I can see the possibility of more camps developing, but I've been advertising for five years now, and I think I've tapped the majority of the market.

There is a need for instructors and there probably always will be, but if you want to make it, you have to really get out there and get your name known.

References

On the East Coast, contact Eastern Surfing Association; 12507 Sunset Avenue, Ste 0, Ocean City, MD 21892; (410) 213-0515 or fax (410) 213-0515. Website: http://www.surfesa.org.

On the West Coast, contact Surfriders Foundation, 122 S. El Camino Real, No. 67, San Clemente, CA 92672; (714) 492-8170.

Surfer Magazine, P.O. Box 1028, Dana Point, CA 92629, (714) 496-5922.

Surfing Magazine, P.O. Box 3010, San Clemente, CA 92674-3010, (714) 492-7873 or fax (714) 498-6485. E-mail: surfing @netcom.com.

Tour Leader

Dreams—The romance of travel, faraway exotic places, and a group of fawning tourists as your charge—what a way to go. Nothing but the best, including the pay and the tips. This is a perfect part-time job, or maybe full-time for the summer season. What a fantasy: See the best of the world and get paid doing it.

Nightmares—Maybe you should call your business "Whiner's Anonymous—Call Me With Your Gripe." That is, providing you can get a job, which can seem like the Impossible Dream. Then there are the bus tours—arrrrgh. Too many days away from home can make a Mexico beach look like Siberia.

Realities—This job takes just the right personality, which is someone who enjoys being in the center of a dust storm. The travel, taken in the right dose, provides a spectacular backdrop, but that's all it is, a backdrop. The job requires meticulous planning and a disposition to handle the grumps with a smile. An ideal summer position, but the best positions are highly difficult to obtain.

What it's all about—Are you the kind of person who taps their fingers while waiting in line at the bank? When you want to leave, but someone is talking to you, do you put your hand in your pocket and play with your car keys? When you drive, if somebody suddenly stops ahead of you in order to turn, but doesn't signal, do you start muttering out loud?

No? Then you could be well-suited for a job as a tour leader. Yes? Well, better keep looking, maybe for a job where you have a better opportunity at controlling your destiny.

Because a tour leader, one who leads groups of vacationers on vacations, could write a book called "ODTAA"—One Damn Thing After Another. There is a remarkable variety of inane little problems you must solve for your guests, and they never seem to stop. The kind of people who fit well into this position are those who can happily glide with the tide, solving those little problems with nary a raised eyebrow, enjoying people and their quirks.

The central appeal of this position is the travel, of course. You actually get paid to go on vacation. The pay is enough to make it an ideal part-time job, perhaps for a school teacher who has the summer off, or a housewife who wants escape from her family for a week now and then, but it is generally not a full-time position. The full-time travel job is being a travel agent, and they work behind a desk with a telephone and computer, not on the shores of the Bahamas.

There is a demand for tour leaders because when some people go on vacation, they don't want to worry about anything or anybody. So they sign up for a package deal with a travel agent, where for a single fee they get a complete vacation, door-to-door, including air fare, lodging, meals, and usually some kind of adventure—either fishing, sightseeing or diving. Typically, about 10 people will sign up for such a tour, and it is up to you as tour leader to make sure everything works out right for them.

So you need a mind for planning and details and a knack with checklists. That much becomes easy after a few trips, a matter of knowing the job. What does not become easy is dealing with the incessant whines and obtuse requests of the guests. No matter how they are phrased, the words always mean "I want..." followed by (your choice): a new pillow, a larger towel, the foreign exchange rate for currency (five times per guest), green taco sauce at dinner, colder beer, better fishing, a comb, or the translation of a phrase in a foreign language. The worst is when guests are alone and simply want to talk to you while they drink—one day after another, for hours and hours and hours—and get sloshed in the process.

This is the real challenge of the job, dealing with the idiosyncrasies of individuals. If you can handle it, you will be very happy in this field, traveling about on trips, some world-class, enjoying the company of your guests, and earning some money in the process. You get a free trip, of course, with all expenses paid. Most of the tours are arranged in late winter, so if you want to get booked for summer, plan on getting arrangements made in December, January or February; most of the trips run between March and September. Tour guides usually work as representatives of travel agents or exotic vacation companies. That is who you contact for a job (expect plenty of competition), and if hired, negotiate with for your fee.

Most tour guides contract a fee for the week, and get bonus money from several sources. The fee ranges from $350 to $650 a week, depending on your experience, abilities, and the policies of the company you are representing. If you are bilingual and leading a group to a foreign-speaking country, you will rate on the high end of the scale.

There can be significant bonuses. You can collect commissions for inspiring guests to take excursions that cost them extra, like a bush plane trip to a remote lake for fishing, a scuba diving class, or a helicopter tour. Other sources of money are individual tips, and they can add up to a significant amount, too. If you get a group of high rollers and lead them onto something world-class and unforgettable—like snorkeling for huge lobsters, then eating the giant crustaceans for dinner—you might pick up another $150 or $200, maybe more, in tips at the end of the week.

Another way to secure large tips is to take photographs of each of the guests during their moments of splendor, and make sure they know that you will send them a print after the trip. That adds a nice touch that often will go rewarded.

As a seasonal, part-time job, being a tour guide can be a real winner, especially on the exotic tours. Working with old-timers on the bus circuit is another matter, although it's a way to gain experience. Either way, however, it is not a promising career for a full-timer. There is little work in the winter months (just some cruises and bus tours), and the year-round grind of being away from a steady homefront can turn the travel into drudgery.

If it rains, the fish don't bite, everybody is whining, one guest accidentally burns you with a cigarette and someone else spills alcohol on you, and you feel a desire to feed them all to a pond of hungry alligators, then it is time for a break.

Probably the best trick to enjoying this job in the long run is your perspective on the world. Over the course of a few years, for instance, you might run a particular tour 20 or 25 times. If you have the ability to look at everything as if it is the first time you have ever seen it, then this is a job you will enjoy forever.

Career Case Study

Sherry Wilkins, Utah   *Sherry Wilkins is a tour director for Tauch Tours, specializing in tours from Salt Lake City to Yellowstone National Park. In the winter, she works at a ski shop. Her experience includes running tours in Hawaii and New England. She enjoys outdoor activities such as hiking and backpacking, and once hiked the Appala-chian Trail from Maine to Georgia. She is married, has two children, and lives in Salt Lake City, Utah.*

Requirements—You have to have nerves of steel. It's a very demanding job, because we're dealing with people who are paying big bucks and they expect a lot for their money. Good organizational skills are important; you're constantly arranging things like dinner reservations and various activities, and you have to be very organized and detail-oriented to pull it off. Time is of the essence when you're touring.

You should be able to retain knowledge well. You're constantly commentating, and you should be able to answer any question that's thrown out at you. Our company doesn't allow the use of notes, although some do. It looks much more professional to be an expert on the area you're in. And there's always something new to learn. I've been doing the Salt Lake-Yellowstone tour for eight years and there's always something new to learn.

You have to have compassion for people and some basic people skills. You have to be very diplomatic, because there is always potential for problems and complaints, and you are the one who's expected to take care of everything. You can't be afraid to take control.

Flexibility is a big one. When the motor coach breaks

down and it's 90 degrees out, or a restaurant doesn't have your reservations, you have to stay calm and improvise. You can't let things get to you. Responsibility and reliability are two key requirements. We've had a few flaky leaders who just couldn't handle the pressure and left during the tour.

I think it's really important to have a bit of medical knowledge, especially CPR training. I don't know if it's a standard requirement from company to company, but ours pays for it. You're dealing with a lot of older people, and you've got to be prepared for anything, especially when you're touring in a place where the altitude is high. And you have to be in good physical condition yourself. I'm on my feet all day long; I stand and mingle with the people, and it can be exhausting. It's a 24-hour-a-day job, so you don't get a lot of rest.

Prospects—There's a lot of competition. I constantly have people on my tours say, "How do I get into this? It's such a perfect job!" But a lot of people don't realize just how much work is involved. There are schools and courses available. I went through a program in New York about ten years ago, and personally, I think it was pretty useless. It does, however, give you a good idea of what you're getting into by letting you know that it's not all glamour.

When I got in eight years ago, there were very few women; it was mostly a male-dominated profession. About 70 percent men, I'd say. But now the balance has tipped, and tour directors are probably about 65 percent women. I still get clients who skeptically say, "You're the first woman tour director we've ever had."

I think luck has a lot to do with it, along with your personality and the way you come across. Tour companies look for people who are very sure of themselves, very sharp and colorful. You can't have a blah personality. Previous travel experience would definitely give you an edge, as well. A seasoned traveler knows about the glitches that can occur. I know a lot of people out here who want to get into the field, but often they have never been out of Rapid City or wherever they grew up and they would probably be less likely to get the job.

Benefits—What I like most is that basically you are your own boss. You're running the show. My only contact with the company is an occasional phone call and sending some paperwork in. It's a real ego booster, being the master and king. It's very personally fulfilling. It gets in your blood, and it's hard to get out.

You're constantly on the move, which I love. The only time I'm really organized is when I'm on the road. Everything is at my fingertips and I know exactly where to find it. Every group is different and the dynamics are always different. Every trip brings new experiences and challenges. During 1988, for instance, when there were all those fires in Yellowstone National Park, we didn't know from day to day when or where we'd be able to get into the park, so we came up against some creative challenges.

Pay—It varies a lot from company to company. Some give you meal allowances and daily set expenditures, some include all that in your salary. As far as basic salary, you can expect to make $250 to $400 a week. However, tour directors go for the tips. The gratuities make it worthwhile. Standard guidelines range from $1.50 to $5.00 per person, per day. Some directors have the option of making a lot of money from commissions on extra activities, but that's against our company's policy. We don't want our clients to feel pressured or herded to do a particular activity or go into a certain store because we make money from it.

Negatives—It's grueling work. You need endless patience and endurance. You're constantly taking complaints, and when you're completely stressed out and fed up, you have to put on a happy face that says, "Everything's fine."

It's a difficult job if you have a family, because you're away from them a lot, and that can cause a lot of stress. It's hard to establish a relationship when you're on the road all the time. When you get off the road and go back to the real world, it can be a difficult adjustment. You're no longer being looked up to by all these people, you're no longer the leader, and it's tough sometimes.

The future—There are always going to be people who

want to travel, although the level definitely fluctuates with the economy. There have been times when we had 12 directors running the same tour, and now we're down to eight. Most of these tours include everything and it's fairly pricey for the average person. I think that's one reason we get so many older people.

I would like to see a younger clientele, and that may happen soon, because the big tourism capitals like the national parks are becoming so cluttered with cars and people that organized tours may someday be the only way to get in.

Career Case Study

Ruth Daly, California   *Ruth Daly has been Operations Manager for Contiki Tours since 1990. Before that, she worked as a tour escort for three years, and also lived in Venezuela as an exchange student. She has toured many countries, and in addition to travel, also enjoys golf and tennis. She lives in Anaheim, California.*

Requirements—The requirements vary, depending on the company. Here at Contiki, we run tours for people from 18 to 35 years of age, so we're a bit more active than many companies. We look for someone with a college education, although that's not a real requirement. Extensive travel experience can be accepted in lieu of a college education. We do prefer people who have experience traveling on their own, so they have a sense of what it's like to be in a foreign country and have to take care of yourself.

You definitely need to be someone who's outgoing and doesn't mind public speaking. You should have a great sense of humor and be able to deal with all kinds of difficult situations. When something goes wrong, you've got to keep a calm façade if nothing else. Very good organizational skills are a definite asset. But most importantly, you have to be somebody who likes working with people and enjoys teaching as well.

Prospects—I receive about 400 resumes a year for five positions, so you can see it's quite competitive, but the job market is growing a great deal. There are many applicants who just aren't cut out for the job. It sounds like such a great thing to do, but sometimes after they've done a couple of trips, they realize that it's not what they thought it would be.

You have to possess certain personality traits to do well. Someone who has a hot temper, for instance, is probably not going to be the best person for the job. You should remember that most of these jobs are seasonal; you work from April through October and that's usually it. Of course, there are some tours in wintertime, but not as many as summer, and the winter tours are generally given to escorts with seniority.

The best time to start submitting resumes is in January, when most companies start the hiring process. If someone were to call me in the middle of summer, I'd say , "Sorry, you're six months off."

It's really important to research the company that you're looking at. You can usually tell by the company's brochure if the tours are the kind you want to run and the clients are they type you want to deal with. It's important to know what you're getting into.

Benefits—A lot of people enjoy the independence. You're sometimes on tours for 50 days at a time, and you're your own boss; you're in charge of the tour.

Meeting people all over the world is another benefit; you make lots of new friends. It's very rewarding to expose others to beautiful areas. I went to the Grand Canyon 20 times one summer, and each time it was exciting to show it to other people. It never got boring. One nice aspect is that you get constant feedback. You get reaction to your performance on the job every day, which provides a lot of instant gratification. It's very rewarding when at the end of a trip people say, "Thanks for the best two weeks of my life."

Pay—Escorts make their money in a number of different ways. All companies pay for your lodging and meals on tour, plus a lump sum. Then you have the opportunity to earn commissions from the sale of optional excursions on the tour, such as helicopter rides over the Grand Canyon. There are also tips. Tips vary a great deal. Some companies, usually open-age, high-end establishments, will specify guidelines, such as $2 per day for both the escort and the driver. Other companies leave it to the discretion of the client. Overall, depending on the tour company, you can make from about $40 a day to $100 a day, even more for bilingual tours. For example, a Los Angeles tour in English would cost about $80, but the same tour in Italian would be $130.

Negatives—There's a certain lack of privacy. If a client has a problem, you're going to be the first one they come to, so in the back of your mind you're always thinking about making sure everything is going well.

It's hard to stay healthy, since you're eating in restaurants three times a day, and you can't really do any regular exercise.

It's very hard to have a relationship with anyone. When you're on the road 300 days a year it's hard to maintain any kind of normal relationship. None of our guides are married.

The future—I think it's a growing industry. The baby boomer generation is getting older and traditional motor coach touring is becoming geared toward them. Motor coach tours here in America are becoming very popular, because it's an inexpensive and comfortable way to travel. These days with the high cost of independent traveling, more and more young people are discovering that motor coach tours are a really good option as well. It's cheap, it's easier, and it's becoming more acceptable. People are beginning to realize the benefits of having someone else take care of all the little details for them.

References

International Tour Management Institute (ITMI), 625 Market Street, Suite 610, San Francisco, CA 94105; (415) 957-9489.

United States Tour Operators Association (USTOA), 211 East 51st Street, Suite 12B, New York, NY 10022; (212) 750-7371 or fax (212)421-1285. E-mail: ustour@aol.com.

High Country Tourist Association, 1490 #2 Pearson Place, Kamloops, BC Canada V1S1J9; (604) 372-7770.

Tree Planter

Dreams—You spend all your time out in the woods, tromping around beautiful places near lakes and streams, getting paid as you go for putting three-inch trees in the ground. Once you get the hang of it, the money is great for a seasonal job. Not only that, but by planting trees you have the satisfaction of making the planet a better place.

Nightmares—There is nothing fun about it. Being a tree planter means hard work, long days, lugging around a 60-pound bag full of seedlings, and being under pressure to put one in the ground every 30 seconds to reach your quota. The show must go on, and that includes in terrible weather, no matter how hot or how heavy the rain.

Realities—Hard workers will discover a demanding job, yet one set in marvelous surroundings, and good seasonal pay when you get your speed up. But you do the same thing, over and over, and your mindset while you work will determine victory or failure.

What it's all about—It would help to be half Johnny Redwoodseed and half octopus to have a job as a tree planter. But since you are human and stuck with two arms and two legs, you will have to settle for having the right frame of mind.

Don't get the experience of being a tree planter confused with John Muir's rhapsodies about the great outdoors, about the "perfect quietude" of nature and the ensuing "freedom from every curable care." Sure, tree planters spend their time in the forest where that outlook is possible, but the problem is that they never stand around long enough to notice the quietude.

In a week, it is common for a tree planting crew to put 100,000 seedlings in the ground in four or five days. Tree planters are up before dawn and try to put a seedling in the ground every 30 seconds, which adds up to 960 trees planted for every eight hours of work. Some do it even faster, or for longer hours, and plant as many as 1,500 trees a day. Why so fast? Because you get paid according to how many trees you plant, ranging from seven to 15 cents a tree, not how many hours you work.

At that rate, say 12 cents per tree at 1,000 trees per day, tree planters end up making about $120 a day, which comes to $600 per week, and $7,800 for a three-month job. Of course, there is no average to the average. The price per tree can vary according to size, with a higher fee paid for larger trees, but it takes longer to plant the larger trees, and there is often no way to make the 1,000-tree-per-day quota.

The work is just plain hard. You are bent over a lot, carrying a heavy bag (as much as 60 pounds) full of seedlings, and the trees must go in the ground regardless of weather conditions. In the course of a few months, you will likely see it all, including some beautiful, cool days, but you will also get your share of barnburners, rain, and in the mountains, snow.

In addition, this is not a year-round job. The planting season is determined by the climate of your respective area. While there are tree-planting contracts available in the summer, most of the work is in the late winter and spring. Because of weather problems—snow and cold ground temperatures—in northern tier areas such as Canada and Alaska, planting operations are shut down in the winter there. In addition, drought in late summer and fall usually puts an end to tree-planting operations. So it is seasonal work, on an area-by-area basis.

That is why the better money in this profession does not come for those who plant trees one by one, but for those who have a year round job growing the seedlings to plantable size, then selling them to the Forest Service and private timber companies (more on that later).

The idea of getting paid 10 or 15 cents every time you put a seedling in the ground sets up a pressure-cooker dynamic that a lot of people just can't take. Instead of savoring the mountain scenery, the smell of conifers, and the chirping of chipmunks, squirrels and birds, most tree planters are doing multiplication in their heads while they work, trying to project the day's earnings—or worrying about doing the job fast enough to make their quota. There is little enjoyment in either. A better approach is to achieve a mindset where you can both appreciate your surroundings and continue to get the trees in the ground.

This is a job that is likely to be available virtually forever on a seasonal or part-time basis. In some areas where timber cuts are high, such as in the northern tier states and Canada, reforestation is vitally necessary. The best job prospects are with private timber companies with large land holdings, as well as with regional Forest Service agencies.

A bonus is that the number of trees planted is not tied to the number that are cut down, but rather to the number of seedlings available for planting. This is an insider's note that few are aware of. Nursery operations that grow seedlings can sell virtually every tree they have available. If you have a large enough nursery, that's where the big money is in this field.

As for tree planters, some are worried that reduction in timber cut rates in the 1990s will trim down this job in the process. That is true only in a few highly localized examples, but the prospects remain good across much of the northern tier states in America, and are outstanding in Canada. There are many reasons. One is because reforestation was very poor in most areas until the 1950s, and foresters are still climbing out of the hole from deficit cutting. Another reason is because trees are also being bought and planted to help stabilize slopes and stop erosion, a bonus for this industry. Finally, for every tree being cut down, there are two to five being planted, so even with a limited timber harvest, there remains a fundamental need for tree planters.

It is true that many young adults try tree planting on for size, then discover they don't like the fit. "Not what I expected." Well, expect hard work. Expect being surrounded by a beautiful environment. Then, most importantly, remember that with each seedling you put in the ground, you are turning the world into a better place. You might return in 40 years and find a magnificent specimen where you planted a three-inch seedling. That is where the true satisfaction awaits.

Career Case Study

Bill Kamin, Washington   Bill Kamin has worked in the timber industry since he graduated from the University of Montana in 1958. He is an avid outdoorsman and a former mountain climber. His travels have taken him from the Olympic mountains in Washington to Mount Kilaminjaro in Africa. Bill and his wife live in Shelton, Washington.

Requirements—The person who wants to be a successful tree planter has to be in good physical health, with strong muscle tone and in good shape. You don't necessarily have to be young, but generally people in the 18 to mid-30 range can perform the job on a daily basis most easily. You should not have emphysema or heart trouble, because there's a lot of rough terrain you have to climb up and down, terrain that is steep, somtimes full of slash, with a lot of obstacles to get around. Plus you're carrying a shovel and a bag full of trees, wearing warm, ususally heavy clothes, and sometimes rain gear. You're packing a lot of extra weight.

There are really no educational requirements, although some experience in forestry would help a person understand a little bit about the way a forest works, the type of terrain we deal with, where to step and not to step in the forest, etc. But that type of knowledge comes from just being familiar with the outdoors, too.

You do have to be able to repeat a monotonous task continually and not let it get to you mentally and psychologically. There is basically no mental challenge to this job, which appeals to some people. Other people who have a little less patience might find it very difficult.

Prospects—There is quite a bit of competition, at least here in the Northwest, within the Hispanic population. Many are used to heavy physical labor, and they're in the market looking for work. Generally, white men in the 18 to 30 age group aren't applying; the working conditions are poor and the pay is not that great.

I hired some of the first tree-planting women to work in this area, and they were not physically prepared in most cases. Many quit within two or three days. That's not to say there aren't women who can do it; we have had a couple of women who outplanted the men, but honestly, women don't generally do this kind of work. I think there are a lot more women who could do it out there today than there were 20 years ago, however; it's primarily a matter of getting yourself in adequate physical condition. Women do have the advantage of a degree of patience that many men don't have, and in that respect they have the potential to be better tree planters. I think they are, in general, mentally a bit more capable of handling this type of work.

Very few private timber companies or state and federal agencies hire many in-house tree planters. It's seasonal work, so hiring someone full-time doesn't make a lot of sense. Consequently, when the time to plant comes, there isn't a readily available pool of people around to form a planting crew, so almost all tree planters are contracted out. Contractors are generally people who deal with many aspects of forestry on a year-round basis. They have a certain number of full-time employees, and in the winter, when they're focusing almost exclusively on tree planting, they hire an additional crew.

Benefits—If you like to work outdoors, you've got a good healthy work environment. There is no smoke, no pollutants and no traffic. The surroundings can be very beautiful in some areas, which is important to some people. It is satisfying to know that you're renewing a resource, that because of your work there will be a new crop of trees down the road. What you do benefits not only who you're working for, but the people in the region you're in, and the earth in general.

Pay—Once you get adept at planting, you can make a lot of money. Planters are generally paid on a piecework basis rather than an hourly rate, and that generally ends up translating to an hourly rate of $8.50 to $14. An average planter can make about $10,000 to $12,000 a season. How much you make depends on how hard you work.

Negatives—You have to deal with very adverse weather conditions. If it's snowing or freezing weather, we usually don't plant; but rain is common planting weather. The terrain can be very rough, also—steep ground, heavy debris, obstacles to get up and over and around. It's very strenuous work, and those who have never done a lot of physical labor have a lot of aches and pains until their bodies get in shape. It's surprising how many different muscles you use to plant a tree.

The work is seasonal; the season starts in mid-December and goes to about the beginning of May. In the timbered states located in the east and southeast, it's probably a bit longer, except in the higher-altitude regions. Regardless, the winter months are generally when the planting is done, and when the season is over, it's over.

The future—I think it's a profession that will be with us as long as there are people. I can't ever envision a time when this job could be done mechanically because of the type of terrain that is planted. There are machines that plant on flat land very efficiently, but when you're dealing with uneven ground, nothing compares to the cost and efficiency of human labor.

Career Case Study

Wayne Connor, California

Wayne Connor has worked as Contract Administrator for Simpson Timber since 1972. He holds a bachelor's degree in forest management from Humboldt State University, and his work experience includes working for the U.S. Forest Service and the Stanford Research Institute. He enjoys motorcycle trips, and has toured in many parts of the world. He is married and lives in McKinleyville, California.

Requirements—There are no educational requirements. You have to have some rudimentary knowledge of how to make a tree survive, and be able to learn some basics about trees; for instance, when you plant them you don't want to leave the roots exposed too long or they'll dry out. Most of that type of information is taught on the job. You have to be in really good shape. You're dealing with steep terrain, often negotiating a lot of brush, and you're carrying a tree bag that weighs about 60 pounds when it's full. You sometimes have to walk a mile or so into the site, and you're going back and forth four or five times a day to get more trees.

You have to be able to get along with others in a tight environment. Many times you'll be packed in a pickup truck with a bunch of other sweaty guys for two hours in the rain.

Prospects—The majority of all tree planters work for contractors who are hired by various timber companies and agencies such as the forest service. There's a lot of turnover. Everybody thinks they can be a tree planter. They think it's really neat to be out dancing around in the forest putting trees in the ground, but it's really tough work. These guys are usually expected to plant between 1,000 and 1,500 trees a day. I've seen a lot of guys quit after half a day, having experienced a rude awakening.

There are usually a core group of people hired by the contractor who work year-round. More seasonal workers are added in winter. If you're in shape and can handle the labor, there are lots of opportunities out there.

Benefits—Probably the biggest benefit is being able to work outside, as well as knowing that you have a part in creating a future crop of trees. There's a lot of camaraderie and socializing, which is fun. And the work may be hard, but it keeps you in really good shape.

Pay—Tree planters are paid by the tree, not by the hour. They receive between seven and fifteen cents per tree, depending on the type of tree. The really top guys can make a couple of hundred bucks a day, but that's rare. I'd say the average tree planter makes about $70 a day.

Negatives—It's ultra-demanding. The worst part is the long hours in winter weather conditions. You start out a typical day at four or four-thirty in the morning, drive a couple of hours to the site, bag up your trees, then plant all day, clean up, and get dropped off around dark. It's not something you can do long-term; it wears you out. It's comparable to being an athlete, I think, after a while your body just can't do it anymore.

The future—Tree planting is usually used for restocking clear-cut areas, and since there hasn't been as much clear-cutting lately with all the environmental concerns, there's no need to replant, especially within the Forest Service. But you can never tell what's down the road.

References

American Forest & Paper Association, 1111 19th Street NW, Ste 800, Washington, D.C. 20036; (800) 878-8878.

California Department of Forestry, 1416 9th Street, PO Box 944246, Sacramento, CA 94244-2460; (916) 653-7772 or fax (916) 327-7744.

New Mexico Forestry & Resources Conservation Division, PO Box 1948, Sante Fe, NM 87504-1948; (505) 827-5830 or fax (505) 827-3903.

U.S. Forest Service district offices can provide contacts of companies hiring tree planters.

Tugboat Operator

Dreams—The rest of the world are like cows in a herd compared to you on a tugboat. You are out there—man, machine and the sea—and give quarter to no one. It's an elemental existence, but a perfect mix between the physical and intellectual, and the pay is about the best you can find working for somebody else. Ah, life is perfect.

Nightmares—It's dangerous. If a rope snaps and wraps you up, you're history. The weather and the hours can be ridiculous, and the worse the weather, the more you have to work. Sometimes you can work all night long. If you snivel about it, you're apt to get thrown overboard.

Realities—This is the classic "hard work, good pay" kind of job. Deckhands do face some danger and unusual hours, but are paid high wages. To be a certified operator requires extensive book and field training, but you might earn $60,000 or more for four days of work per week. A bonus is a bright future for the job.

What it's all about—The ultimate job in the outdoors is one where you can experience the forces of nature on a regular basis and also make a lot of money. You can do that on a tugboat. Working on a tugboat will demand the best from you but provide the best in return. It is a challenging job, regardless of your charge. From deckhand to captain, all that is asked of you is your best, and that is exactly what you are expected to deliver.

If you do, you will have a life where you live by the rhythms of the sea, be challenged physically (as a deckhand) and mentally (as a captain), and be rewarded with excellent pay. Deckhands often make $35,000 to $40,000 (more with overtime) and that's with no education required, and captains earn $50,000 to $60,000—and that's no-risk dough, because someone else owns the boat and business.

There are many appealing aspects to the job. One is that there is something simply awesome about being on a tugboat. These are big, powerful ships with names like "Hercules," "Thor" and "Poseidon." They are used to maneuver monstrous-sized freighters and tankers into port, sometimes tugging, sometimes pushing. They need muscle and a tug has it. As a deckhand you also need plenty of muscle, but as a captain, you need a feather touch.

Deckhands need no tugboat experience, nor education, to get a start. However, most do have plenty of time on boats, either as a deckhand for a commercial fishing boat or party boat. What employers are looking for are hearty people in good condition with a feel for what the sea gives and takes.

The job can be very dangerous. Deckhands work with the ship lines, the giant ropes used to secure barges and some large ships. Given the tremendous forces at play, if you get pinned down to a cleat, the rope breaks and you are struck in the backlash, or if you get tangled up with some of the giant machinery aboard, your life story can be over. All done. Just like that. You learn quickly to be sharply aware of operations at all times.

That is why even highly trained and skilled operators usually first spend a year or two as a deckhand. It gives tug captains the appreciation for the jobs that deckhands are accountable for. At the same time, it gives captains more respect on board from the crew, since the crew will know that the captain is one of them.

That is the kind of spirit a tugboat company owner desires from the crew—the best. After all, the investment in the boat alone is often in the $3 million range, and owners want it operated at its peak.

It is a great challenge to meet the requirements to operate a tug. The goal is a tugboat license, but it doesn't come quick or easy. If you attend a maritime academy, figure four years, similar to what it takes to get a bachelor's degree in college, crowned by a difficult Coast Guard test. If you pass that test, you will be allowed to captain virtually any ship.

Much of the training is on the water. In some cases, that can give commercial fishing captains or party boat skippers an edge in the training process. But newcomers are welcomed, since they are not bringing any bad habits with them from working for years in an undisciplined setting.

The future looks very promising for tugboat companies. Because of the fear of oil spills, most ports require that oil tankers be guided to their destinations. Because of the necessity of dredging ports, tugs are needed to pull the barges to the dumpsite. Virtually all the freighters need not just one tugboat, but several to help them dock safely. In addition, the big international ships can arrive at all times, which not only creates demand, but can add significant overtime hours if you want them.

Another plus with this career is that unlike many maritime jobs, working on a tugboat doesn't mean being away from your family for long periods of time. Captains, mates and deckhands on the international ships may sail around the world, but many become the loneliest people in the world, prisoners of their job, which doesn't allow for a stable family life. A tugboat operator, meanwhile, can have a family. Four days on and three days off is a typical shift. Imagine pulling down the big bucks, then spending three days off each week—that's standard operating procedure for tugboaters.

In the process, you will become keenly aware of the unharnessed power of the sea, of tides and currents, of wind, and the battle against it with the harnessed power of your tug. It is a battle you must win, every time. The rawness of the job has a distinct appeal, but so does the mental challenge. Put it together with a passion for the sea and high wages, and you can get a level of satisfaction rarely found anywhere.

Career Case Study

Mel Sugiyama, California Mel Sugiyama
*has been a tugboat operator since 1985. Prior to that he
sailed as a second mate and worked as a party boat
deckhand. He also worked on a commercial tuna seiner
in the South Pacific, catching fish for Starkist and
VanDeKamp foods. He enjoys fishing, camping,
gardening and cooking. He is married, has one son, and
lives in Vallejo, California.*

Requirements—There are a couple of ways to go about
getting in. For someone coming in off the street, the first
requirement is a Z-card, a seaman's document similar to a
passport, which is issued by the Coast Guard. There are
various requirements that have to be met for that, such as
CPR training and other technical skills. After you receive the
necessary Coast Guard documents, you have to have a specified amount of experience as an ordinary seaman; if you want
to operate a tugboat, this ends up being around two years.
Then you're eligible to take the Coast Guard exam for your
license.

The other way to do it is the way I did it: I started out
working on fishing boats, got a license to run party boats, and
then went to the Merchant Marine School here in San Francisco. I worked at various maritime jobs, and then graduated
from the California Maritime Academy, which is an accredited four-year school where you receive training to attain the
license that will allow you to run a tugboat. Actually it allows
you to operate any vessel in the world. You come out of the
academy with a bachelor of science degree and are ranked as
a third officer in the Merchant Marines.

A good part of the training you receive there is hands-
on, so academy graduates bypass the two-year experience
requirement. Going through the academy hasn't been the
traditional route in the past, but more and more academy
graduates seem to be coming on the tugboats now.

Prospects—There is a big demand for tugboat operator
jobs. The reason is because you're working in the maritime
field, and it's a job where you usually have the option of going

home every night, unlike the people who are out at sea for six months at a time. If you have a family, this is a very attractive job to have. At a lot of the tugboat companies, even if you've gone through all the training and have your license, you must start from the bottom up. They want you to work as a deckhand until they're satisfied that you're qualified to operate the vessel. These tugs are $2 million to $5 million boats, so they're not going to let just anyone off the street take charge.

The length of time to qualify to be an operator can vary; sometimes it's a couple of years. Operators are selected according to seniority, and the turnover rate is very low, so you've basically got to wait until a position opens up. It's generally pretty hard to get into this field.

Benefits—You're out working on the water, and you go to work in fairly casual attire, basically whatever you want. The schedule is great at my company; I work for four days straight, then have four days off. When I get called out to work, it's very rarely during commute hours, so I avoid traffic.

You're not limited to living in the area you work in. A large percentage of our employees and even one of the company owners lives way up north, out of the city. They commute each week, and they usually stay on the boats when they're working, but during their time off they can return to their homes in more rural areas.

Pay—We're union members, as most tugboat companies are. Our pay scale is currently set at around $27 an hour for operators. We also have full medical, dental and optical benefits. The number of hours you work depends on the volume of vessel traffic. We have a minimum four-hour call-out, which means that if we get called out for a job that only takes ten minutes, we still get paid for four hours. And if there's less than four hours between jobs, we're paid straight through for all the time in between.

A typical operator's pay ranges between $50,000 and $60,000 a year. You can definitely make more money if you want to work more days. You can cover for somebody who is off or help out a vessel that's short-handed on your days off. Even deckhands make a pretty good wage. One deckhand/

engineer we have here is making a salary in the operator range because he's working so much. A typical deckhand makes about $35,000 to $40,000 and you don't even need a high school diploma for that.

Negatives—The hours can be very long, and often there's very little time to sleep. The jobs are frequently spaced closely enough together so that there's hardly any time in between, and it's easy to get burned out. There's quite a bit of stress when you're out working. There are a multitude of accidents that can occur with very expensive boats.

There is a danger factor, although it mostly affects the deckhands. They are working with the ship lines, which are fairly heavy, and if they break, which they can do, a deckhand could get killed. Falling overboard, even though the crew is equipped with life-saving work vests, is another danger. With all the moving machinery on board, there are a lot of different ways you can get hurt. I've heard that this is one of the most hazardous jobs you can have, which I'd have to agree with.

The future—We're starting to see more younger people coming in to the profession, instead of the salty old guys in their 60s and 70s. That seems to be a trend. The companies have been expanding consistently in the past six years that I've been working in this area. I predict that it will continue to pick up. Since the Exxon Valdez spill, tankers may soon be required to have escorts in and out of port, which will provide substantially more work for us.

In addition, we do several other types of jobs. Barge work is an example, where we tow barges to and from their destinations. We also crew oil-response vessels, so if there's an oil spill, we go out there and clean it up. It's a little slow right now with the economy in the state it is; there doesn't seem to be as much container traffic, but I don't think it'll stay that way. I think that if the economy improves, the amount of work will increase.

Career Case Study

Michael Dobson, Alabama   *Michael Dobson has worked as a captain for Mobile Bay Towing since 1987. He is married, has two children, and lives in Mobile, Alabama. He is an avid sports fan, and enjoys playing golf and tennis.*

Requirements—You have to have a certain number of years of experience on the waterfront before you can approach the U.S. Coast Guard to apply for your license. The amount of experience depends on the class of license you want; there are different licenses for different vessels, but I think the minimum is three years. There is a pretty sophisticated test given by the Coast Guard.

It's not really necessary to go through any schooling. I never did. All you really need is the experience. You have to be able to relate well to people, to be able to say "yes sir" and "no sir" without a problem. That's our job, to assist the ships as they come in and out of the port.

Prospects—There are just two harbor companies here in Mobile, which only handles harbor tugs. There are only three tugs in each company, because that's all the harbor can handle. So it's pretty competitive, and there is very little turnover. Most people who get into it love this type of work, because having a harbor job lets you be on the ocean without having to get an offshore job on a vessel, which is really rough. So once you get on a boat, you take care of your job and don't let it go.

You could also work for a barge company, but the competition there is unreal.

Benefits—I love being on the water, and I like the freedom of the job. I have complete control over the vessel and the crew. It's not like being a foreman on a job site, where you have somebody looking over your shoulder all the time. If you do your job, they pretty much leave you alone.

Pay—The pay varies quite a bit, depending on how long you've been with your company and what your title is—

---

whether you're a relief captain or a regular captain or what. You have a base salary, which usually isn't a whole lot, but you get a certain amount of money for every ship you dock at night, plus overtime pay. That's where you make your money.

Negatives—The number of hours you put in can be strenuous. We work seven days on, seven days off, 24 hours a day, and at our company there are just four men working. Sometimes it's really slow, but if there's a lot of work, you just run until the work's done and rest when it's over. When the ships come in and out, you have to be there, even if you've already put in a 12-hour day.

The future—I don't see the market going either way. It's seasonal work, and some times are busier than others. You have your ups and downs, just like in any business. It seems to be leveling off more, though. We are getting more big ships in, and the bigger the ships the less work we have, but there is a good portion of smaller ships that are balancing it out.

Reference

Master Mates and Pilots Union, 700 Maritime Boulevard, Linthicum Heights, MD 21090; (410) 850-0973.

Maritime Administration, US Department of Transportation, 400 7th Street SW, Washington, D.C. 20590; (202) 366-4000 or fax (202) 366- 5063. E-mail: paomarad@post - master2.gov.

Licensing & Education Branch, G-MPV-2, US Coast Guard, 2100 Second Street SW, Washington, D.C. 20593; (202) 267-2229.

Video Show Producer

Dreams—As the star and producer of your own outdoor video show, you make millions of dollars and are in demand everywhere. You are recognized in airports, and take your pick of any adventure in the hemisphere. The biggest problem you have is trying to turn on the TV without seeing yourself.

Nightmares—Why does nobody else realize you're a star? Then when you look real close at your film clips, all you see is crap. That's all your sponsors see, too, none of whom will give you any money. Your equipment is Mickey Mouse, your trips are timed with bad weather, and the IRS thinks you've got an expensive hobby.

Realities—Expect a high overhead, meager sales on the video market and impossible odds on the national market. The best bet is a niche in the growing cable or satellite field, but marketing skills are just as critical as production, and your production must be flawless.

What it's all about—The most important thing to get in focus isn't your camera if you are planning a foray into video. Rather it's your outlook. These are the options: 1) A how-to video. 2) Promotion videos for vacation destinations. 3) Short, timed pieces tailored for a local TV market. 4) A half-hour show designed for regional telecast, either via cable or an independent station. 5) A formal production for a national market, either through a network or satellite.

It's true that a handful of professionals who hit the national market can make a cool million, as in dollars where a one is followed by six zeros (a lot of it through product endorsements), but most others either barely scrape by or quickly drop out of sight. That includes some talented folks, too. If you get involved with outdoor video, you need to be more than a talent, you have to be an expert at marketing and promotion in both the television and outdoor manufacturer circles, and every inch of film must be of superb quality.

In addition, expect little or no help along the way. If you want it done, either you will have to do it yourself or pay someone to do it for you. The latter can really cut the top off your profits, especially if you are in a local or regional market.

The basic problem is that it is easy to do a bad video, and even if you pull off a good one, it is still difficult to obtain sponsors or market it to the public. In terms of TV, if people besides yourself can't make money on it, they will have no interest in you or your product. Of the five primary markets, here are capsule summaries:

1) How-to video:

Typically, the how-to outdoors video is the logical starting place for most producers. Some are so bad, where pa grins and holds up a fish while ma runs the camera, that you either cringe in pain or laugh in embarrassment for the "hero." Another problem, even with the good ones, is when the film bores in on such a specific (and often obscure) skill that the potential market and sales become quite small.

Most of the good ones sell 1,000 to 3,000 copies, rarely more, which isn't enough to make it worthwhile. If your topic isn't too localized and you can get royalties from rental services across the country, you can do much better, but most video stores buy them outright and pay no royalties. The price is critical, with anything over $19.95 scaring off buyers. It can be cheap to make copies of a video off a master copy, but until you sell a few thousand, you don't start making much money per unit. Taking this route can be like taking a walk across the desert without water.

One of the best ways to make a how-to video make money is by offering it in conjunction with another outdoor product, as a package deal. For example, suppose you make a deal with Berkley, the giant tackle company, to make a video to show exactly how to rig and fish Berkley soft plastic Power Baits. In turn, Berkley markets the video with a Power Bait kit, a package deal. That can work.

2) Promotional videos:
Resorts and lodges with quality promotional videos can hit a variety of specialty markets. A new source of income for resorts and lodges is the corporate dollar, where corporations book trips in order to have off-site board meetings and brainstorming sessions. The way to attract that business is to provide a 10-minute video that shows the attractions, accommodations, hospitality and privacy.

That's where you come in. You can arrange to shoot these videos and provide copies in exchange for a free trip and a fee. You get treated like a millionaire at the top vacation sites in the western hemisphere. Profits are not large, but what the heck, it's one way to see the world.

3) Timed pieces for local markets:
This is where you shoot a two to four-minute specialty piece, and then sell it as part of another show, perhaps the local news. To make it work, you usually have to hand it to the TV station for free on a silver platter (making your income from a sponsor), or buy the air time yourself. Usually these pieces start with a 15-second teaser, then an advertisement (or several) that pays for both your time and the station's time, then a show that is timed and tailored for the local market.

There are problems with this approach in both large and small markets, however. In large markets, the TV station can often produce the same film cheaper and better by using their own crews. In small markets, sponsors don't pay much for advertising, so the profits are often quite small.

4) Half-hour show for cable or regional telecast:
For an independent professional, this is the best future market to tap. The success of cable and satellite television is resulting is more channels being available in homes—hundreds for those with a satellite dish. Dozens and dozens of specialty shows by independent producers are carving a

huge slice out of the network production pie.

The bottom line, however, is your ability to find sponsors who will pay for the broadcast time, your expenses and salary. Getting sponsors can be like a revolving door, where you try to walk in and just as quickly you are walking out. Some excellent regional outdoors shows on satellite have lost their slots simply because nobody will pay for them. That is your challenge.

5) National market:

If you connect, you will become rich, famous, go anywhere you want to film shows, and be in demand by sponsors. You will suddenly be in demand for all kinds of things: speaking engagements, endorsements, magazine columns, books. When someone sees you on national television, you are instantly transformed into something rare and special, and everyone will want to jump on your coat tails for the ride.

The odds? Put it this way: Don't go quitting your day job before you sign a contract. ESPN is considered the ultimate showcase for an outdoors show, and they get a new proposal for a show virtually every working day of the year. Syndication with the satellite sports networks is more viable. To get it, though, you will need an exceptional production every time out.

When you add all this up and put it in your cash register, it can read "purchase void" mighty easily. This is a tough profession, but like the most difficult roads, the rewards for those who succeed are beyond what most people can imagine.

Career Case Study

Mark Sosin, Florida—Mark Sosin is an award-winning writer, photographer and television producer with an impressive list of credits that span virtually all phases of outdoor communication. He is most famous as the producer and on-camera host of "Mark Sosin's Saltwater Journal," which is broadcast to all 50 states and several foreign countries on ESPN. More than 3,000 of his articles have been published in major magazines and he has written 24 books on the outdoors.

Requirements—I can tell you the bottom line: You have to sell your idea. It doesn't matter where you came from, what your background happens to be, or what you do now, you have to find someone willing to put you on the air. You must find a buyer for your product.

Television encompasses several levels: local, regional, syndication (different stations in various markets), network, and cable network. A local station would be the most logical place to start. Possibly, you can do a two or three-minute spot during their news or sports programming on outdoor-oriented subjects (hunting, fishing, camping, environment, etc.) The station supplies the crew and the editing suite. Unless you're a strong negotiator, payment usually isn't very much.

If you want to have an actual program, you have to get airtime in the markets you want to reach. Local stations are probably the easiest to sell. Syndication (regionally or nationally) takes specialized training to sell. The major networks have shunned outdoor programs in recent years. That leaves the cable networks if you want a national audience. Airtime is bought, bartered, or you can sell a combination of the two. You may be able to find markets that will buy your work and pay you, but that's the exception.

There are two ways to host a show. You can be a reporter and interview others (assuming you develop interviewing skills) or you assume the role of the knowledgeable person (I hate the term "expert"). To be a recognized authority on a subject, you have to have credentials. Formal education is not required in either case (although it certainly won't hinder you), but you do need field experience.

Television is expensive to produce, particularly when you are striving for network quality. You can hire a person with a camera to shoot it for you. Then you must go to an editing suite for the post-production work. You should have a working knowledge of the techniques, some technical experience and an idea of costs. The alternative lies in owning your own equipment and establishing your own production company. State-of-the-art equipment costs a king's ransom if you plan to work with the same gear the big boys do.

Airtime is costly. A typical cable network may charge upwards of $10,000 per week for a 30-minute show, and that's not prime time. If you buy the airtime, you have to resell it to sponsors at a profit. That hopefully pays for your production costs. Frequently, you have to have a pilot show to sell both the cable network and your sponsors. Count on that costing you several thousand dollars.

Prospects—Breaking into the market today on a national basis borders between extremely difficult and almost impossible. You have a much better shot locally or regionally. The competition is out there. ESPN told me that they get 200 proposals for new shows every year. Three to five people will approach a likely sponsor in a given week. It's becoming more demanding. I foresee a shake-out coming. The shows that survive will have to be high quality and quality takes money. You might say that we are going to see an upgrading in programming because of competition. The "good ol' boys" stuff may not cut it anymore.

Most sponsors manufacture and sell products to outdoor enthusiasts. Selling your ideas to markets outside the outdoor field—major corporations—is extremely tough. The ad agency guys on Madison Avenue have one image of the outdoor person: a tobacco-chewing, jeans-wearing redneck with a southern drawl and a pickup truck. They don't view these "second class citizens" as a viable market for their client's product.

Benefits—I enjoy working for myself and I love working in the outdoors. That's something I need to do, personally. Television to me represents an exciting challenge. We try to develop new approaches and techniques on a daily basis. I like to do things that others can't or won't do. There is tremendous personal satisfaction in capturing difficult shots or coming up with strong ideas. Too many people in this business think in terms of simply "getting a show." That implies compromise and less than one's best work.

Certainly being on national television gives you exposure that no other medium can match. Not many people recognize writers or photographers in airports. The visibility can benefit other aspects of your work because your name is known to a broad audience.

Pay—For me, it varies from year to year. I don't even know what I make. That may sound funny, but I run a company. If there is money left over at the end of the year, that's profit, but you have to leave some of it in the bank to cover continuing costs and begin the next season's work. It's an ongoing process. If we come up short at the end of the year, I have to make up the difference. There's a lot of risk involved.

I own all of my own equipment now. When you're starting out, you have to rent equipment and use an outside post-production house for editing. Putting your own production company together takes a lot of money, and unless you have it yourself, you'd better find a banker who is willing to lend it to you.

From what I hear, some show hosts make a respectable living. A few may make a very comfortable living in the high six-figures, but a lot of that money comes from product endorsements and deals with companies rather than their actual production work. My personal concern centers on producing a quality product and quality takes money. That's one reason I haven't gotten rich from this. I believe that if you deliver the best product, the money will come.

You can go the safe route, too. Years ago, I was paid a flat fee for being a field producer. Someone else was taking the risks then, but they had control over the quality of the production and they kept any profit. It was a way to learn the business without assuming the risks.

Negatives—Television is very demanding and it takes a lot of hard work if you want to do a quality job. People think you simply go outdoors and have a good time like everyone else, catching more fish than the average angler dreams of landing. A typical 30-minute show takes us three to five days to shoot and at least that long to edit. You fish for the cameras, so to speak, and not for fun. My relaxation centers on fishing when there are no cameras, microphones or TV crews around.

Producing television shows is very expensive. Not only do you have to rent or buy equipment, but the out-of-pocket costs become astronomical. When it rains or the seas are too rough and you can't shoot, you still have to pay people and handle other costs. When a show turns out less than satisfactory, you don't put it on the air and then you have to eat that cost. It's a hard business and there are always problems.

Perhaps the most significant negative aspect of the business lies in breaking in and establishing yourself. Getting airtime and attracting sponsors frequently requires a track record and you can't prove yourself without the opportunity and support.

The future—Some people have aired outdoor shows continuously for more than 30 years. If you continue to produce a quality product, you should be able to find a market for it for many seasons. I personally believe the market for this type of programming will increase in the next few years. Most cable companies offer subscribers between 30 and 35 channels right now. I predict that it won't be long before that number approaches 100 channels. One or two of those may be all-outdoors networks. Television eats material almost faster than it can be produced. More markets mean a greater demand for original work as well as reruns.

Being on television opens up possibilities in allied fields. Once you become known, you can write, get into radio, serve as a consultant, and lecture or do personal appearances. As people begin to recognize your name and your face, you're looked upon as an authority in the outdoors.

Career Case Study

Nancy Pearlman, California   *Nancy Pearlman is an award-winning environmental broadcaster and television personality who has made safeguarding the earth's ecosystem both a vocation and avocation. Since the 1970s, when Pearlman coordinated the first Earth Day in Southern California and founded the Ecology Center of Southern California, she has worked with hundreds of conservation organizations, serving as administrator, founder, advisory council participant, and member of boards of directors.*

Requirements—To complete any video work successfully requires a massive amount of time and a major commitment to completing project goals in a flexible manner. Due to the very nature of outdoor photography, unforeseen circumstances constantly arise. Thus, flexibility is absolutely necessary. Time schedules are not always predictable; if you want a shot of a certain animal, you sometimes have to wait for hours. You must deal with unexpected weather and distractions like aircraft noise. Traveling at night for the early-morning and early-evening wildlife shots may be required as well. You need to put in long hours.

There is a great deal of competition in the field of video production, but although there are many who can talk, there are few who can actually produce. To be successful, it's essential to be knowledgeable in a variety of areas. I believe a person should be well-read in the field that he or she is covering, and that can be accomplished either formally, through education, or informally, through outside reading.

Your area of concentration depends on what aspect of the business you're focusing on. If you want to write, you need to have an excellent command of the English language. If you're going to be working behind the camera, you need to know how to operate the equipment. If you're going to be in front of the camera, you have to be familiar with your subject and have a commanding presence.

Everyone involved has to be capable of operating in somewhat primitive circumstances. When you're out in the wilderness, the restrooms are in the bushes, the catering truck is not going to show up at noon to serve a gourmet lunch, and you will sometimes have to hike up steep hills lugging all your equipment.

Prospects—Breaking into outdoor television and video is difficult because there is so much competition. But just because someone has the ambition doesn't mean he or she knows how to shoot. Top equipment is a priority, but if you can't use it properly, it's basically worthless.

One way I've seen people break into the field is by donating a piece of work to a non-profit organization that might not have the means to do it themselves. That's one way to learn all aspects: writing, producing, directing, camera, audio, and editing. The key is to get established by proving yourself. You just have to go out and do it. You have to be willing to put in the time and effort with no immediate return. And don't aim too high at first, because getting established takes time and experience.

Benefits—The primary reward is knowing that you're educating the public about our marvelous earth and natural resources; you're creating a wonderful program that millions of viewers will be watching and responding to.

You meet incredibly interesting people. It's been my experience that some of the most informed, dedicated, intelligent, friendly people are those who are out there working in the field, the ones who are studying mountain lions or habitats or whatever. Those people are the true saviours of the earth and it is a pleasure to work with them.

Working outdoors is far more fun than being limited to indoor television production. You are able to get away from the noise and congestion of the city and do something creative and healthful; it's good for the soul.

Pay—There is absolutely no set pay scale. There are so many variables to consider that it is really up to the individuals as to how much they make. With documentaries, you might find yourself putting money you might otherwise make back into the project. If you are willing to explore different avenues and wear different hats, your chances of making money increase. It basically comes down to what you're willing to do. When you become extremely well known and specialized, you can make a substantial living in the tens and even hundreds of thousands of dollars, but that happens infrequently.

Negatives—On the average, there is little money to be made in the environmental documentary field. Very few documentarians become wealthy. Many are content to make an adequate living and enjoy the projects and processes.

If you're primarily a creative person, you may not like the business aspect of distributing your work. That's the dull and often boring part of outdoor video, but I believe that if you're going to spend the time and money on a piece, it's essential and crucial to distribute it and get it seen.

The hours are endless. I'm completely committed to my work and I'm always aware of possible stories and subjects. If you are dedicated, you're always working. A specialist might work selected hours and selected days, but television is generally not nine-to-five work. You simply stay until the shoot is done.

The future—The future is going to bring much more of the wild outdoors to video and television screens. That is a positive trend, but there are conditions to be aware of. Just as books that talk about saving certain areas prove useful in that regard, the information unfortunately helps destroy them by encouraging visitation. With video, we have to show the places so viewers will want to protect them, but the very nature of publicizing the areas will attract more people, and that would ultimately contribute to the areas' destruction.

I believe that there's a larger and growing market. People want to see what is left of our beautiful lands and natural resources. Today's technology is allowing more effective and inexpensive methods. More people are getting into the field, and so more opportunities will be created. However, I predict that there's going to be a saturation point reached soon.

References

Educational Communications, P.O. Box 351419, Los Angeles, CA 90035-9119; (310) 559-9160. E-mail: ecnp@aol.com.

Outdoor Writers Association of America, 2017 Cato Avenue, Suite 101, State College, PA 16801; (814) 234-1011.

Local and regional organizations for communicators will also provide access to people in the field.

Trade magazines that focus on television production and post production are invaluable sources for information on equipment and techniques.

Wildlife Biologist

Dreams—You get the Nobel Prize as the world's anointed guardian of wildlife, spend your time communing with little furry things, and get paid darn well for a rural area. But it isn't the money that's rewarding, it's the knowledge that you have "saved the world." Soon, there will be a movie about how you lived with a family of Musk-ox.

Nightmares—All you get is lab time and nobody pays any attention to your work. In fact, it just seems to get filed and buried forever. A real nightmare is getting staffed in a city. Or what if you can't get a job at all?

Realities—This is a rewarding career with plenty of field time in many diverse areas and a real shot at protecting or restoring wildlife populations. A pro-active biologist can greatly improve the world, piece by piece. But you can expect tough back-room politics where bureaucrats will try to undermine your work.

What it's all about—Everybody loves little furry things. That's why getting your first job as a wildlife biologist can be difficult. The idea of working to protect those little critters is exactly what so many college graduates envision when they start applying for jobs with the U.S. Fish and Wildlife Service or national parks.

The problem is, everybody has the same idea. And whenever a lot of people think they want the same thing, reality has a way of allowing only a few of them to get it. So what can you do? Flip burgers? Drive a taxi cab? Well, there are many other answers. But read this loud and clear: If you know in your gut that becoming a wildlife biologist is the life you want, and you are willing to do everything possible to prepare yourself (we'll get to that) and make yourself employable (we'll get to that, too), you will eventually end up with a job and a career in this field.

The process can be accelerated if you are female or a minority, particularly African-American or Hispanic, because government employers are making a significant attempt to add diversity to this white, male-dominated profession.

Preparing yourself means you can't spend your college summers perfecting your suntan or your dart game. It means working, even volunteering, as an assistant in a role at least remotely related to what you have planned for yourself. It doesn't matter where—in a national park, national forest, range managed by the Bureau of Land Management, state, county or regional park, even a zoo—as much as it matters that you do it. You need to rub shoulders with the pros, mesh with the fabric of the life of a wildlife biologist, get field time and see real problems solved by real people.

Meanwhile, you need to go to a college where their wildlife science program is accredited; you need to perform, getting the best grades possible, and learn how to do your lab work with precision, no matter how long it takes initially (it gets easier later). Learn to write concise reports, learn to speak in front of people, and learn the sciences. You will be paid back later for the effort.

Don't worry so much about attending a big name (and expensive) college. It matters more that the program is accredited and that you perform.

An inside tip is to conduct a little detective work about professors in order to learn which ones have been professionals in the field, and which ones are just acting the part. Then get to know these professors who have field time. Take them out to lunch, meet with them after school for a beer, and pick their brains for everything you can think of. After all, these people have done it; they likely have done it right. You will not only learn the nuances of the field, prime stuff not available from anybody else on a college campus, but may network yourself right into a summer job they know about, or maybe even a permanent position.

When it is time to start looking for work, you'll know the business inside and out. You'll have extensive field time from your summer jobs, a good academic record, and you'll have a contact (your professor buddy) who can point you in the right direction. On the other hand, if you merely get a wildlife degree and start looking for a job, you might as well buy a submarine and try to find the Loch Ness Monster. After all, you will be bringing little practical knowledge to the party.

Once you get into the club, though, you will never want to leave, although you might want to try several chairs out. Remember those little furry things? It's your job to protect them, help populations recover, address problem areas and fix them. It is fascinating work, with a decent amount of field time and studies, as long as you don't let yourself get bottled up in a lab.

Because most of the employment opportunities are in government, as you move up the ladder you will find the bureaucracy pervasive, with the decisions of your overlords often undermining your good science. Some biologists react by doing nothing, never saying a word, merely doing their work and filing it away in a folder that may never be opened again. That is why it has become a joke in government that when you want to stonewall an environmental proposal, you just "put a biologist on it and have 'em study it." Everybody laughs, too.

So what do you do? Take a militant approach and quit? Then how do you eat? No, the response that works is to remember these things: 1) With everything you do, you are trying to make the world a better place. 2) You can't win them all. 3) You can win the ones you care about most. 4) If you lose because of in-house politics, don't take it personally.

What you should take personally is the job you do, day-in, day-out, where one day you will be able to look back and say, "See all those little furry things—I protected them."

Career Case Study

Dan Rosenberg, Alaska   *Dan Rosenberg is a biologist for the U.S. Fish and Wildlife Service in Alaska. He calls it a dream job in a dream location.*

Requirements—The minimum educational requirement is a bachelor of science degree in some related field, such as zoology, wildlife biology or wildlife management—primarily the terrestrial-related fields. Other useful areas of concentration would be ecology, statistics, technical writing, and computer skills. Generally, most people who jump straight into permanent positions have a master's degree. The more common route is to find a temporary position and work your way up to a more permanent type of job. The summer is a typical time to find these temporary positions. That's when agencies need assistants to do field work and other research.

Prospects—The job market is extremely tight. The majority of the jobs available are with the state or federal government. A third avenue of opportunity would be something like a consulting firm. When the economy is in such a state as it is today, jobs in all areas tend to dry up, but this market has always been difficult to break into. Of course, when events such as the Exxon oil spill occur, more jobs are created, but those don't occur very often.

As I said, temporary jobs are the starting point for most people. They can be difficult to obtain, too, although I'd have to say that the market for temp jobs doesn't seem quite as competitive as it was five or ten years ago. There are far more temporary positions available through the federal government in comparison to the state government, and it seems to be easier to break in there.

Benefits—You have the opportunity to work with wildlife and to promote something that you believe in—the betterment of a species or area. Here in Alaska, I get to observe unique assemblages of wildlife that are not found in many other places. You also have the chance to travel to some remarkable places. My first job was in Barrow, Alaska, which is the northernmost point in North America, and I worked on a study on whale migration off the coast—that was really fascinating.

The opportunity to work outdoors is a definite benefit. Wildlife biology is a long way from molecular biology; it's more focused on being outside, studying animal populations and their habitats, managing wildlife areas for public use, and so forth. What you do depends a lot on where you are. The field runs the whole gamut.

Pay—Obviously there's a tremendous range of incomes, depending on where you enter the market. But here's an example: If you started out with a master's degree, in a full-time position with the state you could probably expect to make around $2,800 per month. When you've reached a position close to the top, which takes about 20 years, it could go up to about $5,000 per month. That's really topping out. And that's no longer an outdoor-oriented job.

Negatives—The longer you stay in this field, the more you become encumbered by political processes. Political processes often drive out the biology side of the job. If your goal is to hold the position as a long-term career, you'll begin, after some time, to spend less and less time outdoors, and eventually you'll find yourself in an office permanently.

Bureaucracies are sometimes difficult to deal with. A lot of your time is spent trying to get things done rather that actually doing them. If you're in a management position, you may often end up dealing with the public, so you spend a lot of time dealing with their concerns and the politics involved. That can be a plus or a negative, depending on how disruptive the issue is.

The future—I think that most people who start out as biologists tend to stay with it as a life-long career. I don't see any kind of trend where people are using these jobs as stepping-stones for other related fields, although there are opportunities to move within agencies; for example, from a position with the state government to one with the federal government. Some people also take jobs with private companies, consulting firms or environmental organizations. I can't see the need for biologists ever diminishing.

Career Case Study

Harry Hodgdon, Maryland
Harry Hodgdon is the director of The Wildlife Society.
He has worked in the field for more than 20 years,
specializing in threatened habitat.

Requirements—Biologists must have at least a bachelor's

degree, and most have a master's in wildlife management or wildlife biology. The more experience you have, the better. A lot of students do work during their undergraduate studies and often companies will hire students who are working on their theses.

Prospects—The market is pretty intense; there are a lot more graduates looking for jobs than there are jobs available. Approximately half of all graduates with a bachelor's degree and two-thirds of all graduates holding a master's degree will find a job within one year.

Often individuals are hired on a temporary basis at first, especially within the government agencies; they'll work for six months, or perhaps a year. The more temporary experience you're willing to accept, the better your prospects. Almost any graduate who's willing to take temporary positions and stick with them can find a job within two years.

Benefits—Most people are drawn to the career because they want to work with and perpetuate wildlife resources for people. Ten or twenty years ago the field was concentrated specifically on working with wildlife, and it has lately become more general, more directed toward working with people. Take the spotted owl controversy in Northern California, for example: That's clearly more about people than wildlife. The view now is that humans and wildlife are all part of the same system and should be considered equally important. We have to design programs that benefit both. It's very rewarding to have a part in that.

Pay—I would estimate that someone in an entry-level position makes around $14,000 to $16,000 with a bachelor's degree, and $18,000 to $20,000 with a master's. That usually goes up proportionately with experience. Two-thirds to three-fourths of all wildlife biologist positions are within state or government agencies, and they have set pay scales; they're based on a rating system.

Negatives—Most of the jobs are not high-paying positions, and relocation is sometimes required, especially in government agencies. For some, the travel might be a negative, for others an advantage. Depending on what kind of job you hold, you may have to keep unconventional hours. If you're doing research, studying a species or habitat, you are dependent on the species' schedule. For instance, if you're studying a nocturnal species, there's no way you're going to get out of working at night.

If you've come into the job expecting to be outside with wildlife the whole time, it can be frustrating to find out that you spend 80 percent of your time at a desk on the phone.

The future—I think the field will continue to grow, but not rapidly. In the past, biologists used to be more oriented toward individual species, and now the scope will be broader in terms of looking at wildlife and their habitats together. As use of existing habitats continues, there will always be a need for people to study and regulate them.

References

The Wildlife Society, 5410 Grosvenor Lane, Ste 200, Bethesda, MD 20814; (301) 530-2471. E-mail: TWS@wildlife.org.

National Ecological & Conservation Opportunities Institute, PO Box 511, Helena, MT 59601; (406) 442-0214.

US Fish & Wildlife Service, 2625 Parkmont Road, Building A, Olympia, WA 98502; (360)753-9460.

National Fish & Wildlife Foundation, 1120 Connecticutt Avenue NW, Ste 900, Washington, D.C. 20036; (202) 857-0166 or fax (202) 857-0162.

International Association of Fish & Wildlife Agencies, 444 North Capitol Street NW, Ste 534, Washington, D.C. 20001; (202) 624-7890.

The Job Seeker, Route 2, Box 16, Warrens, WI 54666; (608) 378-4290. E-mail: jobseeker@sparta.msilbaugh.com.

Most state and federal agencies have career information available.

Wildlife Manager

Dreams—You love all those critters—deer, ducks, pheasants—and now your job is to create perfect homes for them. You get plenty of field time, and the right mix of physical work and intellectual challenge. The rewards are extraordinary, not just in pay but in seeing with your own eyes the benefits you are providing for wildlife. Hey, just look at all the deer!

Nightmares—What's this? You hate hunting but didn't know that hunting is a standard management tool, plus a way to help pay the freight? Then you'll have genuine nightmares because it will be your job to manage the hunting program. But that's if you get hired; getting a job is downright impossible without field experience to complement book-learned degrees.

Realities—This is a profession where expertise and field experience are blended, with hunting often an essential part of the program. On a private ranch, you may even be a hunting guide as well, or help manage a cattle business. On public land, a drawback is an oversupply of paperwork. For the well-prepared who are persistent in their job search, the reward is a satisfying career where you make the world a better place for wildlife.

What it's all about—A lot of people do not understand nature's ways. They don't understand that for every 150 fawns that are born, 100 typically die because of lack of food, disease, or the sharp teeth of predators. Wildlife typically produces far more young than the habitat can provide for, creating a scenario in which large numbers of animals will die protracted or violent deaths. It's nature's way.

That is why hunting is a valid management tool. Since adult deer outcompete the young for food, cropping a segment of the adult population through hunting creates space in a habitat for more young to survive. In other words, by hunting the few, you benefit the many.

That can be the hardest lesson for prospective wildlife managers to learn, especially college graduates who have not been exposed to hunting. Many students enroll in wildlife biology classes because they love nature's creatures and are considering a career in which they will protect them. Many are aghast when they learn that hunting and killing the very animals they love is a key tool for managing the most healthy wildlife populations as possible.

Well, it comes with the territory, and if you have an inherent distaste for hunting, then you will need to resolve that conflict before moving into this career. You need to know that up front.

Wildlife managers typically oversee large tracts of land— often private ranches, sometimes state or federal-owned refuges or woodlands. The premise of the job is to help guide an ecosystem to support the most vibrant wildlife populations possible, primarily by helping to create water sources, food sources, and areas of cover for protection against predators. It also includes hunting, in order to keep a herd relatively young and healthy. That is also where your salary often comes from, either from fees charged to sportsmen for access to privately-owned land, or from hunting license fees and excise taxes on guns and ammunition if you work for the government to manage public lands.

On private ranches, many wildlife managers are expected to double as hunting guides during the season; so expertise in firearms, woodsmanship, and handling game can be a factor in getting hired.

The most secure wildlife manager jobs are in government, managing wildlife areas and refuges. The pay is standardized according to your rating, ranging from $28,000 to

$45,000. The best paying jobs, on the other hand, are on private ranches, topping out around $75,000. But this includes very little security; the landowner could have a mediocre financial year, and boom, you're outta there.

This is a profession, and like any specialty, you must master your craft. A bachelor's degree is a necessity, and a master's is advised, and even then, you have no guarantees. A lot of private ranch owners, in fact, are leery of schoolbook-bred wildlife managers. They prefer practical experience. That means working as an assistant, or even a volunteer if you have to, at a wildlife area or refuge while in school, either on a part-time basis year-round if possible, or in a full-time seasonal position in the summer.

There is no substitute for field experience. None. It is often the only difference between someone who gets a job as a wildlife manager and someone else who is book-trained in wildlife management, but can't get hired anywhere and ends up trying to sell life insurance in some ugly city.

The job will provide quite different experiences depending on if you are working at a public wildlife refuge or on a private ranch. On public lands, there is a considerable push to provide services for non-hunters, especially for bird watchers. Hunting is still part of the picture, but not the primary concern year-round. A prediction is that this focus will increase, eventually to the point where special wildlife taxes on equipment (such as binoculars and hiking boots) will be charged to non-consumptive users, and the conservation burden will finally be equaled between hunters and non-hunters.

Private ranches also do not exist solely to provide hunting opportunity for pay. Most are also working cattle ranches, and the wildlife manager duties are likely to spill over into the cattle operations. The wildlife manager who can do both thus becomes extremely valuable to a ranch owner, in some cases indispensable, and it is in these cases where the high salaries come forth. The money goes a long way, too, because these ranches tend to be in rural areas where housing prices are very low compared to urban regions.

The life can be a good one. You spend a lot of time out there on the range, often getting there with a four-wheel drive, making sure that water, food and protection are abundant for wildlife. There's a lot that can be done, building ponds and guzzlers for water, planting corn and milo for food, downing manzanita and brush for cover. The hope in the future is to manage entire ecosystems, and not just have a "deer program." With the right outlook, expertise and persistence at securing a position, a career as a wildlife manager could be a dream job.

Career Case Study

Chuck Harrison, Canada

Chuck Harrison has been in the outdoors field since 1983, working in the private sector as a guide and wildlife manager. He is owner of Gold Creek Outfitters, and enjoys hunting and fishing. He lives in a small town on the Canada/Idaho border.

Requirements—A bachelor of science degree in natural resources is a minimum requirement. As the market gets more competitive, a master's degree should definitely be looked into, although it's not a requirement. It's very important to develop experience while you're going to school. This is not a job that you can just jump into after graduation; you have to start out small and get your name known, working for a consultant or wildlife manager in the field. You need connections. For instance, I worked in the private sector for three or four years before I actually worked in any kind of permanent position.

Your ambition and goals should be clear. If you want to do something like this—a job that's fulfilling but won't make the kind of money that, say, a doctor or lawyer will make—you have to have a lot of drive. You must establish your dedication from the beginning.

Prospects—The current market, at least in the private sector, is good. I see it continuing to improve. There are lots of opportunities available to work with both private and state groups. I think the state and federal markets will continue to be pretty competitive. It looks brighter for the private sector as more jobs are turned over to them. I predict that as the federal agencies limit their hiring, the private sector will take over more of the burden, creating more jobs. I see more and more people willing to spend money on wildlife for recreation purposes, and that trend can only enrich the possibilities for potential employees.

Benefits—The biggest benefit is the quality of life. I love wildlife and I love recreation, and being outdoors is very rewarding. You have the satisfaction of improving resources, which is gratifying. There are many opportunities to see a lot of the country, and you're able to travel quite a bit. The nature of the job keeps you active, both physically (out in the field), and mentally (researching and developing wildlife resources). A big advantage for me is being able to see things people usually don't see; we get to witness a lot of interesting wildlife interaction.

Pay—Salary varies greatly between federal and state agencies and the private sector. When you're working for the government, you're usually limited to the GS scale. Internships, which are generally what people start with to break in, just pay a basic minimum wage. Then, once you get a bit more established, you can make anywhere from $15,000 to $50,000 at the state or federal level, and from $15,000 to $75,000 in the private sector.

Private work is more lucrative because there is such a diverse number of opportunities available. There are many ways to develop resources and wildlife and make money at it; you can offer a consulting service, you can do float trips, things like that.

Negatives—There are a lot of long hours and long days, especially in the private sector. When you work within the government, you pretty much have eight-to-five hours, but you have more freedom working on your own, and you can reap the benefits of those long hours. The amount of travel can be a positive factor, but it can also be a negative. I spend a lot of time away from home, which is hard sometimes.

The future—I see more private land owners needing to diversify and manage their property. People are starting to not only farm or ranch, but develop their land for wildlife. As that happens, more people will be needed to manage the areas successfully. I also see a trend toward more non-consumptive use; we're seeing a greater interest in wildlife viewing, wildlife photography, petting zoos, things of that nature. Because of the variety of job possibilities, I think the future looks very bright.

Career Case Study

Ron Regan, Vermont

Ron Regan has worked as a wildlife manager for the Vermont Fish & Wildlife Department since 1980. He worked for the department seasonally prior to that while attending the University of Vermont. Ron is married and has two children, with whom he lives in Barre, Vermont. He enjoys reading, classical music, church-related activities, and outdoor recreation.

Requirements—Requirements vary somewhat from state to state. A bachelor's in biology or wildlife is often all that is technically required, but due to the intense competition a master's is almost necessary. Some states probably do require a master's. An entry level position may not require any experience, but for more complex jobs, two or three years experience is preferred. You have to be fairly independently motivated and task-oriented. You should enjoy working with people; the job is not all running around capturing wild animals, contrary to popular belief. There are lots of meetings and various dealings with other resource managers.

The ability to adapt to a changeable work load is a definite requirement, especially if you're working for a state agency. Most states have fairly small staffs, and when emergencies come up, you're the one who has to take care of them, so you have to adjust quickly.

Prospects—The market is not all that great. The problem is that most wildlife biologists land jobs with state or federal agencies, which offer a limited number of positions, and have a high rate of job retention. Since there aren't that many positions to begin with, there's not a very high rate of turn-over. There are a larger number of opportunities in private consultant work, which is beginning to develop, but it's a fairly new area of growth.

Benefits—One thing that I appreciate about my job is the rich diversity of work; it's a very nice blend of field work and office work. There is also a pleasant diversity within the office work—it requires writing skills, computer skills and mathematical skills. I find that to be very rewarding. It's also fun to work with a wide variety of people.

There is also a great deal of satisfaction in knowing you're managing a living resource. I view myself, as do many others, as a steward of a resource, helping to perpetuate ecosystems on a day to day basis.

Pay—This is not the kind of profession where you're going to get rich. I would say an entry level position pays somewhere around $22,000 a year, and it goes up with experience. Someone with ten years experience would be making a salary in the low $30,000s.

Negatives—I think one of the biggest drawbacks can be dealing with political entities. You often have to cope with the viewpoints of the politicians, which don't always coincide with what we think should be done. It's frustrating trying to gain support for programs at the political level, but that's something you have to learn to live with, I think. You just have to remember that persistence is required.

The hours are pretty diverse. They can be very routine sometimes, and other times there will be a fair amount of nighttime and weekend work. If you're involved in any kind of research that requires specific sampling periods, you're not going to have a typical work day. That can be agreeable to some people, and it may bother others.

The future—I don't think the state or federal markets are going to improve much. They're going to continue to be highly competitive. There is not a whole lot of room for expansion in the wildlife profession. If anything, I think there will be an emphasis on higher degrees of education. But for persistent people who have the flexibility to move around and take summer jobs, there will always be openings. It's not a closed door by any means, but it is going to continue to take work to get in.

References

The Wildlife Management Institute, Suite 725, 1101 14th Street NW, Washington, D.C. 20005; (202) 371-1808.

The Wildlife Society, 5410 Grosvenor Lane, Ste 200, Bethesda, MD 20814; (301) 530-2471. E-mail: TWS@wildlife.org.

The Job Seeker, Route 2, Box 16, Warrens, WI 54666; (608) 378-4290. E-mail: jobseeker@sparta.msilbaugh.com.

International Association of Fish & Wildlife Agencies, 444 North Capitol Street NW, Ste 534, Washington, D.C. 20001; (202) 624-7890.

Environmental Job Opportunities Bulletin, from Institute for Environmental Studies, University of Wisconsin-Madison, 550 North Park Street, 15 Science Hall, Madison, WI 53706; (608) 263-3185 or fax (608) 262-0014.

Contact the career development departments at universities known for their natural resource programs.

Windsurfing Instructor

Dreams—This is a "job?" You go windsurfing all the time, get paid $50 an hour for groups, and are treated like an idol by your students. Plus you get discounts on gear, kickbacks on sales, and then a three to five-month vacation in the winter. Hey, where do I sign up?

Nightmares—You know you're great, but nobody else seems to know it, no matter how much you tell them. For some reason, nobody wants to take a lesson from you, and then when a few kids finally sign up, there's no wind. Finally, you give up. "I just wanted to go windsurfing anyway."

Realities—Bad weather and a bad attitude are killers, but you can control both. Base your operation in a fair weather location and stay composed with your students, no matter what. With a flair for promotion and skill at communication, a master windsurfer can work up quite a clientele.

What it's all about—What starts out as a curiosity can sometimes turn into a life's passion. That is exactly what happens so often with windsurfing.

A newcomer's interest is often kindled by the sight of a windsurfer cutting across a lake or bay or through ocean breakers. It looks effortless, fast and exciting. The vision has a way of sticking in your mind, and before long, you say to yourself, "I'd like to try that." Then comes the awakening: While windsurfing is fast and exciting, it is anything but easy, and can be downright humiliating the first few times out.

That's where the windsurfing instructor comes in. The instructor can bridge that fragile time for a newcomer when expectations always outdistance skills. While the initial learning process can take a beginner months on their own (if they have enough stamina to keep at it), a good instructor can shrink that time down to weeks. That is why there is a market for wind-surfing instructors, and why this is a viable career.

It takes an instructor with a multi-faceted personality to make it, though. Of course, you must be a master windsurfer, one who knows all the tricks of the trade, from squeezing out every bit of push from a light breeze to cutting down a gale to manageable proportions. Then you have to be able to communicate these skills in a way that is not threatening or condescending. Fail at the latter and it won't matter if you can rip through high breakers at 40 mph.

You also have to have a strategy to consistently attract pupils, a way to keep them, and finally, a way to make some bonus money. That can all be done. How? This is how: You must be headquartered near a large urban area that is consistently windy, where there are good windsurfing waters nearby. Or you can be located at a major vacation destination on a seasonal basis. San Francisco, Miami, the Great Lakes, Houston and New Orleans are good examples of the former, and Lake Tahoe, Las Vegas and Atlantic City are examples of the latter. With a potential large pool of students at areas such as these, you will have a decent chance at financial success.

But how do you attract pupils, then manage to keep them long enough to pay off? There are many answers. You can link up with a windsurfing shop or surf shop for referrals, and post bulletins on supermarket punchboards. You can advertise in high school, community college and college newspapers (which is great value for the money), and inspire mainstream media (newspapers, radio, TV) to feature you as a unique outdoor personality. Let no promotional opportunity be dormant.

That can get the flow of students started. You can keep them by offering package deals, where you provide the equipment, wet suit (if needed), a four-part (or longer) course, and a graduation certificate. Another tip is to use a waterproof camera to take action photographs of your students, then include an 8 x 10 photo as part of the package price. You can make additional money by setting up connections with dealers or manufacturers, where you get cut in if your students decide to buy their boards, or more rarely, where you get demo products on consignment.

The best way to keep the price down for individual students, yet jack the profit up for you, is to offer group rates, perhaps as little as $5 or $7.50 per student, then run hourly lessons for groups of six to ten, making $30 to $70 an hour. This works best at resort areas, such as Lake Tahoe, where there can be a steady flow of curious newcomers. On an individual basis, the rate is usually about $12.50 an hour for beginner lessons, and as much as double that for intermediate or advanced.

Annual earnings? There is no average to the average, because of each respective area's variables in length of season and number of prospects. If you set up a business in Puget Sound, Washington, for instance, where it rains for about nine straight months, you might need to sign up for food stamps.

Obviously, that is why the southern tier states are more attractive locations. They get hot, sunny weather, regular coastal breezes, and plenty of people who like to dream of a sport where they are free like the wind. It's quite a vision, cutting across the water surface, skipping over boat wakes like a flying fish, hanging on for the ride while the wind takes you yonder.

The fantasy is just enough to inspire the curious to check it out. And there you are as an instructor, all ready to help.

Career Case Study

Vicki Harraghy, Texas

Vicki Harraghy started teaching windsurfing in 1981, has been a certified master instructor since 1983, and opened Texas Excursions in 1986. Her past work experience includes teaching high school and dance, doing construction work, and even being an artist ("a starving artist"). She lives with her husband in Corpus Christi, Texas.

Requirements—The most important thing is to be interested not just in windsurfing, but in teaching people. I have been a teacher my whole life—my mother told me I was a very bossy child. I have a degree in secondary education; I taught both high school and dance classes for several years before I started teaching windsurfing, but I think I could be happy teaching just about anything.

I've found that a lot of people who apply for jobs as windsurfing instructors just want to windsurf. They love the sport and figure that it's an easy way to do what they want to do and make money, but you really have to be in it for others. You've got to have empathy, to remember what it was like to be a beginner. I teach some intermediate and advanced lessons, but 75 percent of my students are beginners.

The sport by nature tends to attract self-motivated people, over-achievers, and when they realize just how hard windsurfing is to learn, they tend to feel a little lost and insecure. You have to put yourself back in that place and identify with them. As far as technical skill is concerned, you basically just have to be better than the level you're teaching. I've known some wonderful instructors who really weren't great sailors, but they had the people skills that made people want to learn.

You do have to enjoy windsurfing yourself, of course. I find that the enjoyment I have of the sport makes me want to motivate and turn other people on to it. I have taught people from age 6 to 83, and I've found that if there's a will, there's a way.

Prospects—The sport has not grown in the past few years the way I expected it to, so I don't think it's really competitive. I think there are more people trained to be instructors than there are actual practicing instructors. A lot of people take training courses and end up doing nothing more than improving their own sailing. The season is just too short for most people to consider it as a full-time job. I think that the market is probably best in Florida, where there are calmer winds and a longer season. Here in Texas, as well as on the west coast, the wind often blows too hard and you have to end up canceling lessons more than you'd like.

Benefits—It keeps you healthy. You have to keep yourself in good condition, because if you've got aches and pains all the time, you'll be miserable. I love the broad range of people that I meet. No matter whether it's an 80-year-old woman or an eight-year-old kid, hearing them say, "I didn't think I could do it, but I did!" is very rewarding. I've seen incredible positive lifestyle changes in many people. They get hooked on sailing, and realize that they could use a much lighter sail if they lost those extra 15 or 30 pounds, and that it's a real hassle to run back to the beach for a cigarette when you're all wet and dripping.

It's nice to be able to choose your own working hours, too, although actually the clients dictate my schedule. But if I don't want to teach at a certain time, I don't have to.

Pay—The pay scale depends on the area you're in. In Miami, it's not uncommon for instructors to make $25, $30, even $50 an hour. But here in my area it ranges from about $10 to $15 for beginning lessons, $25 for advanced. One reason for my low rates is that the economy in Texas is not great right now. I'd rather charge lower prices and have them come back a whole bunch of times than charge a lot for a one-shot lesson.

A lot of beginning instructors make as little as $5 an hour. Of course, that's per customer, and if you're real ambitious you could teach six people at once. It depends on how motivated you are. I average three to six lessons a day usually, but in the summertime I've taught as many as 22 lessons in one day for three or four days straight. Of course, I was real tired after those days, but like a farmer, you have to make hay when the sun shines. I know that come December, January and part of February, I won't have anyone knocking at my door.

Instructors also can get benefits, like discounts and equipment, which ends up being really profitable, because equipment is so expensive.

Negatives—The wind and the sun are hard on your hair and skin. I'm 44 years old, and I think my skin is at the point where it doesn't want to be out in the sun anymore. I also have a lot of aches and pains that I probably wouldn't have if I did something else. But I love what I do, so I live with it.

The future—I don't know what the future holds. I think that the sport badly needs some standardization. It can be inconvenient and expensive; for example, if you buy Bic equipment you have to buy Bic parts. No other brands are interchangeable. And it wouldn't be a bad idea if they—the powers that be—would try to get the prices down. They're catering to racers and professionals with light, high-tech equipment. The average person wants simplicity.

I compare it to me and my car: I don't know how the motor works, I just put gas and water and oil in it and it goes. That's how a lot of people look at windsurfing. They're not interested in camber-inducers and space-age materials and all that stuff. The industry needs to look at what the average person wants. They "high-tech" themselves too much.

I see more people interested in learning, especially senior citizens. I'm extremely excited about the number of people over 60 who want to learn. Many ads portray windsurfers as a bunch of young flat-bellies, so I'm surprised, with that kind of public image, that so many older people are trying it. I think that people in general are becoming more and more health-conscious, and when they retire, rather than sitting in a chair and taking up knitting, they're getting out there and going for it.

Career Case Study

Steve Levine, Florida   *Steve Levine has been in the windsurfing business since 1978, and is the co-owner of Tackle Shack Water Sports in Florida. He enjoys diving (and has taught it professionally), racing, water skiing, jet skiing, and is a licensed boat captain. He lives with his family in Pinealis Park, Florida.*

Requirements—First of all, you've got to have a good healthy interest in windsurfing and really enjoy being in the water a lot, like three or four days a week. Some people can't take the sun, and people who can't stand being outside all day in 90-degree weather with 60 percent humidity aren't going to make it.

Here in Florida, as well as in the Caribbean, Mexico, and much of Southern California, this is a year-round operation;

we teach every weekend of the year, even when it's cold, so we want people who will make a commitment to stick around for at least a couple of years. I don't hire any part-time, summer-only people. I'm not going to train someone and sponsor him through school if he's planning on leaving in six months. It takes a lot of drive.

A good instructor needs to have a good understanding of people; he needs to be strong yet insightful and personable, not cocky. He needs to know how to applaud people in an activity where the applause of one means a lot to many. He has to be able to challenge students and set up a peer pressure environment. He should be very knowledgeable about equipment: proper sizing, repair, and what to use for different weather conditions. He's got to do his homework on where he's teaching.

Another angle to consider is the sales angle. At my shop we sell gear as well as teach lessons, and lessons become a selling tool. As you teach, you become a salesman in a small way as well. A lot of people are sales-adverse and want to be just a nice guy, but it's hard to make money in a business like this without pushing a little.

Prospects—It's highly competitive. It's important to be good and honest. It's good if you're a humble person. I would rather have someone at any age, in good physical condition, with no background other than a healthy interest in sailing. It's a real challenge for men or women. There are opportunities.

Benefits—Your boss has empathy for you when the wind is blowing 20 miles per hour and you want to come in two hours late. You're involved in the fastest growing business in the industry. You have the opportunity to meet a lot of nice people and try all the new equipment as soon as it hits the market. It's an exciting career.

Pay—Most of my employees start out at minimum wage, around $5, and they have to prove themselves for 90 days, and then they can be considered for instruction. My employees are full-time; they work in my store and on the beach. A good instructor makes about half the tuition of the lesson—$60 bucks a head, and can pick up an extra $100 a week.

Negatives—After baking in the sun seven days a week, you start to realize it's not as glamorous as a lot of people think. In a lot of cases, your social life changes; weekends are our busiest times and you have to be out there working. It's hard work. There's a lot of moving gear around. My instructors are very safety-oriented, they're required to be as safe as they can possibly be, and they're very conscientious about that responsibility. They tend to put their hearts and souls into what they're doing, and it can be mentally stressful when you consider the level of responsibility they actually have. Lives are at stake.

The future—I'm seeing more people getting involved in the sport. It's not a fad. A lot of people do not realize that windsurfing can be a grown-up, pleasant, serene experience as well as an exciting one. It's a multi-faceted sport, and it doesn't cost a lot, once you buy your initial equipment.
It doesn't contribute to pollution, it's not loud, and it's convenient—anyone can do it. Some of my best customers are old enough to be my father. It's a universal sport. From an instructor's standpoint, there are opportunities all around the world. You could go and instruct in France if you wanted to. I believe that it's going to grow to be a stable sport; its introduction in the Olympics has proven that.

References

U.S. Sailing Association, P.O. Box 1260, 15 Maritime Drive, Portsmouth, RI 02871; (401) 849-5200 or fax (401) 683-0840.
Boardsailor Instructor's Group, 4168 Brookhill Drive, Fair Oaks, CA 95628; (916) 965-9463. E-mail: Susana@NS.net.

Writer

Dreams—An outdoors writer actually gets paid to go on adventures, receives red-carpet treatment at wondrous destinations, and is often well-loved by the public. He or she will see and experience the greatness of nature, have the chance to test fine equipment, and make from $500 to $1,000 per story.

Nightmares—Here's a great job for self-abuse and suffering at the hand of non-responsive editors. It means getting low pay per story, spending tortured hours at the keyboard, and then, when planning a trip, dealing with the difficulty of finding someone to take care of your dog. Small newspapers pay all of $10 per column. Argh.

Realities—Musts include quality writing to reach good-paying markets, the ability to be either a No. 1 specialist or widely diversified (or both), and the discipline to write and sell a story a day and keep your ego under control. It's not too difficult to sell to local or regional markets, but very difficult to reach the national level.

What it's all about—Outdoor writing can make you rich or it can make you poor, but regardless of how much money you make, you will always get to travel to fish, hunt or explore. Like most professions, the pay starts out lousy, but for the persistent and talented few who stick to it for years, the rewards can become quite lucrative. These are the outdoors writers who live what seems like a charmed life, earning $100,000 per year while always heading off on another great adventure.

Very few people start out being an outdoors writer as a full-time job. Rather they tend to phase into the career over the course of several years, a transition that occurs as one learns the craft of writing and photography, becomes adept at selling stories, then rises up the ladder by publishing in wide-reaching publications.

The first year or two, when you can make as little as $25 to $50 for newspaper columns and features, you can sell four or five stories a week and still make only $10,000 before taxes. But if you can make it through that first year, good things have a way of happening shortly thereafter. You see, you will learn that all editors really want from writers is a good idea that they can use to sell their product. If you get a reputation for providing it, you're halfway home. Then you have to sit down and write the thing, and write it well. Do that once a day and you can make a lot of money, having a hell of a good time in the process.

But most outdoors writers don't develop the persistence or the craft to make that dream happen. Some have a habit of skipping a lot of writing days in order to fish and hunt a lot— "After all, that's why I'm an outdoors writer." In the long run, that approach can be a killer.

Unless you are on a special trip, you just plain have to write nearly every day. One solution is to fish or hunt at peak times, perhaps just two or three hours, then have the rest of the day to write a story. A well-plotted schedule for writing and adventure can provide the excitement you desire, as well as develop consistent work habits.

Over time you will develop style to go with craft, contacts at newspapers and magazines to go with your ambition, and make a good living to go with plenty of adventure. If you deliver the goods, editors will start calling you for ideas and stories. As the evolution continues, there will come a time when you scarcely need to write a query letter—the standard form of introduction—because the phone seems to ring nearly every day.

One helpful tool to getting established is to become a capable photographer, then produce a complete package for magazines that includes a main feature, photos and sidebar. Always shoot slides, not prints. To learn new markets, buy an up-to-date edition of *Writer's Market*, and as soon as you qualify for membership, join the Outdoor Writers Association of America and regional writers' organizations.

The future is best for outdoors writers who can write in different styles, on many different subjects, and for many different markets, yet also be known as a specialist in one clear field. The best approach is to have an established column in a newspaper and a few magazines, something you can count on for regular income, then branch out by writing features, or maybe a book.

Before you know it, you will be out and about, having the time of your life, when you suddenly realize that you have done it—you not only get to enjoy the outdoors, but you are getting paid for it as well. Some 2,000 members of the Outdoor Writers Association of America do it full-time. There's always room for one more.

Career Case Study

Michael Hodgson, California   Michael Hodgson *is a full-time freelance outdoors writer and photographer. He writes a weekly column for the San Jose Mercury News, is a contributing editor for Backpacker Magazine, and serves as editor of the newsletter for the Outdoor Writers Association of California. He has written eight books and has been published in numerous periodicals. He lives in San Jose with his wife and daughter.*

Requirements—You've got to have a passion for the written word and for the language in general, coupled with a love for the outdoors. It's not necessary to have a degree in English or journalism—I have neither—but it is necessary to understand the written word and to have a desire to learn. One of the beauties of being an outdoors writer is you have the opportunity to expand your knowledge of the outdoors.

You should know how to photograph. That's very important. Often the first words out of an editor's mouth are, "Do you have photos?" You don't have to be an Ansel Adams, but you need to have basic photography skills. Having photographs with your article can make the difference between the circular file and the editor's desk. They're also a visual aid for me; I'll hang photos for my latest project on the wall in front of me to keep scenes fresh in my mind.

Prospects—I think it's really no different whether you get work or not; you've got to practice writing. You've got to have ideas, things you want to share, and you have to find a market to share them with. Smaller town newspapers are one of the easier places to break into. Small, sports-specific news-letters are good, too. Just about every area of the outdoors has one, whether it is bow hunting or bass fishing or nordic skiing or whatever. They don't pay worth beans, but what they allow you to do is find your voice and develop a clip file of established work. Every assignment has to become a stair step.

You have to look at every piece you do for its potential to take you to the next level. Once you get established, you can go on to magazine assignments and major, large-circula-tion papers. First of all, you must understand the market you're trying to get into. Read the magazines and see what it is they look for and what voice they write with. You can parlay small introductory assignments in sections usually reserved for freelancers into feature assignments, perhaps.

Writing for newspapers is invaluable because it teaches you to write quickly and effectively; they teach you how to make your writing tight. That's a must! It's easy to be verbose, but making your writing tight yet readable and effective is a challenge. Joining a professional organization is another valuable tool. I read *Writers Digest* religiously, and I am active in both Outdoor Writers Association of America, and Out-door Writers Association of California. I'm also the OWAC newsletter editor.

The key is to get yourself published. There are all kinds of avenues; millions of places out there need people to do copywriting and things of that nature. Books, if you really want to get into them, can be great, providing your idea can be marketed effectively by a publisher. If you have an idea and feel strongly enough about it to write a whole book on it, by all means do so.

You must always look at ideas and see how they mesh. You can't look at an assignment as just one assignment. I'm always thinking of what else I can do with it; a newspaper story can lead to a magazine feature, and so on.

Benefits—The greatest benefit to me is that I get to share my passion, my energy, my eagerness for the outdoors. I get to try a variety of outdoor activities. I live and work and write my passions, and I get paid for it. What a concept! I am actually encouraged to do the things I love, like backpacking or mountaineering. It can be dangerous, though. You have to make sure you don't become a mercenary for articles. You can't go around with your hand out looking for trips.

Any writer who says ego isn't a part of it is a liar. It's great to see your name in print. It's also fun to feel that you are an advocate for something. Outdoors writers have the power to make people aware of our resources, to help them appreciate the greatest resource we have—nature.

Pay—If an outdoors writer is writing a monthly column for a small regional magazine, he can expect to make around $100 to $150 per column. For features, it's around $250 to $300. With a national magazine, $450 to $500 is standard for a column; features can pay anywhere from $1,000 to $1,500. That's strictly for an established writer; it's very rare that a beginning writer will make that kind of money unless he or she has an incredible story. The pay goes up as you get more established.

Newspapers pay from $25 to $100, $25 being standard. That's a very specific market. But you can work the market; you can write a piece for the local paper and turn around and sell it again to another paper out of the region because it's a non-competing market. You can triple your money. Syndication is another option; it's something to look into once you get established. But it's a very difficult market. Not just anyone can get syndicated. But if you can, there's a lot of money to be made. You can expect to make $5 to $10 per column per paper and if you sell to 100 papers, that's $1,000. That's a lot of money.

With books, it varies with each project. Some writers are paid a flat fee, like $3,000 a book, but the traditional means of payment are royalties: twelve and a half percent of net receipts is standard, and the top-selling writers get 15 percent, and in rare cases, up to 18 percent with large advances. However, a typical advance for a book is only $1,000 to $1,500.

When you combine all the incomes from newspapers to magazines to books, a typical first-year net for a freelance writer is about $5,000 to $7,000. Do not start to become a full-time freelance writer unless you have a spouse or other money source, such as a deep savings account, to support you. The next year it might go up to $15,000, and once you get established it's possible to make $40,000 to $50,000 a year— that's full-time, all the time.

For a part-time dedicated freelancer who has another job, $25,000 is not unusual, but that's spending all your time at it.

Negatives—The hours are long and the pay is low. And every writer deals with rejection. You're always thinking about writing, always generating ideas. Sometimes it gets to be irritating. You can't just go on a hike and relax; every step of the way you're thinking about a possible story. You have to watch that.

As a freelancer, the inconsistent pay is discouraging. When you finally make it, when you're successful, you'll look back and see a long, hard road. Along the way, it's 80 percent blood, sweat and tears and 20 percent writing skills. You have to have a tremendous zest for what you do. As a writer, you're by yourself; you don't have anyone there cheering for you. You have to want it badly, so badly that nothing stands in your way. You must feel comfortable with and know how to market yourself and your ideas. Some very talented writers don't get published because they don't know how to market their work.

The future—Your long-term prospects are solely dependent on the effort you're willing to make. Every waking moment, every hour of every day is an opportunity to generate article ideas and get published. I carry a pad of paper with me at all times. Before I became aware of all the opportunities around me, I had these great ideas, ideas that I know would have made me a million dollars, but they were forgotten for lack of a notebook. Freelancers live and die by their own initiative, or lack thereof.

Career Case Study

Bob McNally, Florida

Bob McNally is a full-time professional outdoors writer, photographer and broadcaster. He served for 16 years as Outdoors Editor for the Florida Times-Union, which he left to concentrate full-time on freelance outdoor writing interests. He averages well over 150 magazine feature stories every year. In addition, he has written or co-written nine books, is the host of the syndicated In-Fisherman Saltwater radio show, and has won many national and regional awards. He lives near Jacksonville, Florida with his family.

Requirements—If you're going to be a professional, you'd better know how to write, and journalism school is a good way to prepare for that. It's not entirely necessary, but it certainly can help. There are a million guys out there who know how to write, and a million who know to fish and hunt, but there are very few who know how to do both. The best way is to try to break into a small publication, like a weekly newspaper or a tabloid, and start doing columns.

Prospects—It's easy to get writing jobs. What's hard is to get good quality work. If you want to write a weekly fishing column for a newspaper for ten bucks a story, no problem. If you want to write a $2,000 story for *Sports Afield* or *Field & Stream* or *Outdoor Life*—the Big Three, they call them—that's very difficult.

The late Al McClane, a very good friend of mine, once told me that *Field & Stream* could purchase 50 to 75 major features a year, in addition to what their staff produced. They were receiving an average of 2,000 queries and unsolicited stories per month. So you can see that the competition is exceptionally keen on that level. Too many guys think that all they have to do is write a story and wow somebody and they're automatically going to get into *Sports Afield*. But you need to be a professional; the top editors don't have time to deal with amateurs.

Benefits—I get to fish and hunt more than the average

guy. That's basically it right there. And I love to write. If you don't love to write, you shouldn't be in this business.

The more different things you do in this business, the more lucrative it is. Most people don't realize the variety that's available. If you go on a fishing trip with a buddy, for example, you can do all kinds of things with it. From that one trip you can write a newspaper story, a couple of magazine stories, go on two or three radio shows; you can sell some photography, maybe get some information for a future book, even get on TV if you're into that.

Pay—By other writing standards, for example a novelist or techno-journalist or someone working for *Newsweek*, outdoors writing doesn't pay a fraction of what they make. I can remember working for $10 a story 20 years ago when I was in college. How much you make depends primarily on how hard you're willing to work. For $100, you can get your name in little publications with no problem.

But there comes a certain point for a full-time professional where it's not worth the time and labor. If you're not earning at least fifty bucks for a couple of hundred words, forget it. But you have to remember that with every one of those little stories you do when you're starting out, you're learning. I look back on some of the stuff I did five years ago and I cringe. I look back on some of the stuff I did ten years ago and it's like first grade. So that's the only way to do it, to put your time in. If you're a junior journalism school major and you're working construction to pay your way, it's okay to work for $50 a story. Send queries.

You often have to supply your photography, too. If I were to sell a story to *Redbook* or *The Atlantic*, one of the bigger well-known magazines, they don't expect photography to come with the story. But if you were to write the same story for *Outdoor Life*, they'd expect the full package for the same amount of money. But don't be entirely discouraged by the pay for outdoors writing, at least in the early stage.

There are some good, full-time outdoors writers who are making six-figure incomes. And there are some who have made over $1 million solely from outdoors writing. There definitely is a financial upside to outdoors writing if you work hard, are good, and stay with it.

Negatives—I can't go fishing without thinking about work. I love fishing and hunting more than anything, but it's always work, all the time. I get incredible attacks of guilt if I'm not always working. I go on different trips all the time, and if you're not thinking about what you're going to do with that trip, you're in trouble. You'd really better love writing and all facets of it.

There are plenty of writers who really specialize, and I look at that as a negative. These guys concentrate on one thing and one thing only, like bass fishing, and sure, they might be more knowledgeable and have more insight on bass fishing than me, but that's all they do. I move with the seasons of the year; I go on a few turkey hunts, get in on the bass fishing while it's good, look forward to the saltwater fishing. I'm going fishing in Latin America, Canada and the Bahamas soon. In the spring, I'll start training my dogs. I've gone crazy with the variety. It really opens up your possibilities.

Newspaper writing was fun because I got to write what I wanted when I had no other market for it, but sometimes you get some sports editor telling you to write about what he thinks is the most important thing, and you know it's worthless. Or sometimes someone will change your work without telling you. This guy once put a headline on a story I had written about quail hunting: "Quails are no sitting duck." Editors and copywriters are a hassle to deal with sometimes. If you're a pure wordsmith, you'd better go into another field.

The future—If you have any talent at all, you will shine. As I said before, a lot of guys can fish and hunt and a lot of guys can write, but it's tough to get the two together. Personal contacts mean a lot, but everyone has to spend an awful lot of time in the trenches.

Career Case Study

Tom Huggler, Michigan—Tom Huggler is a full-time writer, photographer and book author specializing in outdoor subjects. He has written eight books on the subjects of hunting, fishing and outdoor fiction, and has won numerous writing and photography awards. He is

*the camping editor for Outdoor Life and a monthly
columnist for North American Hunter and North
American Fisherman. Huggler and his family live in
Lansing, Michigan.*

Requirements—I think a person should have some training in writing, and that can be in journalism or it can be an
English degree. I'm a former high school English teacher and
I've got two degrees in English. You also need to have a very
strong interest in the outdoors and a certain amount of
experience in the outdoors. Those two things go hand in
hand—informal and formal training. You don't have to be an
expert. A lot of people feel that if they're not experts in the
field they're writing about, they're not going to do well. But
if you have skills in writing and reporting, that seems to fall
into place.

Prospects—I think the way that most of us got started
was that we did an awful lot of magazine reading and became
familiar with the market that we were interested in, with
particular publications and their styles, what they published
and didn't publish. Suddenly the light went on inside our
heads and we said, "I can do this just as well, if not better."
We'd see stories others had written and say, "That's absolutely wrong, that guy doesn't know what he's talking about,
and I can set him straight." Then we'd go to the markets with
which we were most familiar, the ones that we read and
knew.

My first piece was written at 12 years old, a story for a
little obscure trapping magazine published in Pennsylvania.
They let people tell their personal stories, and I wrote a story
about muskrat trapping. Then *Outdoor Life* made the mistake
of paying me 300 bucks when I was 17. Little did I know it
would take 15 years to sell another story to *Outdoor Life*. You
just have to say, I love these stories and I can tell these stories,
too. I think desire and ability are the keys. You make your
own luck. The first-time writer needs to experience a kill, he
needs to score with a market.

A lot of writers wouldn't agree with me—they'd say to
query first, but I'd recommend writing the manuscript, then
sending it in blind. And then forget about it, forget you ever
wrote it. It's probably the hardest thing for young writers to

learn, but you must disassociate yourself from your work. Once you've sent it, you must forget all about it. The worst thing you can do is sit and stew and fret over it and worry about rejection, because chances are it will be rejected.

But if you're lucky the editor may see a spark and write you a little note saying, "Gee, you've almost got it," or, "It's good, but we just used something like that a couple of months ago." I find that editors want quality stuff and they don't care how they get it, whether they're queried or sent it outright.

Anyway, what happens is that you begin to make a track record for yourself, and then when you decide to write for another magazine or another market, you can say "I did" instead of "I can do."

Benefits—There are many. First of all, you have found someone you can work for, namely yourself. You know the person you work for. That's good because you try harder, but it can be bad because you can sometimes try too hard. Many outdoors writers have a touch of masochism and a strong dose of work addiction. I say that from personal experience because I'm that way myself. You call your own shots—how much you'll work, when you'll work, when you'll play.

There's a pretty strong support system out there among outdoors writers. Writing can be one of the loneliest professions, but I've found that there's a strong camaraderie among people in this field. I don't know if that's true of other writing fields. We tend to feed off each other and help each other. Not a day goes by that I'm not on the phone talking to somebody, commiserating with them, sharing ideas, or helping them try to solve a problem with an editor.

Another advantage is that the full-time freelancer gets to travel. You must travel if you're going to produce work, even if it's only out to your backyard at first. Eventually you have to expand your circles of experience. I've taken some of the greatest trips of my life all across North America since I've become a writer. It's a healthy job. We don't always sit in little dark rooms and write; we get to be outside, sucking in good air, getting exercise. And we are able to gain an even stronger appreciation, understanding and respect for natural resources, animals and their habitats, and landscapes.

The outdoors are a constant discovery—there's just not

enough time to discover it all in the 80 or so years we're allotted. I'm still growing, and I still pinch myself after ten years of full-time writing because I enjoy it so much. The outdoors are everywhere, literally. There are so many different facets of it, whether you're the silent sport type, like a backpacker, or a hook-and-bullet guy, or a woman riding a bike. It's just limitless.

Pay—There are various tiers in the writing field. For an entry-level writer who's not interested in making a lot of money but wants to write, he can work for free or for an average of $25 to $50 a week for newspapers, or perhaps $50 to $100, depending on the paper. Mid-range is around $250 to $600 a story. Upper range is $600 on up to $1,500. That's pretty much the top. There are magazines like *Audubon* and *National Geographic* that will pay substantially more, but they're not the mainstream markets for most outdoor communicators.

As far as annual sales, incomes can range from $5,000 for a part-time freelancer to as much as $100,000 or more for someone who's heavily diversified. By diversified I mean not just writing for magazines, but working for various companies, selling art, possibly getting some book royalties, giving seminars and speeches—full-time freelance outdoor communicators. Some are able to make $40,000 or $50,000 with a newspaper and another $40,000 or $50,000 freelancing. But the range is quite wide.

Negatives—Historically we're frowned on by the so-called "legitimate journalists." We have hands-on experience. Most journalists see or hear and report; we go out and do and then report. We're constantly fighting for legitimacy. A certain segment of the public says all we do is play, and they don't realize how hard some of us do work.

I can't imagine any other writer-types who make less money than outdoors writers. You need a journalism degree to get into a newspaper, but an outdoors writer can waltz in and say, "I love to hunt and I want to write about it," and an editor may very well say, "Okay, go ahead."

There are too many quasi-outdoors writers, that is, doctors and lawyers who have the means to fly up to Denali

National Park for the weekend and take photos and write a story. They're taking money out of the pockets of legitimate communicators because they are happy to see their name in print. They're not in it for the money, and so they're willing to do it for practically nothing.

Just about all the markets pay a relatively low rate, and there is a lot of competition. That's not to say that the cream can't rise to the top, but it is highly competitive.

This may be the only field where a writer is expected to be a photographer as well. In most cases, you need to supply the full package to an editor to be successful.

The future—I think outdoors writing is among the easiest of the writing fields to break into, and anyone with a tremendous amount of talent and/or motivation can do it. I think a lot of writers look at outdoors writing as a springboard for something else, such as dabbling in fiction or poetry or writing screenplays.

It depends on your goals. Some communicators are strong environmentalists whose goal is to persuade people. They are successful, too, because they're not out to make a lot of money. They're after a cause. With the increased emphasis on environmental issues, quality outdoor recreation, and the need to return to family traditions and other values, I think the future bodes well for the outdoors writer.

References

Outdoor Writers of America, 2017 Cato Avenue, Suite 101, State College, PA 16801; (814) 234-1011. OWAA can also provide contacts for regional outdoors writers organizations.

The Dow Jones Newspaper Fund, PO Box 300, Princeton, NJ 08543-0300; (609) 520-5930 or fax (609) 520-5804. E-mail: newsfund@plink.geis.com. (Write for journalism career and scholarship information.)

American Society of Magazine Editors, 919 3rd Avenue, 22nd Floor, New York, NY 10022; (212)752-0055 or fax (212)888-4217.

Society for Environmental Journalists, PO Box 27506, Philadelphia, PA 19118; (215)247-9710.

The book *Writers Market* provides listings, guidelines, contacts and pay rates for hundreds of magazines.

Youth Camp Director

Dreams—A youth camp director becomes the hero of every youngster he helps. You get all the outdoor action anyone could dream of while teaching about nature, hiking, swimming, canoeing, and fishing. And the pay really isn't so bad, either.

Nightmares—Anarchy, total anarchy. Nobody listens to you, and after you throw a fit, the kids decide they hate you. Your plans are continually disrupted, and so is your sleep because Johnny is afraid the boogey man is going to get him. If you have to eat one more hot dog, you're going to turn into one.

Realities—If you count your blessings in smiling faces, you'll be very rich. That's good, because the pay is only fair. Adventures are many, the friendships golden, the food . . . well, better watch the cholesterol.

What it's all about—The first thing to remember about youngsters is that they don't have an "off" button. They are always "on," and except when they pull the plug each night and finally go to sleep, you have to be on, too, to keep up with them.

A lot of adults just can't handle that. Some have a difficult time with two or three children; imagine having a dozen. You can't? Then move it on little doggy, because empathy is the name of the game. So is leadership, outdoors know-how, first-aid training, and most importantly, the equanimity to be happy in a world where 25 misguided missiles might be fired at you simultaneously.

Sound like a nightmare? Actually, the opposite is true for people who make directing a youth camp their career. Most of them say things like "I really like doing this," or "Best job in the world," and even "Wouldn't trade my life with anyone." That is because there is tremendous enjoyment in watching a youngster progress and gain confidence in an activity, then smile at you as if you were king of the world. After you get their respect, they'll do practically anything to get your appreciation.

It usually becomes obvious at the outset whether or not someone is cut out for this kind of work. The best advice is to take a job as an instructor at an established youth camp and then see if you like it. You will know very quickly; this isn't the kind of position that results in a neutral response. You will love it or hate it; but hey, if you got this far you will probably love it.

Relating with youngsters is a dynamic experience. These little people will arrive to camp a bit nervous, some away from their families for the first time in their lives, many with no experience in the outdoors. They might be afraid of jumping in a lake, getting lost, thunder or lightning, getting cold, or wild animals. For instance, during the day they might joke about raccoons, bears and the boogey man, but at night some youngsters will be afraid of them, really afraid. You need the awareness to take notice, then tell them, "Don't worry, I'll take care of everything."

The future looks good for youth camps. The key is that it has become suitable for parents to take a week or two on vacation away from their children, which are then signed up for a youth camp.

Although it can scare both children and parents to be separated, after the first time through, it turns out be more of a relief than a shock, and allows children to gain confidence and develop abilities to prosper on their own. These little success stories can breed return business for several consecutive years, and in many cases, the same children that once vowed "I won't go!" will demand, "I must go!"

As a career, it is not difficult to get started as an instructor, and as a director, is a stable pursuit in the long run. Alas, the pay is only fair, with $30,000 about average for a director working in someone else's company. That's on the low side compared to many other pursuits in this book. Nobody gets in this line of work because of the money.

On the other hand, if you own your camp, it can be very profitable. But then there's the cost of getting in, of buying an established camp. If you try to set up your own, even if you know a premium location, you will discover a bureaucratic spider web awaiting you. Acquiring use permits, insurance, building permits, water connections, septic . . . well, government bureaucrats will put you through an experience worse than anything a group of kids could deal you.

The most special part of being a director of a youth camp are all the connections you make with children. At first, they will be fearful of you; after all, you aren't mom or dad. But by the end of their stay, you will rate up there with Santa Claus and the Little League coach as Important People. For years, they will remember you as the hallowed guider who maybe helped them catch their first fish, jump into the lake for the first time, paddle a canoe, and protected them from the bears.

These rewards can't be documented in a paycheck. But they are just as real in the smiling faces and bright eyes of a youngster who has declared you a hero. Sometimes that's enough, plenty enough.

Career Case Study

Jim Wiltens, California   *Jim Wiltens has worked as director for Deer Crossing Camp. His background includes working as a marine biologist and an analytic chemist. He has been featured in several outdoor related magazines, and has authored several books, including one about behavior motivation with children. He lives in Sunnyvale, California.*

Requirements—There are four major categories to consider for any youth camp position, whether it is as a counselor or director: safety, responsibility, skills and licensing. Minimum safety requirements are CPR and first aid certification. Anything beyond that—a lifeguard certificate, search and rescue training, advanced first aid, emergency medical training, paramedic training—is definitely smiled upon. The specific requirements depend on the individual camp. Most of the ones I've listed are way beyond what's actually required. Responsibility goes hand-in-hand with those safety techniques. Parents are handing over their most precious possessions—their children—and you are accountable for their well-being.

The skills required vary. I hold an instructor or expert rating in every area in the camp—that's important to me. I'm certified as a windsurfing instructor, a kayaking instructor, a diving instructor, a first aid and CPR trainer. I have a black belt in martial arts and teach martial arts. I have a bachelor's degree in botany and a master's in biology. All these things allow me not only to be able to participate with the kids, but to judge the true abilities of prospective employees.

It's important to me to hire the best counselors I can find, and when I interview them, I can cut through the fluff and find out if they really know what they're talking about.

I also have experience in child psychology and recreation management. I worked in motivational psychology with athletes for some time, learning to bring out the very best in each person. I think the most important requirement of starting your own camp is an entrepreneurial spirit. My parents instilled that in me at a very young age. When I was 14, I owned my own swim school. I started my first backpacking company when I was 18. That spirit is essential to succeeding; it's too hard otherwise.

When we bought Deer Crossing Wilderness Camp, I had never worked in a summer camp before. The camp was a former Boy Scout retreat, and it took two and a half years to rebuild and open it. I was lucky to have a supportive family; it became a family project, sort of a Swiss Family Robinson thing. It was very difficult—there was no road in, so everything had to be carried and boated in. We were all working full-time jobs, and I lived in a tent in order to save as much money as possible. Every vacation, every weekend was dedicated to the camp.

I learned then that I wasn't going to be just a guide backpacking kids into the mountains. I had to become an electrician, a plumber and a carpenter. Any camp director will learn that you must have multiple skills. You're always going to have to do some things yourself, even if you have the resources to hire professionals.

You have to care more about lifestyle and people than money. The return won't make any sense from a money standpoint. Most of all, it's a choice—the knowledge that I'm doing it because I want to.

Prospects—There are not a lot of director jobs available. The ones that become available come in one of four ways: 1) by nepotism—your family has a camp, and you inherit it; 2) by marriage; 3) by entrepreneurial means; 4) by working your way up in an established camp or organization (such as Boy Scouts or Campfire Girls) and waiting for the position to open.

The best way is to start as a counselor and work your way up. Camps are so hungry for instructors now that they're going overseas to find them. It's been difficult to find young people with the work ethic here. You will learn more as a counselor in one season of camp than in four years of college—I've been told that by people who are in school, majoring in recreation.

You usually start as a counselor and slowly work your way up, becoming a head counselor, then assistant director, etc., until someone dies or moves on and a position is available.

Benefits—Practicing motivational psychology, bringing out the best in each kid, is great for me. It's the ultimate experiment—an incredible growth experience.

It's an extremely ego-satisfying job. The children that come to the camp leave their other everyday environments—home and school—and are in the camp environment 24 hours a day. We have the power to influence them in positive ways. When their self-esteem is up, I get happy. When I see a kid become ecologically aware, I'm excited.

There's a development of new friendships every year, with people from countries all over the world. A lot of the kids have become close personal friends, and even when they graduate from the program, they keep in touch. I just went on a second honeymoon with my wife, a whitewater kayaking trip in Costa Rica, and we took one of our campers. When this kid first came to camp, he was terrified of whitewater, and on this trip he was paddling some incredible territory. I felt like a dad.

When I'm out of doors, I feel charged and excited. I have more energy. There are tremendous health benefits. I get involved in all the activities with the kids, I get to do all the things that I enjoy.

Pay—When you work in the woods, you find that money does not grow on trees. I worked for nothing during my first year. The pay scale varies dramatically; a director can make anywhere from $7,000 to $30,000 per year, and that's working full-time. If you own your own camp, it's possible to make more money, but usually only in the massive operations like the ones on the east coast, and those aren't very common.

Negatives—Here's the ugly duckling side: Like a duck, you're got a bunch of eggs you're responsible for 24 hours a day. That can be emotionally draining. Whenever there's a problem, whether it's with camper or a counselor, they come to the director. You're a confidante, a confessor and a psychologist, and you have to stay up and be there for them so that they can perform to their full potential. You have to make sure that everything goes right with all these parents' most precious things—their children. And you can get parents who are extremely demanding.

In the off-season I have more flexibility, but I have to deal with the business end—writing press releases, things like that. There's an unbelievable amount of paperwork.

It's a demanding job, and it does pull you away from your family. Your family can break down when you're away. Fortunately for me, my wife enjoys what I do and is able to come up and stay with me on her vacations.

The future—It's been said that the summer camp environment will become more popular with parents and children as time goes on. We've been seeing expansion every year, and I believe that the idea will continue to grow in popularity, although it will become more expensive.

It's important to follow marketing trends and what's happening all the time. Private camps have a special flavor that is a result of the director of the camp—there are the old "ma and pa" operations and there are the psychology-oriented, modern-type camps, and there will always be a demand for both.

The camp director who participates and is involved has to eventually give more authority to others, because everyone ages; you just can't do it all forever.

Career Case Study

Margaret Whitehead, New York
Margaret Whitehead is the director of the Campfire
Council's Aloha Camp in Buffalo, New York.

Requirements—Here at Campfire, directors are required to have a bachelor's degree in some education-related field. I imagine that a recreation degree would be acceptable, too. The state requires that you are a minimum of 25 years old. Those are the only necessary requirements here.

In my opinion, it's important to have good administrative skills and be adaptable in your thinking. You have to keep up with the times and be willing to be flexible in your programming. There are some directors who have been in the business for years, and they want to do the same things over and over. That just doesn't work; times change and kids change. If you're only open to one way of doing things, your program won't be appropriate.

You have to be able to be sympathetic to the feelings of others but at the same time remember that ultimately you're in charge, and sometimes you have to make difficult decisions, according to what's best for the camp. You have to both get along with everyone and remain an authority figure.

Prospects—Director positions are extremely hard to come by. Many camps are closing in this area, at least. Sixty percent of the camps in western New York have closed in the past ten years; many of those were church-related camps. This is due to a combination of things: liability insurance, economics, health department requirements. In other parts of the country, where the camping season may be a little longer, the case may be different. There is certainly no lack of children.

I would recommend that someone who wants to be a camp director start out as a counselor and work at different camps, not just one. That was a mistake that I made; I worked at the same camp for years. Working at different kinds of camps—church-related, non-profit, community-oriented— gives you a broader perspective and a variety of experiences to draw on. That will make you more valuable to an employer.

Benefits—Being with different kinds of people is wonderful. There's a new staff every year, and although there are many repeat campers, there are always new ones. Meeting such a variety of people is a lot of fun.

Building a concern for the environment in children is very rewarding. I've recently been working on a program in which we go into urban schools and present a three-part project on trees. A few weeks ago, we brought a group of third-graders out in the woods, and when they got off the bus, they just couldn't deal with it, they didn't know what to do with all the trees and things around. A few of them just started running off into the woods. At the beginning of the day, they found some bugs and caterpillars, and there was lots of screaming and squealing, but by the end of the day most of them were letting the caterpillars crawl on their hands. They wanted to take them home.

That's extremely rewarding, to see the effect of nature on children. Another benefit is the opportunity to develop new projects and programs. You're always looking for new activities and ideas, and the freedom to be creative can be really gratifying.

Pay—Salaries really vary, depending on what type of agency you're with. The type of organization I work for pays about $16,000 to $18,000 per year, but I know of other agencies in the area who pay up to $10,000 more. The size of the camp is a determining factor. If you're heading a local camp with only 30 children at a time, you're going to make a much lower wage.

Negatives—The hours are rough, and the pay is low. During the summer, you work about 96 hours per week. You begin working at 6:30 or 7:00 in the morning and go until midnight. Summer is very intense, and as one gets older, that schedule is harder to maintain.

You can't take summer vacations—you're on your summer vacation. It's not your typical nine-to-five job. At most jobs you work eight to ten hours a day and go home at night. At camp, you literally live your work.

The future—This industry really fluctuates. Over the past two years, we've seen an increase in the number of campers. Sometimes a bad economy is good for camping, because families can't afford to go on family vacations, but they want their kids to still have the opportunity to do something outdoors, so they send them to camp. Right now it appears to be on the upswing.

References

American Camping Association, 5000 Slate Road, 67 North, Martinsville, IN 46151; (800) 428-2267 or (317) 342-8456 or fax (317)342-2065.

American Camping Association, Northern California, 1726 Lincoln Avenue, PO Box 151493, San Rafael, CA 94901; (415) 459-2235.

Peterson's Guide, 202 Carnegie Center, PO Box 2123, Princeton, NJ 08540; (800) 225-0261 or fax (609) 243-9150.

Camping has listings for available director jobs; phone the American Camping Association, (800)362-2236.

For a nationwide Guide to Accredited Camps, phone (800) 428-CAMP.

Appendix I
Careers Ranked by 20 Categories

Solitude

Travel

Working with People

Long-term security

Easiest Seasonal Job Openings

Appendix II
Alphabetical Index to References

Adventure Travel Society, Inc., 6551 South Revere parkway, Ste 160, Englewood, CO 80111; (303) 649-9016.

Alaska Air Carriers Association, 4040 B Street, Anchorage, AK 99503; (907)277-0071.

America Outdoors, PO Box 10847, Knoxville, TN 37939; (423) 558-1812 or (423) 558-1815.

American Camping Association, 5000 Slate Road, 67 North, Martinsville, IN 46151; (800) 428-2267 or (317) 342-8456 or fax (317) 342-2065.

American Camping Association, Northern California, 1726 Lincoln Avenue, PO Box 151493, San Rafael, CA 94901; (415) 459-2235.

American Fisheries Society, 5410 Grosvenor Lane, Ste 110, Bethesda, MD 20814; (301) 897-8616.

American Forest and Paper Association, 1111 19th Street NW, Ste 800, Washington, DC 20036; (800) 878-8878.

American Forestry Association, 2101 E Street NW, Washington, DC 20037; (202) 293-3806 or fax (202) 647-0265. E-mail: assa@ms3644wpo.us-state.gov

American Mountain Guides Association, PO Box 2128, Estes Park, CO 80517; (970) 586-0571.

American Red Cross, Health and Safety Services, 8111 Gatehouse Road, Falls Church, VA 22042; (703) 206-7180.

American Resources Group, 374 Maple Avenue East, Ste 210, Vienna, VA 22180; (703) 255-2700.

American Sailing Association, 13922 Marquesas Way, Marina del Rey, CA 90292; (301) 822-7171 or fax (310) 822-4741.

American Society of Magazine Editors, 919 3rd Ave, 22nd Flr, New York, NY 10022; (212) 752-0055 or fax (212) 888-4217.

American Society of Media Photographers, Washington Road, Ste 502, Princeton Junction, NJ 08550-1033; (609) 799-8300 or fax (609) 799-2233.

American Sportfishing Association, 1033 North Fairfax Street, Ste 200, Alexandria, VA 22314; (703) 519-9691.

American Water Works Association, 6666 West Quincy Avenue, Denver, CO 80235; (303) 794-7711.

Association for Experiential Education (AEE), 2305 Canyon Boulevard, Ste 100, Boulder, CO 80302-5651; (303) 440-8844.

Backroads, 801 Cedar Street, Berkeley, CA 94710; (510)527-1889, ext 117 or (800)462-2848.

Boardsailor Instructor's Group, 4168 Brookhill Drive, Fair Oaks, CA 95628; telefax (916) 965-9463. E-mail: susana@ns.net

Boise Inner Agency Fire Center, 3833 South Development Avenue, Boise, ID 83705-5354; (208) 387-5512. (This Center coordinates firefighting for the entire United States.)

California Department of Fish & Game, Education Branch, 1416 9th Street, Sacramento, CA 95814; (916) 653-8120.

California Dept of Forestry & Fire Protection, 1416 9th St, PO Box 944246, Sacramento, CA 94244-2460; (916) 653-7772.

California Maritime Academy, PO Box 1392, 200 Maritime Academy Drive, Vallejo, CA 94590; (707) 648-4222 or fax (707) 649-4773. E-mail: enroll@prop.csum.edu. Website: http://www.csum.edu

Canadian Owners and Pilots Association (COPA), 75 Albert Street, Ste 1001, Ottawa, Canada KiP5E7; (613)236-4901.

Canoe & Kayak Magazine, PO Box 3146, Kirkland, WA 98083; (206)827-6363.

Careers in Ecology, from the Center for Environmental Studies, Arizona State University, Tempe, AZ 85287; (602) 965-2975.

Coast Guard Information Center, 14180 Dallas Parkway, Dallas, TX 75240-9795; (800)424-8883, ext 5003.

Corporation for National Service (Americorps); (202)606-5000.

The Dow Jones Newspaper Fund, PO Box 300, Princeton, NJ 08543-0300; (609) 520-5930 or fax (609) 520-5804. E-mail: newsund@plink.geis.com

Eastern Surfing Association, 12507 Sunset Avenue, Ste 0, Ocean City, MD 21842; (410) 213-0515 or fax (410) 213-0515. Website: http://www.surfesa.org

Educational Communications, PO Box 351419, Los Angeles, CA 90035-9119; (310) 559-9160. E-mail: ecnp@aol.com

Environmental Job Opportunities Bulletin, from Institute for Environmental Studies, U. of Wisconsin-Madison, 550 North Park ST, 15 Science Hall, Madison, WI 53706; (608) 263-3185.

Environmental Traveling Companions, Fort Mason Center, , Landmark Bldg C, San Francisco, CA 94123; (415) 474-7662.

Greater Miami Service Corps, 810 NW 28th Street, Miami, FLA 33127; (305)638-4672.

High Country Tourist Association, 1490 #2 Pearson Place, Kamloops, BC Canada V1S1J9; (604) 372-7770.

International Association of Business Communications, 1 Halladie Plaza, #600, San Francisco, CA 94102; (415) 433-3400.

International Association of Firefighters, 1750 New York Avenue NW, 3rd Floor, Washington, DC 20006; (202) 737-8484 or fax (202) 737-8418.

International Association of Fish and Wildlife Agencies, 444 North Capitol Street NW, Ste 534, Washington, DC 20001; (202) 624-7890.

International Llama Association, 2755 South Locust Street, Ste 114, Denver, CO 80222; (303) 756-9004.

International Sportsmen's Exposition, PO Box 2569, Vancouver, WA 98668; (800) 545-6100/(360) 693-3700.

International Tour Management Institute (ITMI), 625 Market Street, Ste 610, San Francisco, CA 94105; (415) 957-9489.

Inter-Ski Services, Inc., PO Box 9595, Friendship Station, Washington, DC 20016; (202) 342-0886.

The Job Seeker, Route 2, Box 16, Warrens, WI 54666; (608)378-4290.

JOBSource (computerized job data bank). Contact: Computerized Employment Systems, Inc., 1720 West Mulberry Unit B9, Fort Collins, CO 80521; (970) 493-1779.

League of American Bicyclists, 190 West Ostend, Ste 120, Baltimore, MD 21230; (410)539-3399 or (800)288-BIKE.

Licensing & Education Branch, G-MPV-2, US Coast Guard, 2100 Second Street SW, Washington, DC 20593; (202) 267-2229.

Marine Technology Institute, 1828 L Street NW, Ste 906, Washington, DC 20036-5104; (202) 775-5966 or fax (202) 429-9417. E-mail: mtspubs@aol.com

Maritime Administration, US Department of Transportation, 400 7th Street SW, Washington, DC 20590; (202) 366-4000 or fax (202) 366-5063. E-mail: pao-marad@postmaster2.gov

Maritime Institute, 1310 Rosecrans Street #G, San Diego, CA 92106; (619) 225-1783.

Massachusetts Division of Forests & Parks, 100 Cambridge Street, Boston, MA 02202; (617) 727-3180.

Master Mates & Pilots Union, 700 Maritime Boulevard, Linthicum Heights, MD 21090; (410) 850-0973.

Montana Outfitters and Guides Association, Box 9070, Helena, MT 59624; (406) 449-3578.

National Association of Broadcasters, 1771 N Street NW, Washington, DC 20036; (202) 429-5300.

National Association of Interpretation, PO Box 1892, Fort Collins, CO 80522; (970) 484-8283.

National Association of Service and Conservation Corps (NASCC), 666 11th Street NW, Ste 500, Washington, DC 20001; (202) 737-6272.

National Ecological and Conservation Opportunities Institute, PO Box 511, Helena, MT 59624; (406) 442-0214.

National Fish & Wildlife Foundation, 1120 Connecticut Avenue NW, Ste 900, Washington, DC 20036; (202) 857-0166 or fax (202) 857-0162.

The National Fisherman, PO Box 7438, Portland, ME 04112-7438; (207)842-5600 or fax (207) 842-5603.

National Fisheries Institute, 1901 North Fort Myer Drive, Ste 700, Arlington, VA 22209; (703)524-8880 or fax (703)524-4619.

National Marine Fisheries Commission, 1315 East-West Highway, Silver Springs, MD 20910; (301) 713-2239.

National Parks and Conservation Association, 1776 Massachusetts Avenue NW, Washington, DC 20036; (202) 223-6722 or fax (202) 659-0650.

National Recreation & Park Association, 2775 South Quincy Street, Ste 300, Arlington, VA 22206; (703) 820-4940.

National Retail Federation, 325 7th Street NW, Washington, DC 20004; (202) 783-7971.

National Ski Patrol, Inc., Ste 100, 133 South Van Gordon Street, Lakewood, CO 80228; (303) 988-1111 or fax (303) 988-3005.

The National Sporting Goods Association (NSGA), 1699 Wall Street, Mount Prospect, IL 60056; (847) 439-4000.

New Mexico Forestry & Resources Conservation Division, PO Box 1948, Sante Fe, NM 87504-1948; (505) 827-5830 or fax (505) 827-3903.

North American Paddle Sports Association (NAPSA), 12455 North Wauwatosa Road, Mequon, WI 53097; (800)755-5228.

North American Wildlife Enforcement Officers Association, Rural Route 2, Whycocomagh, Nova Scotia, Canada, B033MO; (902) 756-2584.

Office of Returned Volunteer Career Services, 1990 K Street NW, Washington, DC 20526; (800) 424-8580, ext 2284.

Outdoor Writers Association of America, 2017 Cato Avenue, Ste 101, State College, PA 16801; (814) 234-1011.

Paddler Magazine, PO Box 1341, Eagle, ID 83616; (208)939-4500.

Peace Corps, 1990 K Street NW, Washington, DC 20526; (800) 424-8580.

Peterson's Guide, PO Box 2123, 202 Carnegie Center, Princeton, NJ 08540; (800) 225-0261 or fax (609) 243-9150.

Professional Paddle Sports Association, PO Box 248, Butler, KY 41006; (606)472-2205.

Professional Photographers of America, Inc., 57 Forsythe Street NW, Ste 1600, Atlanta, GA 30303; (404) 522-8600 or fax (404) 614-6400.

Professional Ski Instructors of America (PSIA), 133 South Van Gordon Street, Ste 101, Lakewood, C) 80228; (303) 987-9390 or fax (303) 988-3005. E-mail: natoff@genie.geis.com

Public Relations Society of America, 33 Irving Place, New York, NY 10033; (212) 995-2230.

Ski Industries of America, 8377-B Greensboro Drive, McLean, VA 22102; (703) 556-9020 or fax (703) 821-8276. E-mail: siamail@IX@netcom.com

Sno-engineering, Inc., 34 School Street, Littleton, NH 03561; (603) 444-4811 or fax (603) 444-0414. E-mail: snoe@snoe.com

Society of American Foresters, 515 SW 5th Street, Ste 518, Portland, OR 97201; (503) 222-7456.

Society of Environmental Journalists, PO Box 27506, Philadelphia, PA 19118; (215) 247-9710.

Student Conservation Association, Inc., PO Box 550, Charlestown, NH 03603; (603) 543-1700.

Superintendent of Documents, US Government Printing Office, Washington, DC 20402.

Surfer Magazine, PO Box 1028, Dana Point, CA 92629; (714) 496-5922.

Surfing Magazine, PO Box 3010, San Clemente, CA 92674-3010; (714) 492-7873 or fax (714) 498-6485. E-mail: surfing@netcome.com

Surfriders Foundation, 122 South El Camino Real, No.67, San Clemente, CA 92672; (714) 492-8170.

US Coast Guard Academy, Director of Admissions, 15 Mohegan Avenue, New London, CT 06320-9807; (203) 444-8505.

US Department of Agriculture, Forestry Service, PO Box 96090, Washington, DC 20013-6090; (202) 205-8333. (Ask for "A Job with the Forest Service: A Guide to Career Opportunities in Technical Support Positions" and/or "Professional and Administrative Careers in the Forest Service."

US Department of the Interior, National Park Service, PO Box 37127, Washington, DC 20013-7127; (202) 208-4649. (Ask for "National Park Service: Careers" and/or "Seasonal Employment: The National parks."

US Fish and Wildlife Service, 2625 Parkmont Road, Building A, Olympia, WA 98502; (360) 753-9460.

US Forestry Service, 740 Simms Street, Golden, CO 80401; (303) 275-5350 or fax (303) 275-5671.

US Sailing Association, PO Box 1260, 15 Maritime Drive, Portsmouth, RI 02871; (401) 849-5200 or fax (401) 683-0840.

US Sailing Association (racing association), Box 209, Newport, RI 02840; (301) 849-5200.

US Tour Operators Association (USTOA), 211 East 51st Street, Ste 12B, New York, NY 10022; (212) 750-7371 or fax (212) 421-1285. E-mail: ustour@aol.com

Vermont Bike Touring, Box 711, Bristol, VT 05443: (802)453-4811 or (800)245-3868.

The Wildlife Management Institute, 1101 14th Street NW, Ste 725, Washington, DC 20005; (202) 371-1808.

The Wildlife Society, 5410 Grosvenor Lane, Ste 200, Bethesda, MD 20814; (301) 530-2471. E-mail: tws@wildlife.org

YWCA-USA, 726 Broadway Avenue, New York, NY 10003; (212) 614-2700.

Resource Guide

Note: The following are sample selections from THE WHOLE WORK CATALOG. To receive a free copy of the complete 32-page catalog, write or call The New Careers Center, 1515 -23rd Street, PO Box 339TS, Boulder CO 80306. Phone (303) 447-1087, Fax (303) 447-8684.

Part-Time Travel Agent
Monaghan $24.95 **#4092** ©94 pb

This big, 400-page book shows how to open a home-based travel agency, avoiding the high start-up costs of traditional travel agencies. You can make money booking airlines (access computerized airline reservation systems for just $15 a month), tours, cruises, hotels and car rentals. Not only that, you can get free trips from tour operators eager for your business, and even earn your own frequent flyer miles on other people's travel. A detailed guide to the many opportunities created by recent changes in the travel marketplace. *Highly recommended.*

How to Get Paid $30,000 a Year to Travel
Chilton $24.95   **#4626**   ©95 pb

According to the author, you can make $30-$52,000 a year delivering brand new recreational vehicles, limousines, and other specialty vehicles to dealerships around the country (unlike passenger cars, which are delivered by truck). Ordinarily you can use your regular driver's license, you can work full-time, part-time, on vacations, or on weekends—and you can set your own hours. Some companies fly you back home from your trips at *their* expense (but you get to keep the frequent flyer miles). An interesting opportunity for retired people, couples and others wanting to see the country and be paid for it, all fully covered in this detailed guide.

How to Get a Job With a Cruise Line
Miller $14.95   **#1696**   ©94   pb

Cruise lines hire fitness instructors, tour leaders, massage therapists, pursers, photographers, youth counselors, clerks, watersports instructors, and many, many other types of people. Mary Miller's new book will show you who to contact, how to apply, and what to expect from a cruise line job. We especially like the insider's tips from the men and women who do the hiring for cruise ships, and the first-person stories from people on the job.

The Insider's Guide to Air Courier Bargains
Monaghan $14.95   **#2023**   ©95 pb

How to fly at extremely low rates–possibly even free–to destinations all over the world as a freelance air courier. By accompanying time-sensitive cargo (shipped as passengers' luggage on regularly scheduled airlines) you can travel the world for next to nothing. Monaghan shows what air couriers do, why they are needed, typical fares, positioning yourself for free travel, plus a listing of courier contacts in the U.S., Canada and other locations around the world.

Start and Run a Profitable Tour Guiding Business
Briadwood $14.95   **#5294**   ©96   pb

In almost no other occupation do you have the chance to meet and experience such a wealth of different people and cultures as in tour guiding. This new book shows how to run your own tours as an independent guide, work for an existing company, or set up your own tour business, hiring staff to assist you. Covers different types of tours (cruise, land, bus, etc.), how to set rates for your tours, standard commissions in the industry, much more. Includes sample legal contracts.

College Degrees You Can Earn From Home
NCC with Judith Frey$14.95   **#4438**   ©95   pb

It's entirely possible to earn a legitimate college degree, from an accredited school, through home study. It can take as little as three to six months and can cost less than $1,000. The problem is that most colleges that offer such programs never advertise—and you don't want anything to do with many of those that do advertise. This new guide covers 100+ accredited colleges that offer degrees through written correspondence, on-line computer instruction, cable TV, video tapes and more. Subtitle: "How to get a first-class degree without attending class."

Profits From Your Backyard Herb Garden
Sturdivant $10.95   **#4636**   ©95   pb

This book,written by a delightful herb and flower grower on an island off the coast of Washington, is for beginning herb growers. It's short, easy to read, and gives good information for starting a small-scale herb business in your backyard. Covers growing, harvesting, packaging, and marketing culinary herbs to local restaurants and supermarkets, starting a backyard potted herb business and more.

 **Herbs For Sale: Growing and Marketing Herbs, Herbal Products, and Herbal Know-How**   Sturdivant
$14.95   **#4126**   ©94   pb

This companion to *Profits From Your Backyard Herb Garden* covers almost every conceivable herb-related business. The chapter on growing herbs covers profiting from a backyard, greenhouse, or small acreage in culinary herbs, dried flowers, salad greens, potted herbs or gourmet garlic; plus there are chapters on creating an herb farm; making herbal products (medicinal herb teas, herbal extracts, aromatic pillows, body care products, etc.); wildcrafting; teaching about herbs; other possibilities—herb shops, aromatherapy, etc.

Secrets to a Successful Greenhouse Business
Taylor $19.95   **#4672**   ©94   pb

Based on nearly 20 years experience in growing plants and designing greenhouses, Taylor's book shows how to profit from a wholesale greenhouse business—making up to $20,000 per 30'X96' greenhouse in 90 days. Includes solar greenhouse plans (70° inside/30° outside without heaters), who to sell to (nation-wide plant buyers list), when and how to grow the best selling plants, how to profit from hydroponics and organic growing methods, working efficiently so only 7 hours per week are needed to maintain a 96' greenhouse, more. Impressive book.

How to Make Money Growing Plants, Trees & Flowers
Francis Jozwik, Ph.D. $19.95   #2118   ©92   pb

Dr. Jozwik, who has operated a successful greenhouse and nursery business for over 20 years, shows how to make a significant income growing special ornamental crops in your own backyard. He explains why these ornamentals are in such great demand and gives all the nuts and bolts for getting started without technical expertise or spending a lot of money. Detailed examples show the ins and outs of each type of business with actual economic data for specific operations. Photo illustrations throughout.

Flowers For Sale: Growing & Marketing Cut Flowers
Sturdivant $15.95   #2112   ©92   pb

This book gives an easy, step-by-step plan for starting a flower growing and selling business either in your backyard or on a small acreage. Numerous successful flower businesses are profiled, including Saturday Market flower sellers and one grower who takes in $650,000 on less than an acre of flower production. Hundreds of plant varieties with potential as commercial cut flowers are listed, with seed sources and other information. Covers harvesting, pricing, displaying, selling, business and tax information, collecting flowers and greenery from the wild, and much more.

Country Bound! Trade Your Business Suit Blues for Blue Jean Dreams
Marilyn & Tom Ross $19.95   #2576   ©97   pb

This is an extremely comprehensive guide to earning a good living in the country—and having a better quality of life in a cleaner, healthier environment. Covers 23 gutsy tactics for finding the right rural job, strategies for becoming self-employed in your own special Eden, guidelines for buying a moneymaking small town business, counsel about the safest, least-congested places to live, with checklists, charts and maps to guide your selection. All the facts for finding "slower paces and friendlier faces" from authors who traded the Southern California metroplex for a quiet Colorado mountain town back in 1980.

Lawn Aeration: Turn Hard Soil Into Cold Cash   Pedrotti $19.95   #2200

Lawn areation is one of those offbeat businesses that nobody's ever heard of—but that can produce a very good income when you know what you're doing. It costs about $6,500 to buy the equipment and supplies, but if you believe the author—and we think he's extremely convincing—you can make $35,000- $50,000 working full time only 8 months of the year. It's also possible to get started with only $500 or so if you rent your equipment. An intriguing opportunity.

Your Money or Your Life
Dominguez $11.95   #5264   ©92   pb

"If you spend your life energy on stuff that brings only passing fulfillment and doesn't support your values, you end up with less life." It's this focus on "life energy"—the precious and limited time each of us has here on earth—that sets this book apart. Dominguez offers a 9-step plan for achieving financial independence, which they define as "having an income sufficient for your basic needs and comforts from a source other than paid employment." This is a powerful, unquestionably life-changing program guaranteed to permanently improve your relationship with money. *Highly recommended.*

Earning Money Without a Job
Jay Conrad Levinson $9.95   **#0108**   ©91   pb

Hundreds of money-making ideas—some obvious, some surprising—all within the realm of immediate opportunity. Hardly any require much capital, and most can be done from home. This is an exceptionally well-written book that's a pleasure to read. "The real answer to being your own boss is many small jobs. This book is the best guide available."—*The Next Whole Earth Catalog*

Free Money When You're Unemployed   Blum $16.95   **#2865**   ©96   pb
Blum compiles information on some 1,000 sources of foundation funds available for the millions of Americans now unemployed. These funds—for everything from grocery bills to mortgage payments—are available from foundations and are outright grants rather than loans. Includes contact information, eligibility requirements, etc., including special programs for retirees and those needing aid following a divorce or death of a spouse. According to the author, much of this information has never before been made available to the general public.

The Independent Medical Transcriptionist
Avila-Weil $32.95   **#4724**   ©94   pb

If you're willing to learn to do medical transcription this book can be the key to an outstanding career working for yourself—from a home office if you prefer. Covers breaking into the field the right way, learning to do medical transcription (including home study courses), building a successful medical transcription business, detailed information on business operations, marketing, financing your business, and much, much more. Includes tables showing standard regional billing rates and hours of daily transcription needed to generate $80,000/year in billings. This edition is comprehensive (almost 500 pages), authoritative and recommended.

How to Start and Operate a Mail-Order Business
Dr. Julian Simon $39.95   **#0874**   ©93   hc

Mail-order sales are growing almost five times as fast as retail sales, and this book provides everything you need to know to get a mail-order business off to a good start and then keep it running smoothly, efficiently and profitably. We've seen dozens of books on the subject and don't think any of them seriously compete with Simon's, which is the one we regularly refer to in our own office. A professor of economics and marketing at the U. of Illinois, Simon has started, successfully operated, and profitably sold his own mail-order business. The fifth edition includes a chapter on personal computers and lists 500 products that sell successfully by mail. "You can learn more from this volume than in a month of listening to the experts."—*Direct Mail Briefs*

The Work-at-Home Sourcebook Arden $19.95 **#0996** ©96 pb

This new 6th edition gives full contact information for hundreds of home business opportunities (home-based franchises, distributorships, etc.), in addition to listing over 1,000 companies with work-at-home programs—offering jobs ranging from knitting to data processing and from proofreading to marketing and much more. Arden provides details on job descriptions, pay and benefits, how to apply and how to make the most of working at home once you get the job. Includes a section on markets for homemade handcrafts and a section on "learning at home to work at home." No other book even comes close. "Besides being a tremendous financial resource, this book is just plain fun to read..."—*Welcome Home*

Make Money Reading Books
Fife $15.00 **#2735** ©93

A college degree is helpful but not really necessary to break into the freelance reading business, according to Fife. Covers literary services, book reviewing, researching, translating, indexing, manuscript reading, literary representation (becoming a literary agent) and other opportunities. Includes sections on setting up your business, marketing your services (to newspaper, book and magazine publishers, writers, students, businesses, government, non-profit organizations and others), and more. An interesting, well-executed book.

The Information Broker's Handbook
Rugge $34.95 **#2229** ©96 pb

Information brokering is one of the hottest entrepreneurial fields of the 90s, and this is clearly one of the most comprehensive, authoritative guides to the opportunities available. Starting from scratch, author Sue Rugge grew her own information brokerage company to the $2 million annual sales level, and she covers all the nuts and bolts here. Includes a free disk of business forms, information on all the search and retrieval options available today, details on establishing an office, marketing and selling your services, pricing and billing, etc. *Highly recommended.*

How to Make a Whole Lot More Than $1,000,000 Writing, Commissioning, Publishing and Selling "How-To" Information Lant $39.95 **#1898** ©93

Lant has built a one-person information empire, and he's adamant that anyone with motivation can do the same. This is a hefty volume with an impressive amount of detail on making money from books, booklets, audio cassettes and special reports. Full information is provided both for producing your own material and/or commissioning others to do the writing (while you concentrate on marketing). If you really want to ride the information-age wave—working at home with just your computer, fax machine and creative marketing imagination—you'll love this book.

Sunshine Jobs: Career Opportunities Working Outdoors
Stienstra $16.95 **#5470** ©97 pb

Please use the order form (reverse of this page) to order additional copies of this book.

ORDER FORM
THE NEW CAREERS CENTER
1515 - 23rd Street, P.O. Box 339-TS, Boulder CO 80306

Name _____

Street /apt. no. _____

City/State/Zip _____

Daytime phone no. _____
(in case we need to contact you about your order)

Item No.	Title		Total Price	

Need more room? Just attach another sheet of paper.

MasterCard/Visa Orders: (303) 447-1087 8-5, M-F, Mtn. Standard Time 24-hour fax: (303) 447-8684	Merchandise total		
	Colo. residents add 3% tax		
	Shipping (except foreign)	4	50
	TOTAL (U.S. funds only)		

Call today for a free copy of The WHOLE WORK CATALOG. Order with confidence—your satisfaction is guaranteed.

Method of Payment (Sorry, no C.O.D.'s)

☐ Payment enclosed: check or money order for the total amount of _____

☐ Visa ☐ MasterCard Acct. No. _____

Expiration Date: _____   Note: **$20 minimum on credit card orders, please**

signature: _____